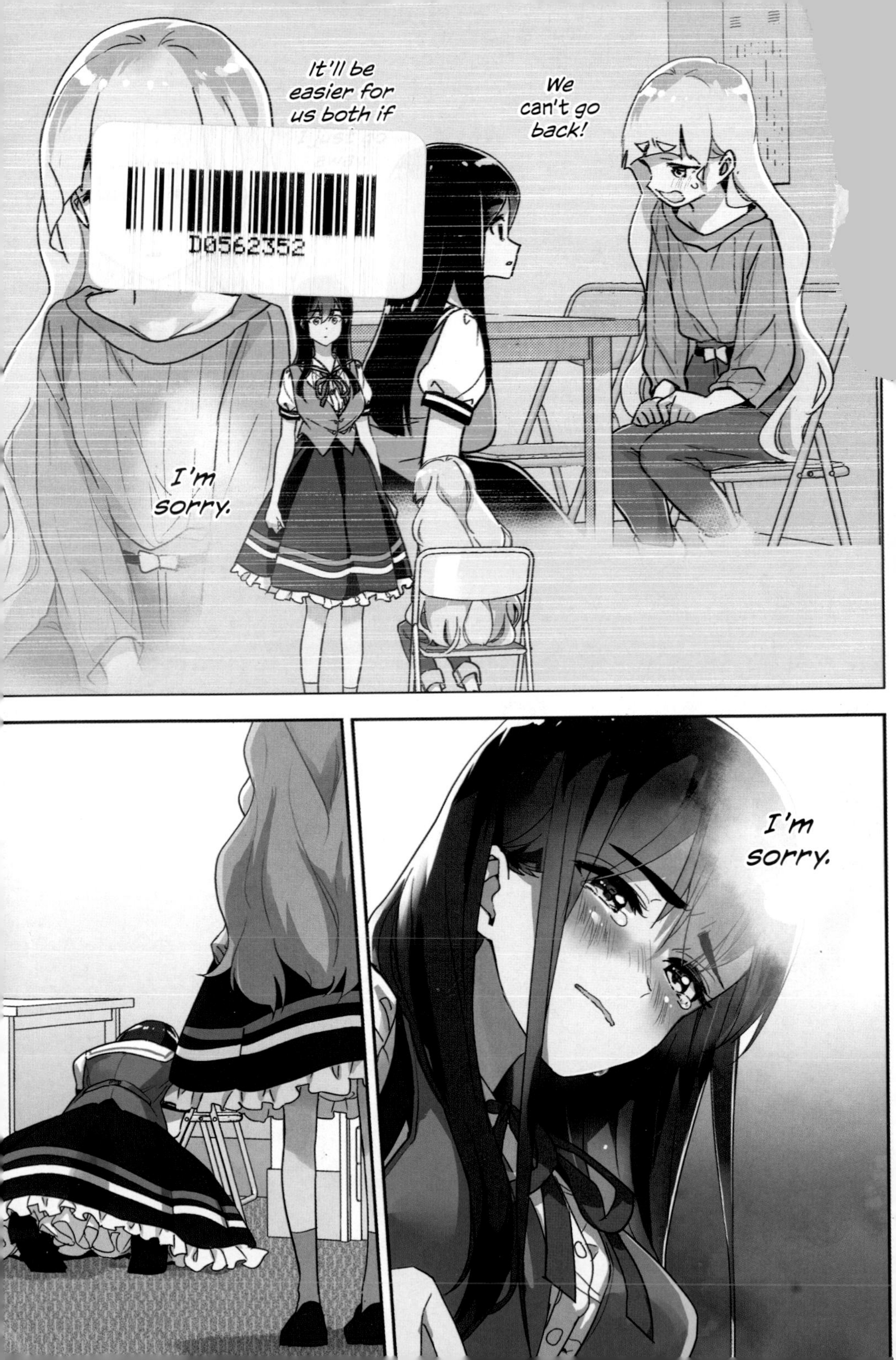
We can't go back!
It'll be easier for us both if
I'm sorry.
I'm sorry.

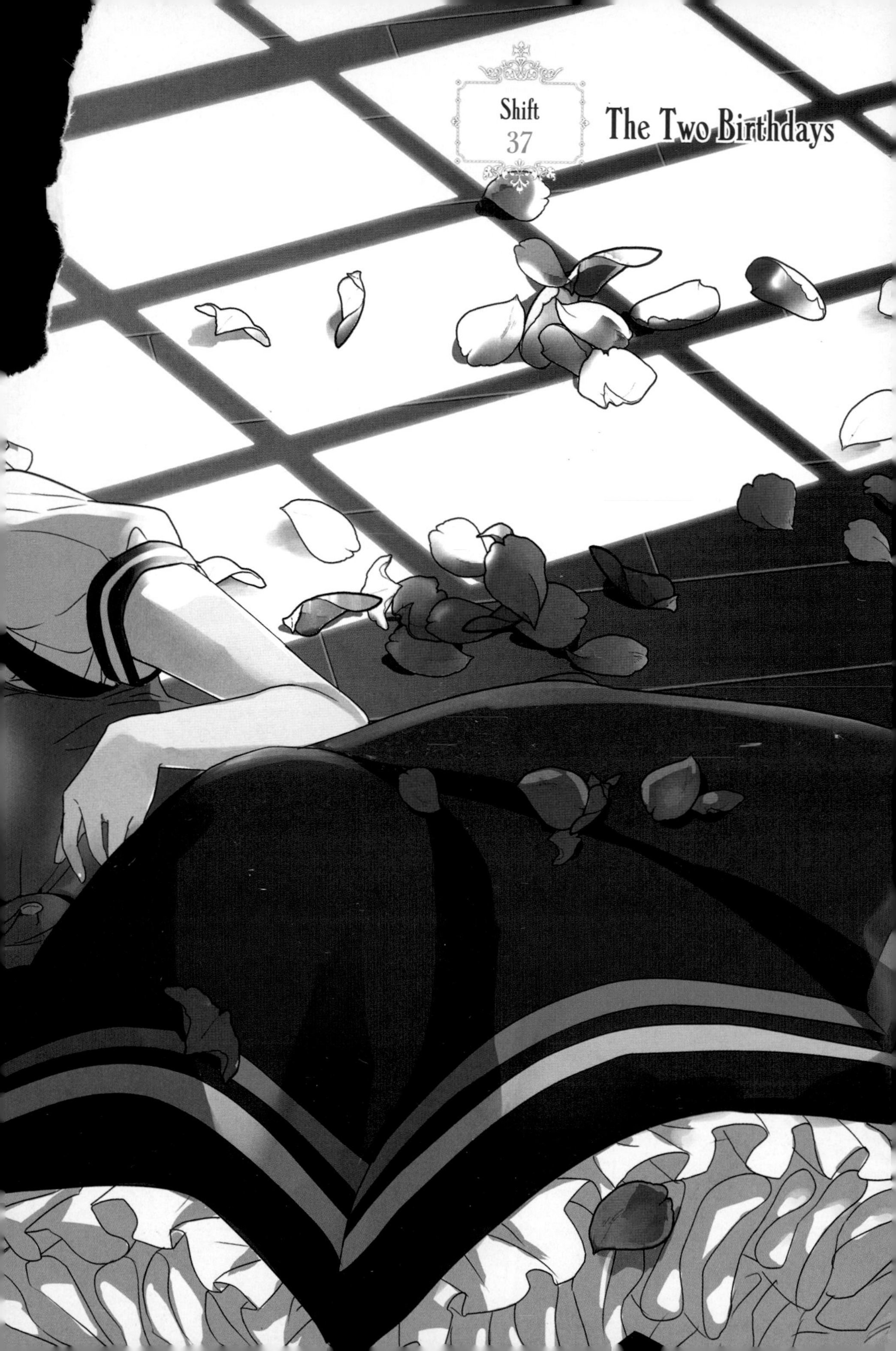
Shift
37
The Two Birthdays

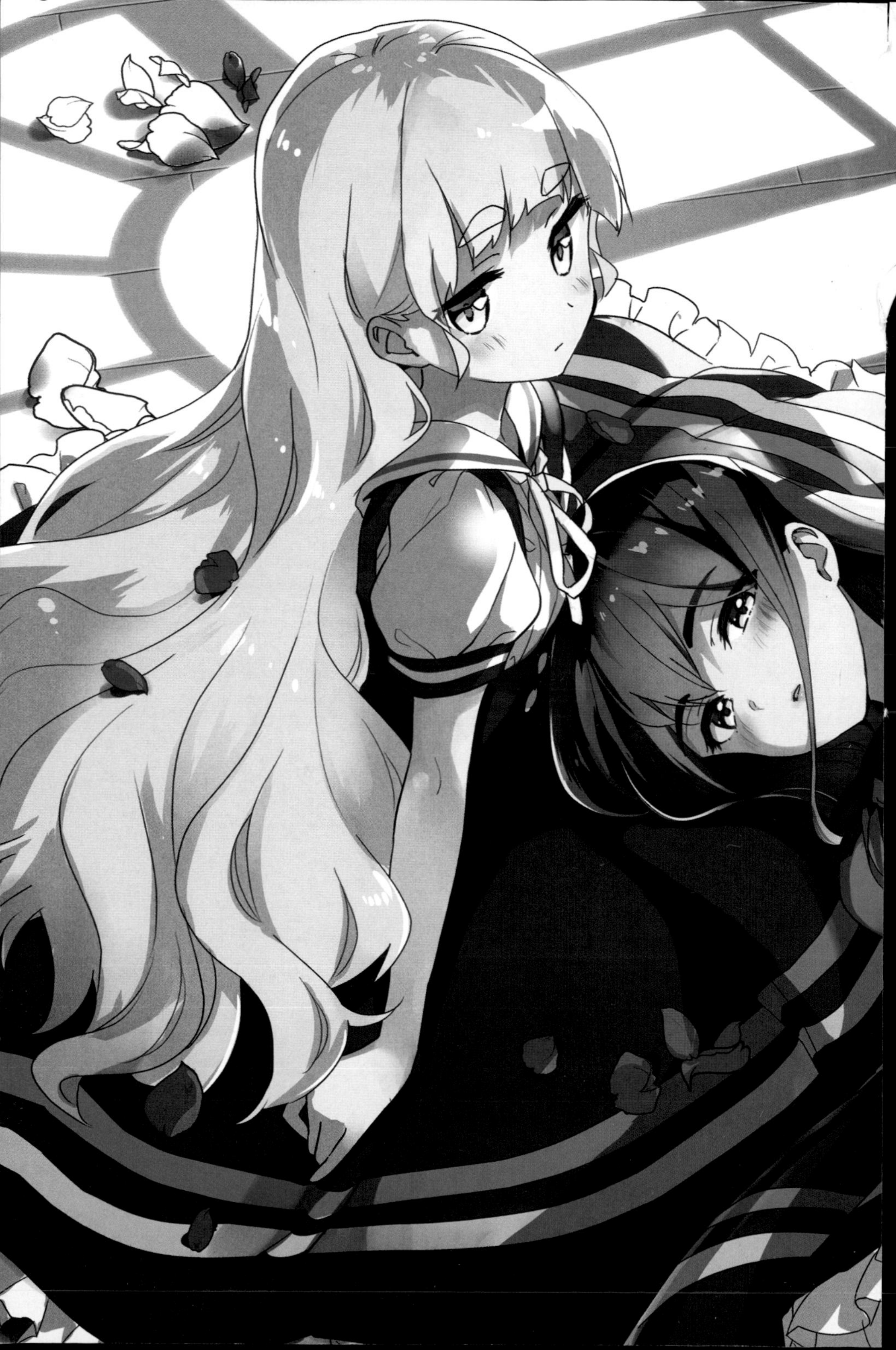

# CONTENTS

8

Schwestern in Liebe!

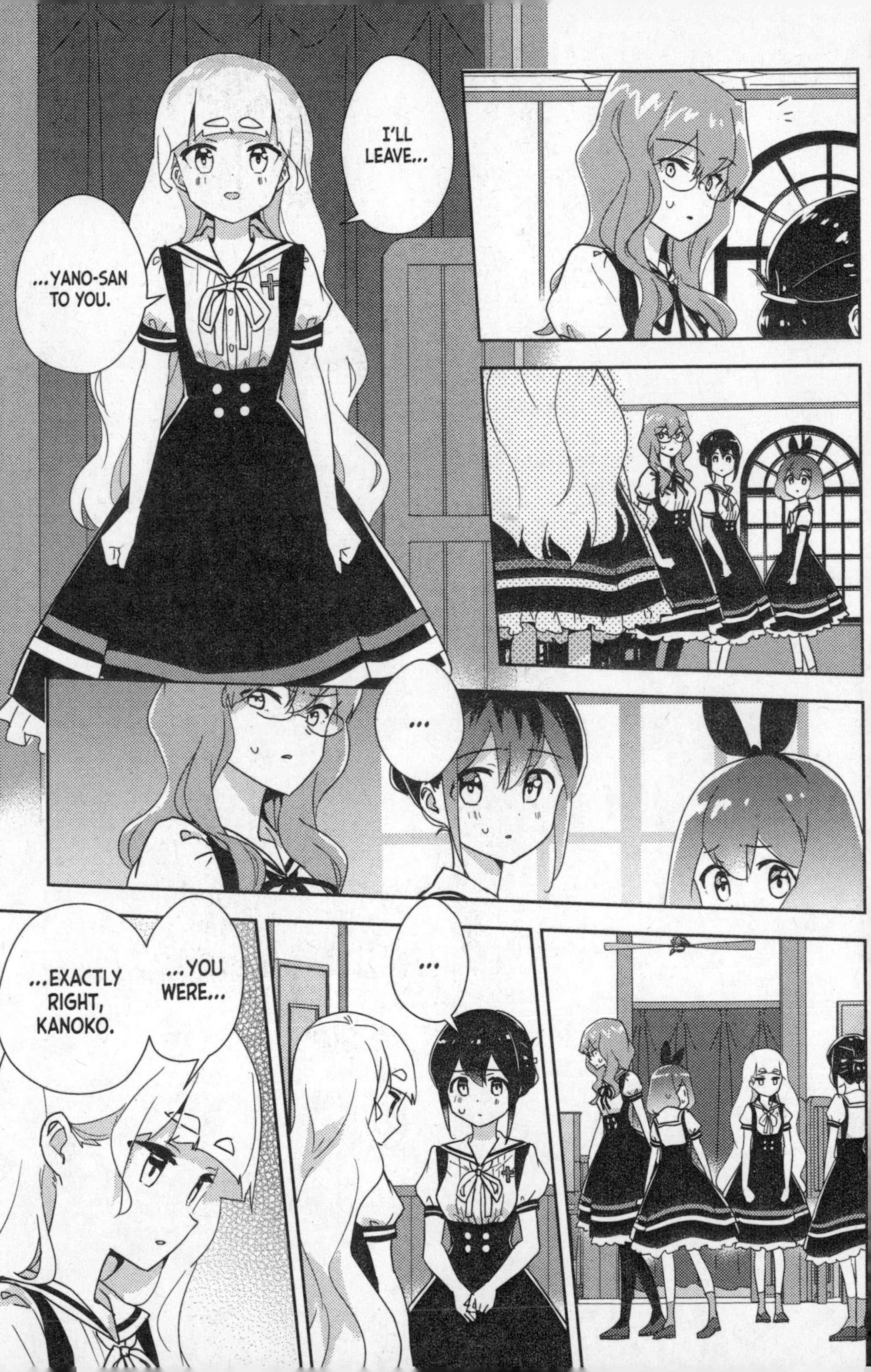
I'LL LEAVE...
...YANO-SAN TO YOU.
...
...
...YOU WERE...
...EXACTLY RIGHT, KANOKO.

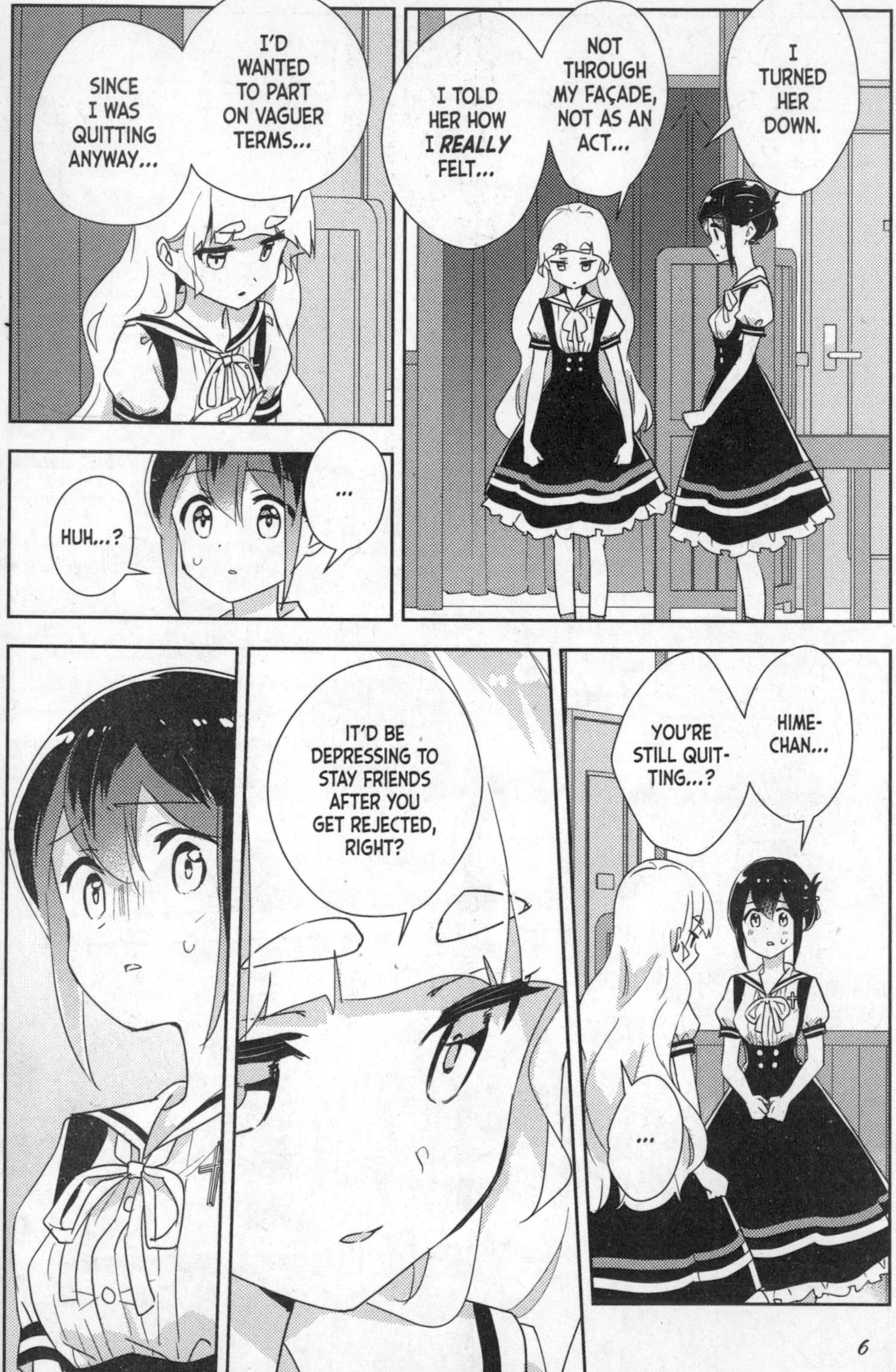
I TURNED HER DOWN.
NOT THROUGH MY FAÇADE, NOT AS AN ACT...
I TOLD HER HOW I *REALLY* FELT...
I'D WANTED TO PART ON VAGUER TERMS...
SINCE I WAS QUITTING ANYWAY...
...
HUH...?
HIME-CHAN...
YOU'RE STILL QUIT-TING...?
...
IT'D BE DEPRESSING TO STAY FRIENDS AFTER YOU GET REJECTED, RIGHT?

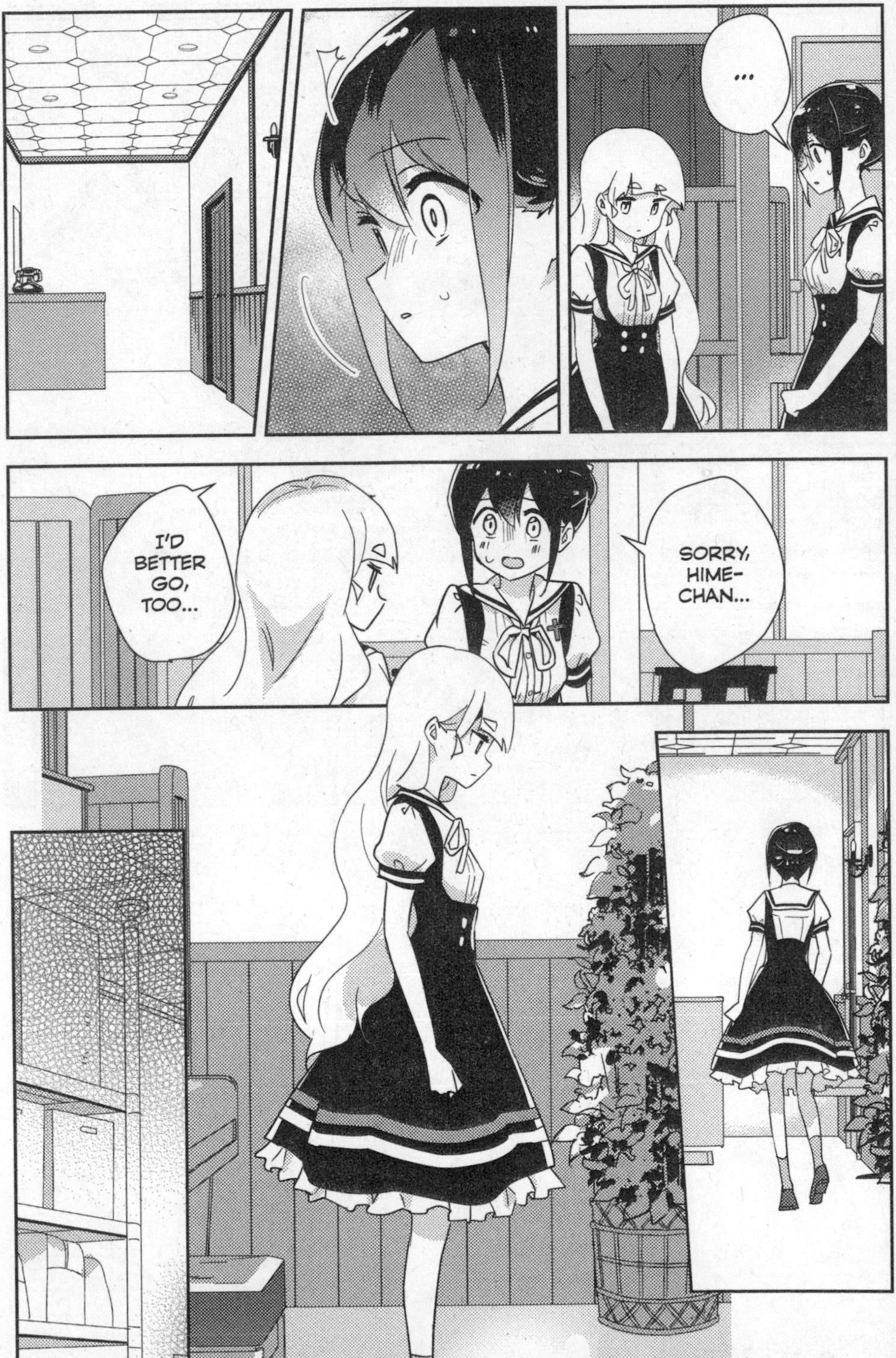
...
SORRY, HIME-CHAN...
I'D BETTER GO, TOO...

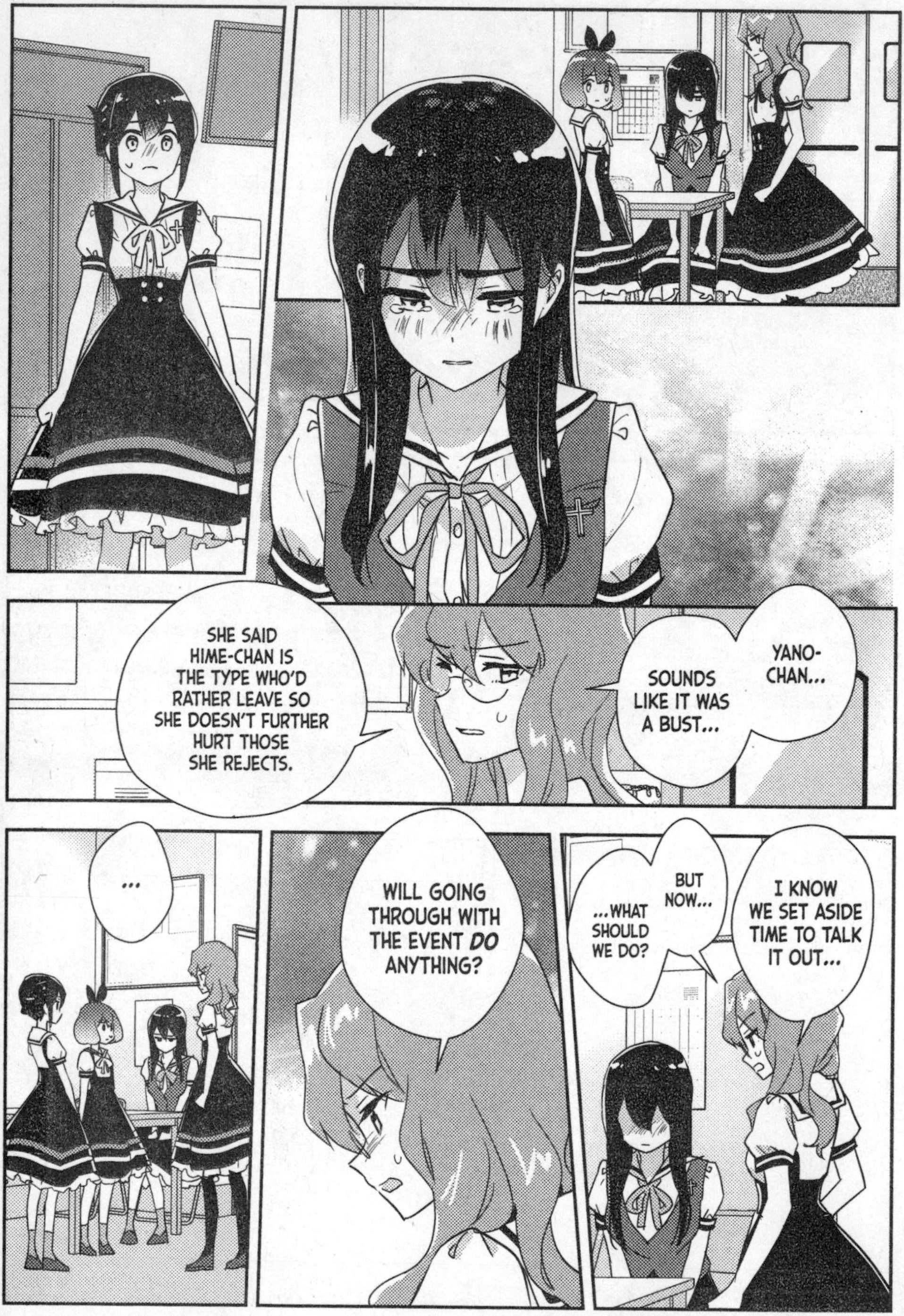
YANO-CHAN...
SOUNDS LIKE IT WAS A BUST...
SHE SAID HIME-CHAN IS THE TYPE WHO'D RATHER LEAVE SO SHE DOESN'T FURTHER HURT THOSE SHE REJECTS.
I KNOW WE SET ASIDE TIME TO TALK IT OUT...
BUT NOW...
...WHAT SHOULD WE DO?
WILL GOING THROUGH WITH THE EVENT *DO* ANYTHING?
...

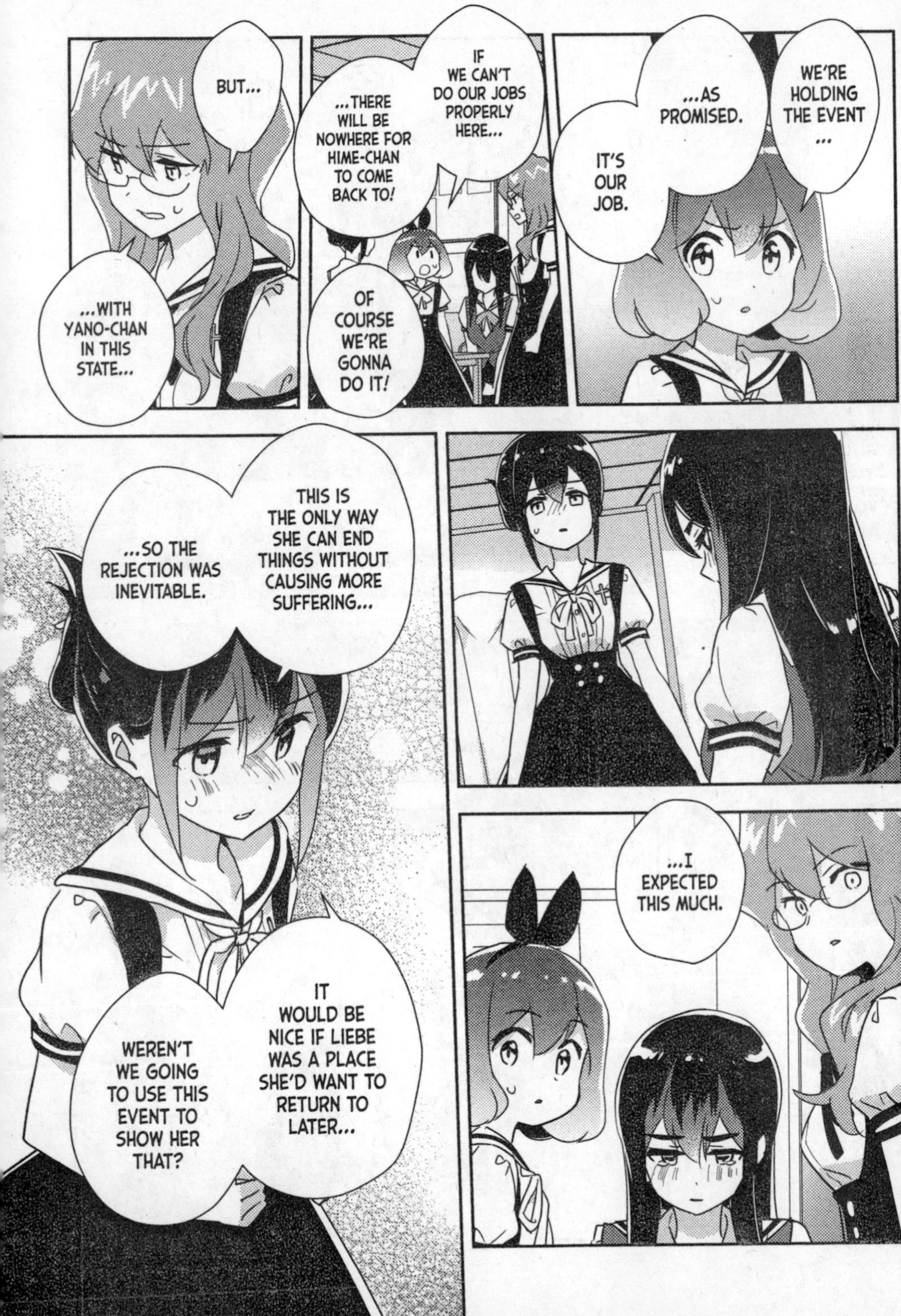
WE'RE HOLDING THE EVENT ...
...AS PROMISED.
IT'S OUR JOB.
IF WE CAN'T DO OUR JOBS PROPERLY HERE...
...THERE WILL BE NOWHERE FOR HIME-CHAN TO COME BACK TO!
OF COURSE WE'RE GONNA DO IT!
BUT...
...WITH YANO-CHAN IN THIS STATE...
...I EXPECTED THIS MUCH.
THIS IS THE ONLY WAY SHE CAN END THINGS WITHOUT CAUSING MORE SUFFERING...
...SO THE REJECTION WAS INEVITABLE.
IT WOULD BE NICE IF LIEBE WAS A PLACE SHE'D WANT TO RETURN TO LATER...
WEREN'T WE GOING TO USE THIS EVENT TO SHOW HER THAT?

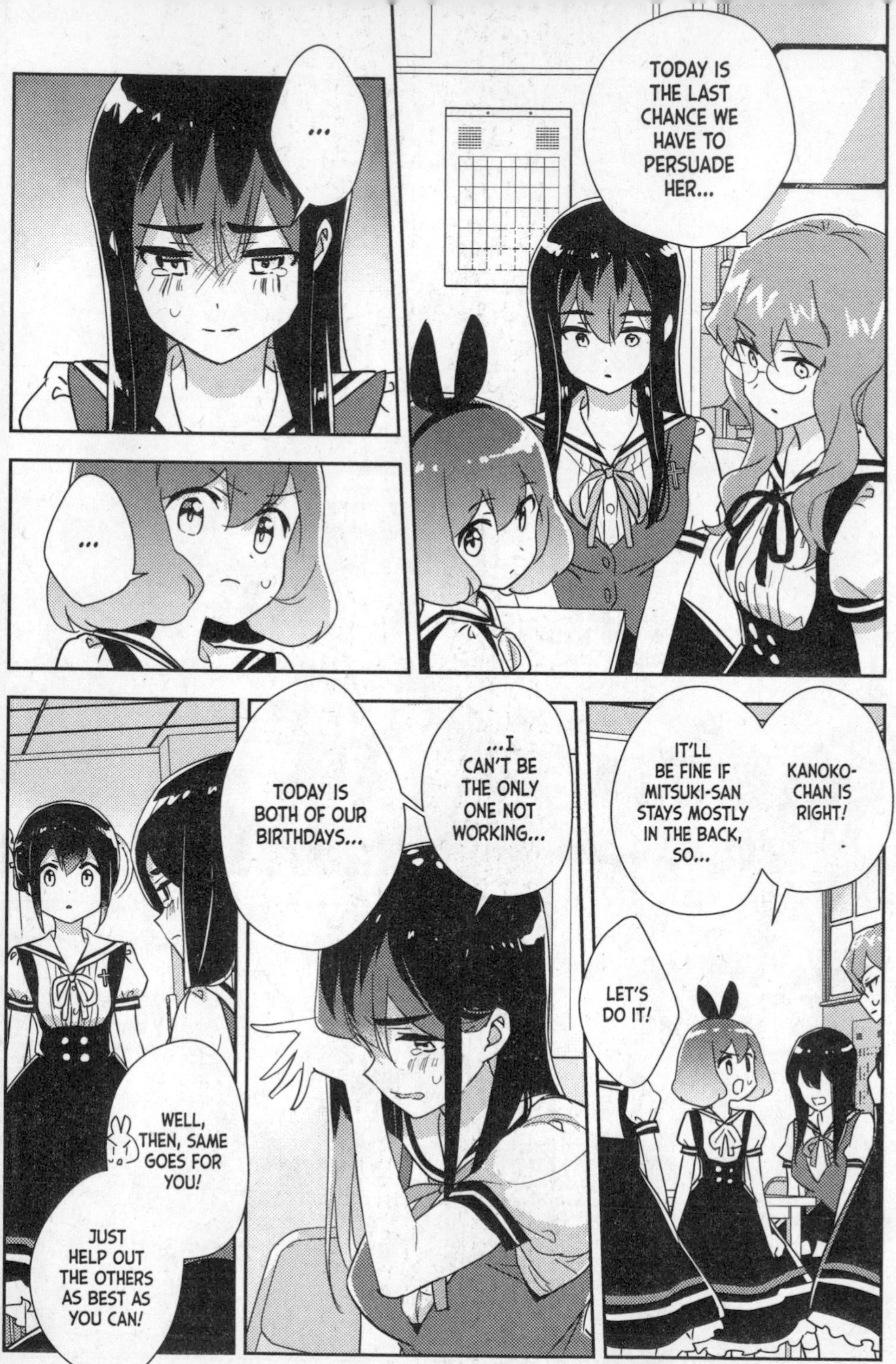
TODAY IS THE LAST CHANCE WE HAVE TO PERSUADE HER...
...
...
KANOKO-CHAN IS RIGHT!
IT'LL BE FINE IF MITSUKI-SAN STAYS MOSTLY IN THE BACK, SO...
LET'S DO IT!
...I CAN'T BE THE ONLY ONE NOT WORKING...
TODAY IS BOTH OF OUR BIRTHDAYS...
WELL, THEN, SAME GOES FOR YOU!
JUST HELP OUT THE OTHERS AS BEST AS YOU CAN!

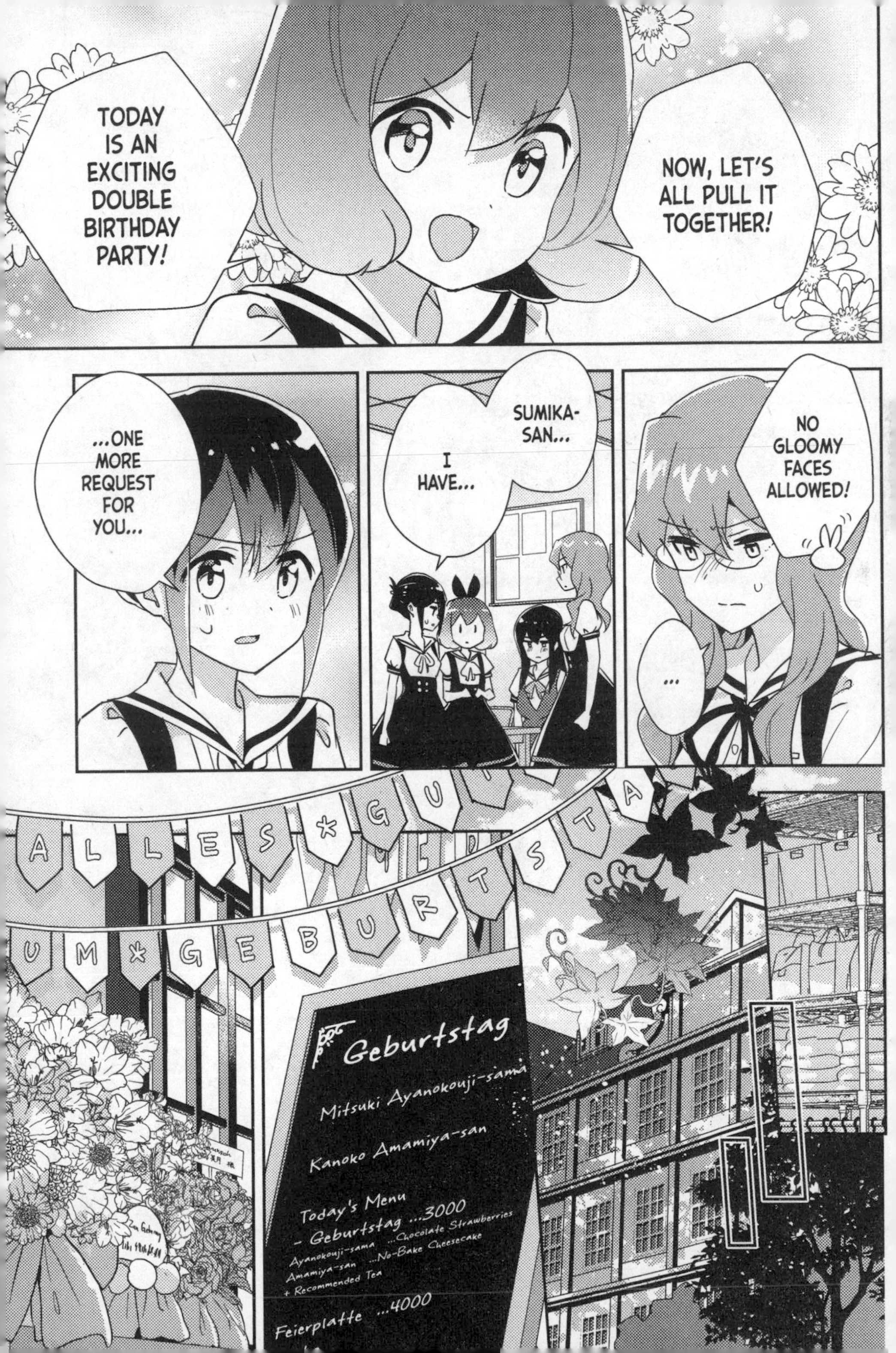
NOW, LET'S ALL PULL IT TOGETHER!
TODAY IS AN EXCITING DOUBLE BIRTHDAY PARTY!
NO GLOOMY FACES ALLOWED!
...
SUMIKA-SAN...
I HAVE...
...ONE MORE REQUEST FOR YOU...
Geburtstag
Mitsuki Ayanokouji-sama
Kanoko Amamiya-san
Today's Menu
- Geburtstag ...3000
Ayanokouji-sama ...Chocolate Strawberries
Amamiya-san ...No-Bake Cheesecake
+ Recommended Tea
Feierplatte ...4000

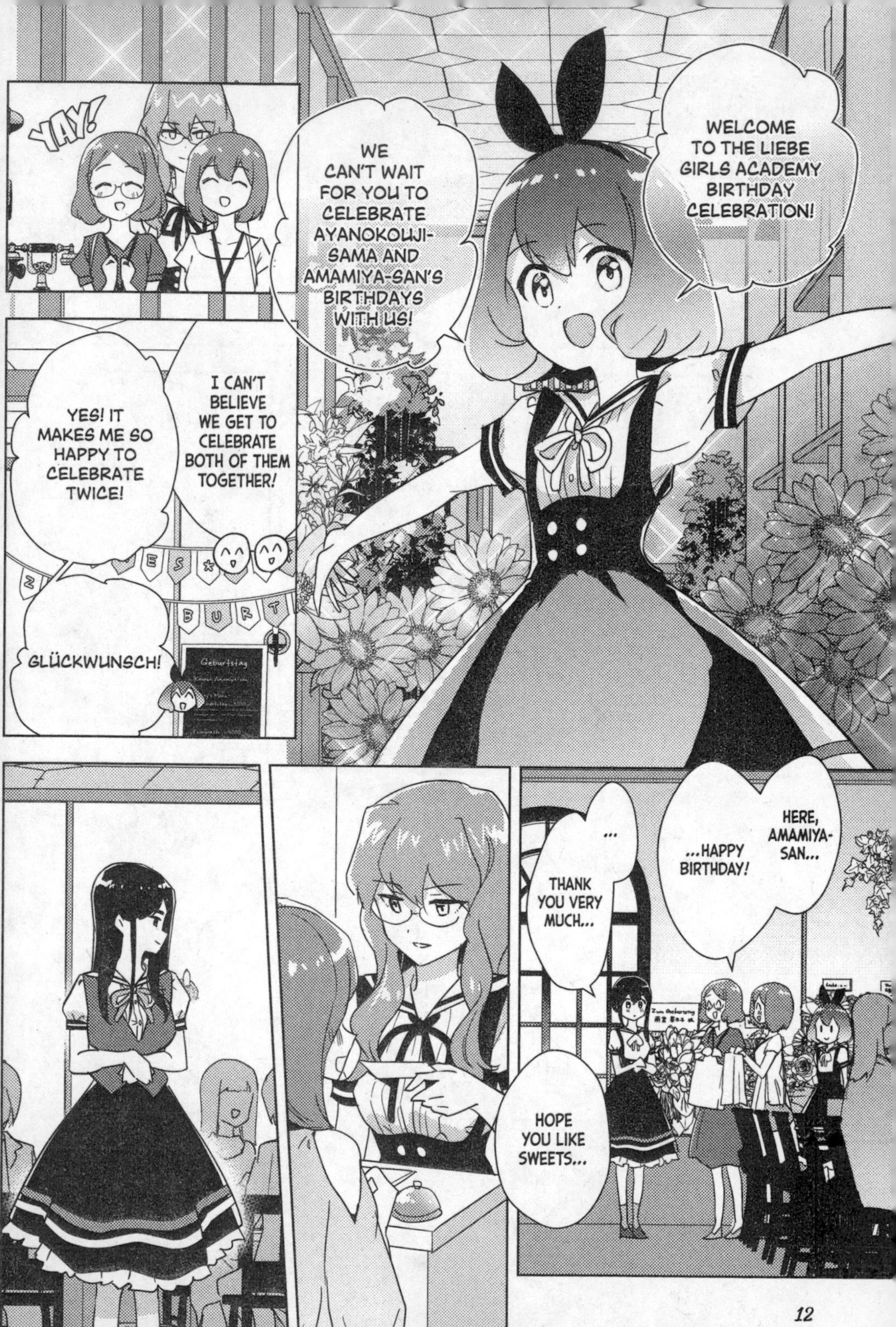
WELCOME TO THE LIEBE GIRLS ACADEMY BIRTHDAY CELEBRATION!
WE CAN'T WAIT FOR YOU TO CELEBRATE AYANOKOUJI-SAMA AND AMAMIYA-SAN'S BIRTHDAYS WITH US!
YAY!
I CAN'T BELIEVE WE GET TO CELEBRATE BOTH OF THEM TOGETHER!
YES! IT MAKES ME SO HAPPY TO CELEBRATE TWICE!
GLÜCKWUNSCH!
Geburtstag
HERE, AMAMIYA-SAN...
...HAPPY BIRTHDAY!
...
THANK YOU VERY MUCH...
HOPE YOU LIKE SWEETS...

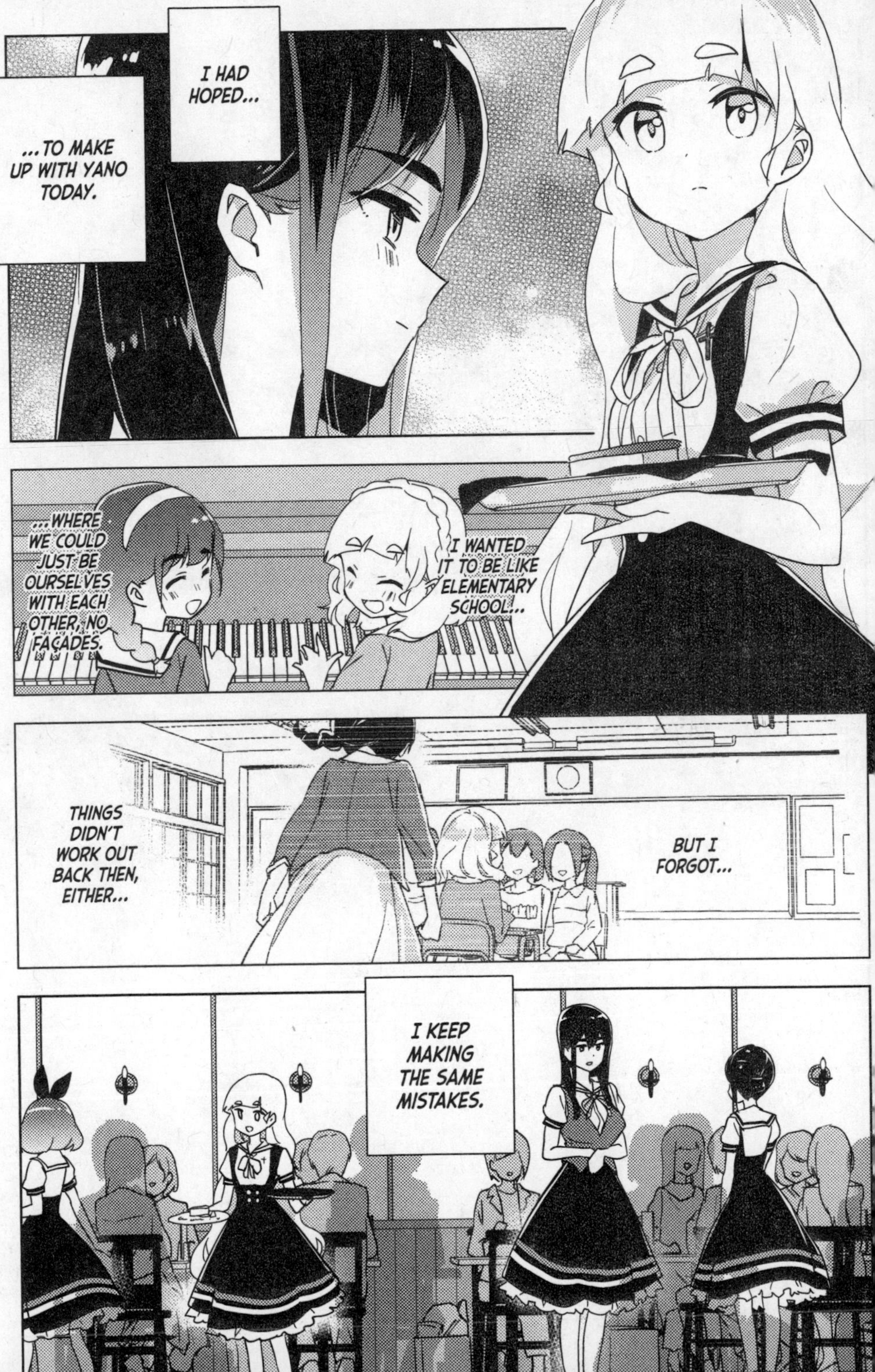
I HAD HOPED...
...TO MAKE UP WITH YANO TODAY.
I WANTED IT TO BE LIKE ELEMENTARY SCHOOL...
...WHERE WE COULD JUST BE OURSELVES WITH EACH OTHER, NO FAÇADES.
BUT I FORGOT...
THINGS DIDN'T WORK OUT BACK THEN, EITHER...
I KEEP MAKING THE SAME MISTAKES.

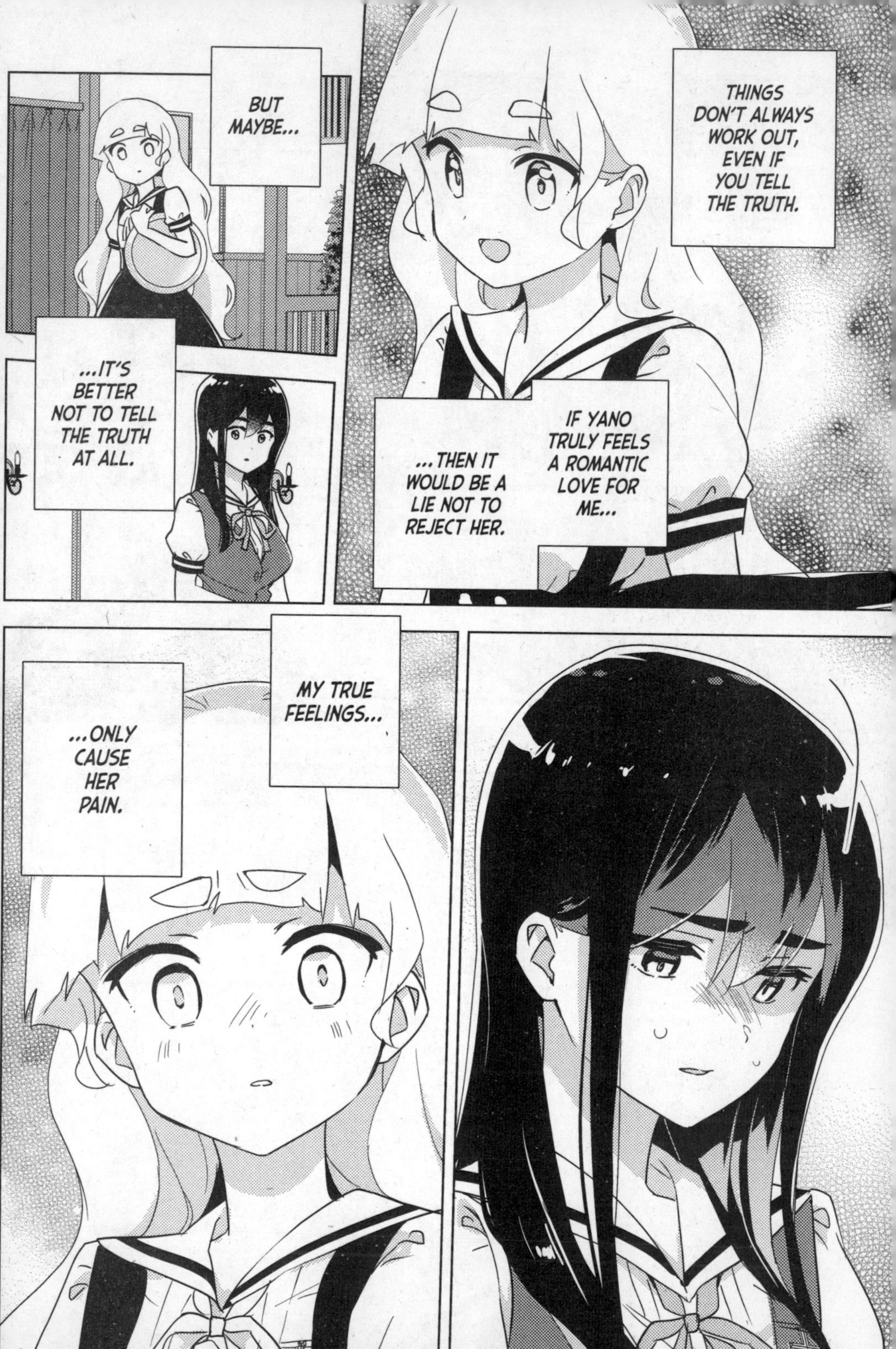
THINGS DON'T ALWAYS WORK OUT, EVEN IF YOU TELL THE TRUTH.
IF YANO TRULY FEELS A ROMANTIC LOVE FOR ME...
...THEN IT WOULD BE A LIE NOT TO REJECT HER.
BUT MAYBE...
...IT'S BETTER NOT TO TELL THE TRUTH AT ALL.
MY TRUE FEELINGS...
...ONLY CAUSE HER PAIN.

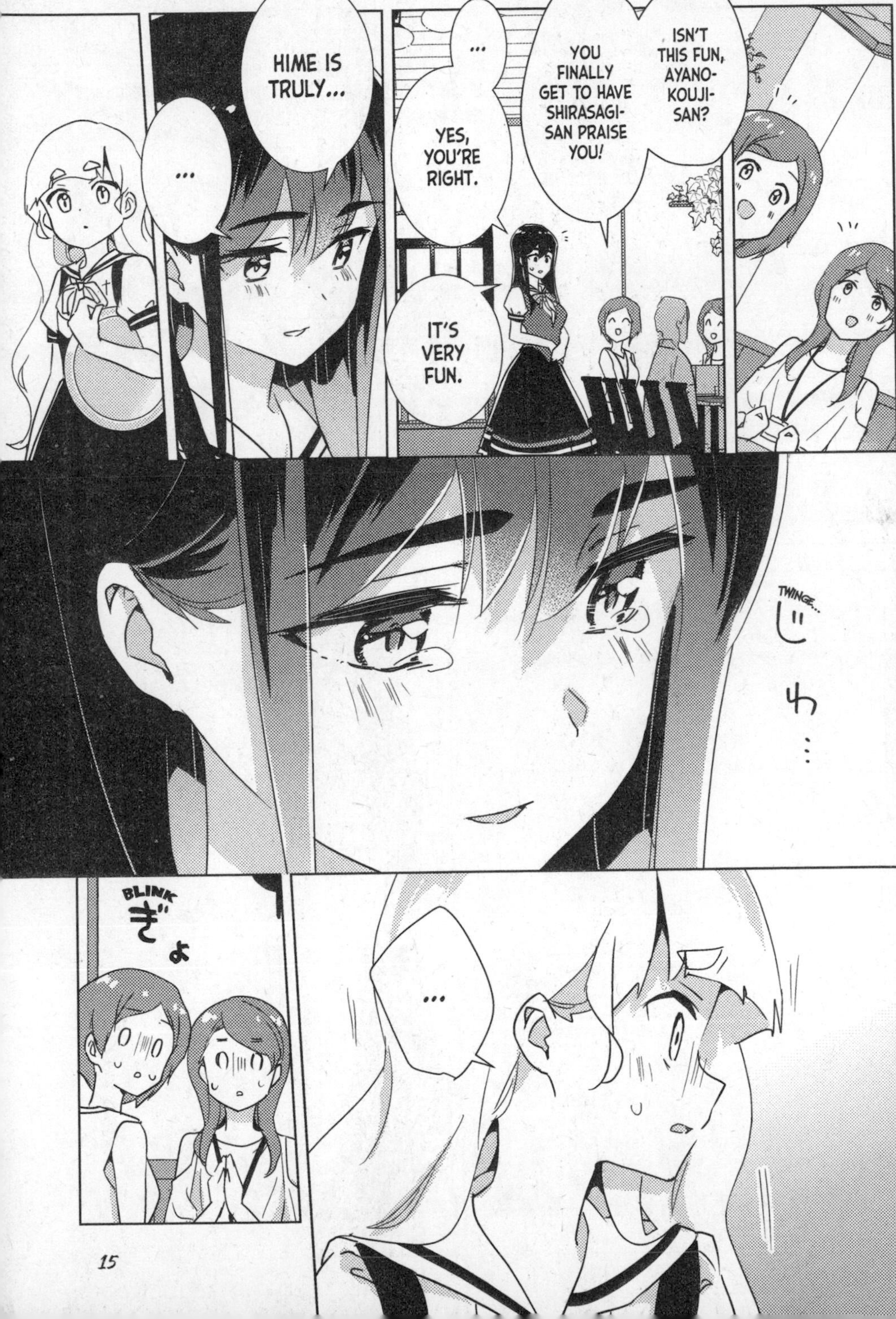
ISN'T THIS FUN, AYANO-KOUJI-SAN?
YOU FINALLY GET TO HAVE SHIRASAGI-SAN PRAISE YOU!
...
YES, YOU'RE RIGHT.
IT'S VERY FUN.
HIME IS TRULY...
...
TWINGE...
じわ…
...
BLINK
ぎょ

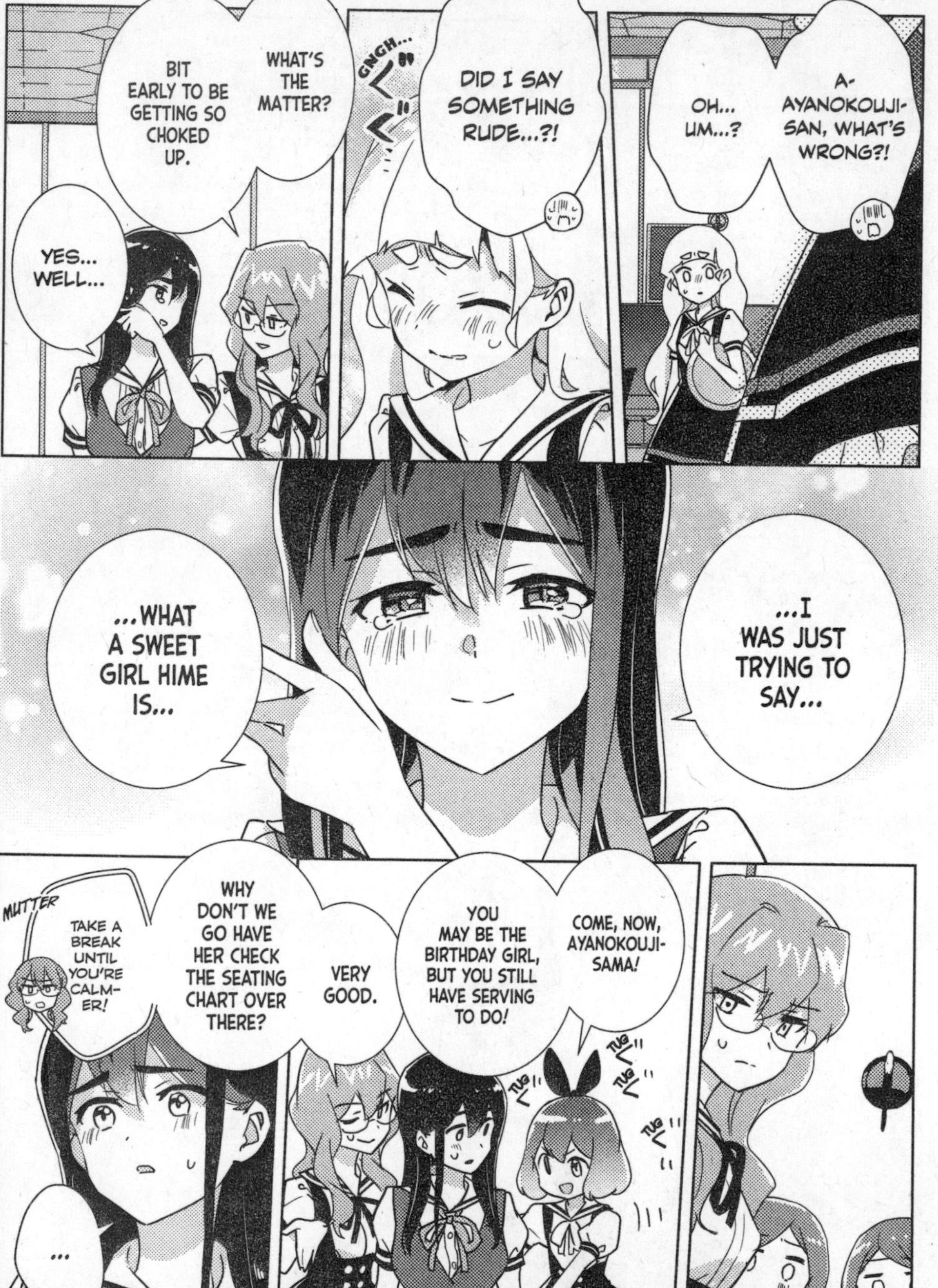
A-AYANOKOUJI-SAN, WHAT'S WRONG?!
OH... UM...?
GNGH...
DID I SAY SOMETHING RUDE...?!
WHAT'S THE MATTER?
BIT EARLY TO BE GETTING SO CHOKED UP.
YES... WELL...
...I WAS JUST TRYING TO SAY...
...WHAT A SWEET GIRL HIME IS...
COME, NOW, AYANOKOUJI-SAMA!
YOU MAY BE THE BIRTHDAY GIRL, BUT YOU STILL HAVE SERVING TO DO!
TUG
TUG
TUG
TUG
VERY GOOD.
WHY DON'T WE GO HAVE HER CHECK THE SEATING CHART OVER THERE?
MUTTER
TAKE A BREAK UNTIL YOU'RE CALMER!
...

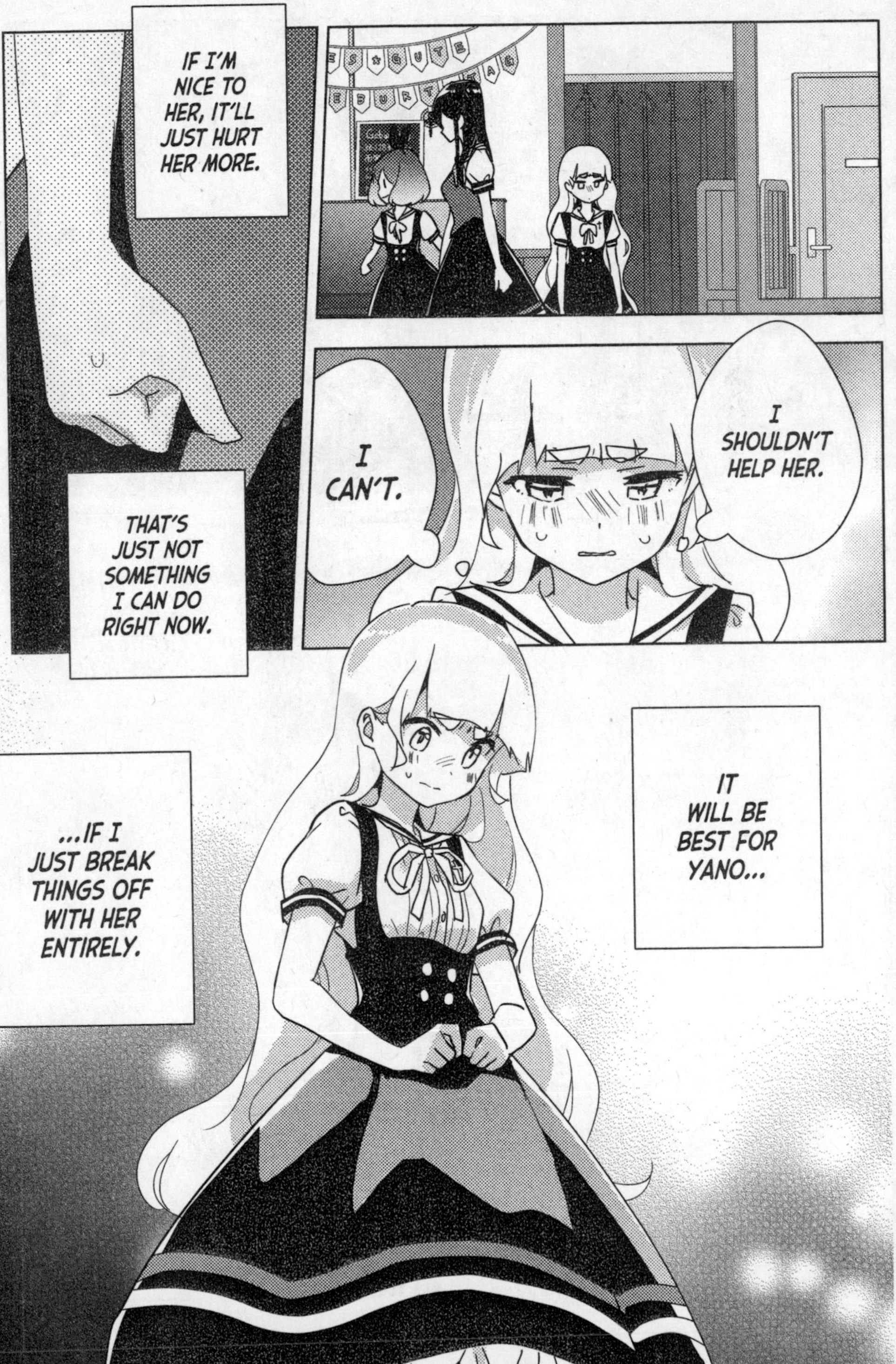
I SHOULDN'T HELP HER.
I CAN'T.
IF I'M NICE TO HER, IT'LL JUST HURT HER MORE.
THAT'S JUST NOT SOMETHING I CAN DO RIGHT NOW.
IT WILL BE BEST FOR YANO...
...IF I JUST BREAK THINGS OFF WITH HER ENTIRELY.

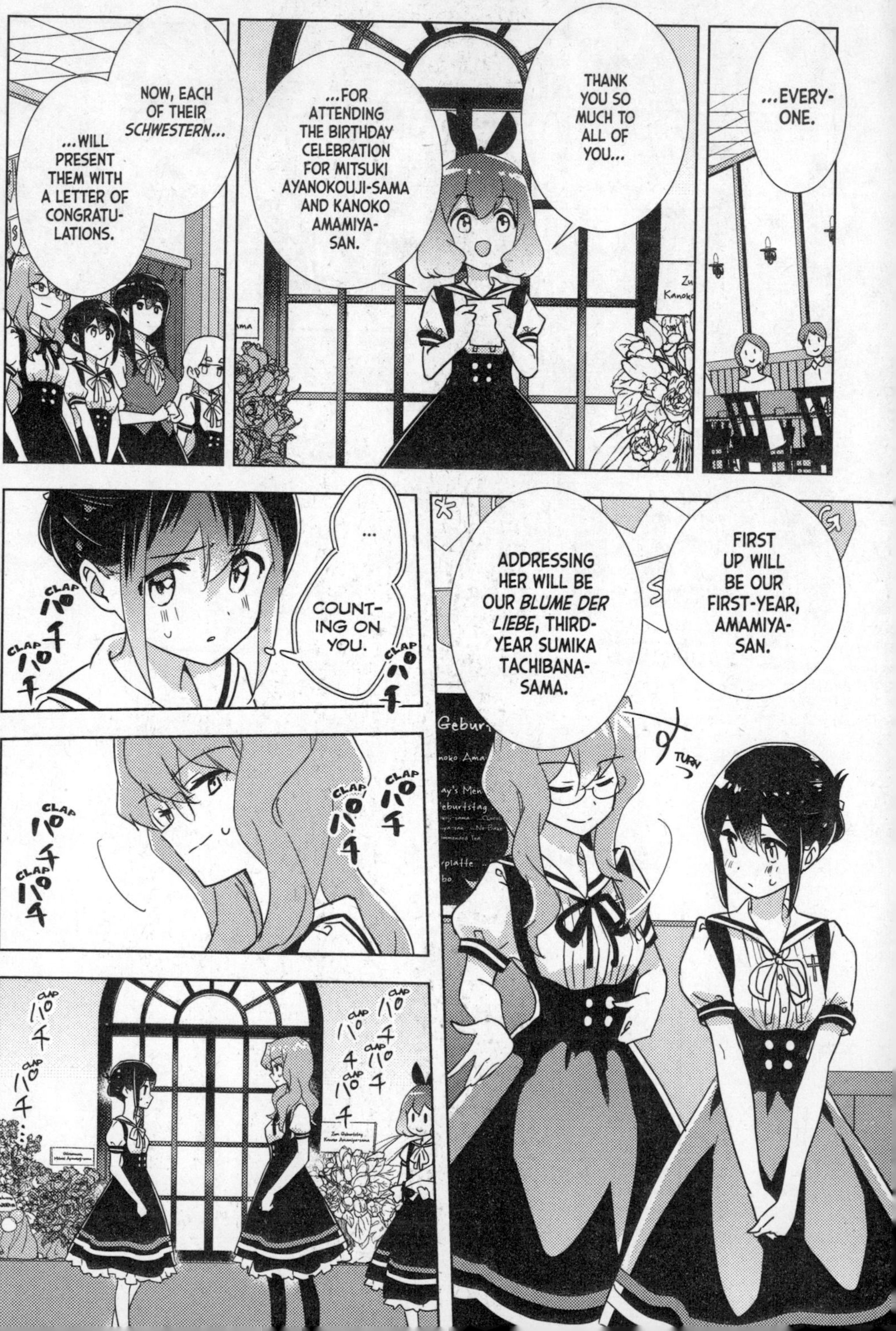
...EVERY-ONE.
THANK YOU SO MUCH TO ALL OF YOU...
...FOR ATTENDING THE BIRTHDAY CELEBRATION FOR MITSUKI AYANOKOUJI-SAMA AND KANOKO AMAMIYA-SAN.
NOW, EACH OF THEIR *SCHWESTERN*...
...WILL PRESENT THEM WITH A LETTER OF CONGRATU-LATIONS.
FIRST UP WILL BE OUR FIRST-YEAR, AMAMIYA-SAN.
ADDRESSING HER WILL BE OUR *BLUME DER LIEBE*, THIRD-YEAR SUMIKA TACHIBANA-SAMA.
TURN
...
COUNT-ING ON YOU.
CLAP パチ
CLAP パチ
CLAP パチ
CLAP パチ
CLAP パチ
CLAP パチ
CLAP パチ
CLAP パチ
CLAP パチ
CLAP パチ
CLAP パチ
CLAP パチ

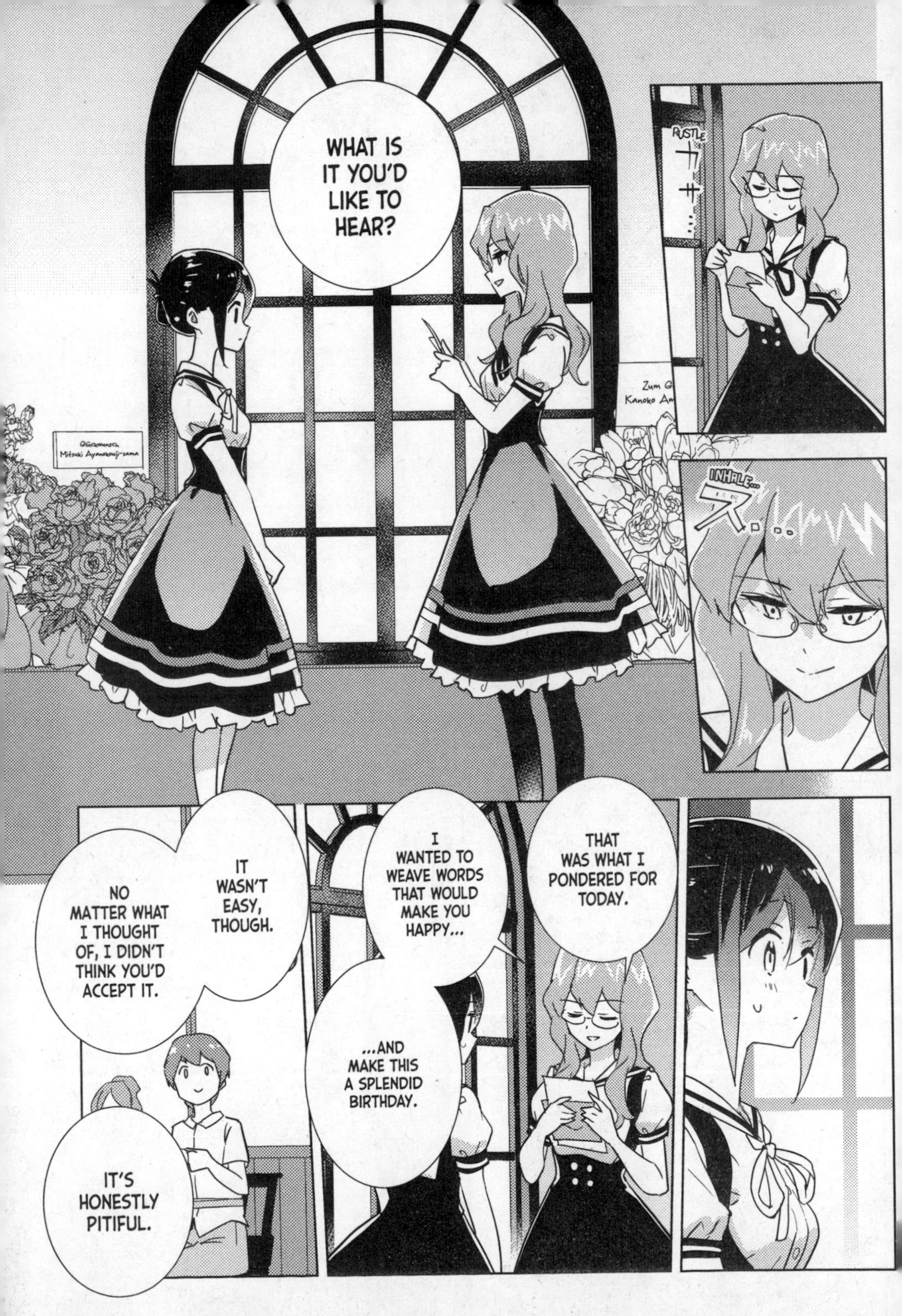
RUSTLE
ガサ…
INHALE...
ス…
WHAT IS IT YOU'D LIKE TO HEAR?
Glückwunsch Mitsuki Ayanokouji-sama
THAT WAS WHAT I PONDERED FOR TODAY.
I WANTED TO WEAVE WORDS THAT WOULD MAKE YOU HAPPY...
...AND MAKE THIS A SPLENDID BIRTHDAY.
IT WASN'T EASY, THOUGH.
NO MATTER WHAT I THOUGHT OF, I DIDN'T THINK YOU'D ACCEPT IT.
IT'S HONESTLY PITIFUL.

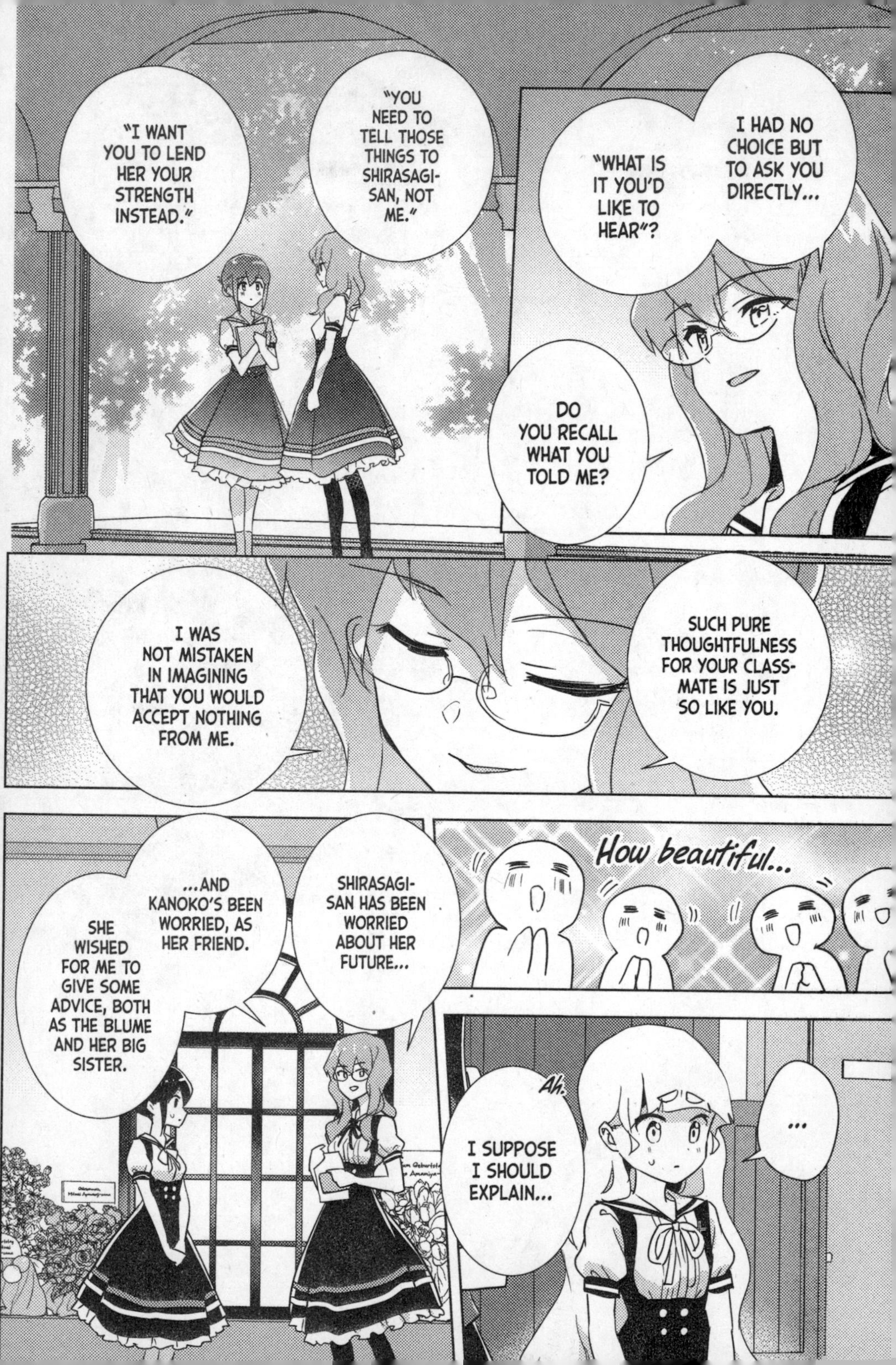
I HAD NO CHOICE BUT TO ASK YOU DIRECTLY...
"WHAT IS IT YOU'D LIKE TO HEAR"?
DO YOU RECALL WHAT YOU TOLD ME?
"YOU NEED TO TELL THOSE THINGS TO SHIRASAGI-SAN, NOT ME."
"I WANT YOU TO LEND HER YOUR STRENGTH INSTEAD."
SUCH PURE THOUGHTFULNESS FOR YOUR CLASS-MATE IS JUST SO LIKE YOU.
I WAS NOT MISTAKEN IN IMAGINING THAT YOU WOULD ACCEPT NOTHING FROM ME.
How beautiful...
...
Ah.
I SUPPOSE I SHOULD EXPLAIN...
SHIRASAGI-SAN HAS BEEN WORRIED ABOUT HER FUTURE...
...AND KANOKO'S BEEN WORRIED, AS HER FRIEND.
SHE WISHED FOR ME TO GIVE SOME ADVICE, BOTH AS THE BLUME AND HER BIG SISTER.

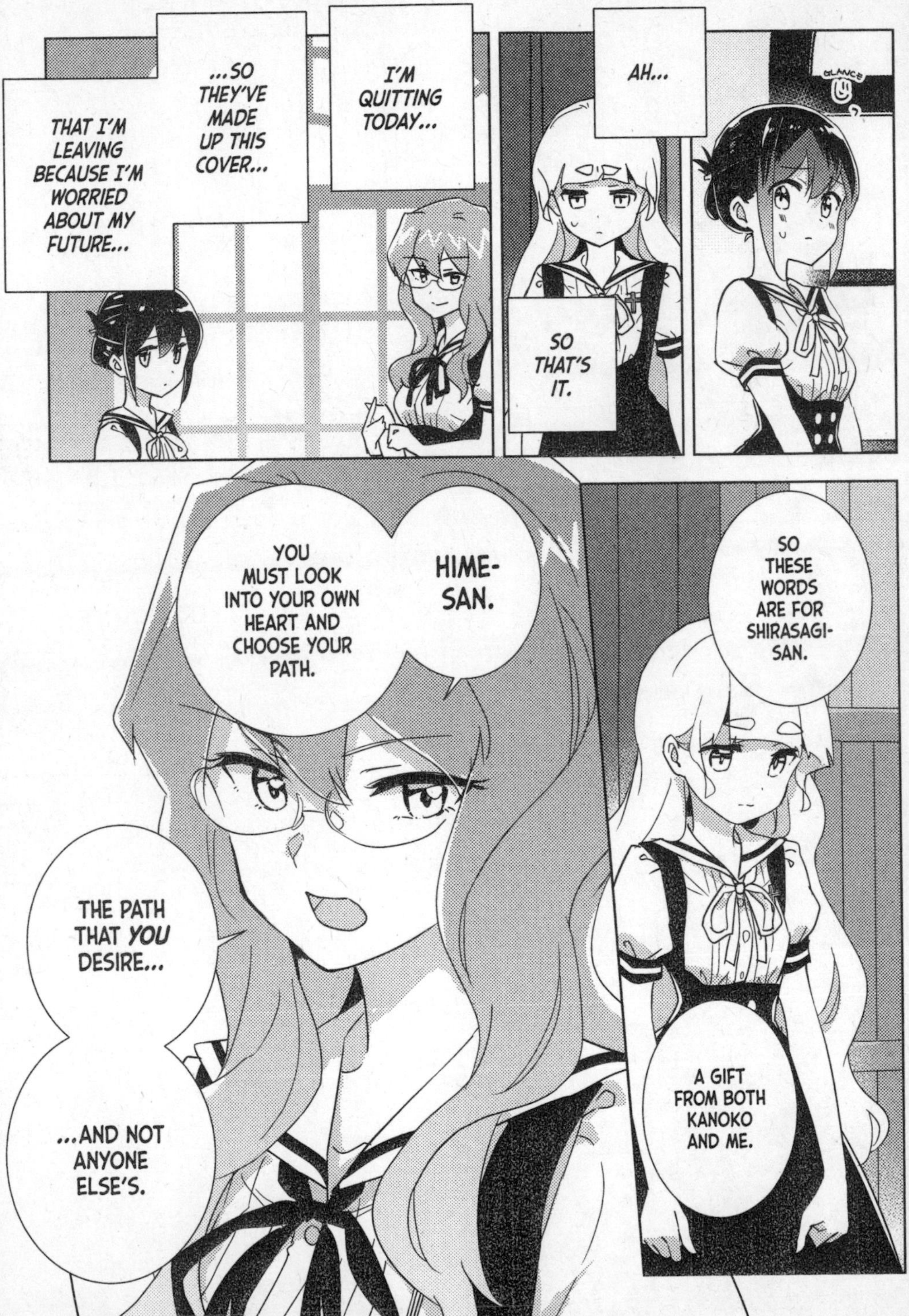
GLANCE
AH...
SO THAT'S IT.
I'M QUITTING TODAY...
...SO THEY'VE MADE UP THIS COVER...
THAT I'M LEAVING BECAUSE I'M WORRIED ABOUT MY FUTURE...
SO THESE WORDS ARE FOR SHIRASAGI-SAN.
A GIFT FROM BOTH KANOKO AND ME.
HIME-SAN.
YOU MUST LOOK INTO YOUR OWN HEART AND CHOOSE YOUR PATH.
THE PATH THAT YOU DESIRE...
...AND NOT ANYONE ELSE'S.

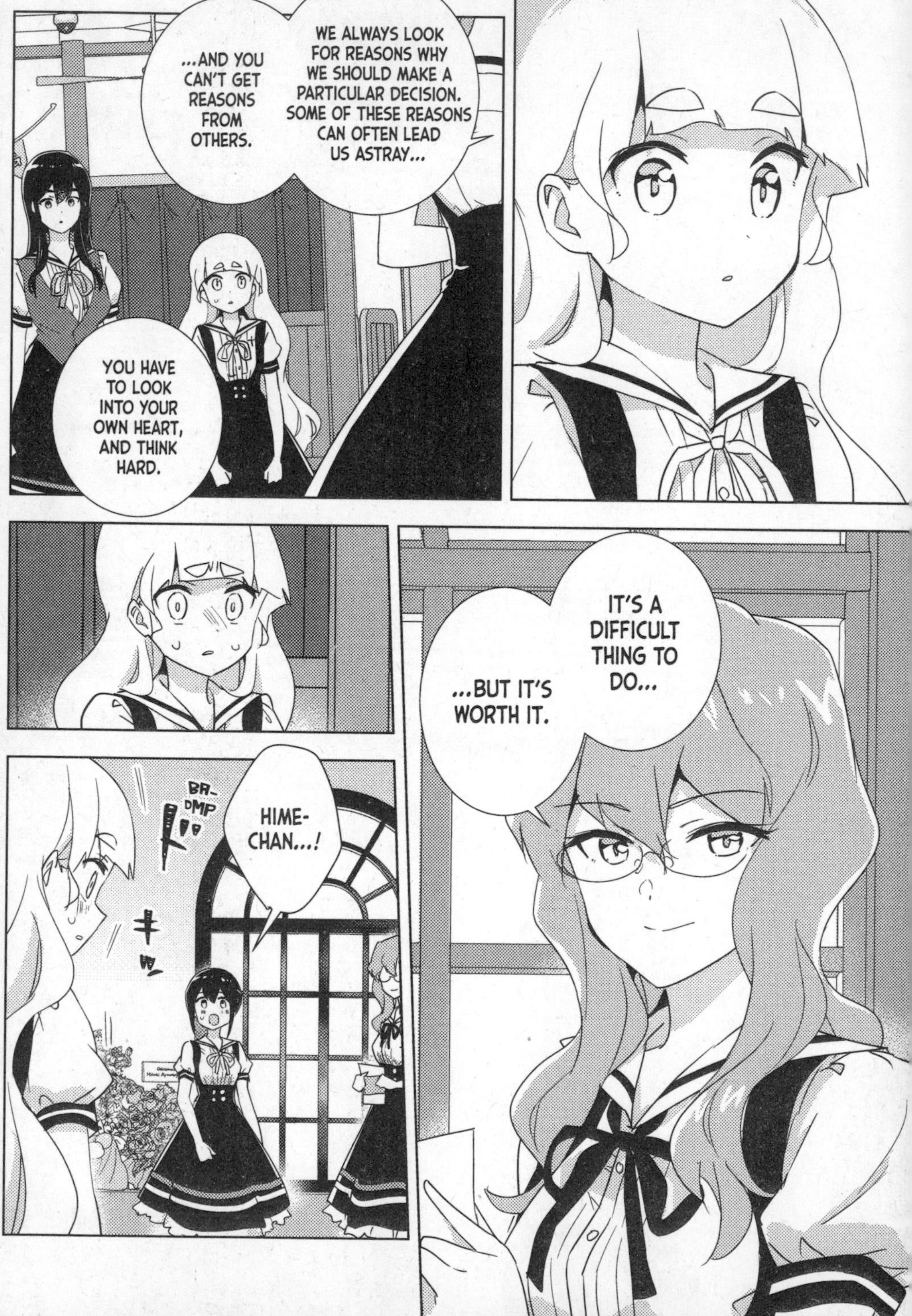
WE ALWAYS LOOK FOR REASONS WHY WE SHOULD MAKE A PARTICULAR DECISION. SOME OF THESE REASONS CAN OFTEN LEAD US ASTRAY...
...AND YOU CAN'T GET REASONS FROM OTHERS.
YOU HAVE TO LOOK INTO YOUR OWN HEART, AND THINK HARD.
IT'S A DIFFICULT THING TO DO...
...BUT IT'S WORTH IT.
BA-DMP
HIME-CHAN...!

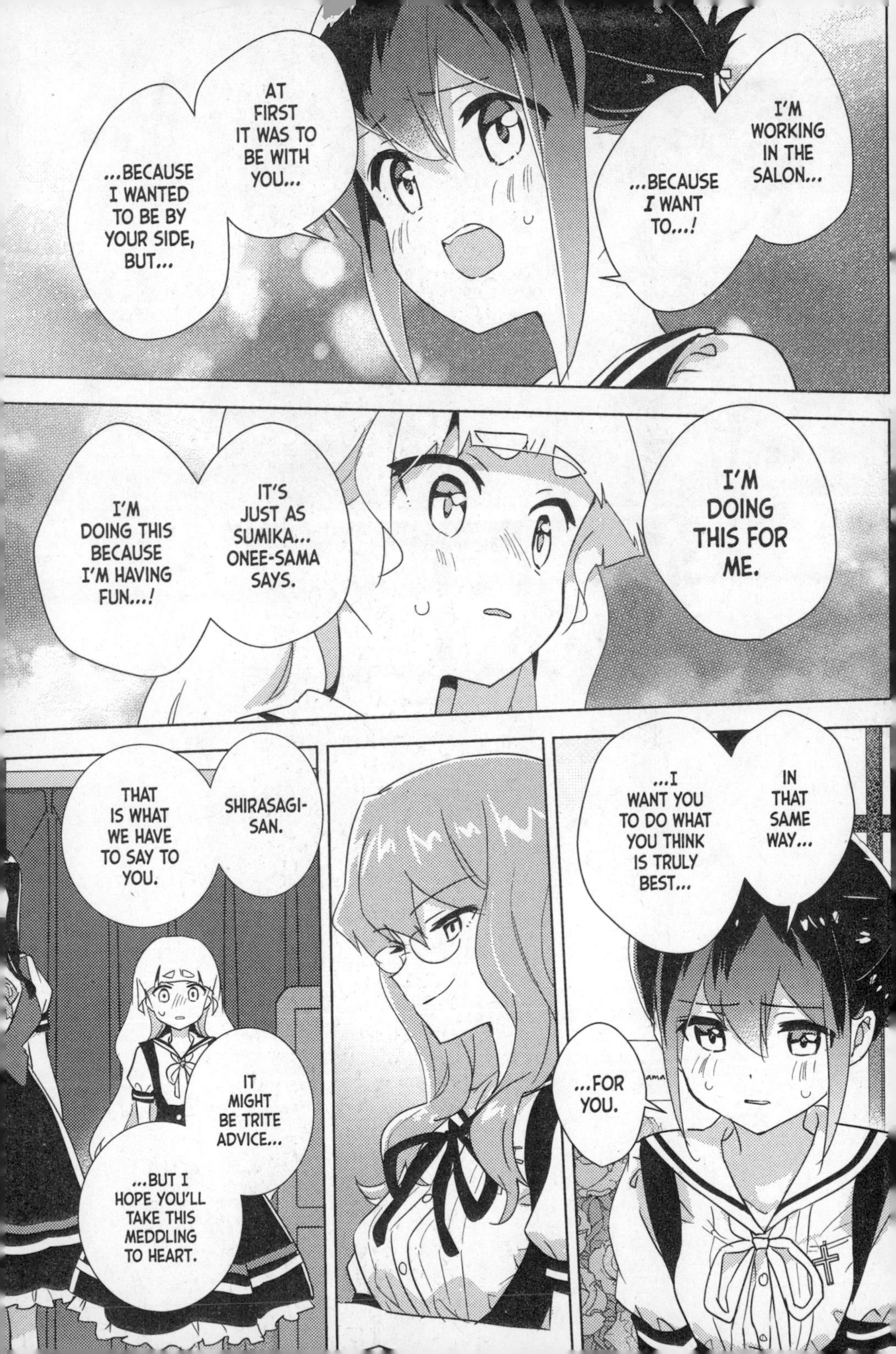
I'M WORKING IN THE SALON...
...BECAUSE *I* WANT TO...!
AT FIRST IT WAS TO BE WITH YOU...
...BECAUSE I WANTED TO BE BY YOUR SIDE, BUT...
I'M DOING THIS FOR ME.
IT'S JUST AS SUMIKA... ONEE-SAMA SAYS.
I'M DOING THIS BECAUSE I'M HAVING FUN...!
IN THAT SAME WAY...
...I WANT YOU TO DO WHAT YOU THINK IS TRULY BEST...
...FOR YOU.
SHIRASAGI-SAN.
THAT IS WHAT WE HAVE TO SAY TO YOU.
IT MIGHT BE TRITE ADVICE...
...BUT I HOPE YOU'LL TAKE THIS MEDDLING TO HEART.

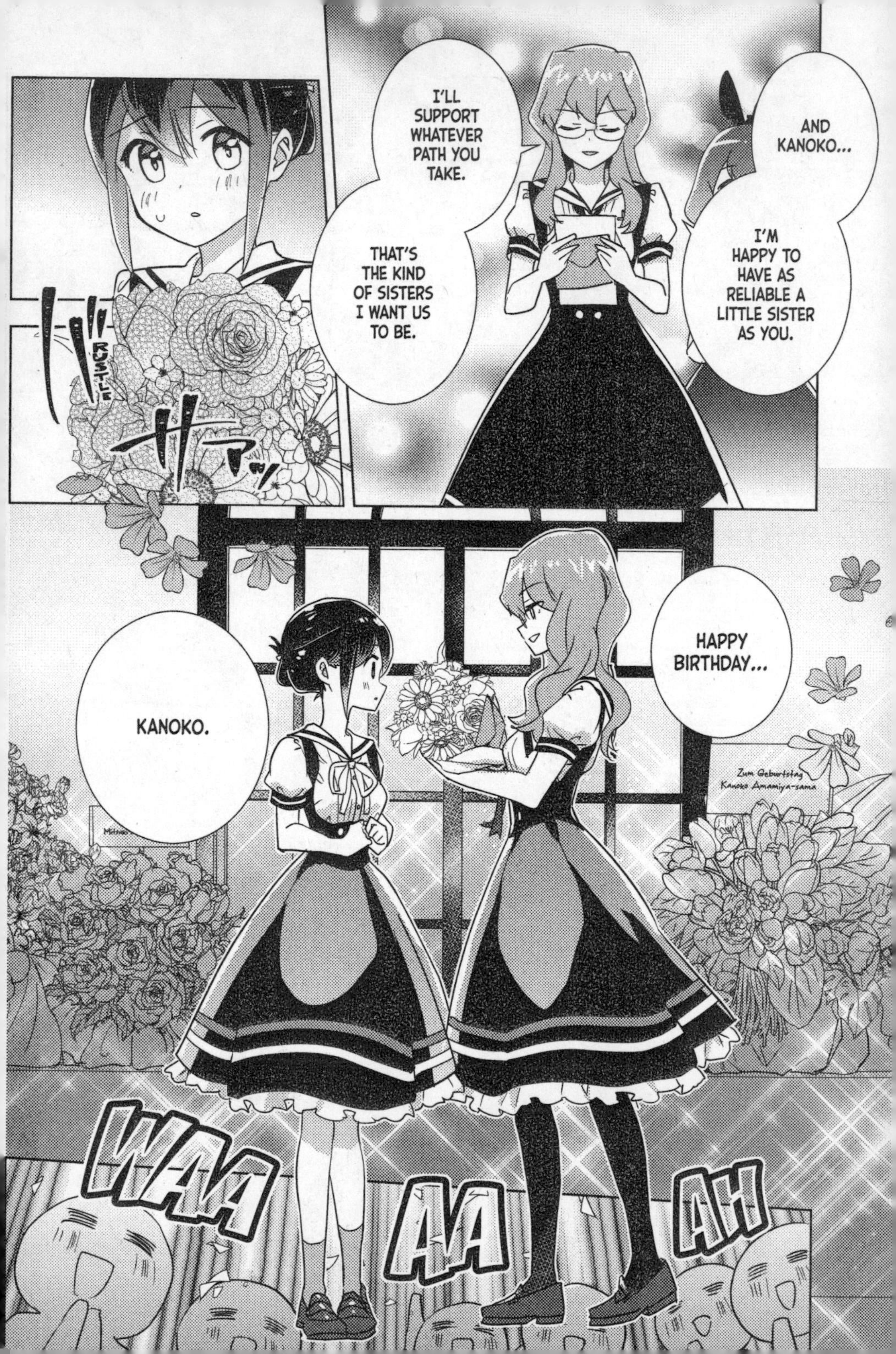
AND KANOKO...
I'M HAPPY TO HAVE AS RELIABLE A LITTLE SISTER AS YOU.
I'LL SUPPORT WHATEVER PATH YOU TAKE.
THAT'S THE KIND OF SISTERS I WANT US TO BE.
RUSTLE
HAPPY BIRTHDAY...
Zum Geburtstag Kanoko Amamiya-sama
KANOKO.
WAA
AA
AH

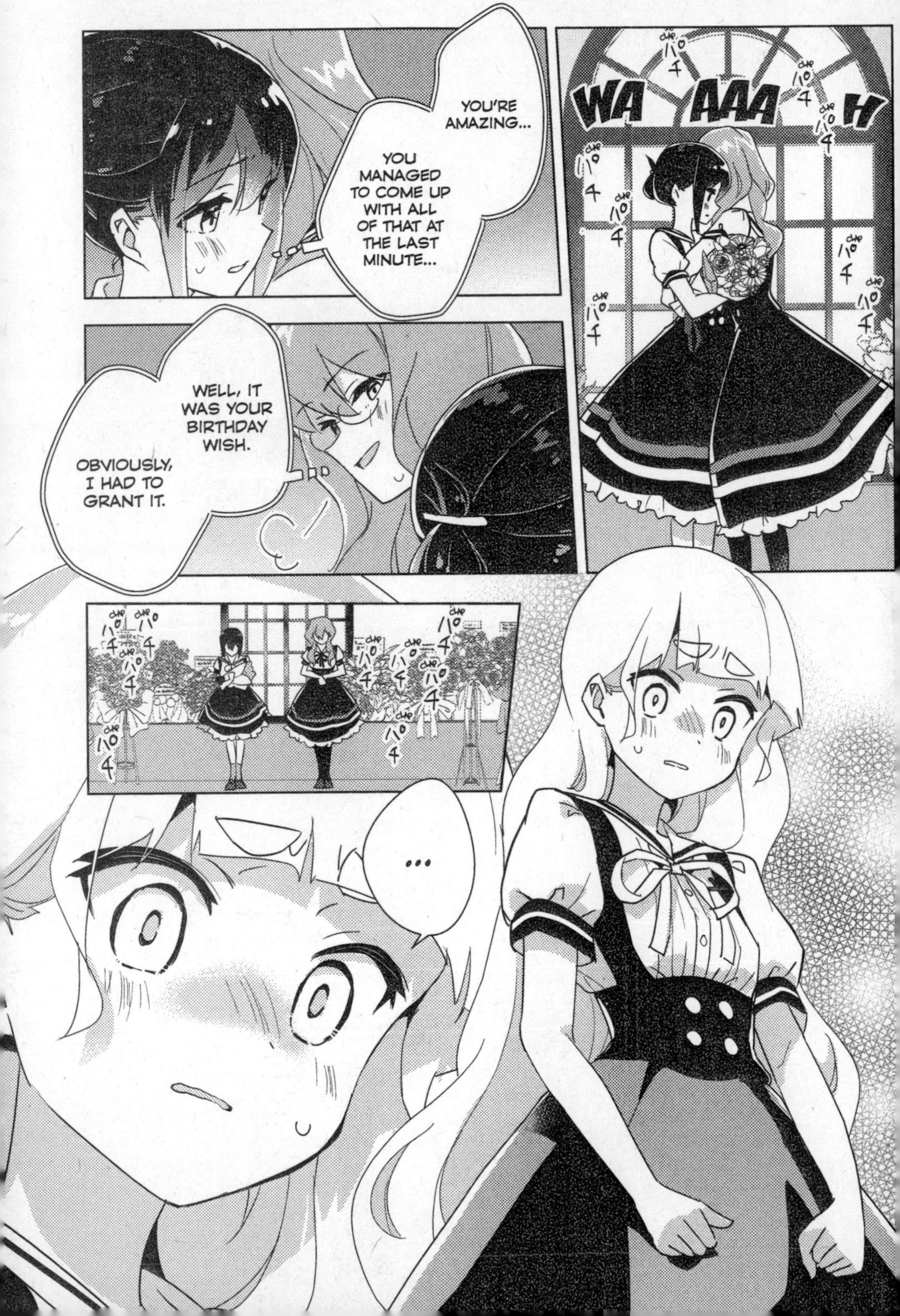

WA AAA H
CLAP パチ
YOU'RE AMAZING...
YOU MANAGED TO COME UP WITH ALL OF THAT AT THE LAST MINUTE...
WELL, IT WAS YOUR BIRTHDAY WISH.
OBVIOUSLY, I HAD TO GRANT IT.
CLAP パチ
...

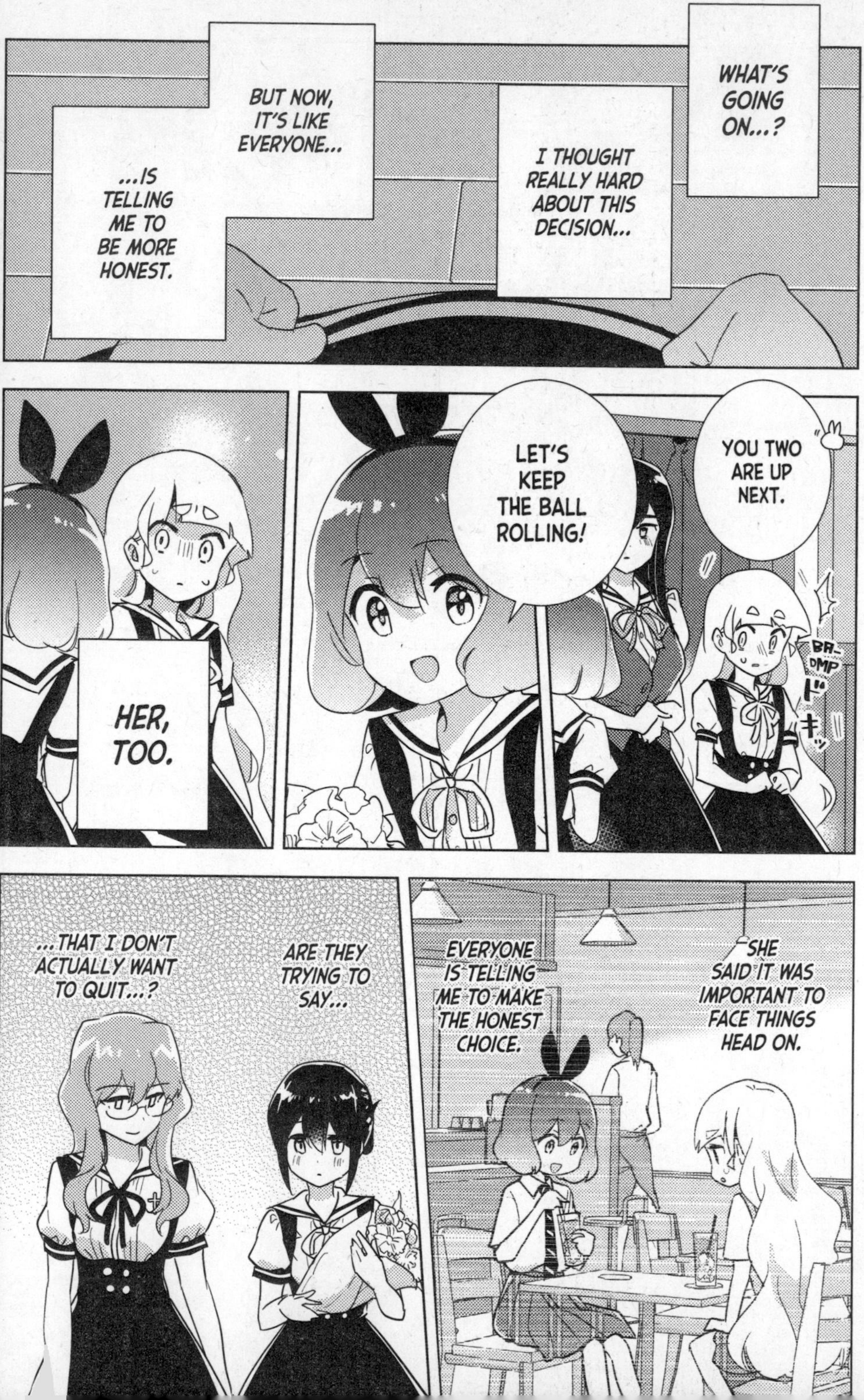
WHAT'S GOING ON...?
I THOUGHT REALLY HARD ABOUT THIS DECISION...
BUT NOW, IT'S LIKE EVERYONE...
...IS TELLING ME TO BE MORE HONEST.
YOU TWO ARE UP NEXT.
LET'S KEEP THE BALL ROLLING!
BA-DMP ドキッ
HER, TOO.
SHE SAID IT WAS IMPORTANT TO FACE THINGS HEAD ON.
EVERYONE IS TELLING ME TO MAKE THE HONEST CHOICE.
ARE THEY TRYING TO SAY...
...THAT I DON'T ACTUALLY WANT TO QUIT...?

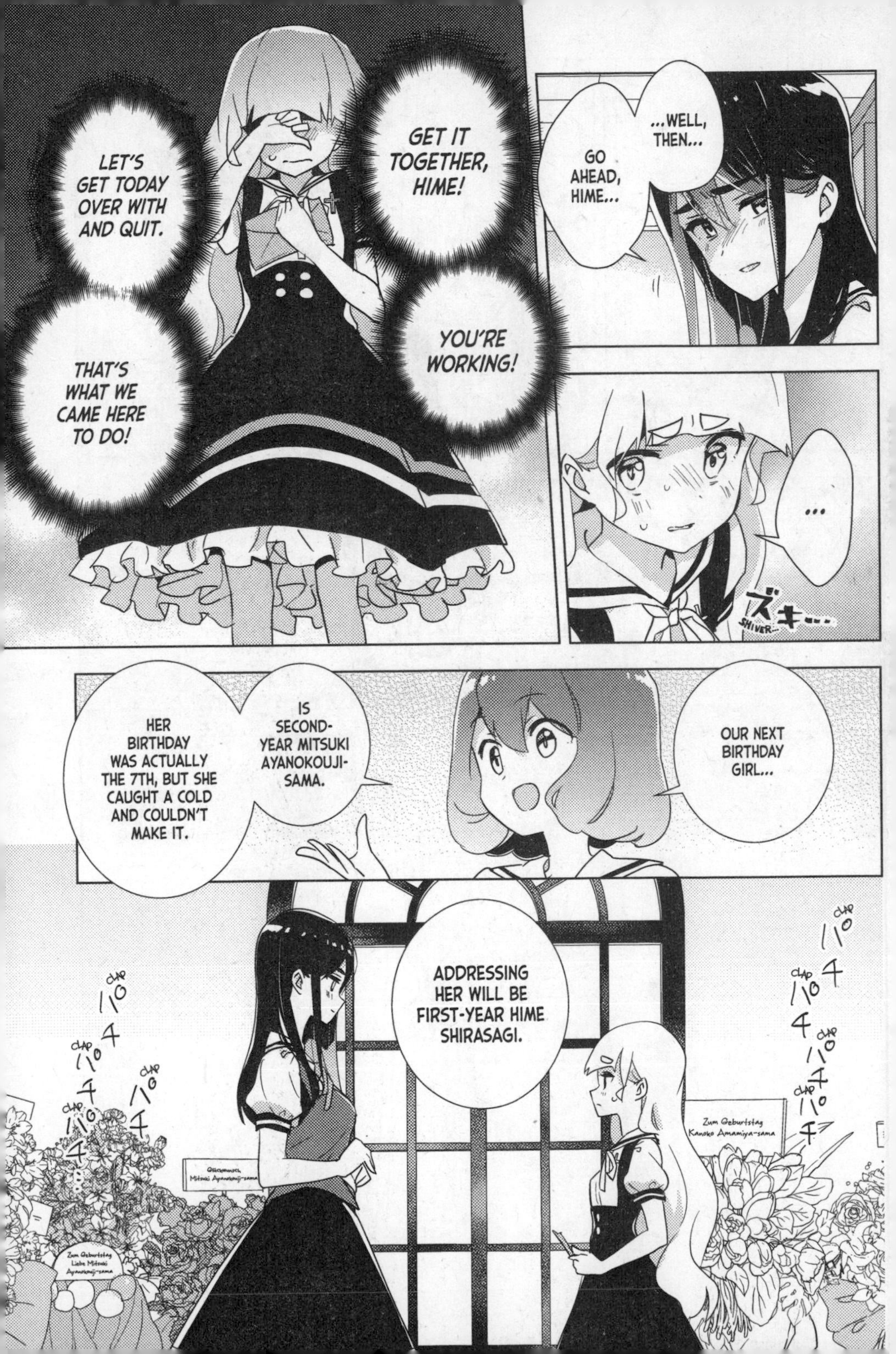
...WELL, THEN...
GO AHEAD, HIME...
...
ズキ…
SHIVER...
GET IT TOGETHER, HIME!
LET'S GET TODAY OVER WITH AND QUIT.
YOU'RE WORKING!
THAT'S WHAT WE CAME HERE TO DO!
OUR NEXT BIRTHDAY GIRL...
IS SECOND-YEAR MITSUKI AYANOKOUJI-SAMA.
HER BIRTHDAY WAS ACTUALLY THE 7TH, BUT SHE CAUGHT A COLD AND COULDN'T MAKE IT.
パチ
CLAP
ADDRESSING HER WILL BE FIRST-YEAR HIME SHIRASAGI.
Zum Geburtstag Kanoko Amamiya-sama
パチ
CLAP
Zum Geburtstag Liebe Mitsuki Ayanokouji-sama

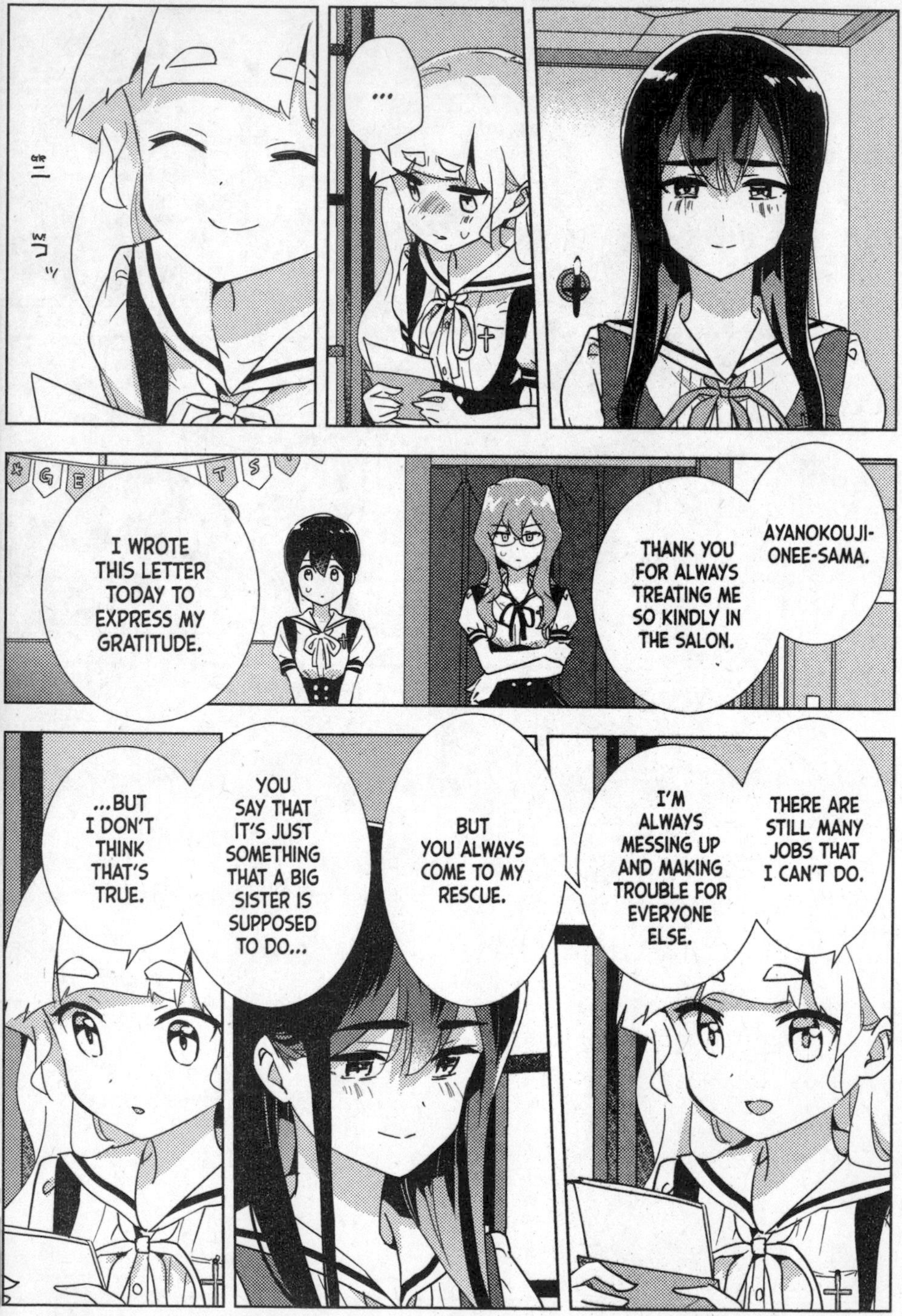
...
ニコッ
AYANOKOUJI-ONEE-SAMA.
THANK YOU FOR ALWAYS TREATING ME SO KINDLY IN THE SALON.
I WROTE THIS LETTER TODAY TO EXPRESS MY GRATITUDE.
THERE ARE STILL MANY JOBS THAT I CAN'T DO.
I'M ALWAYS MESSING UP AND MAKING TROUBLE FOR EVERYONE ELSE.
BUT YOU ALWAYS COME TO MY RESCUE.
YOU SAY THAT IT'S JUST SOMETHING THAT A BIG SISTER IS SUPPOSED TO DO...
...BUT I DON'T THINK THAT'S TRUE.

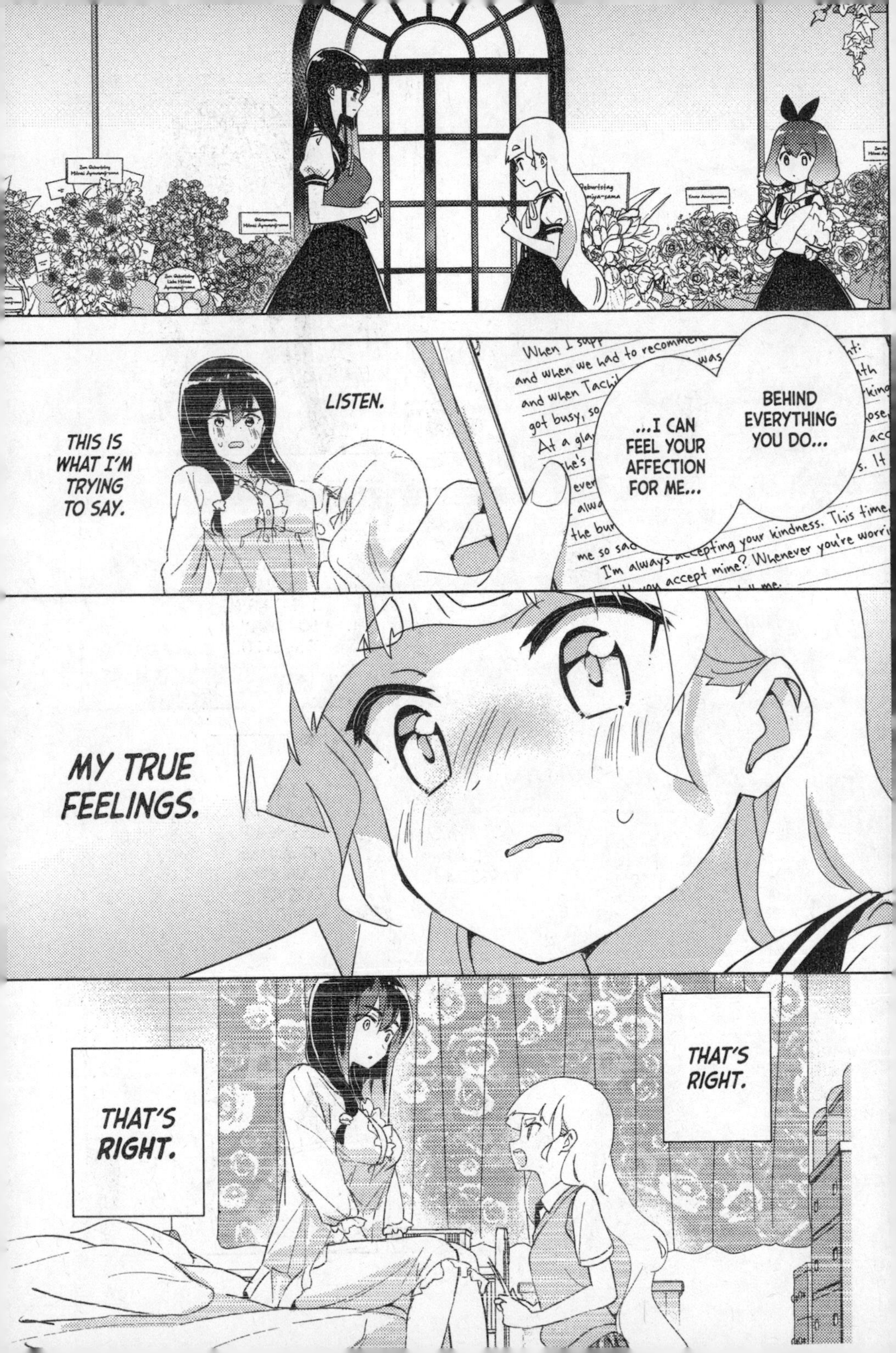
BEHIND EVERYTHING YOU DO...
...I CAN FEEL YOUR AFFECTION FOR ME...
LISTEN.
THIS IS WHAT I'M TRYING TO SAY.
MY TRUE FEELINGS.
THAT'S RIGHT.
THAT'S RIGHT.

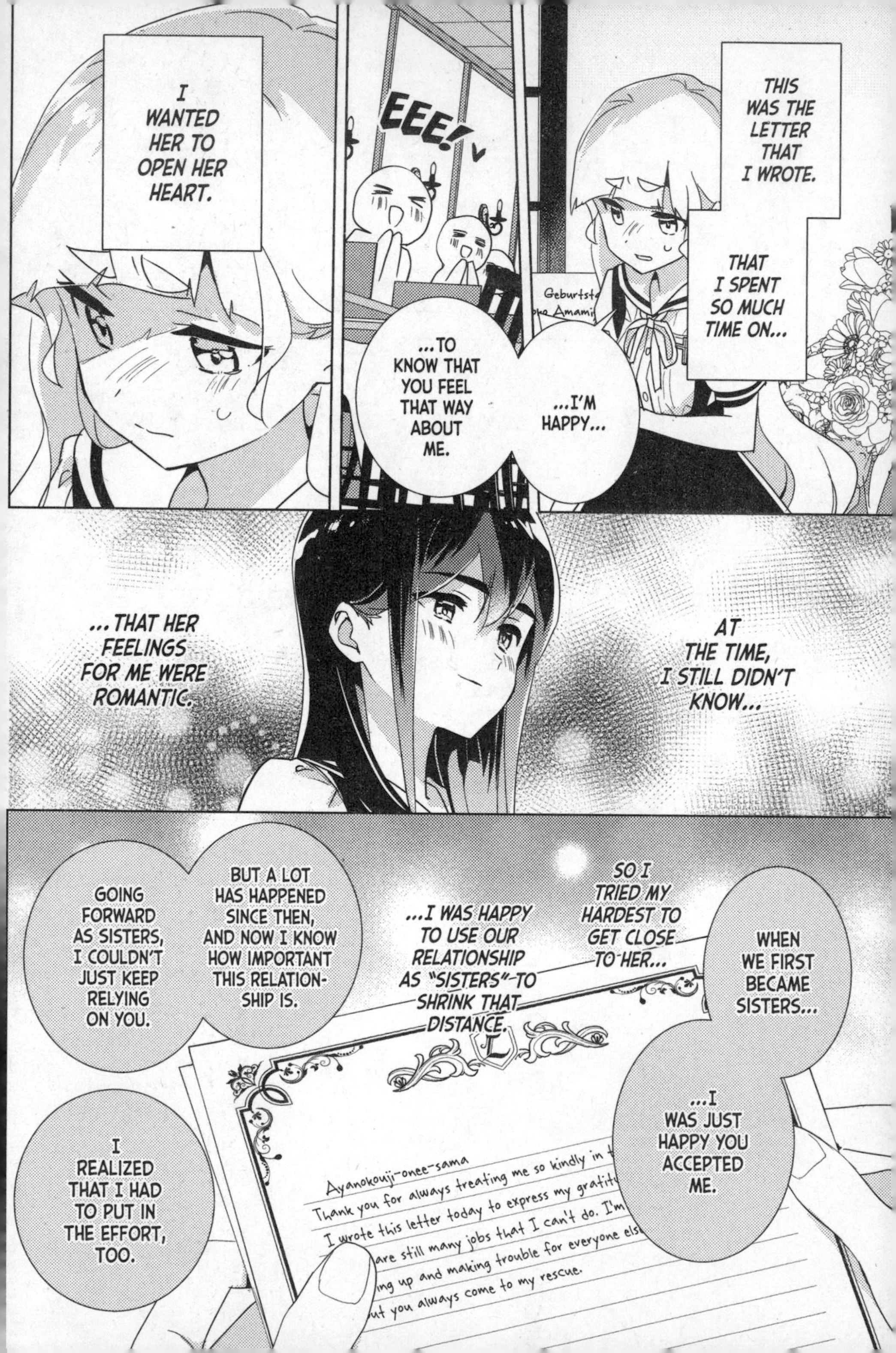
THIS WAS THE LETTER THAT I WROTE.
THAT I SPENT SO MUCH TIME ON...
...I'M HAPPY...
...TO KNOW THAT YOU FEEL THAT WAY ABOUT ME.
EEE!
I WANTED HER TO OPEN HER HEART.
AT THE TIME, I STILL DIDN'T KNOW...
...THAT HER FEELINGS FOR ME WERE ROMANTIC.
WHEN WE FIRST BECAME SISTERS...
...I WAS JUST HAPPY YOU ACCEPTED ME.
SO I TRIED MY HARDEST TO GET CLOSE TO HER...
...I WAS HAPPY TO USE OUR RELATIONSHIP AS "SISTERS" TO SHRINK THAT DISTANCE.
BUT A LOT HAS HAPPENED SINCE THEN, AND NOW I KNOW HOW IMPORTANT THIS RELATIONSHIP IS.
GOING FORWARD AS SISTERS, I COULDN'T JUST KEEP RELYING ON YOU.
I REALIZED THAT I HAD TO PUT IN THE EFFORT, TOO.
Ayanokouji-onee-sama
Thank you for always treating me so kindly in
I wrote this letter today to express my
are still many jobs that I can't do.
up and making trouble for everyone
you always come to my rescue.

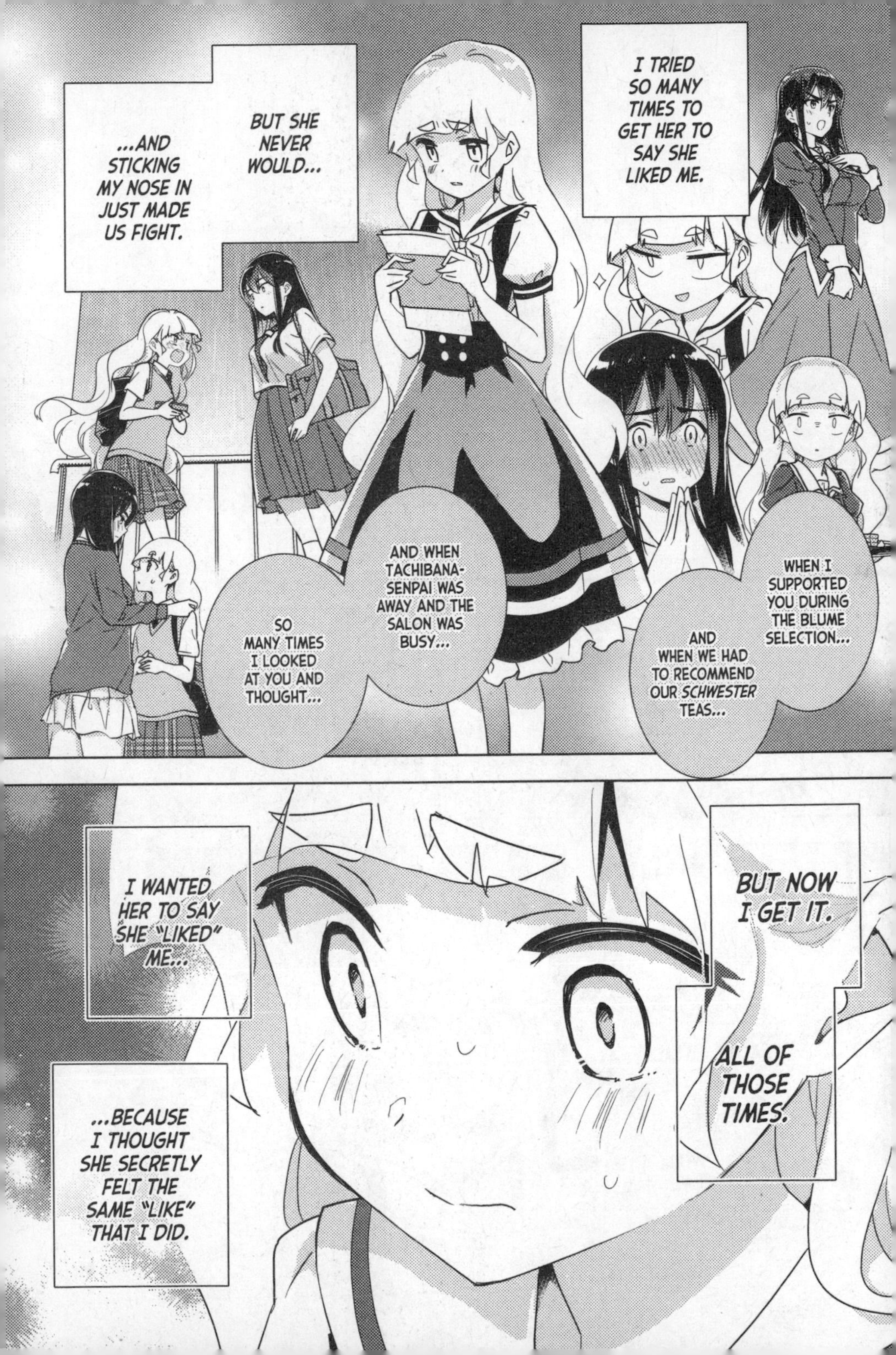
I TRIED SO MANY TIMES TO GET HER TO SAY SHE LIKED ME.
BUT SHE NEVER WOULD...
...AND STICKING MY NOSE IN JUST MADE US FIGHT.
WHEN I SUPPORTED YOU DURING THE BLUME SELECTION...
AND WHEN WE HAD TO RECOMMEND OUR *SCHWESTER* TEAS...
AND WHEN TACHIBANA-SENPAI WAS AWAY AND THE SALON WAS BUSY...
SO MANY TIMES I LOOKED AT YOU AND THOUGHT...
I WANTED HER TO SAY SHE "LIKED" ME...
...BECAUSE I THOUGHT SHE SECRETLY FELT THE SAME "LIKE" THAT I DID.
BUT NOW I GET IT.
ALL OF THOSE TIMES.

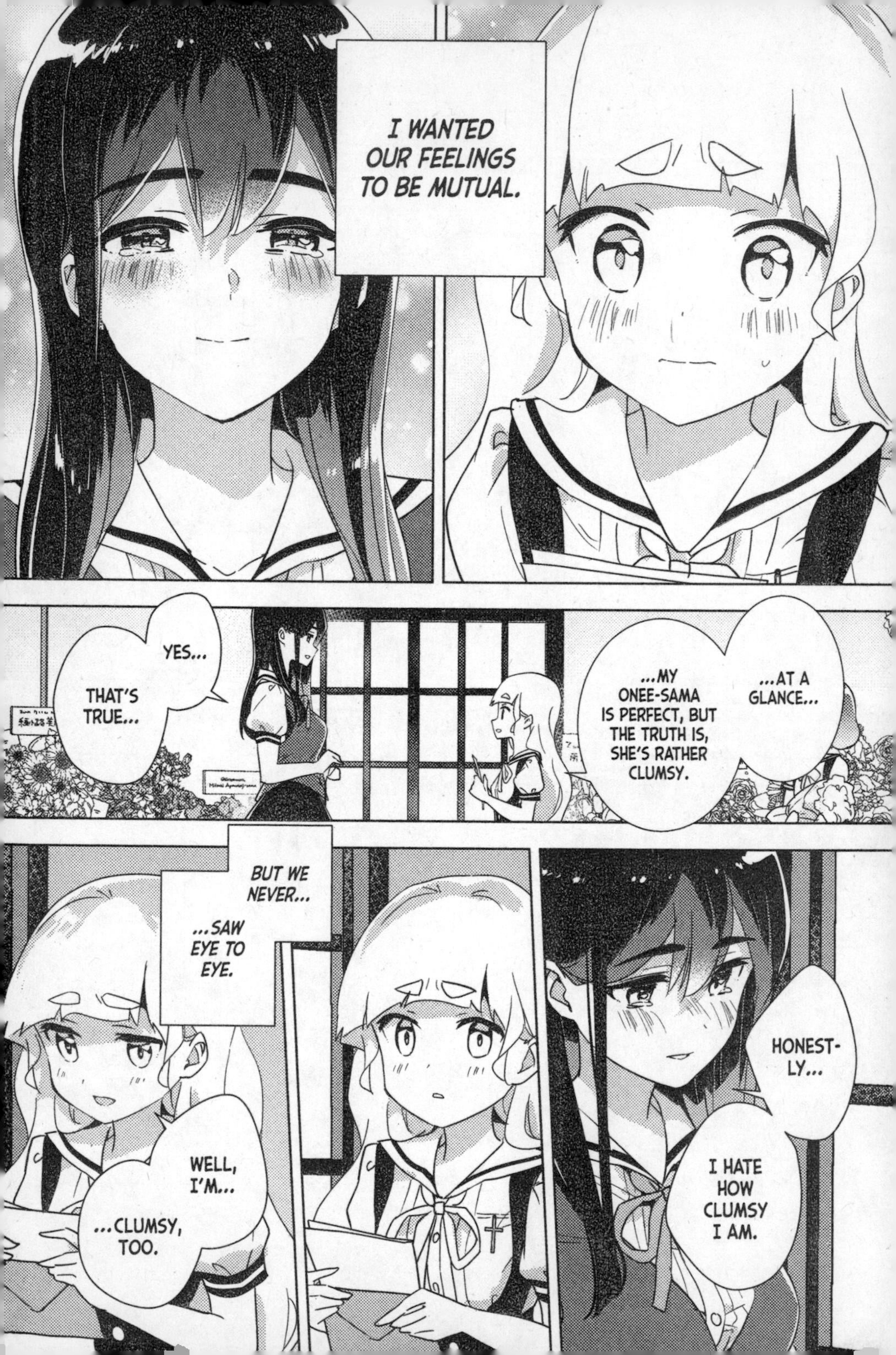
I WANTED OUR FEELINGS TO BE MUTUAL.
...AT A GLANCE...
...MY ONEE-SAMA IS PERFECT, BUT THE TRUTH IS, SHE'S RATHER CLUMSY.
YES...
THAT'S TRUE...
HONEST-LY...
I HATE HOW CLUMSY I AM.
BUT WE NEVER...
...SAW EYE TO EYE.
WELL, I'M...
...CLUMSY, TOO.

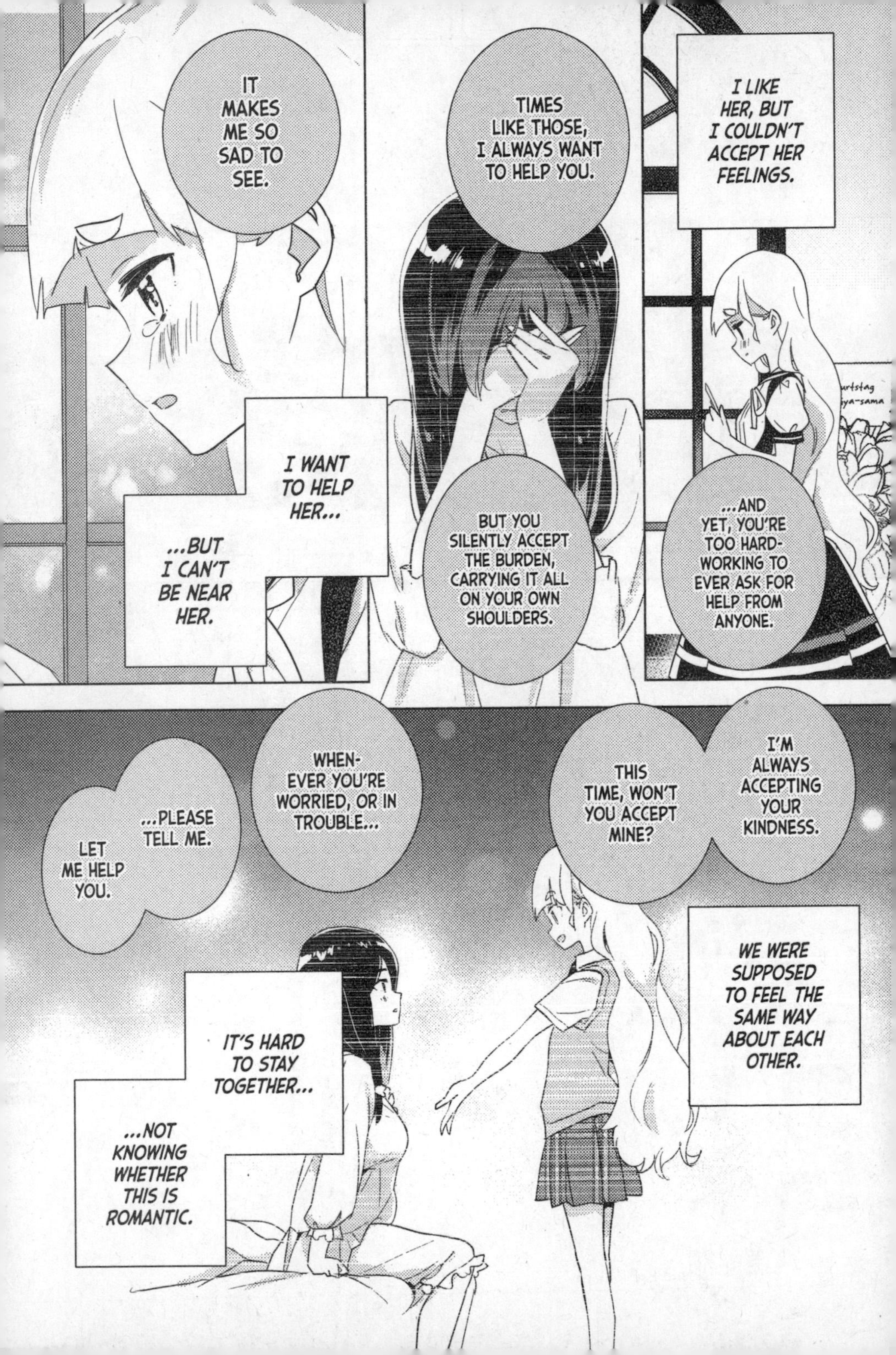

I LIKE HER, BUT I COULDN'T ACCEPT HER FEELINGS.
...AND YET, YOU'RE TOO HARD-WORKING TO EVER ASK FOR HELP FROM ANYONE.
TIMES LIKE THOSE, I ALWAYS WANT TO HELP YOU.
BUT YOU SILENTLY ACCEPT THE BURDEN, CARRYING IT ALL ON YOUR OWN SHOULDERS.
IT MAKES ME SO SAD TO SEE.
I WANT TO HELP HER...
...BUT I CAN'T BE NEAR HER.
I'M ALWAYS ACCEPTING YOUR KINDNESS.
THIS TIME, WON'T YOU ACCEPT MINE?
WE WERE SUPPOSED TO FEEL THE SAME WAY ABOUT EACH OTHER.
WHEN-EVER YOU'RE WORRIED, OR IN TROUBLE...
...PLEASE TELL ME.
LET ME HELP YOU.
IT'S HARD TO STAY TOGETHER...
...NOT KNOWING WHETHER THIS IS ROMANTIC.

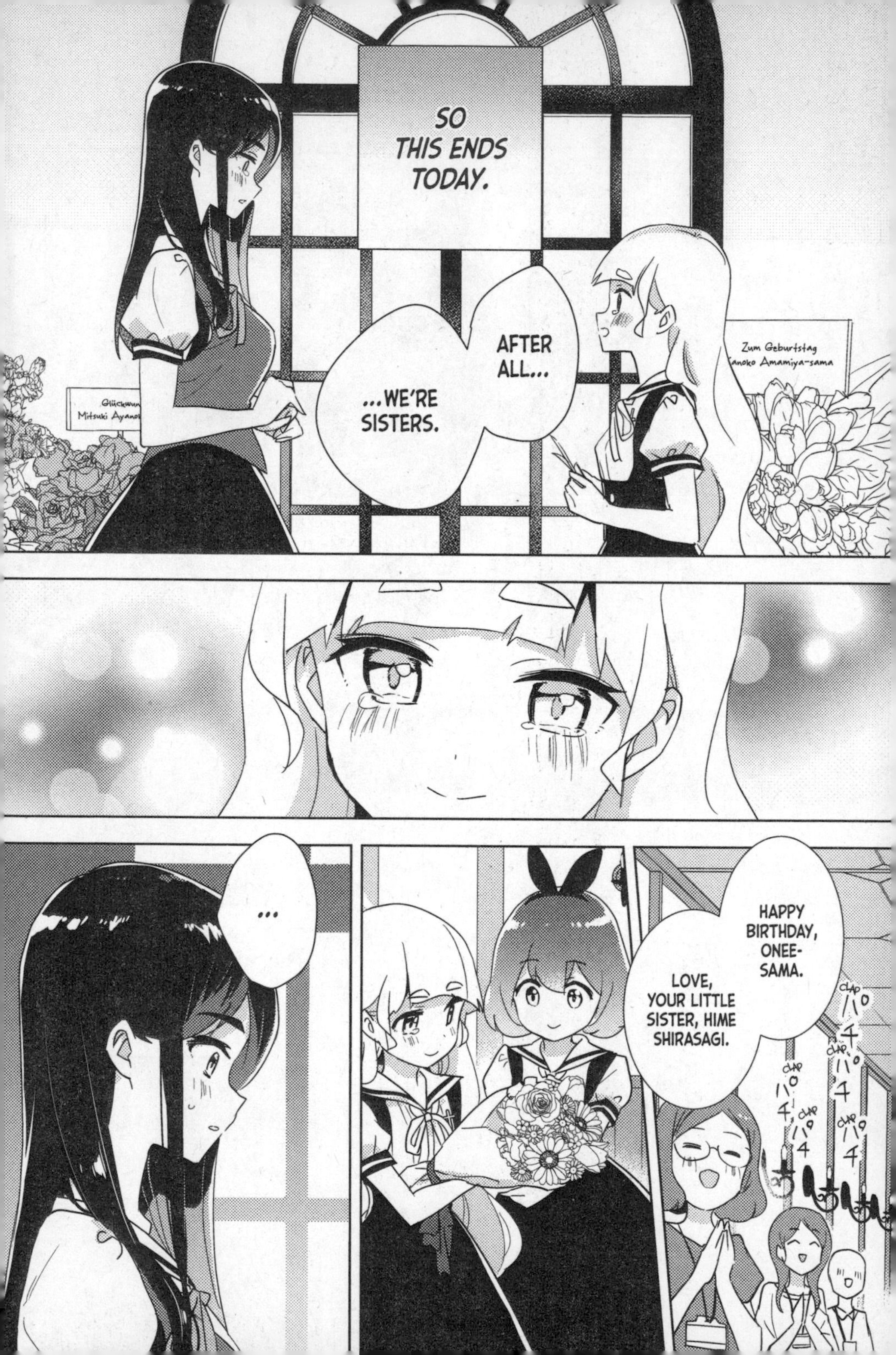
SO THIS ENDS TODAY.
AFTER ALL...
...WE'RE SISTERS.
Zum Geburtstag
HAPPY BIRTHDAY, ONEE-SAMA.
LOVE, YOUR LITTLE SISTER, HIME SHIRASAGI.
CLAP パチ
CLAP パチ
CLAP パチ
CLAP パチ
CLAP パチ
...

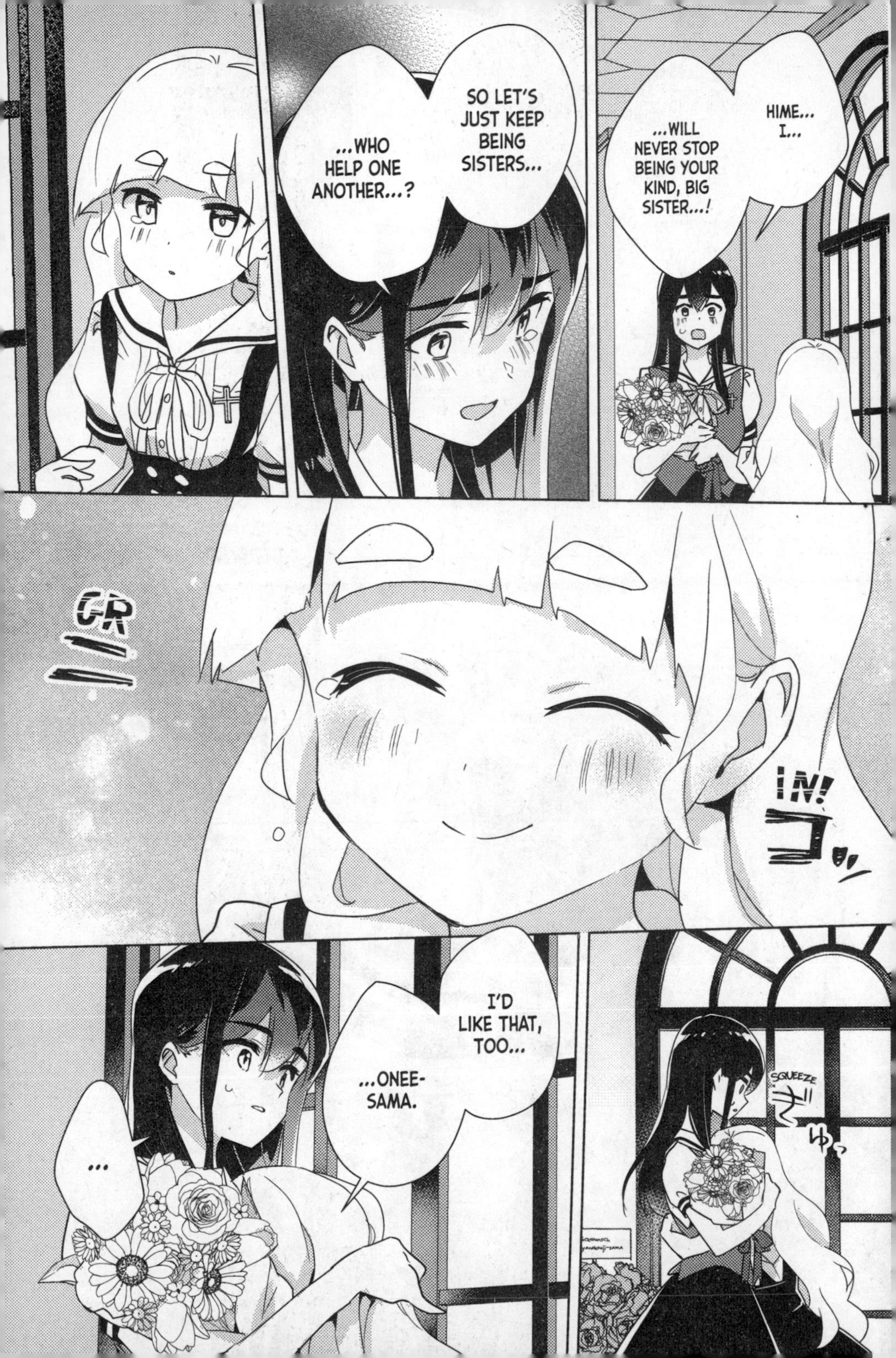
HIME... I...
...WILL NEVER STOP BEING YOUR KIND, BIG SISTER...!
SO LET'S JUST KEEP BEING SISTERS...
...WHO HELP ONE ANOTHER...?
GR
IN!
SQUEEZE
I'D LIKE THAT, TOO...
...ONEE-SAMA.
...

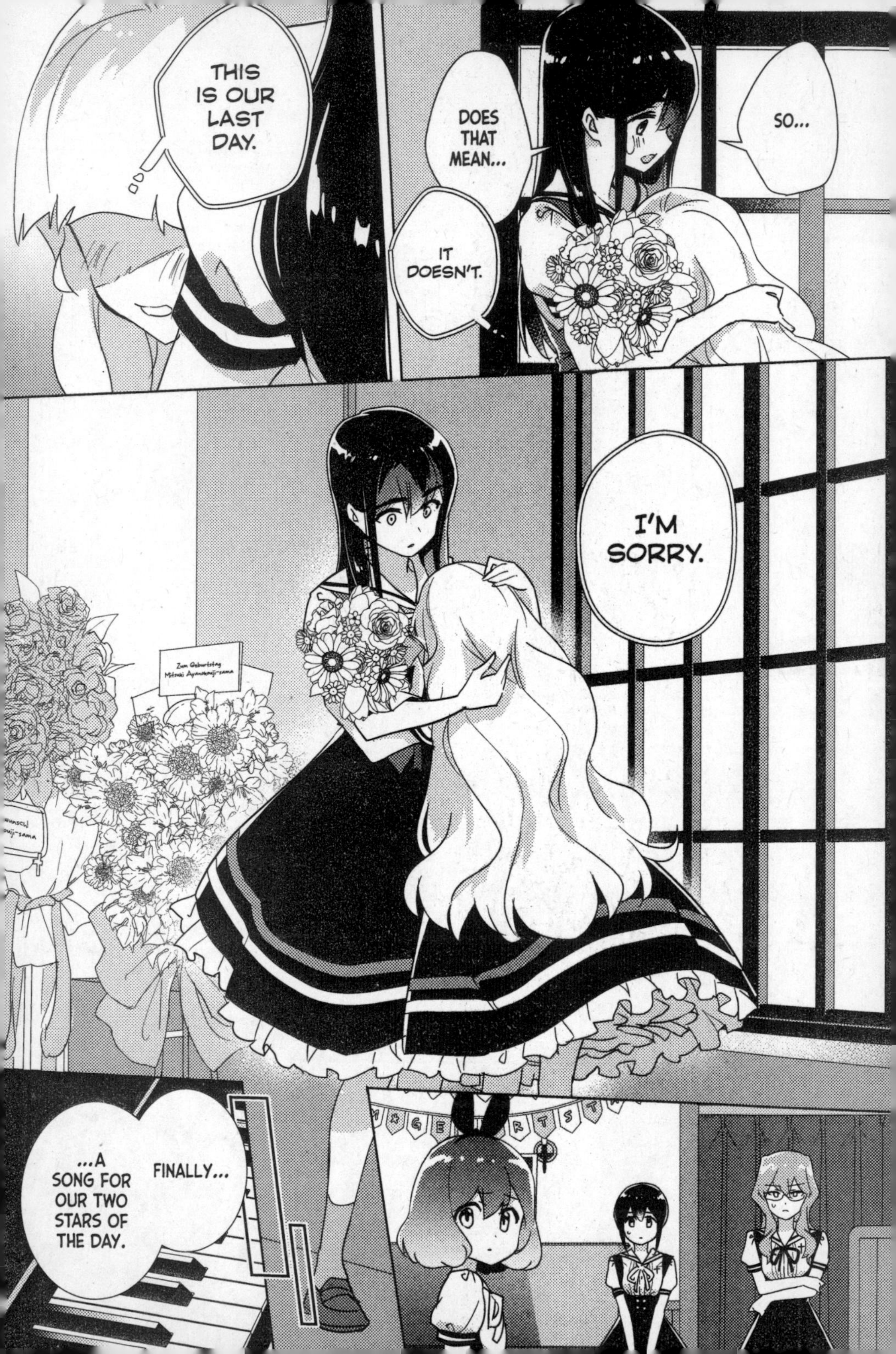
SO...
DOES THAT MEAN...
IT DOESN'T.
THIS IS OUR LAST DAY.
I'M SORRY.
Zum Geburtstag
FINALLY...
...A SONG FOR OUR TWO STARS OF THE DAY.

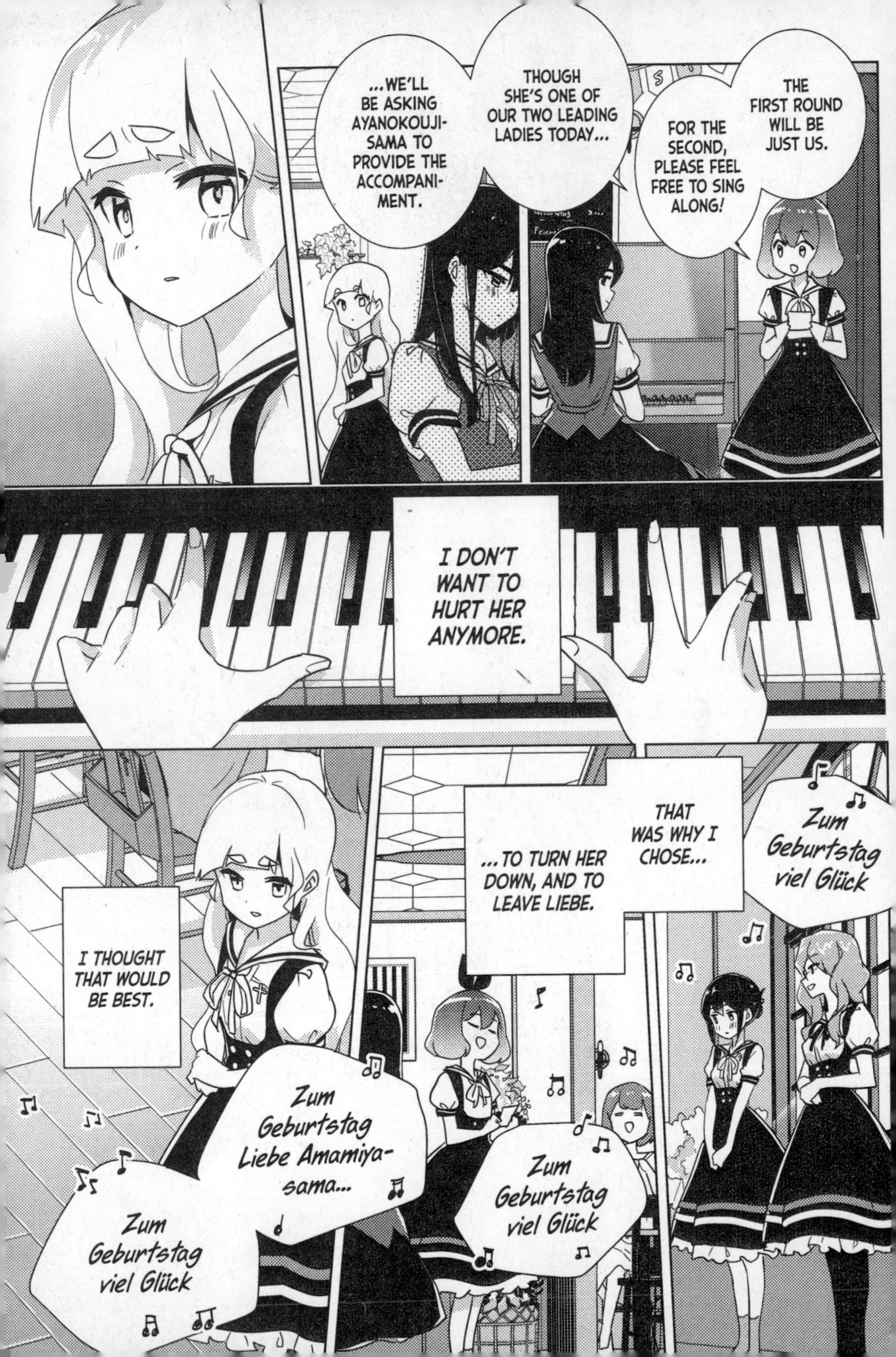
THE FIRST ROUND WILL BE JUST US.
FOR THE SECOND, PLEASE FEEL FREE TO SING ALONG!
THOUGH SHE'S ONE OF OUR TWO LEADING LADIES TODAY...
...WE'LL BE ASKING AYANOKOUJI-SAMA TO PROVIDE THE ACCOMPANIMENT.
I DON'T WANT TO HURT HER ANYMORE.
Zum Geburtstag viel Glück
THAT WAS WHY I CHOSE...
...TO TURN HER DOWN, AND TO LEAVE LIEBE.
Zum Geburtstag viel Glück
Zum Geburtstag Liebe Amamiya-sama...
I THOUGHT THAT WOULD BE BEST.
Zum Geburtstag viel Glück

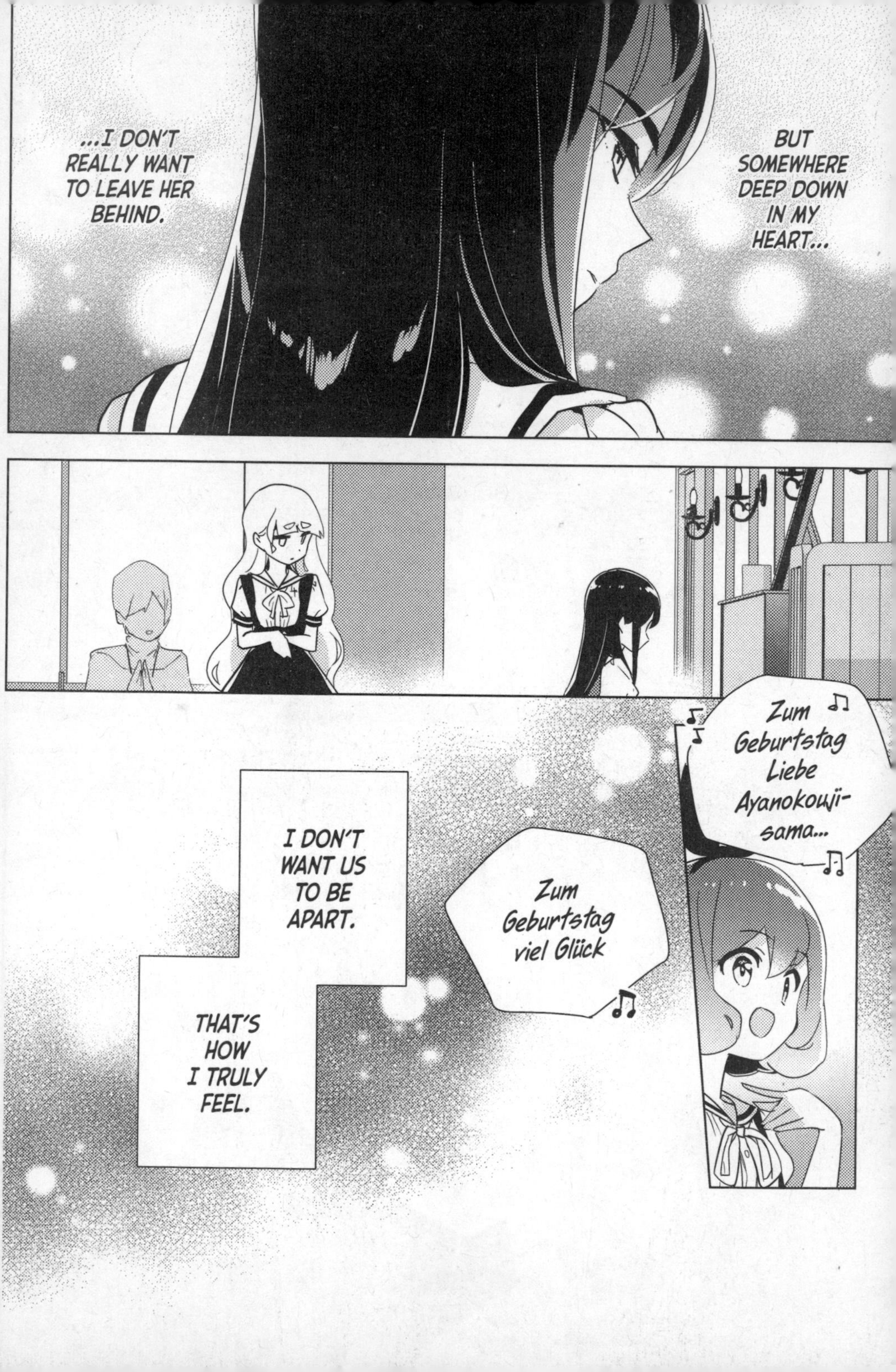
BUT SOMEWHERE DEEP DOWN IN MY HEART...
...I DON'T REALLY WANT TO LEAVE HER BEHIND.
Zum Geburtstag Liebe Ayanokouji-sama...
Zum Geburtstag viel Glück
I DON'T WANT US TO BE APART.
THAT'S HOW I TRULY FEEL.

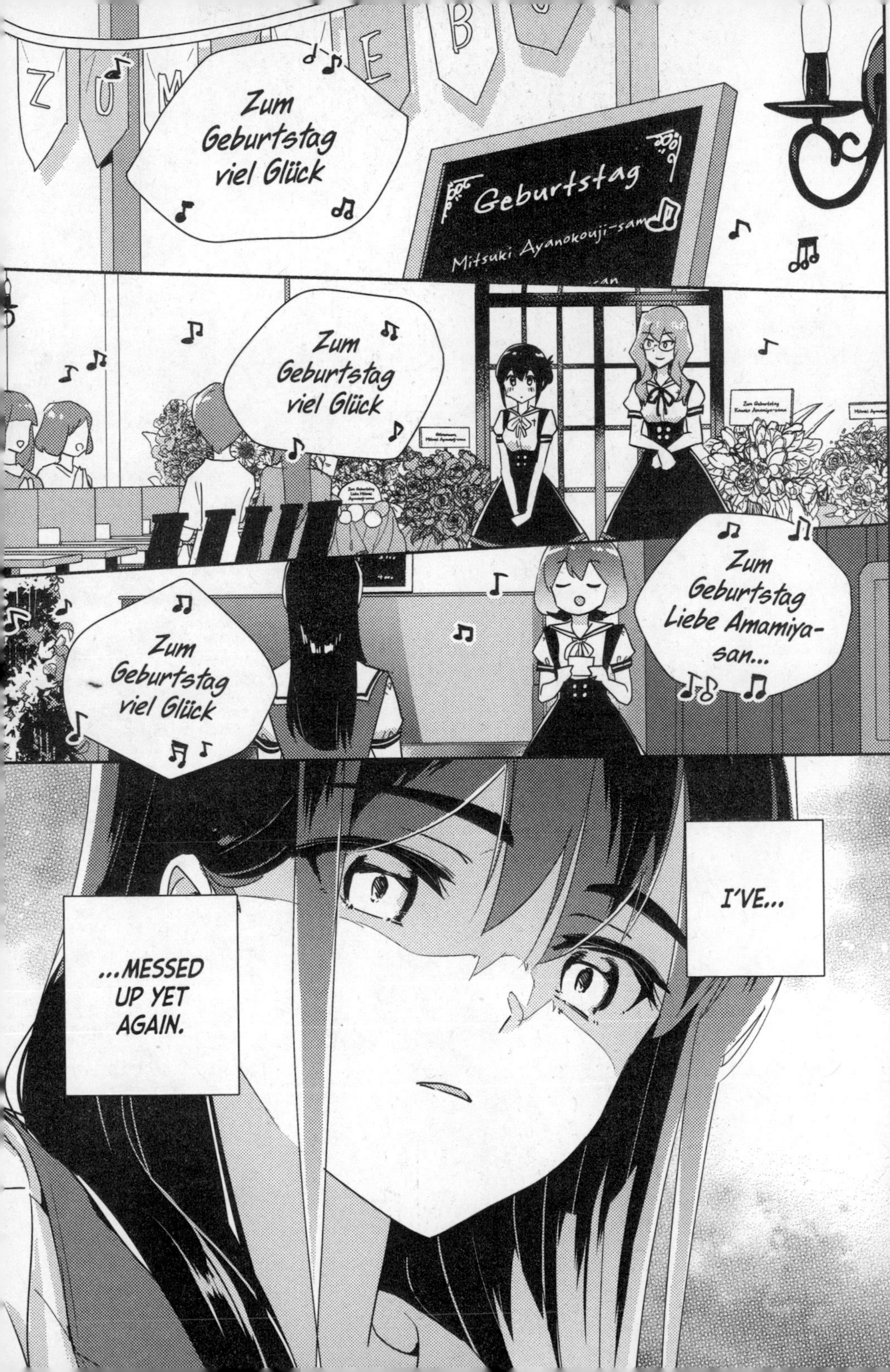
Zum Geburtstag viel Glück
Geburtstag
Mitsuki Ayanokouji-sam
Zum Geburtstag viel Glück
Zum Geburtstag Liebe Amamiya-san...
Zum Geburtstag viel Glück
I'VE...
...MESSED UP YET AGAIN.

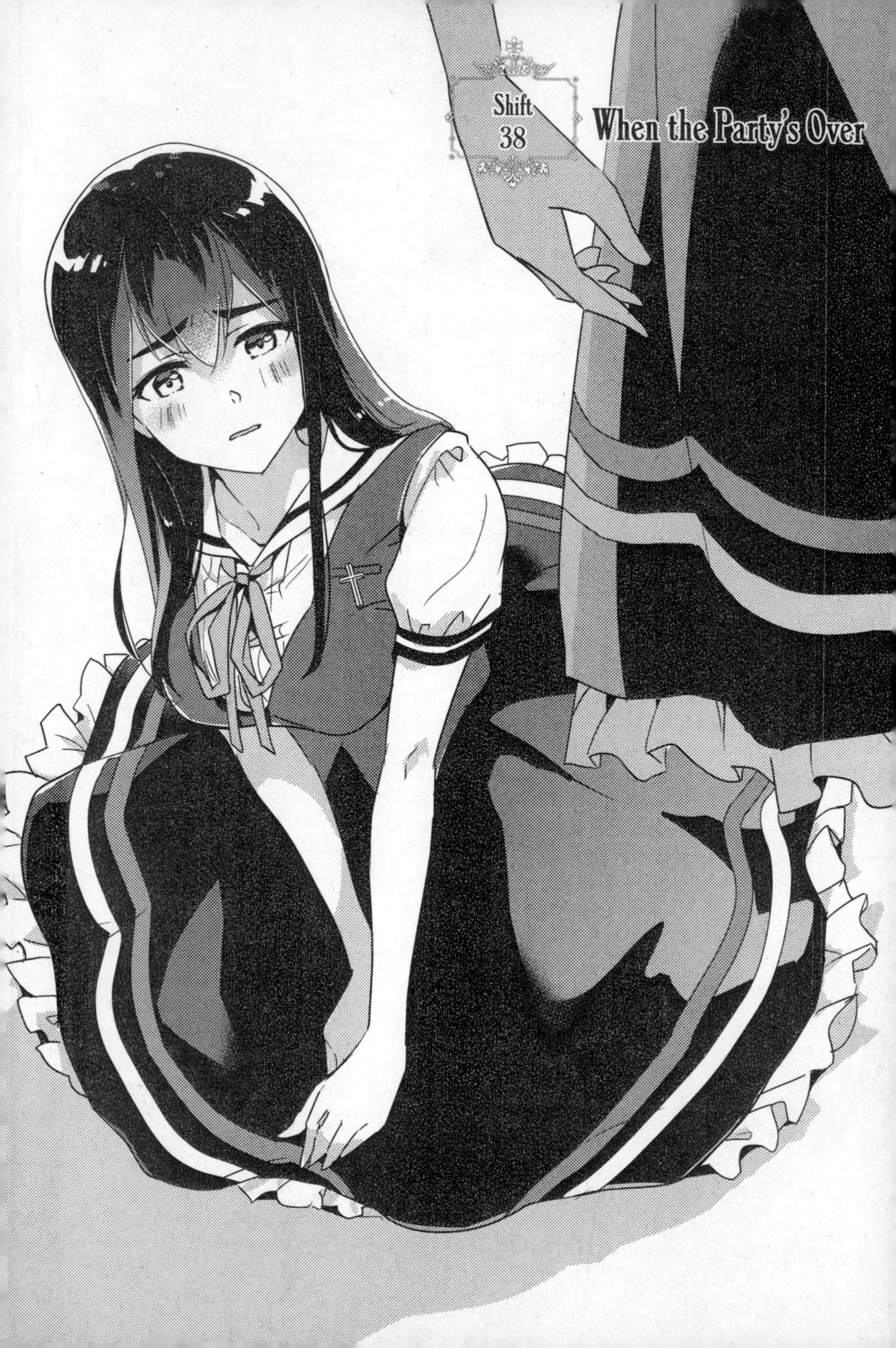

Shift
38
When the Party's Over

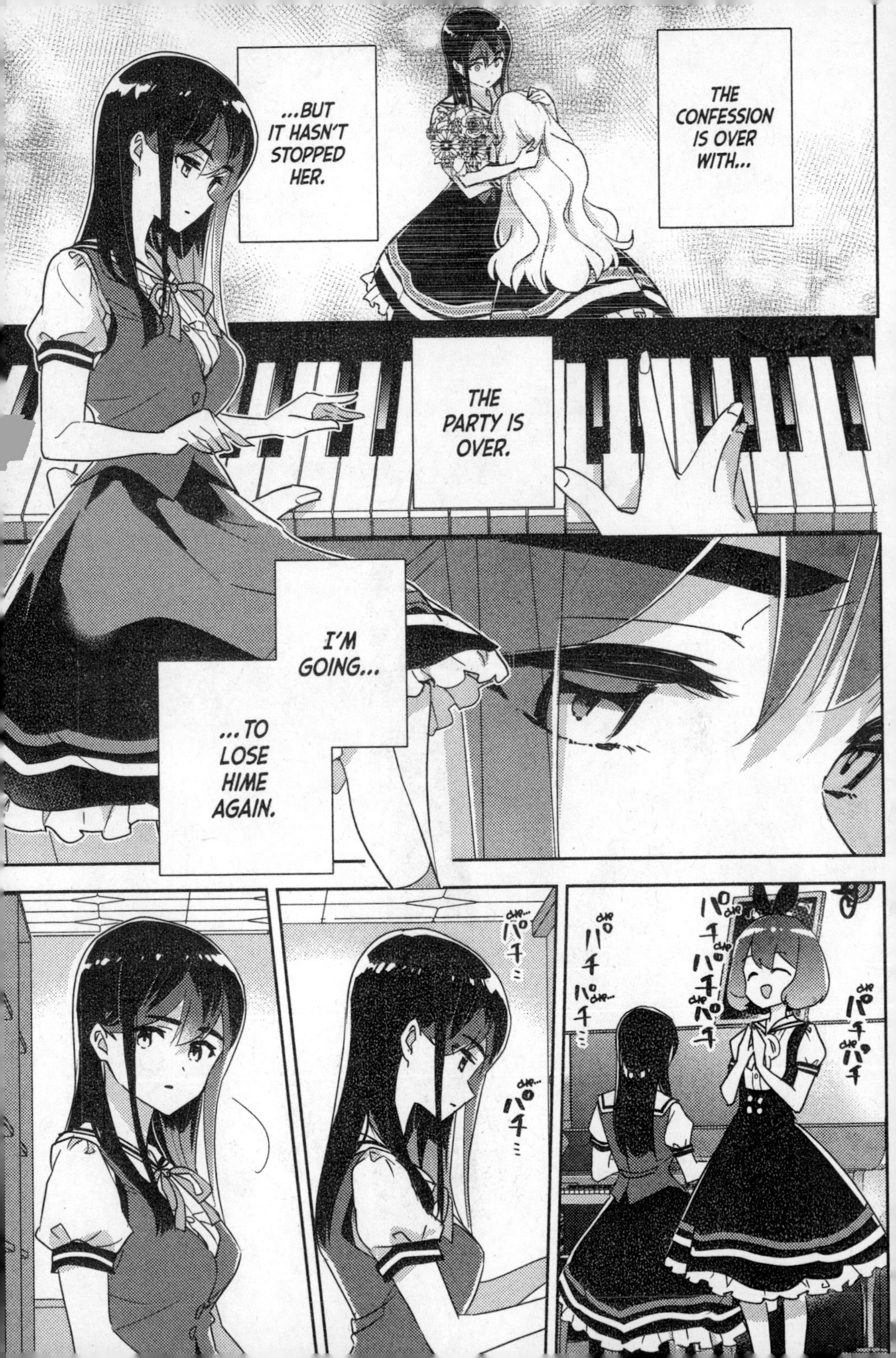
THE CONFESSION IS OVER WITH...
...BUT IT HASN'T STOPPED HER.
THE PARTY IS OVER.
I'M GOING...
...TO LOSE HIME AGAIN.
パチパチ
パチパチ
パチパチ
パチパチ
パチ

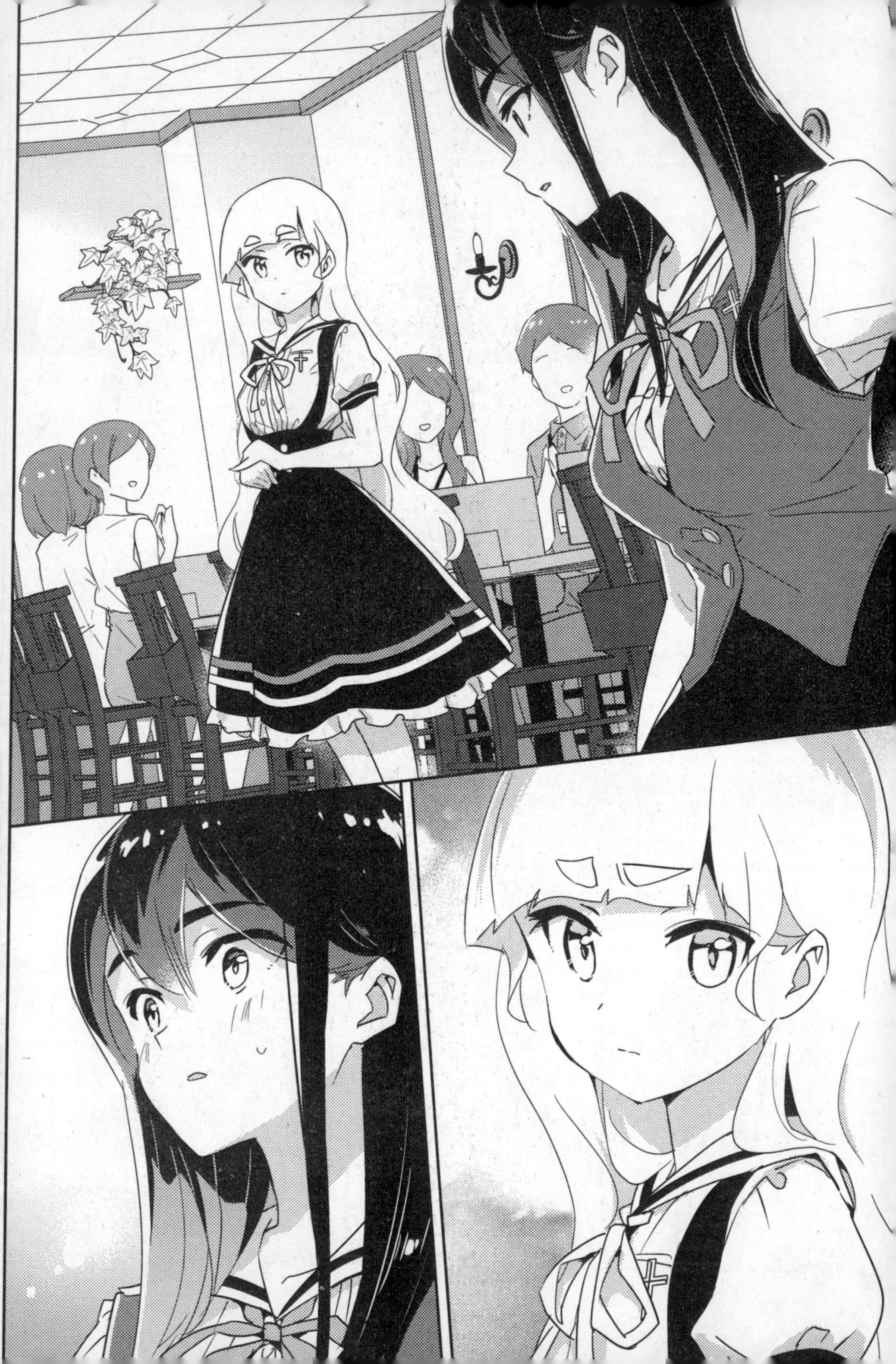

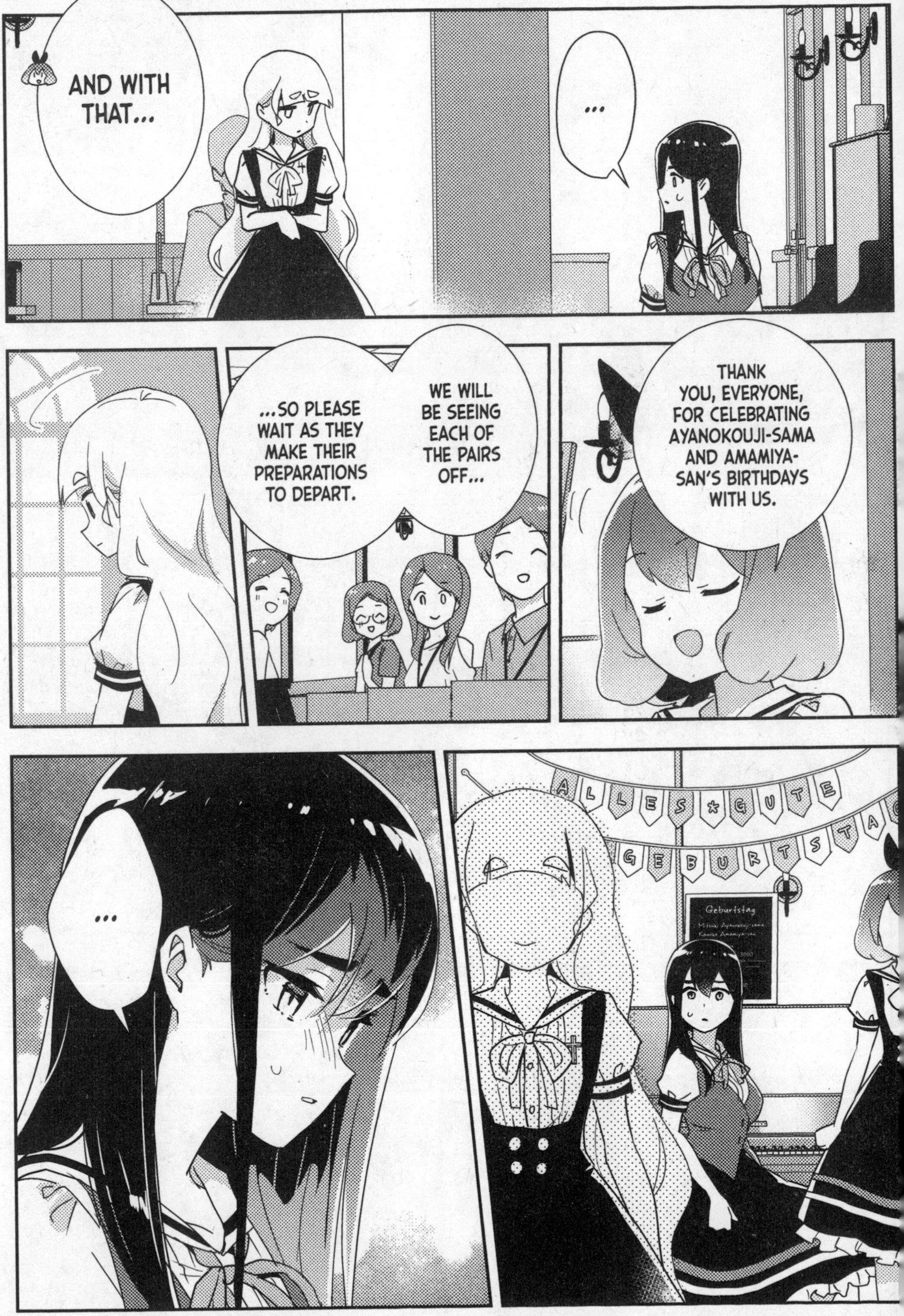
...
AND WITH THAT...
THANK YOU, EVERYONE, FOR CELEBRATING AYANOKOUJI-SAMA AND AMAMIYA-SAN'S BIRTHDAYS WITH US.
WE WILL BE SEEING EACH OF THE PAIRS OFF...
...SO PLEASE WAIT AS THEY MAKE THEIR PREPARATIONS TO DEPART.
ALLES GUTE
Geburtstag
...

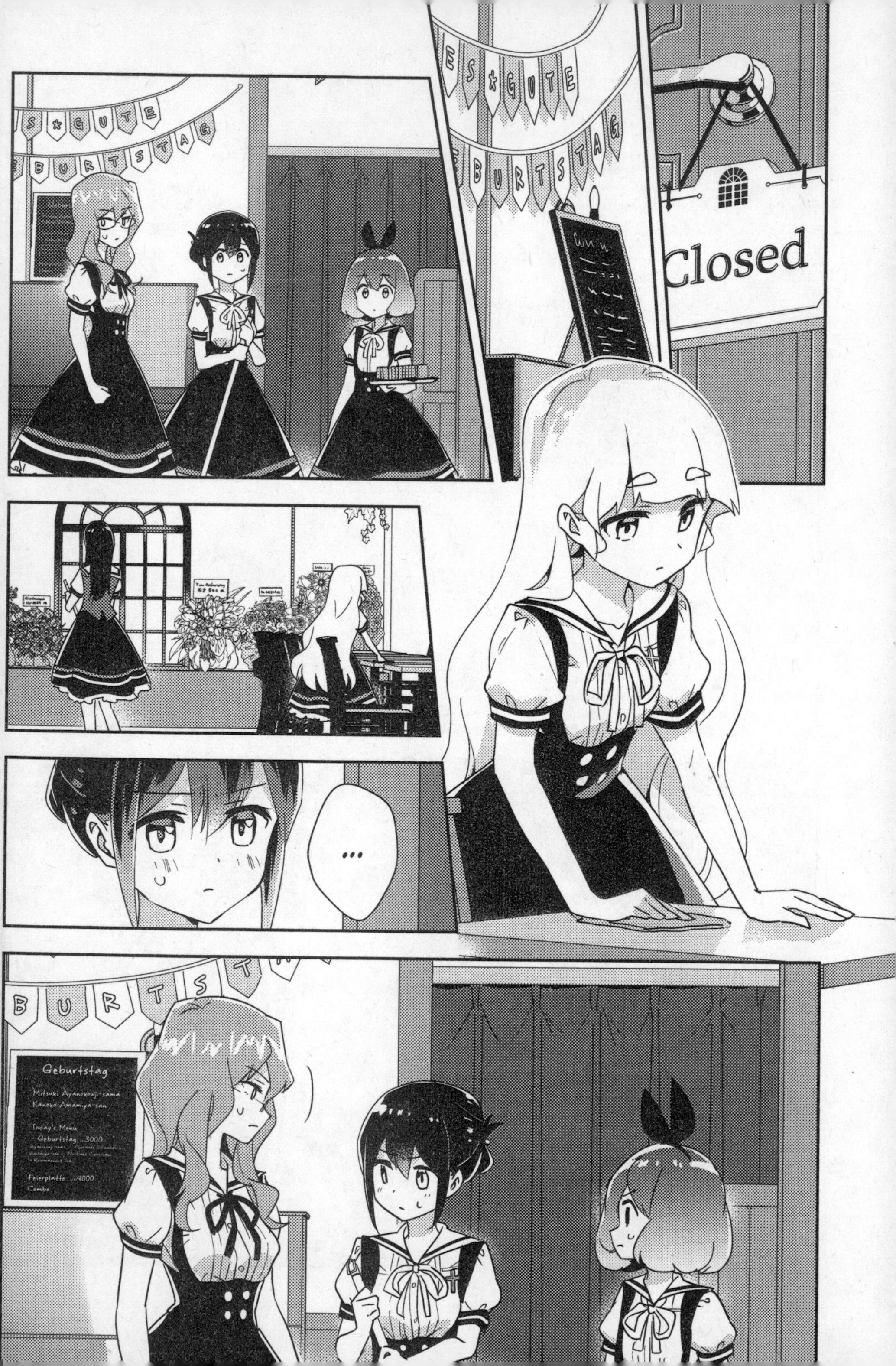
ES★GUTE
BURTSTAG
Closed
ES★GUTE
BURTSTAG
...
BURTST
Geburtstag
Mitsuki Ayanokouji-sama
Kanoko Amamiya-san
Today's Menu
Geburtstag ...3000
Feierplatte ...4000
Combo

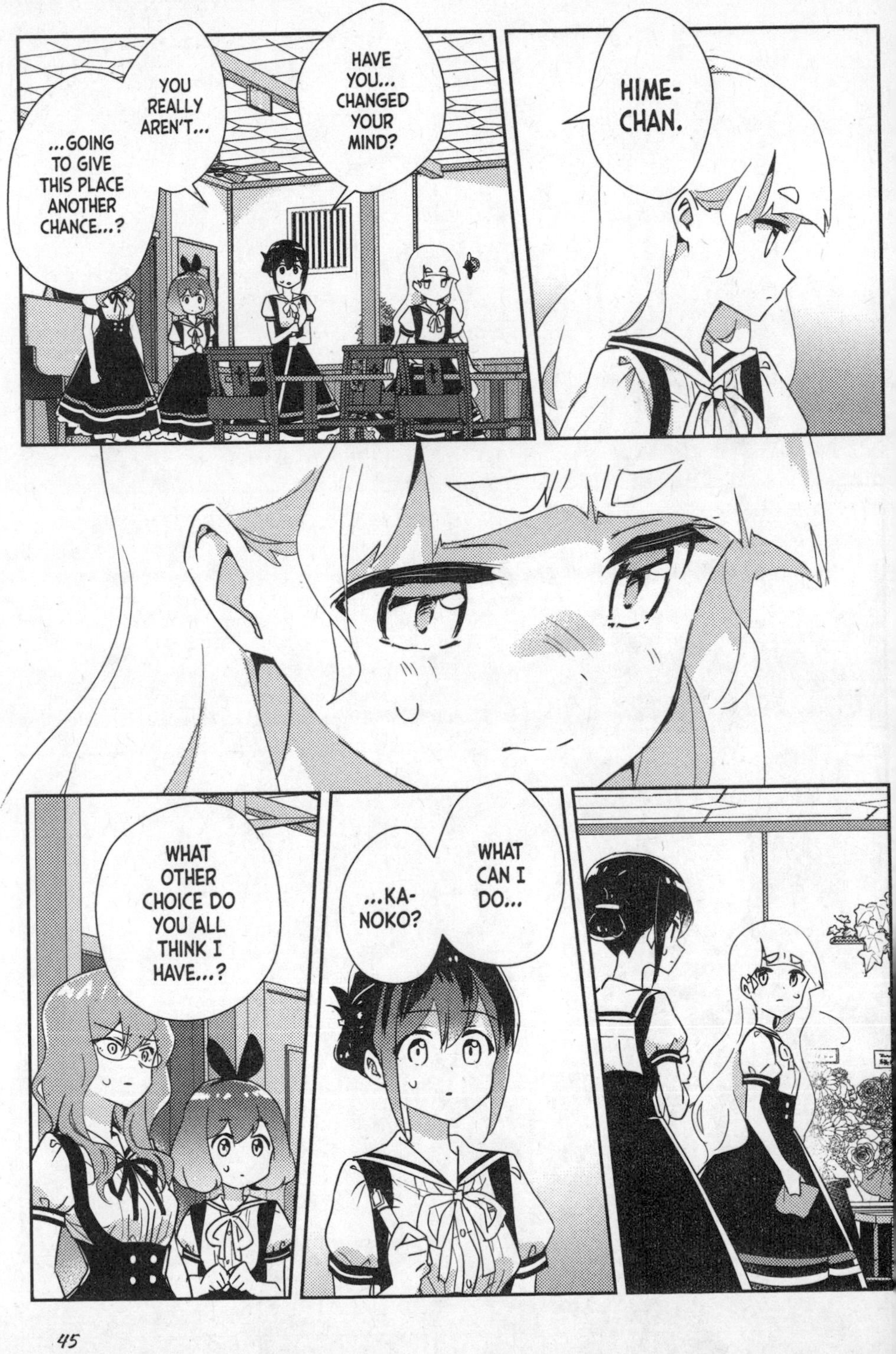
HIME-CHAN.
HAVE YOU... CHANGED YOUR MIND?
YOU REALLY AREN'T...
...GOING TO GIVE THIS PLACE ANOTHER CHANCE...?
WHAT CAN I DO...
...KA-NOKO?
WHAT OTHER CHOICE DO YOU ALL THINK I HAVE...?

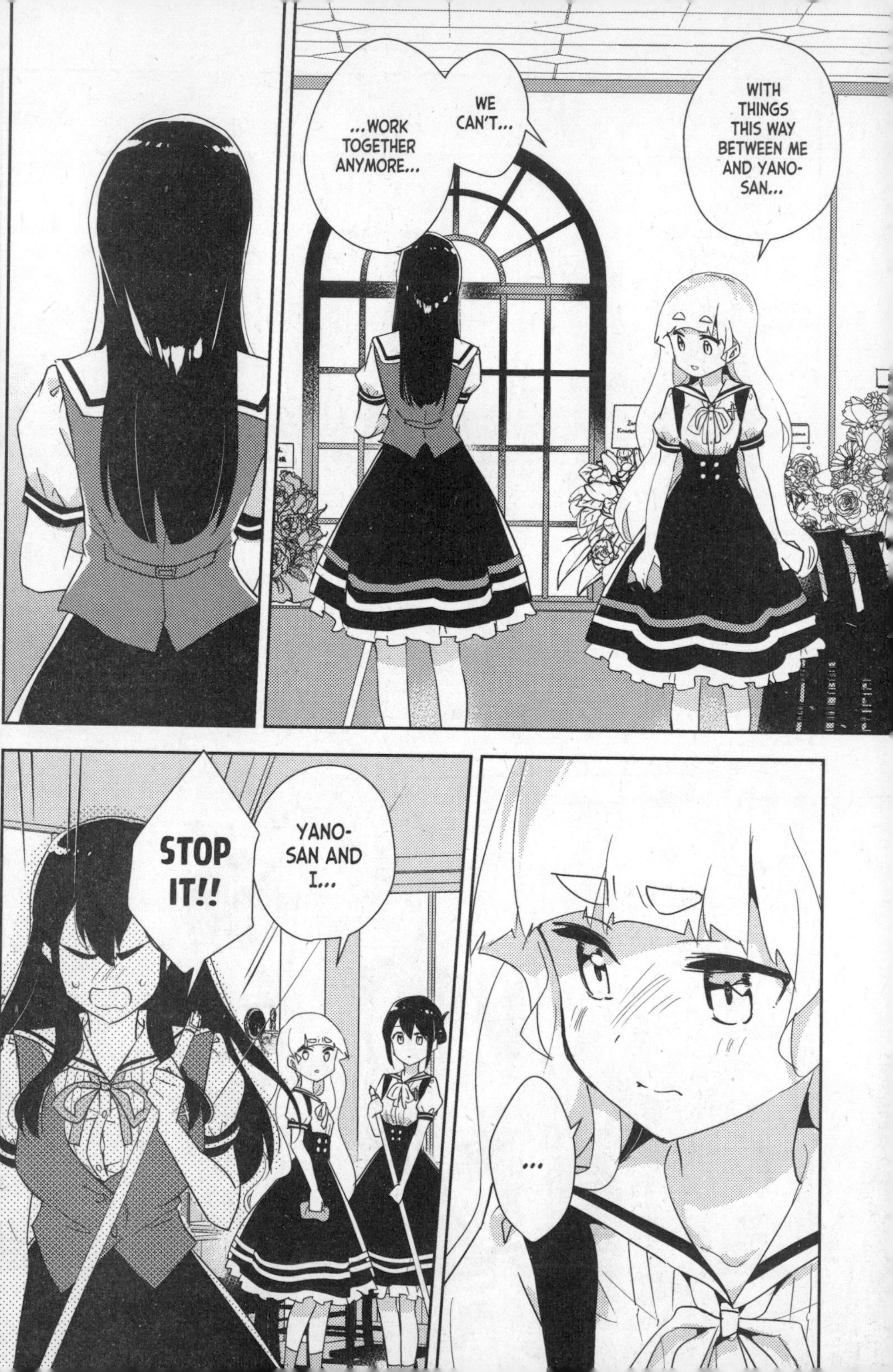
WITH THINGS THIS WAY BETWEEN ME AND YANO-SAN...
WE CAN'T...
...WORK TOGETHER ANYMORE...
...
YANO-SAN AND I...
STOP IT!!

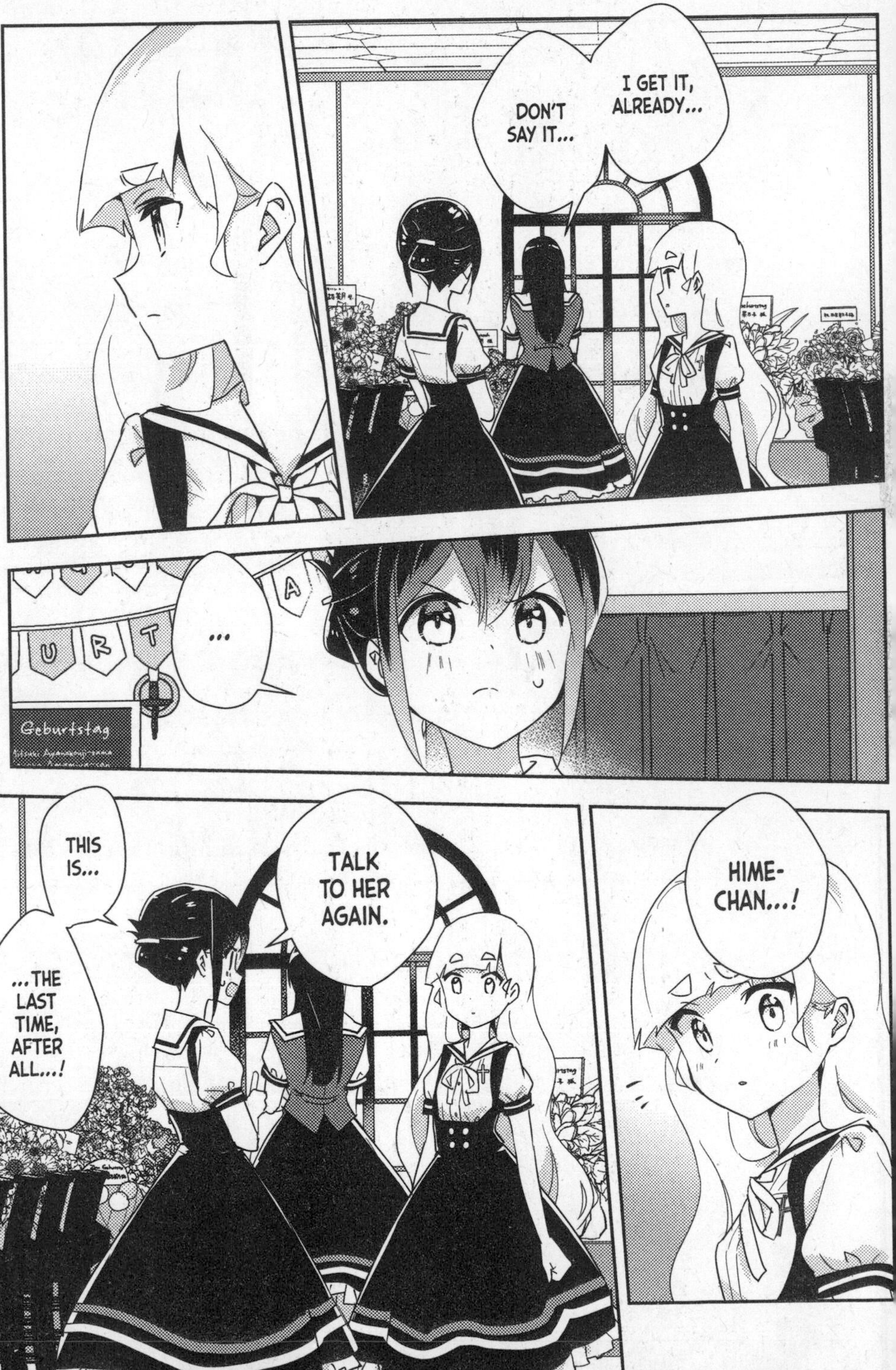
I GET IT, ALREADY...
DON'T SAY IT...
...
Geburtstag
HIME-CHAN...!
TALK TO HER AGAIN.
THIS IS...
...THE LAST TIME, AFTER ALL...!

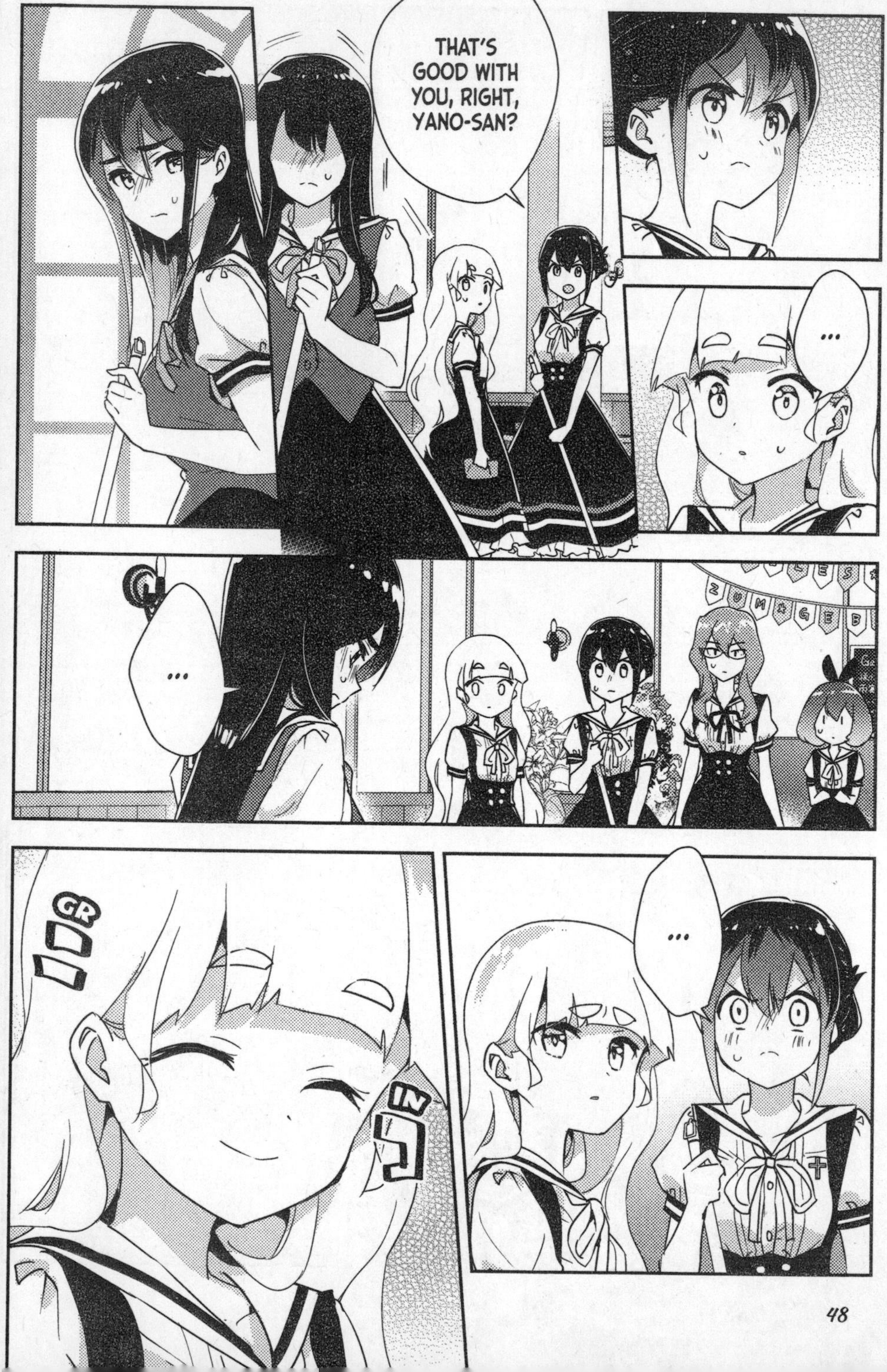
...
THAT'S GOOD WITH YOU, RIGHT, YANO-SAN?
...
...
GRIN

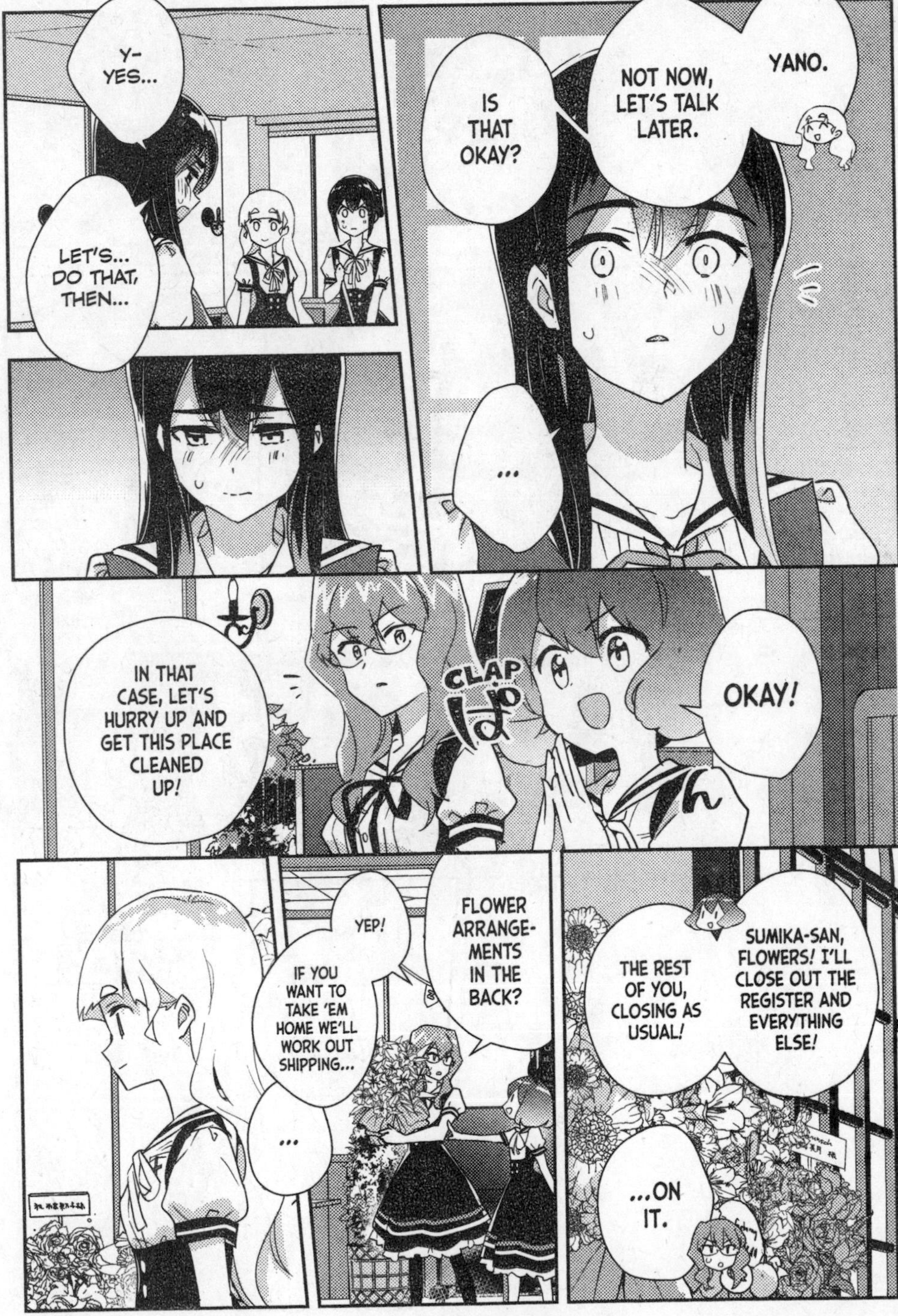
YANO.
NOT NOW, LET'S TALK LATER.
IS THAT OKAY?
...
Y- YES...
LET'S... DO THAT, THEN...
OKAY!
CLAP
IN THAT CASE, LET'S HURRY UP AND GET THIS PLACE CLEANED UP!
SUMIKA-SAN, FLOWERS! I'LL CLOSE OUT THE REGISTER AND EVERYTHING ELSE!
THE REST OF YOU, CLOSING AS USUAL!
...ON IT.
FLOWER ARRANGE-MENTS IN THE BACK?
YEP!
IF YOU WANT TO TAKE 'EM HOME WE'LL WORK OUT SHIPPING...
...

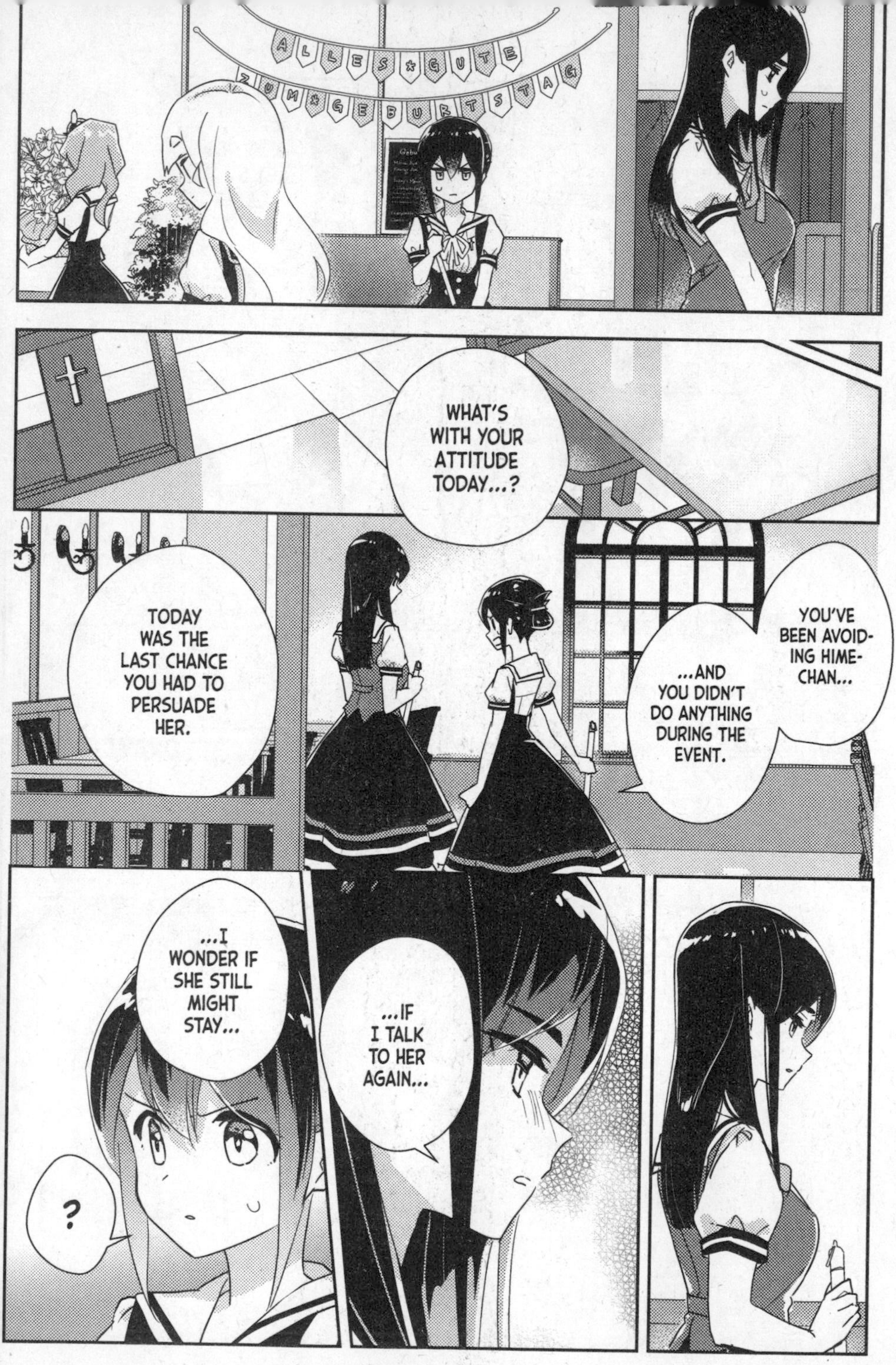
ALLES*GUTE
ZUM*GEBURTSTAG
WHAT'S WITH YOUR ATTITUDE TODAY...?
YOU'VE BEEN AVOIDING HIME-CHAN...
...AND YOU DIDN'T DO ANYTHING DURING THE EVENT.
TODAY WAS THE LAST CHANCE YOU HAD TO PERSUADE HER.
...IF I TALK TO HER AGAIN...
...I WONDER IF SHE STILL MIGHT STAY...
?

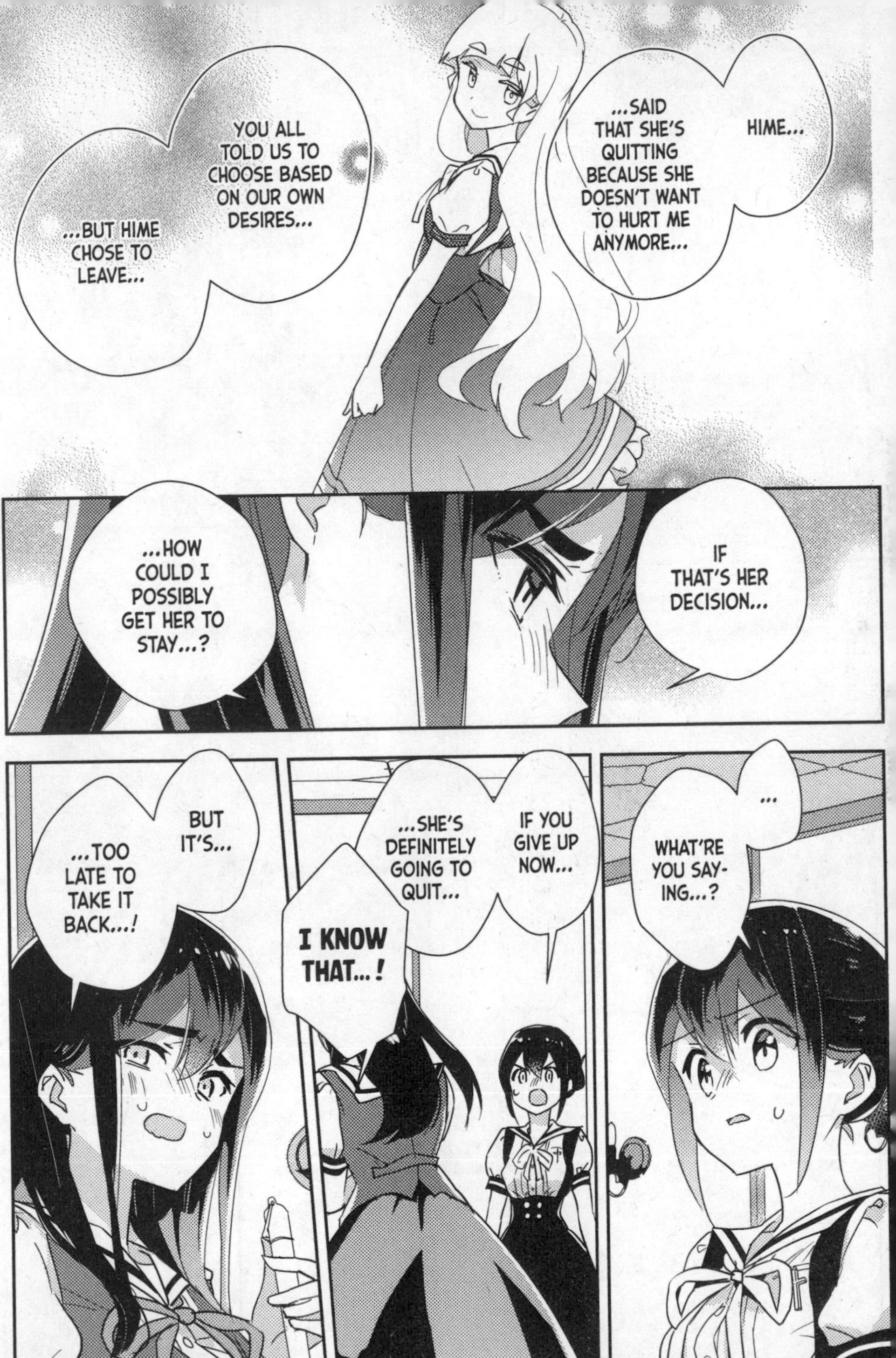
HIME...
...SAID THAT SHE'S QUITTING BECAUSE SHE DOESN'T WANT TO HURT ME ANYMORE...
YOU ALL TOLD US TO CHOOSE BASED ON OUR OWN DESIRES...
...BUT HIME CHOSE TO LEAVE...
IF THAT'S HER DECISION...
...HOW COULD I POSSIBLY GET HER TO STAY...?
...
WHAT'RE YOU SAYING...?
IF YOU GIVE UP NOW...
...SHE'S DEFINITELY GOING TO QUIT...
I KNOW THAT...!
BUT IT'S...
...TOO LATE TO TAKE IT BACK...!

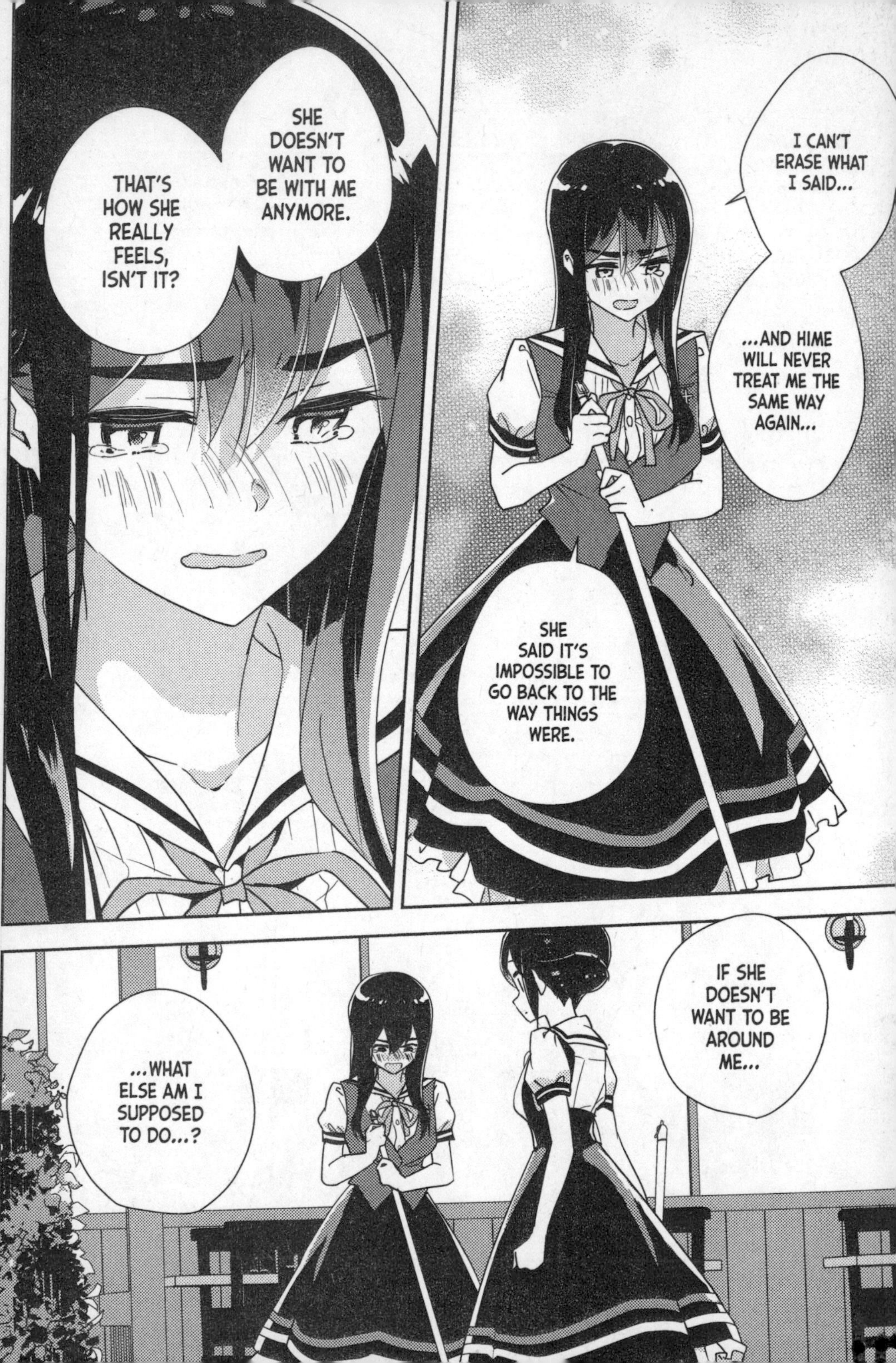
I CAN'T ERASE WHAT I SAID...
...AND HIME WILL NEVER TREAT ME THE SAME WAY AGAIN...
SHE SAID IT'S IMPOSSIBLE TO GO BACK TO THE WAY THINGS WERE.
SHE DOESN'T WANT TO BE WITH ME ANYMORE.
THAT'S HOW SHE REALLY FEELS, ISN'T IT?
IF SHE DOESN'T WANT TO BE AROUND ME...
...WHAT ELSE AM I SUPPOSED TO DO...?

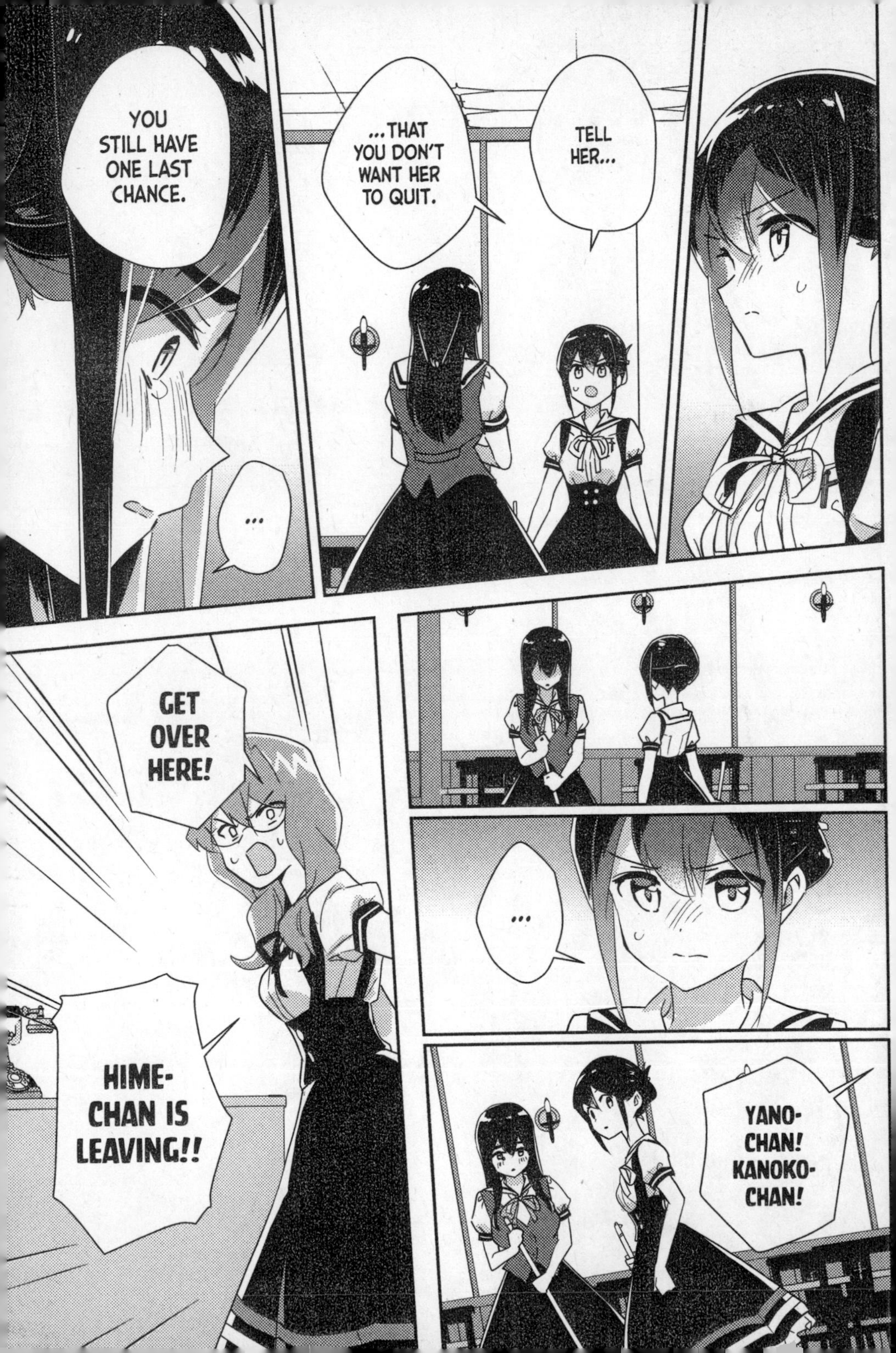
TELL HER...
...THAT YOU DON'T WANT HER TO QUIT.
YOU STILL HAVE ONE LAST CHANCE.
...
...
YANO-CHAN! KANOKO-CHAN!
GET OVER HERE!
HIME-CHAN IS LEAVING!!

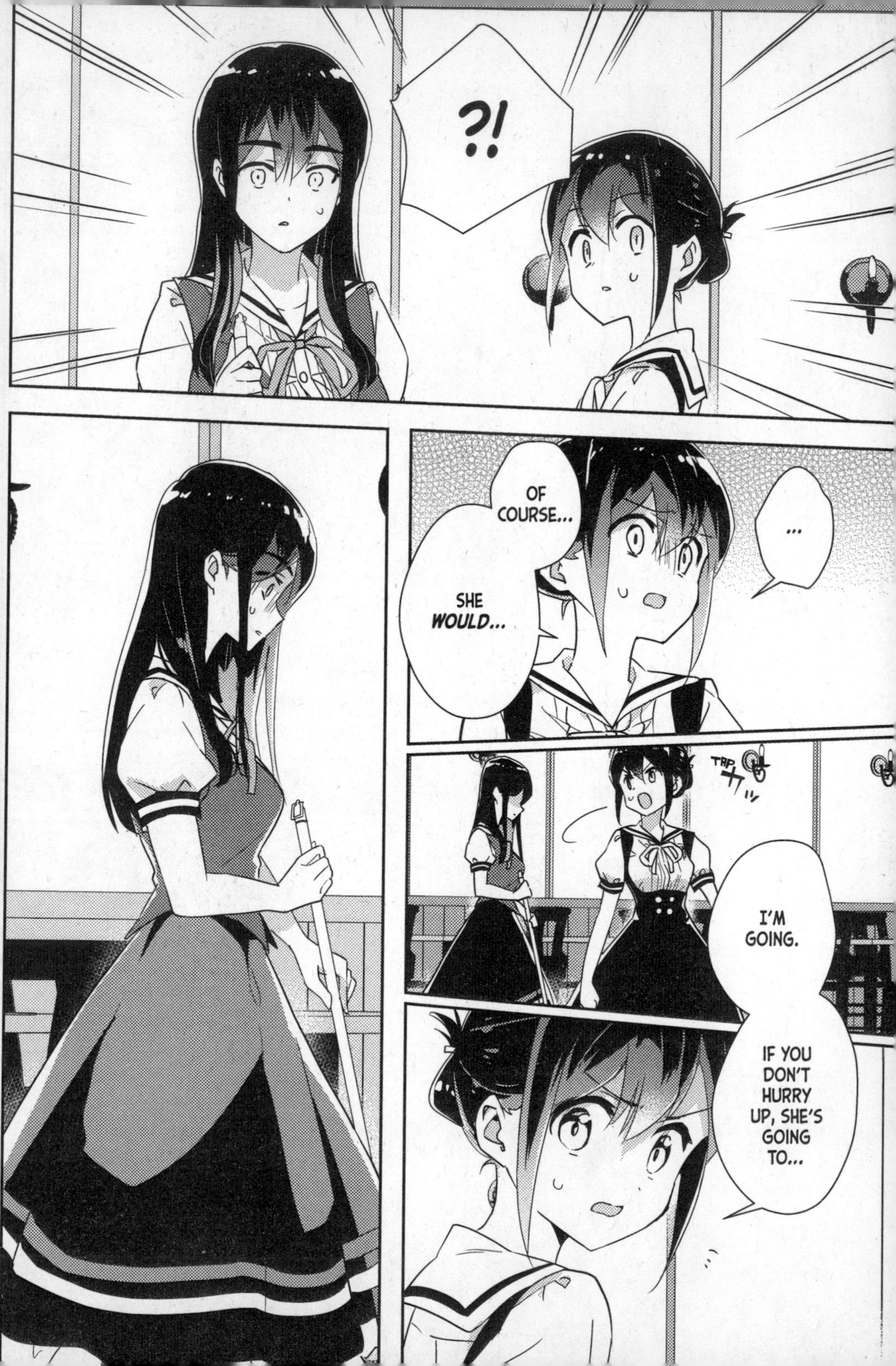
?!
...
OF COURSE...
SHE *WOULD*...
TAP
I'M GOING.
IF YOU DON'T HURRY UP, SHE'S GOING TO...

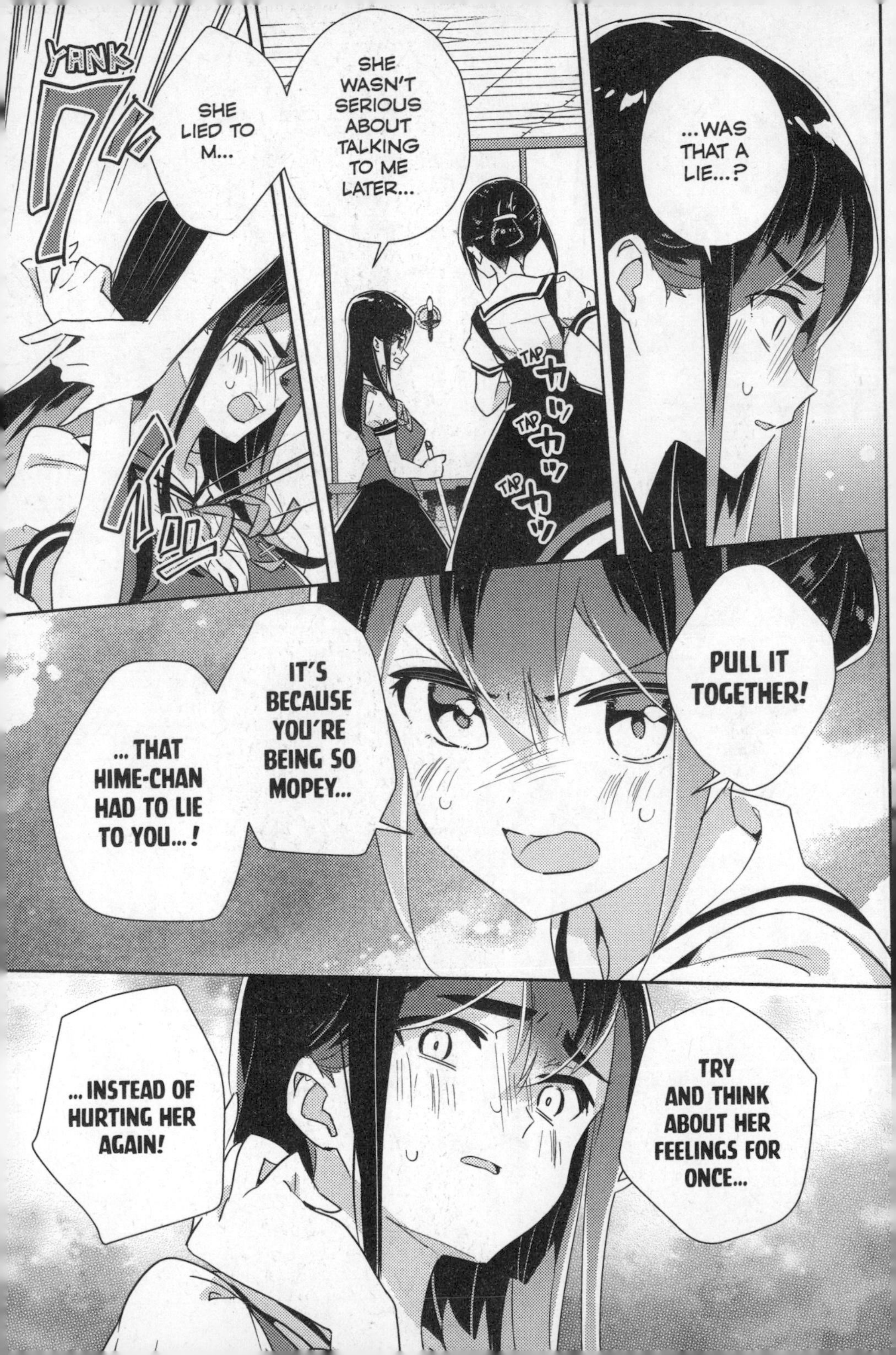
...WAS THAT A LIE...?
SHE WASN'T SERIOUS ABOUT TALKING TO ME LATER...
TAP
TAP
TAP
SHE LIED TO M...
YANK
PULL IT TOGETHER!
IT'S BECAUSE YOU'RE BEING SO MOPEY...
...THAT HIME-CHAN HAD TO LIE TO YOU...!
TRY AND THINK ABOUT HER FEELINGS FOR ONCE...
...INSTEAD OF HURTING HER AGAIN!

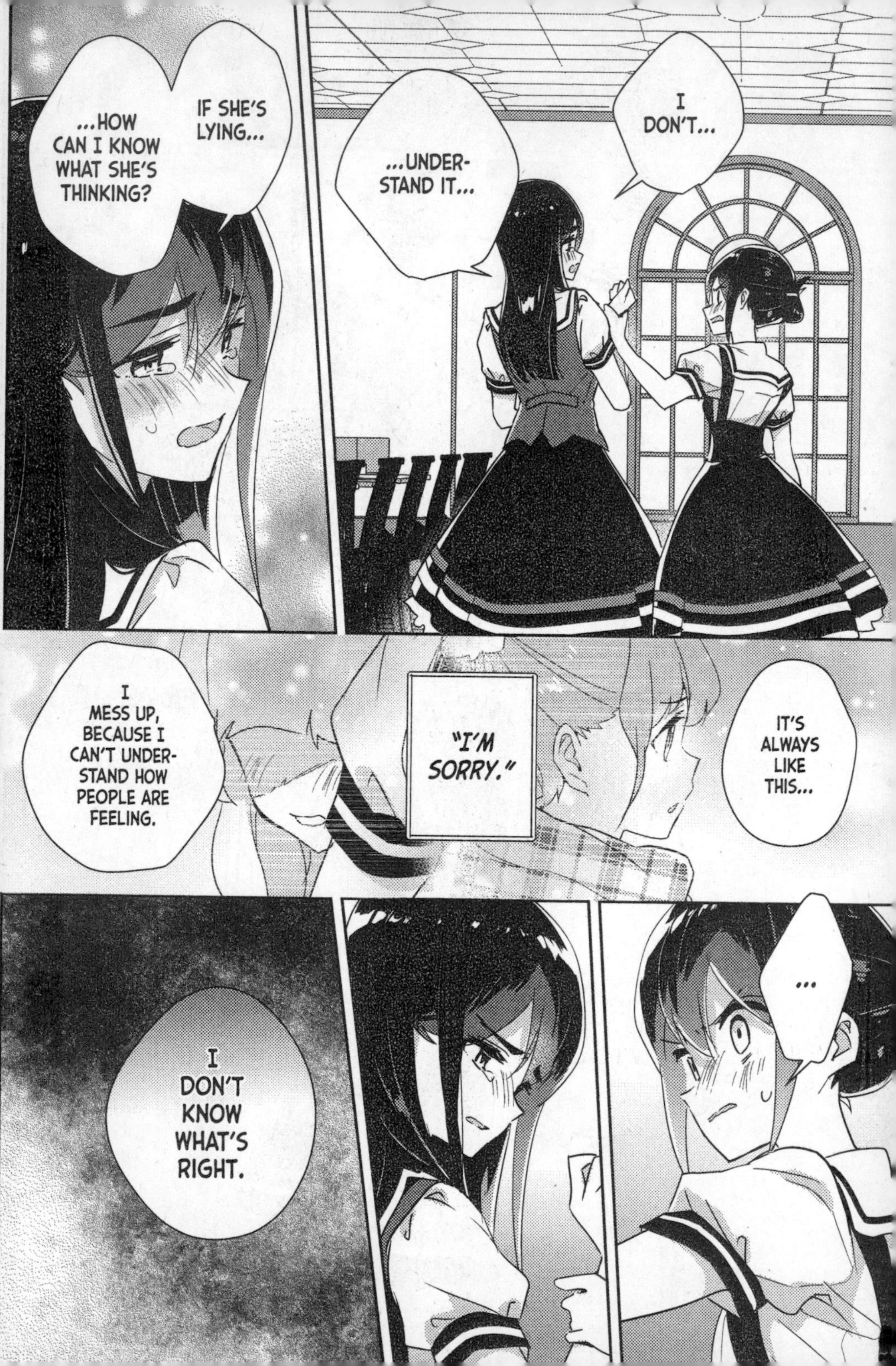
I DON'T...
...UNDER-STAND IT...
IF SHE'S LYING...
...HOW CAN I KNOW WHAT SHE'S THINKING?
IT'S ALWAYS LIKE THIS...
"I'M SORRY."
I MESS UP, BECAUSE I CAN'T UNDER-STAND HOW PEOPLE ARE FEELING.
...
I DON'T KNOW WHAT'S RIGHT.

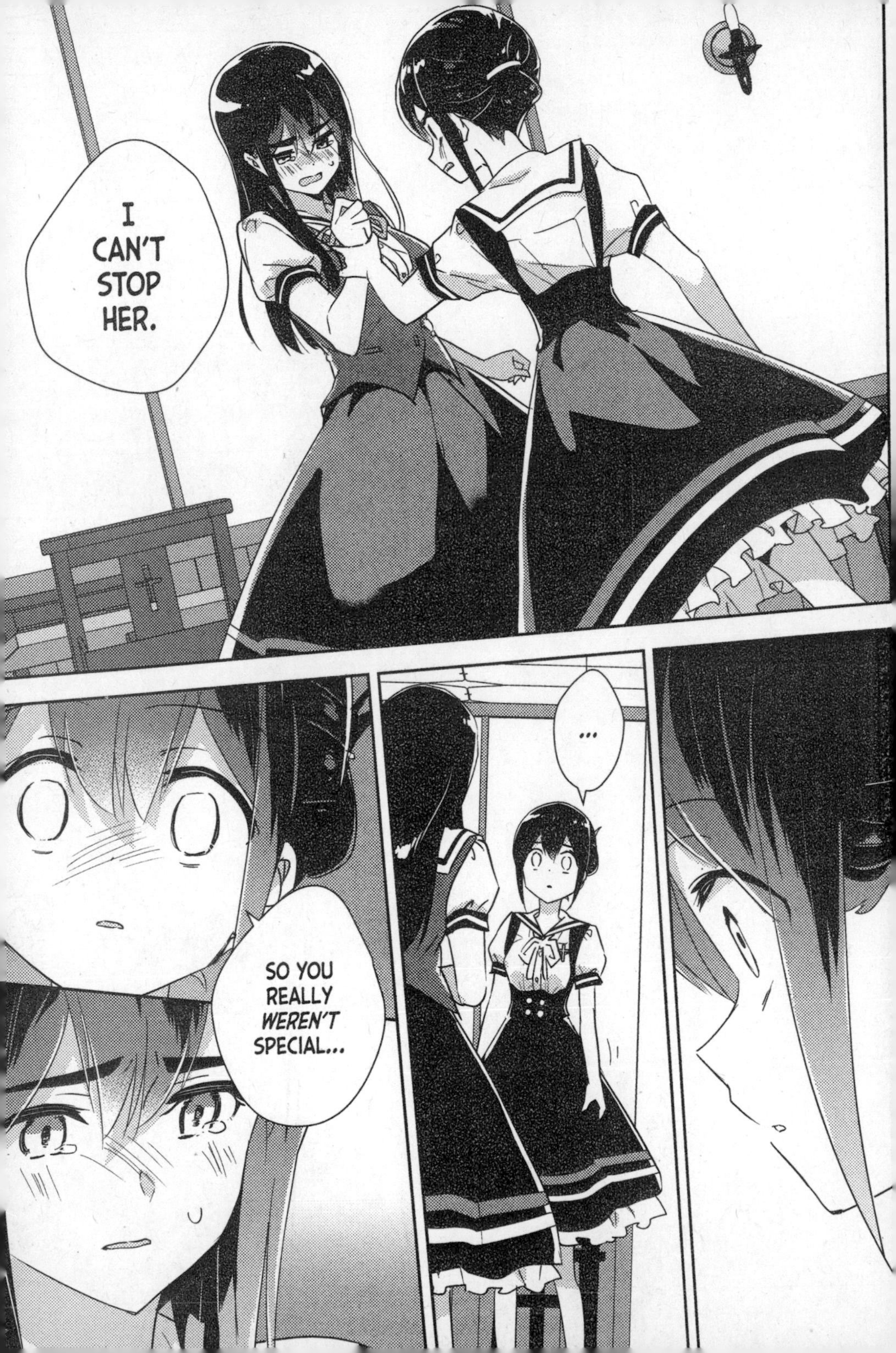
I CAN'T STOP HER.
...
SO YOU REALLY *WEREN'T* SPECIAL...

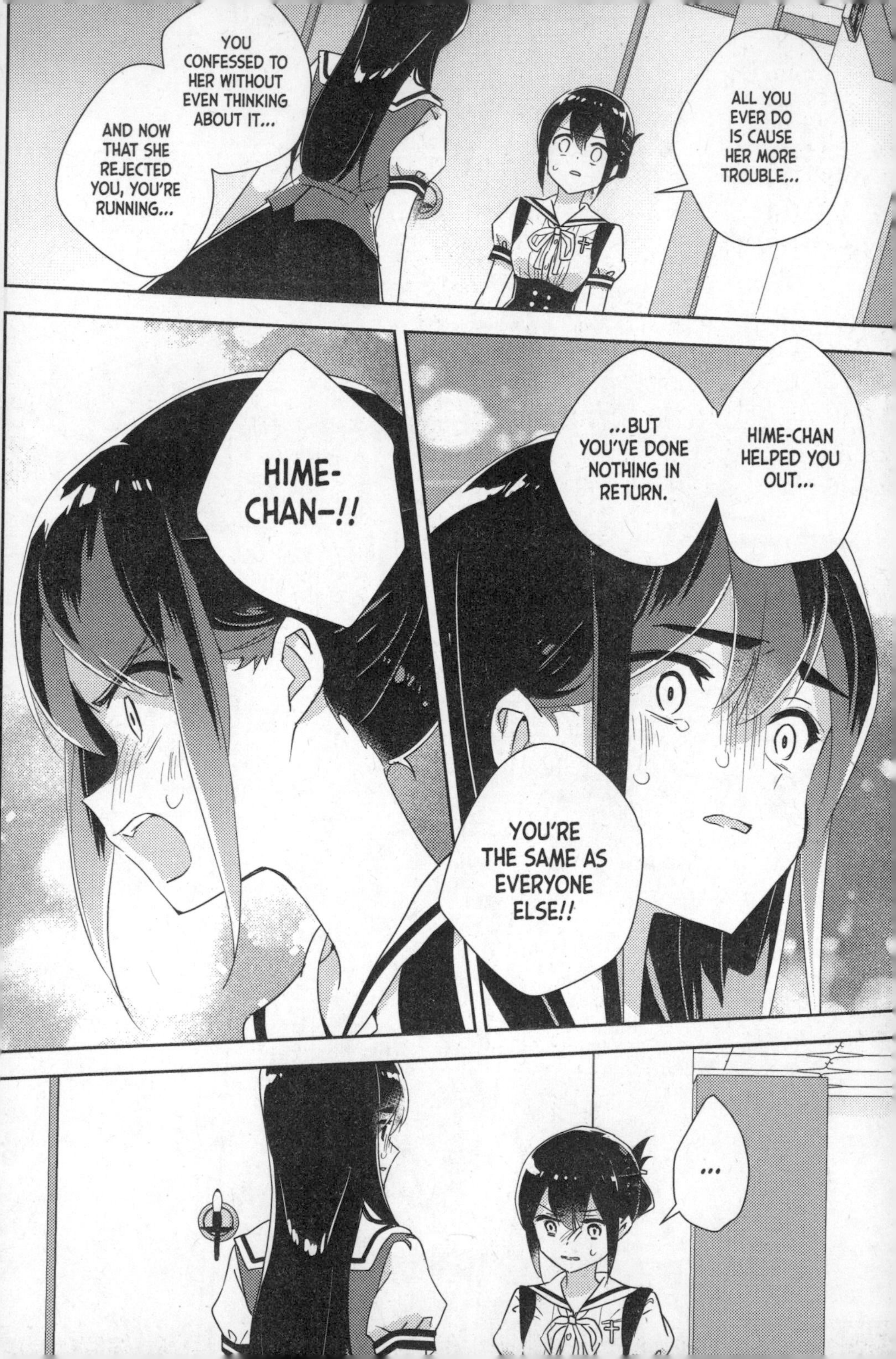
YOU CONFESSED TO HER WITHOUT EVEN THINKING ABOUT IT...
AND NOW THAT SHE REJECTED YOU, YOU'RE RUNNING...
ALL YOU EVER DO IS CAUSE HER MORE TROUBLE...
HIME-CHAN HELPED YOU OUT...
...BUT YOU'VE DONE NOTHING IN RETURN.
YOU'RE THE SAME AS EVERYONE ELSE!!
HIME-CHAN-!!
...

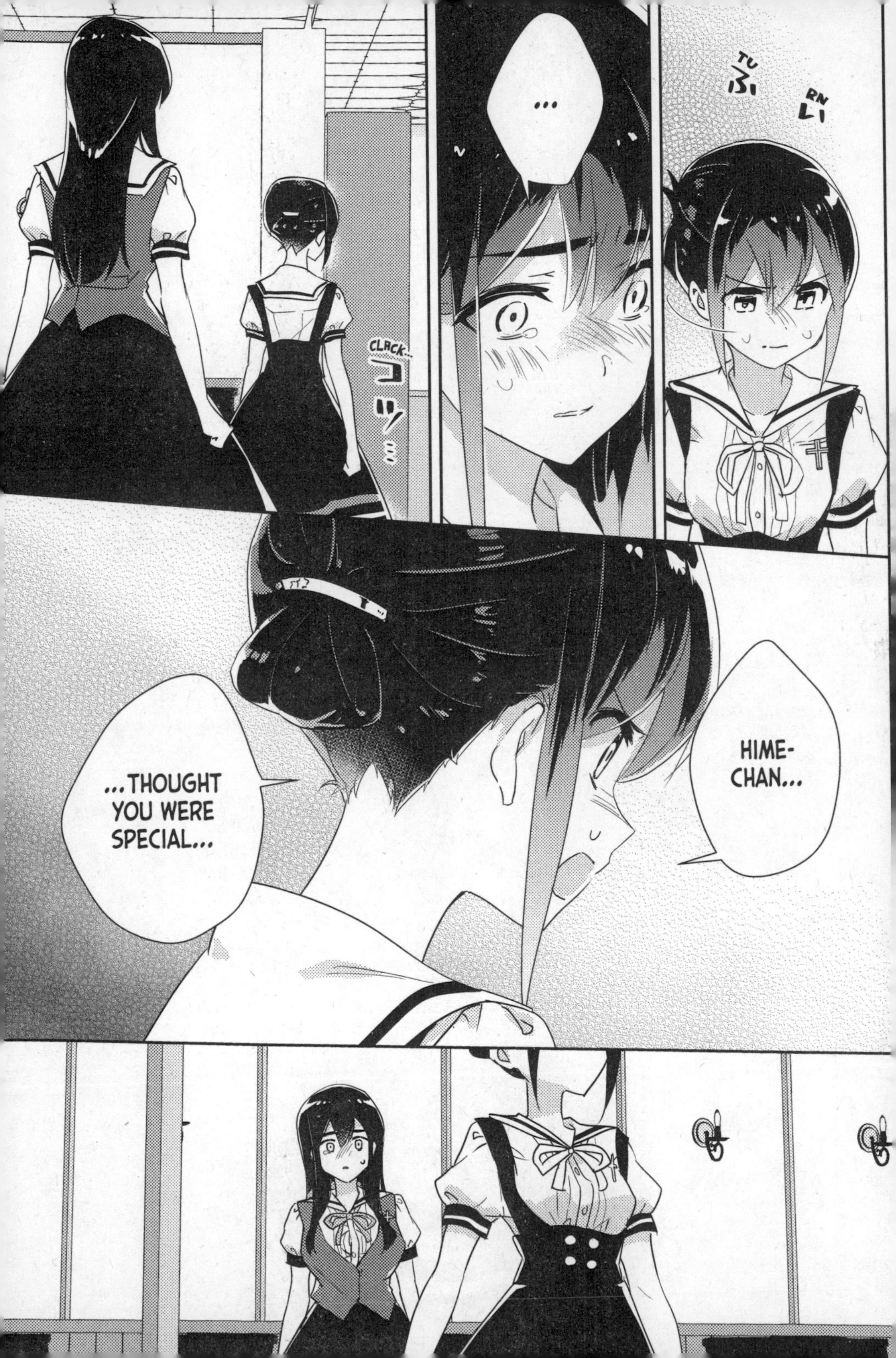
TU ふ
RN い
...
CLACK...
コッ...
HIME-CHAN...
...THOUGHT YOU WERE SPECIAL...

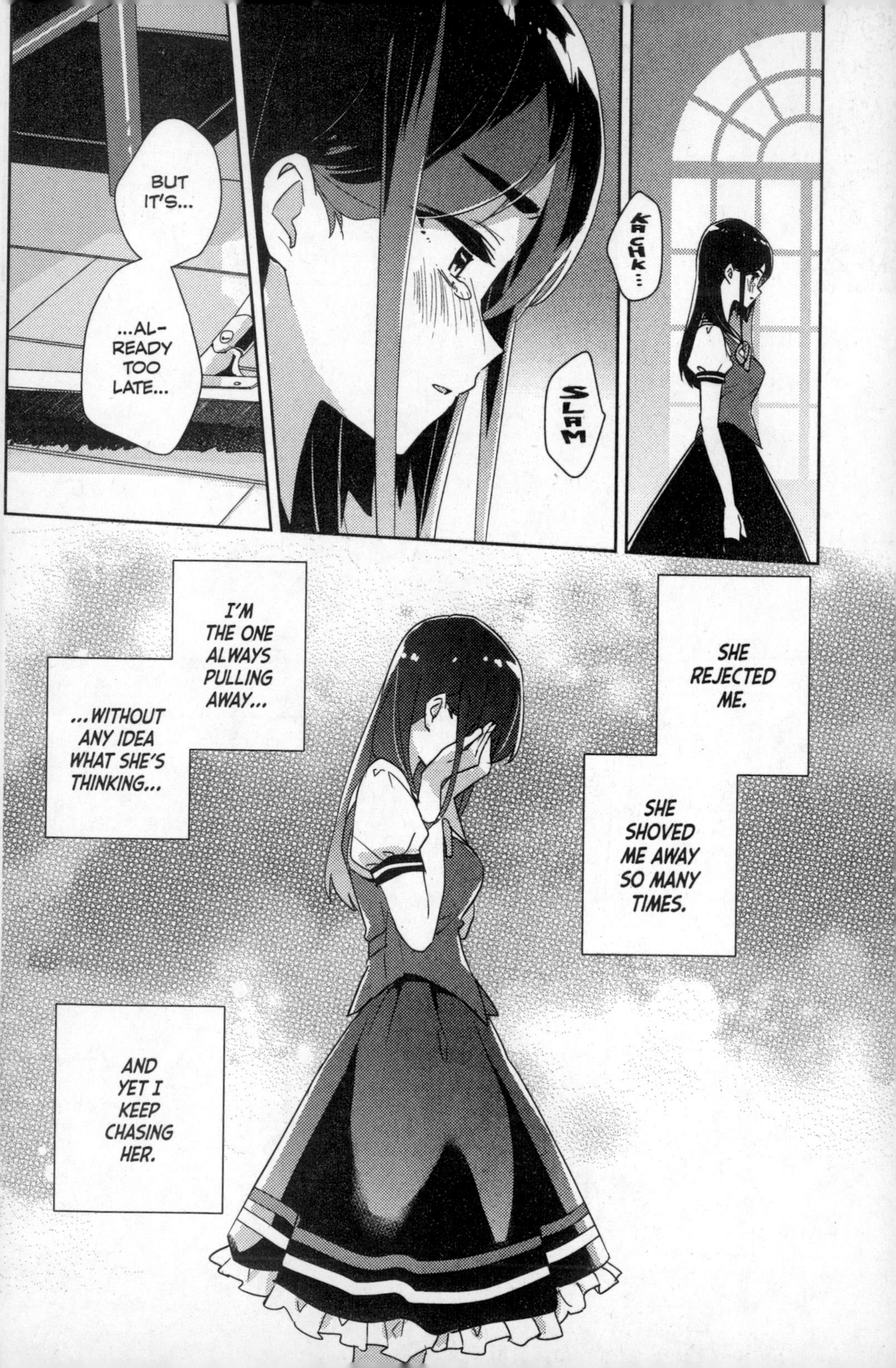
KACHK...
SLAM
BUT IT'S...
...AL-READY TOO LATE...
SHE REJECTED ME.
SHE SHOVED ME AWAY SO MANY TIMES.
I'M THE ONE ALWAYS PULLING AWAY...
...WITHOUT ANY IDEA WHAT SHE'S THINKING...
AND YET I KEEP CHASING HER.

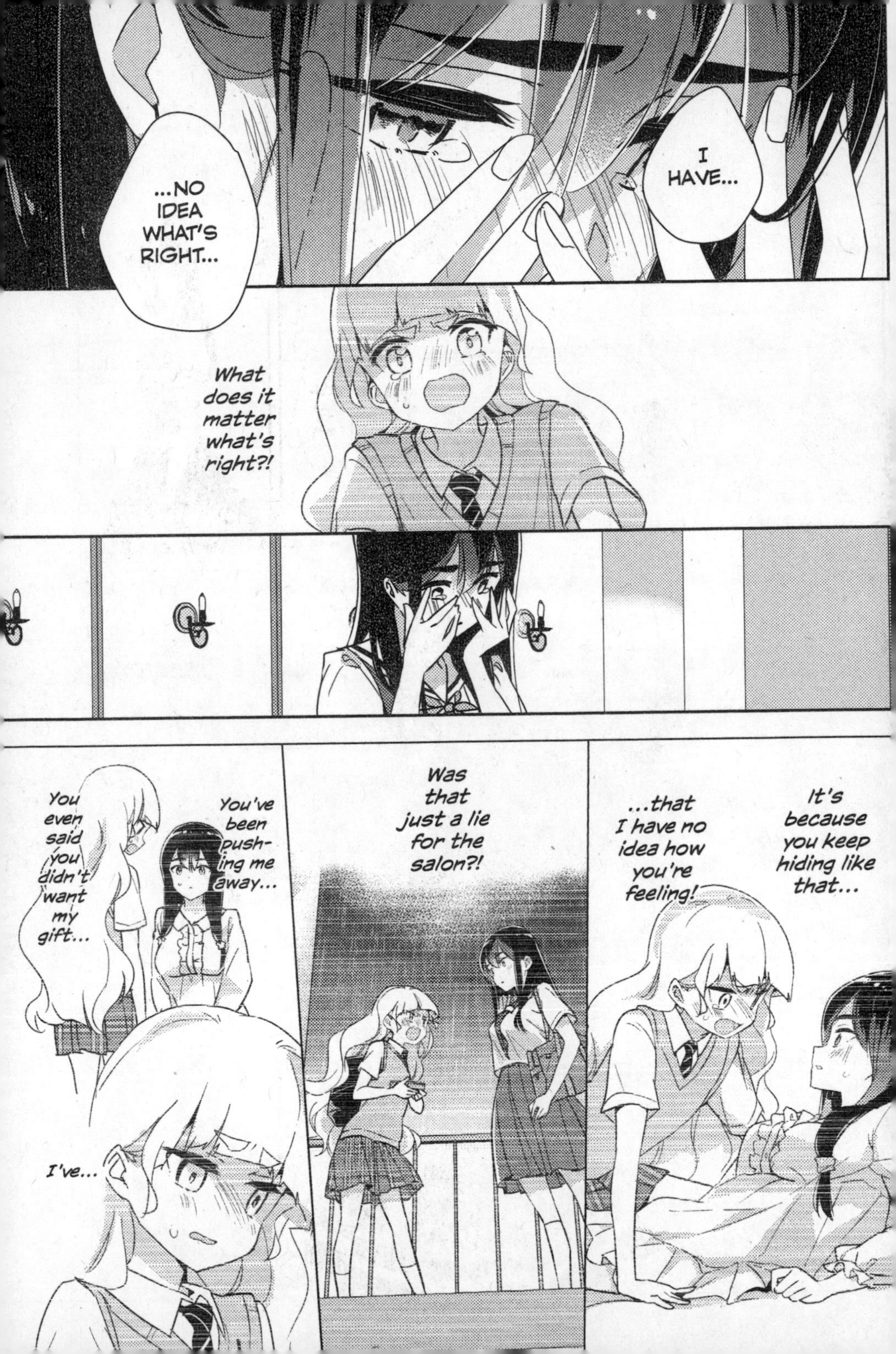
I HAVE...
...NO IDEA WHAT'S RIGHT...
What does it matter what's right?!
It's because you keep hiding like that...
...that I have no idea how you're feeling!
Was that just a lie for the salon?!
You've been pushing me away...
You even said you didn't want my gift...
I've...

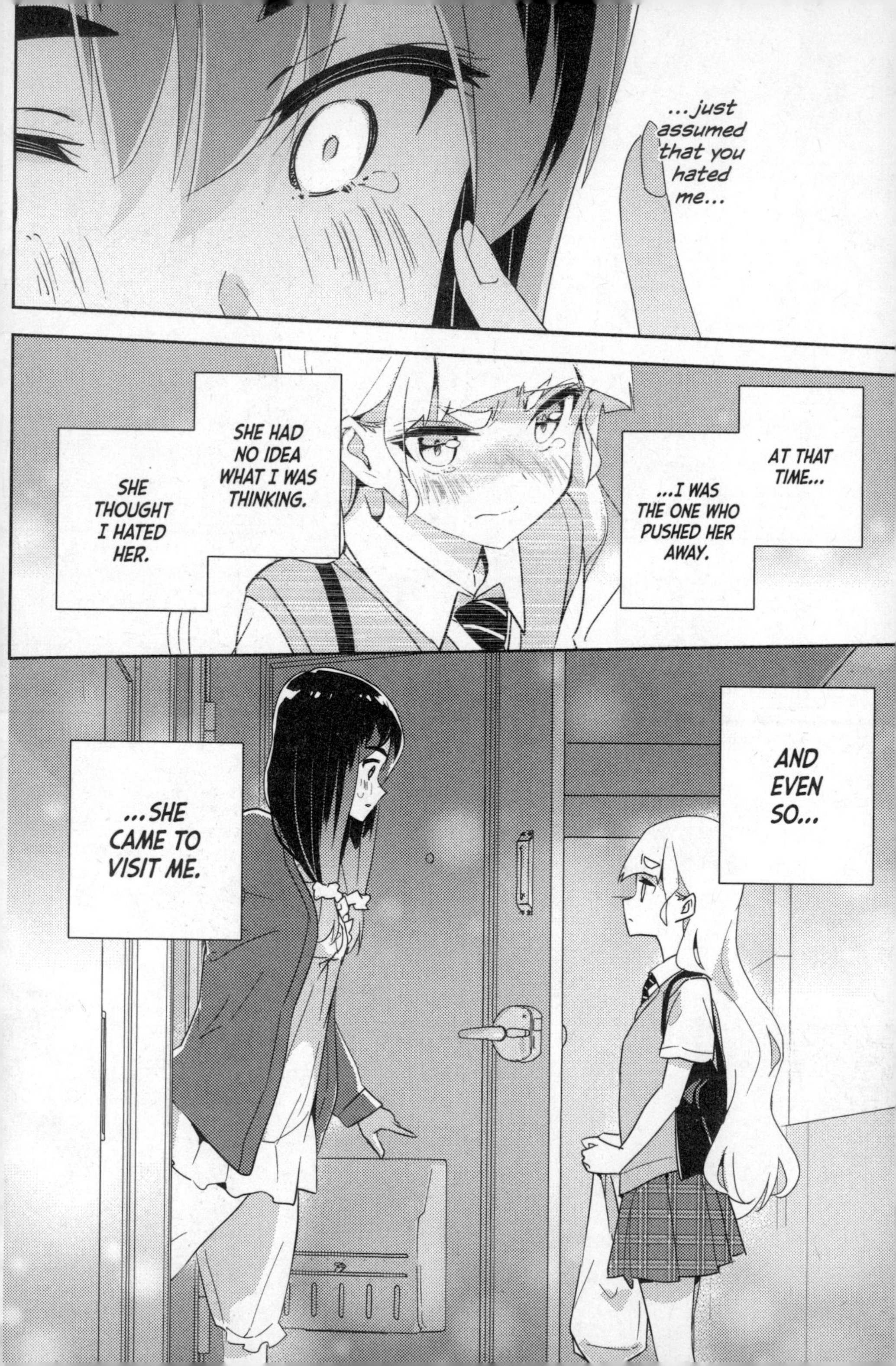
...just assumed that you hated me...
AT THAT TIME...
...I WAS THE ONE WHO PUSHED HER AWAY.
SHE HAD NO IDEA WHAT I WAS THINKING.
SHE THOUGHT I HATED HER.
AND EVEN SO...
...SHE CAME TO VISIT ME.

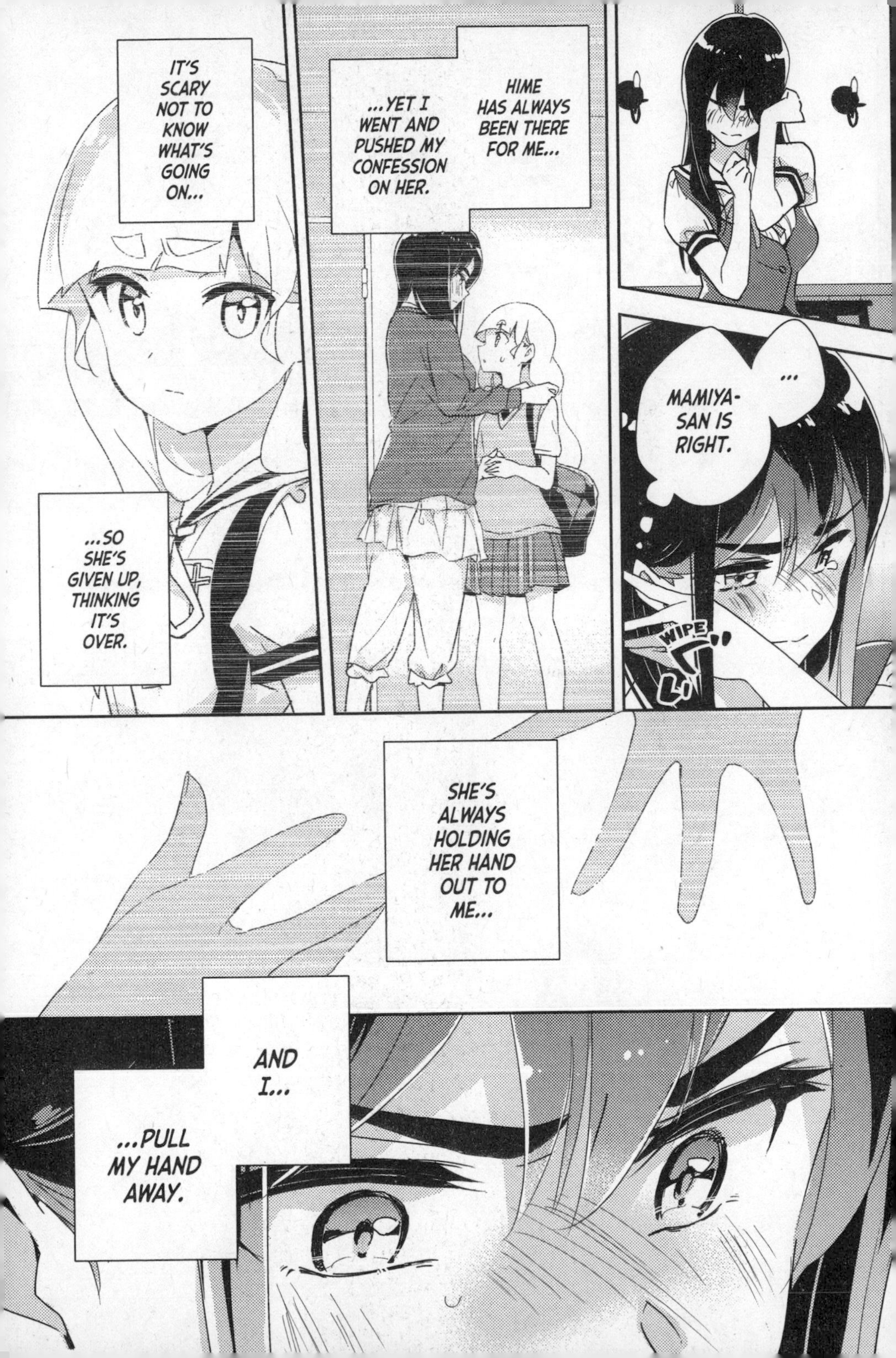
...
MAMIYA-SAN IS RIGHT.
WIPE
HIME HAS ALWAYS BEEN THERE FOR ME...
...YET I WENT AND PUSHED MY CONFESSION ON HER.
IT'S SCARY NOT TO KNOW WHAT'S GOING ON...
...SO SHE'S GIVEN UP, THINKING IT'S OVER.
SHE'S ALWAYS HOLDING HER HAND OUT TO ME...
AND I...
...PULL MY HAND AWAY.

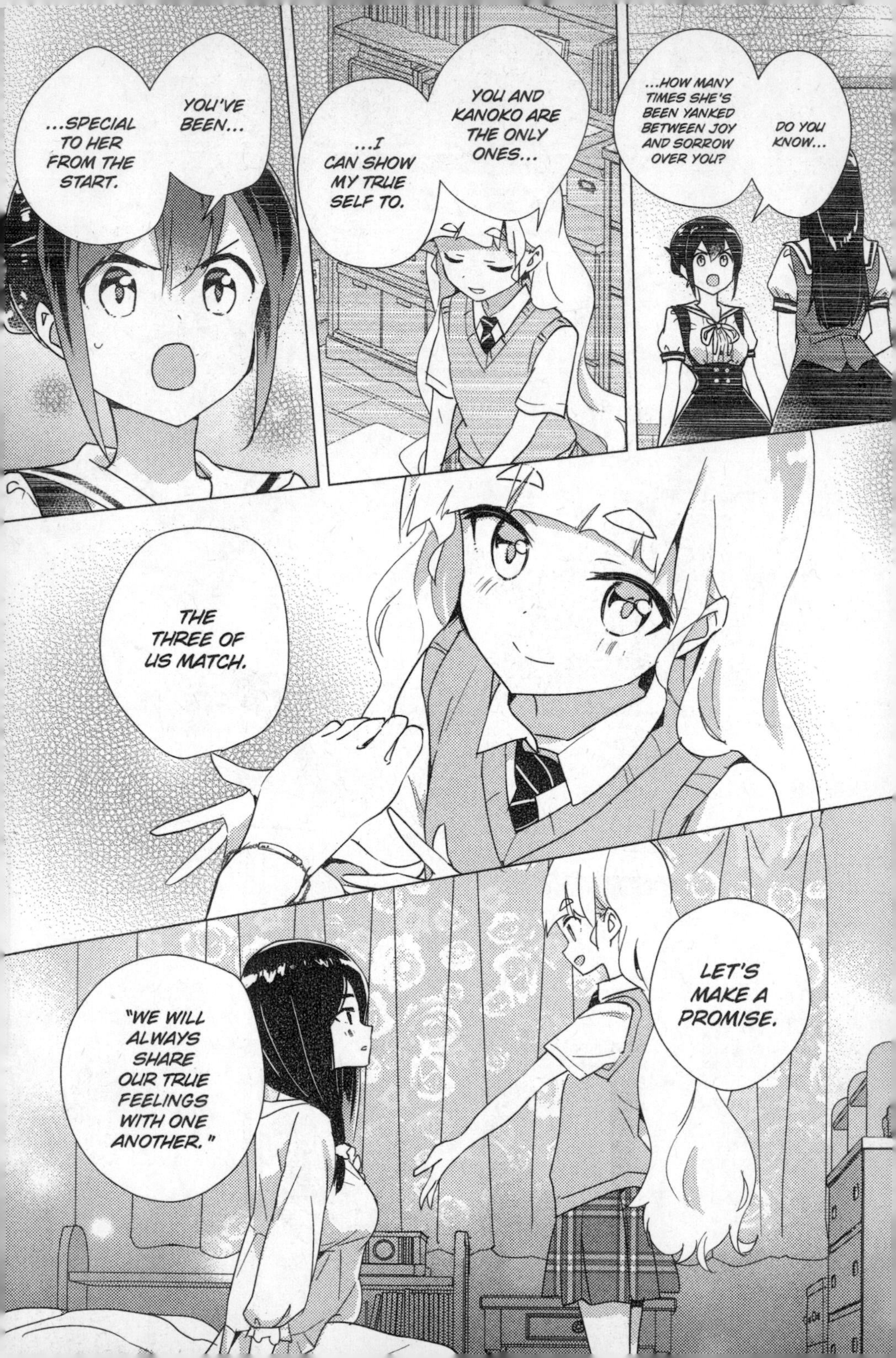
DO YOU KNOW...
...HOW MANY TIMES SHE'S BEEN YANKED BETWEEN JOY AND SORROW OVER YOU?
YOU AND KANOKO ARE THE ONLY ONES...
...I CAN SHOW MY TRUE SELF TO.
YOU'VE BEEN...
...SPECIAL TO HER FROM THE START.
THE THREE OF US MATCH.
LET'S MAKE A PROMISE.
"WE WILL ALWAYS SHARE OUR TRUE FEELINGS WITH ONE ANOTHER."

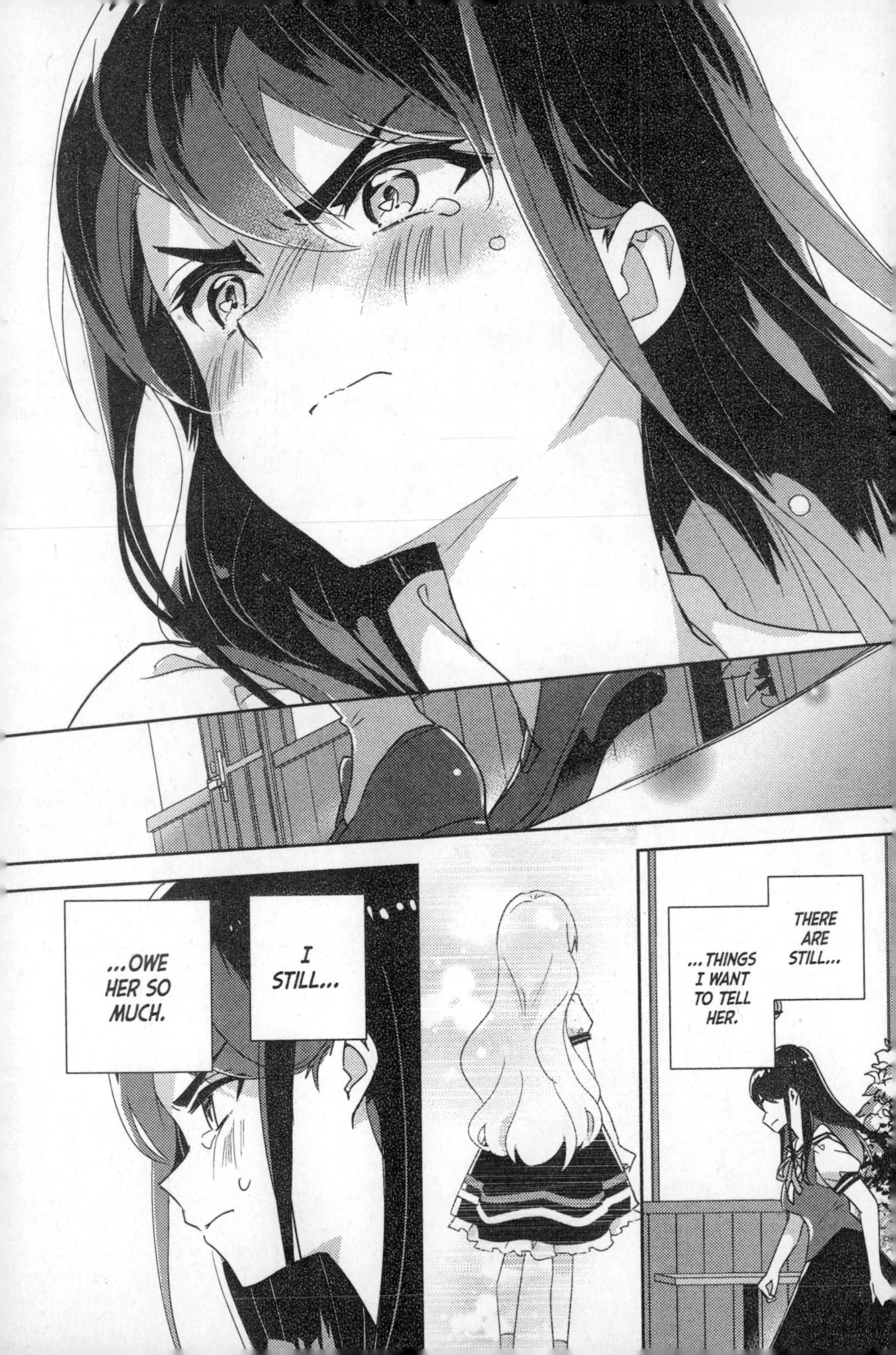
THERE ARE STILL...
...THINGS I WANT TO TELL HER.
I STILL...
...OWE HER SO MUCH.

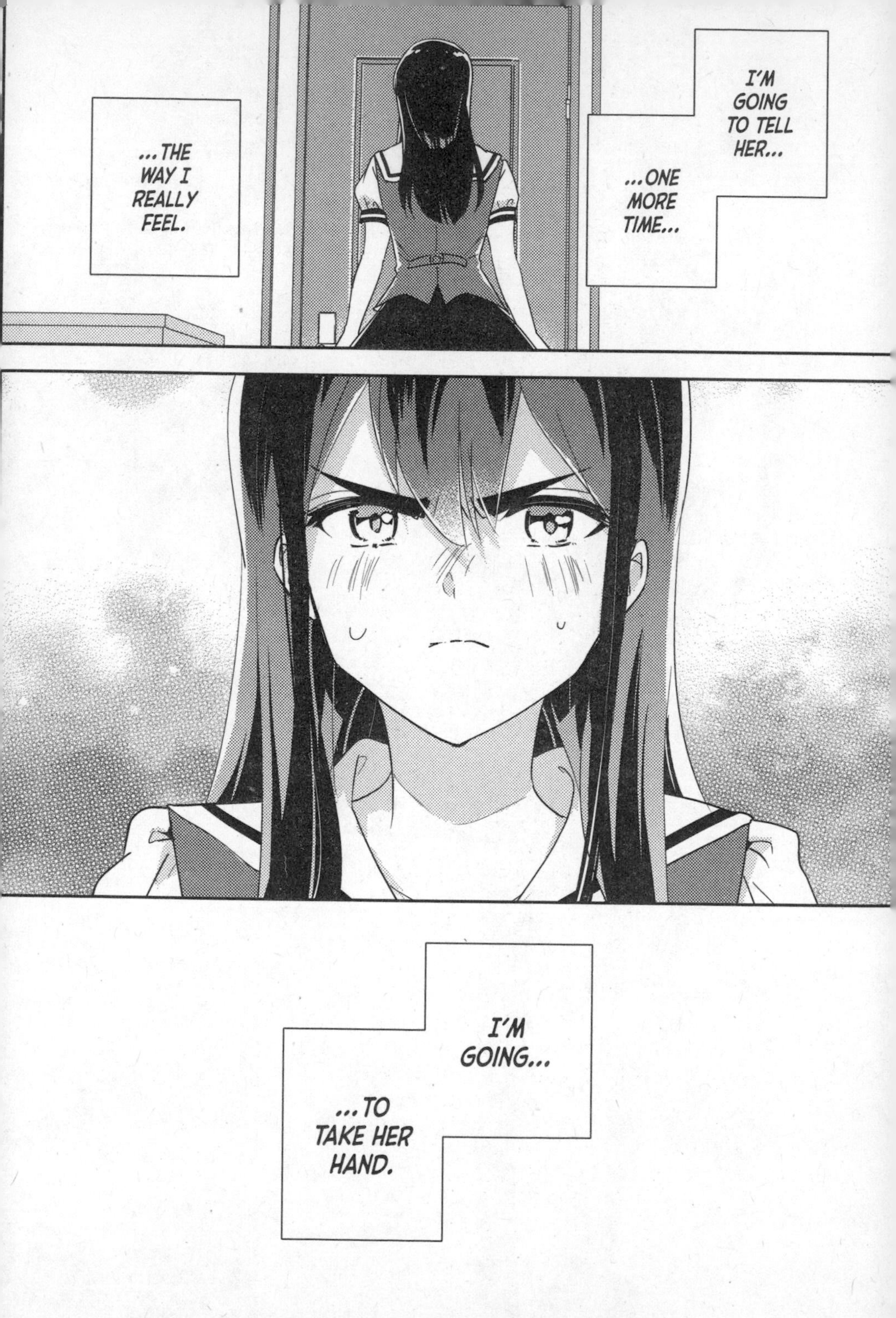
I'M GOING TO TELL HER...
...ONE MORE TIME...
...THE WAY I REALLY FEEL.
I'M GOING...
...TO TAKE HER HAND.

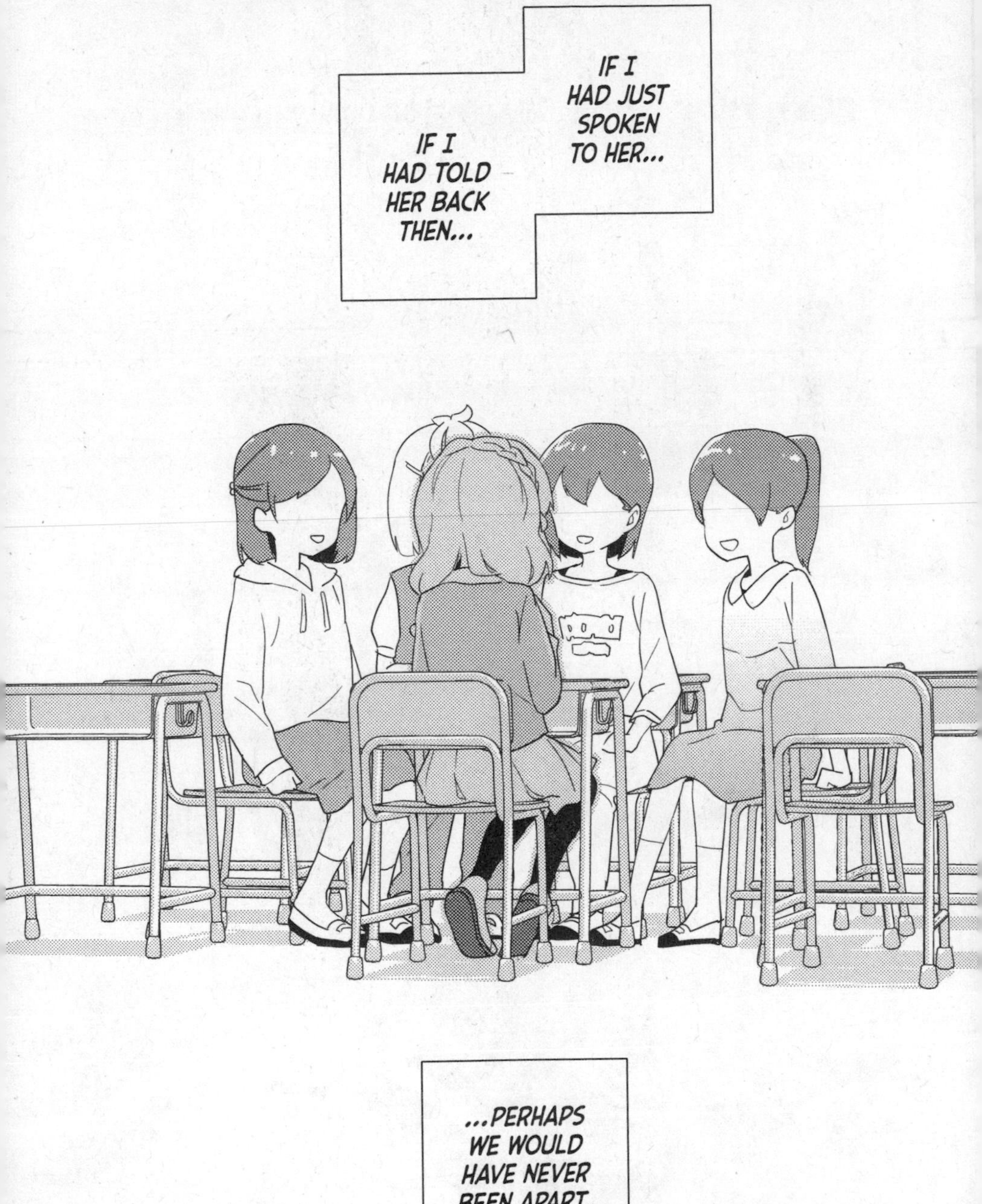
IF I HAD JUST SPOKEN TO HER...
IF I HAD TOLD HER BACK THEN...
...PERHAPS WE WOULD HAVE NEVER BEEN APART.

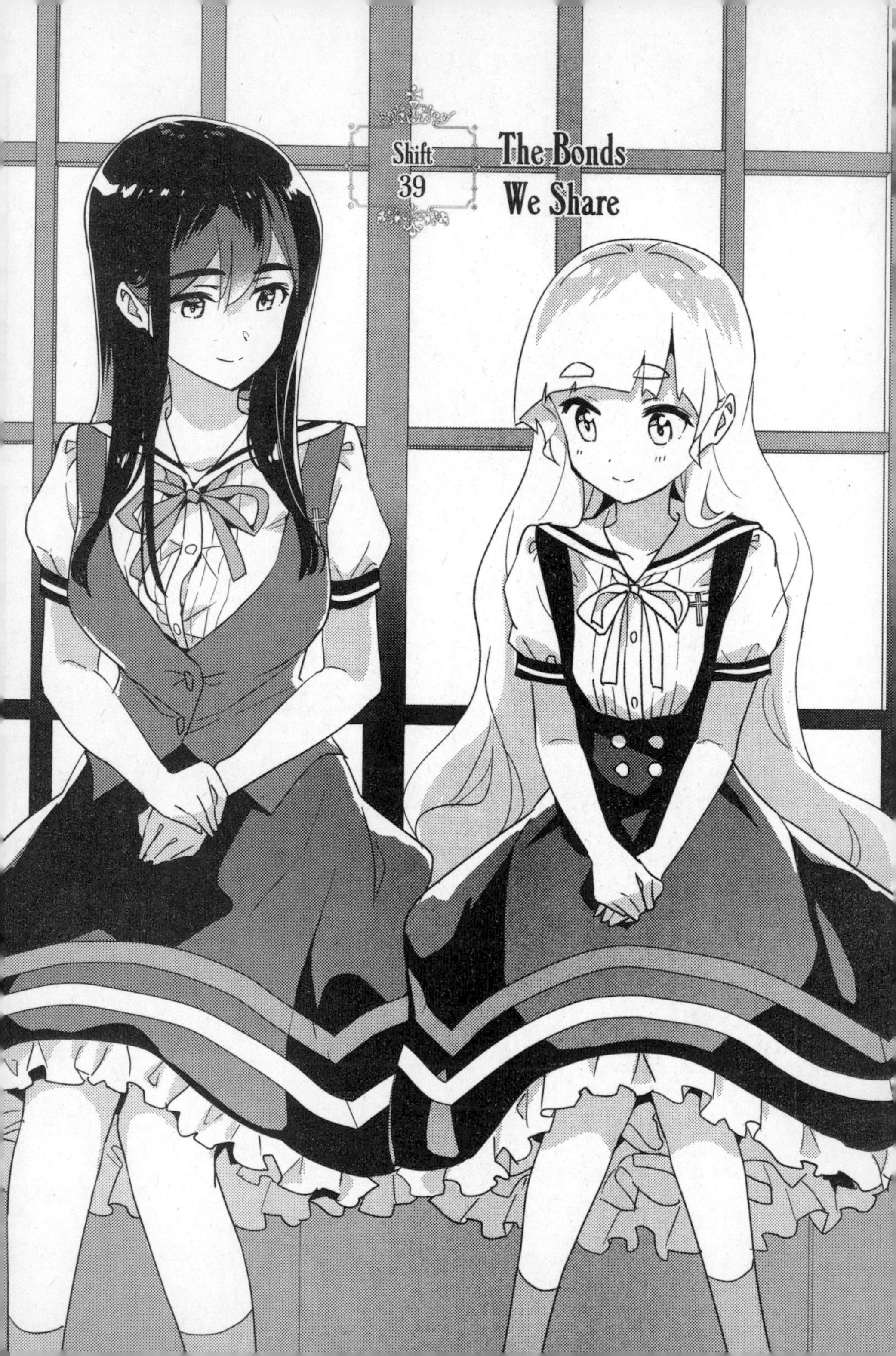
Shift 39
The Bonds We Share

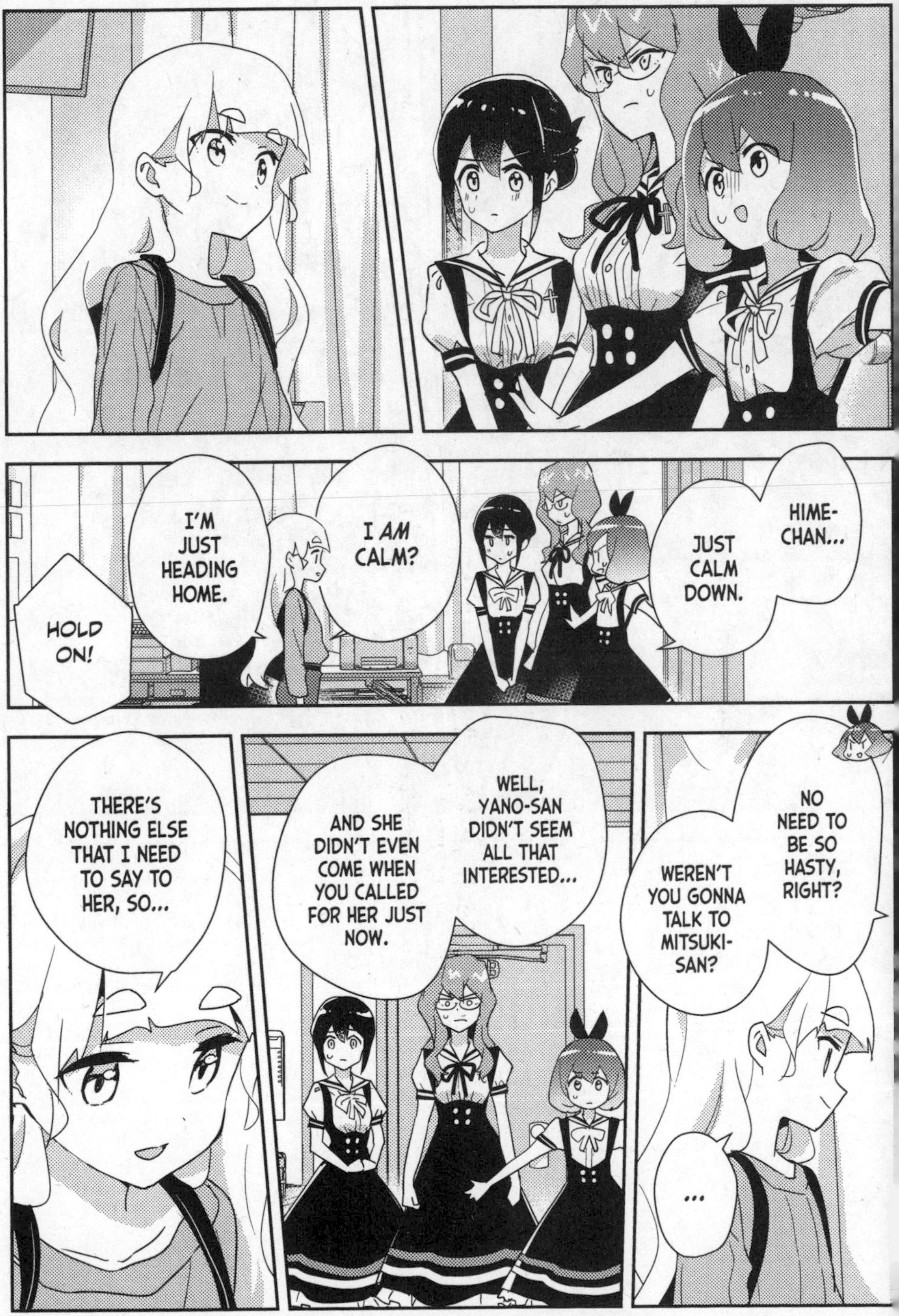
HIME-CHAN...
JUST CALM DOWN.
I *AM* CALM?
I'M JUST HEADING HOME.
HOLD ON!
NO NEED TO BE SO HASTY, RIGHT?
WEREN'T YOU GONNA TALK TO MITSUKI-SAN?
...
WELL, YANO-SAN DIDN'T SEEM ALL THAT INTERESTED...
AND SHE DIDN'T EVEN COME WHEN YOU CALLED FOR HER JUST NOW.
THERE'S NOTHING ELSE THAT I NEED TO SAY TO HER, SO...

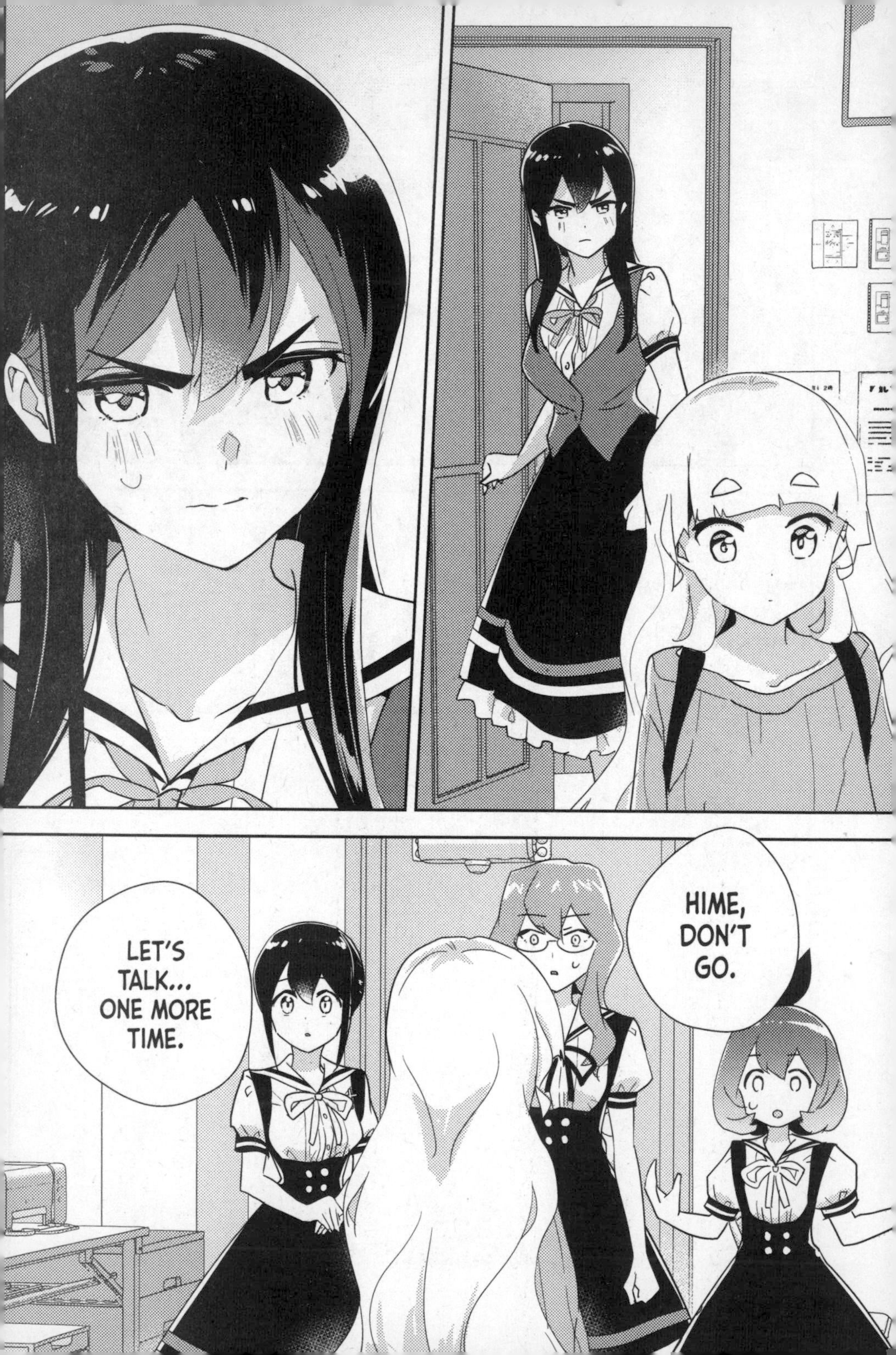
HIME, DON'T GO.
LET'S TALK... ONE MORE TIME.

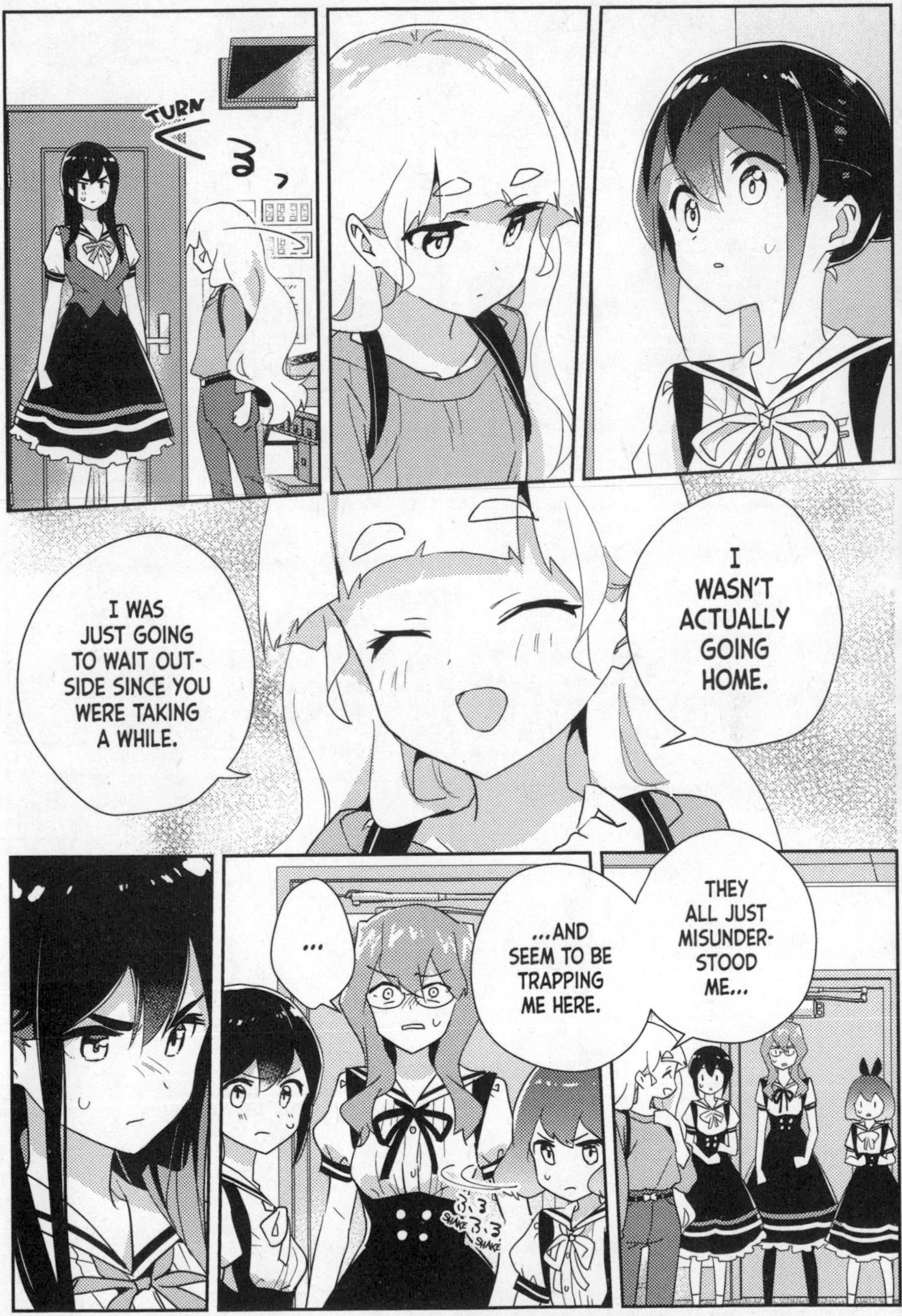
TURN
I WASN'T ACTUALLY GOING HOME.
I WAS JUST GOING TO WAIT OUT-SIDE SINCE YOU WERE TAKING A WHILE.
THEY ALL JUST MISUNDER-STOOD ME...
...AND SEEM TO BE TRAPPING ME HERE.
...
SHAKE SHAKE

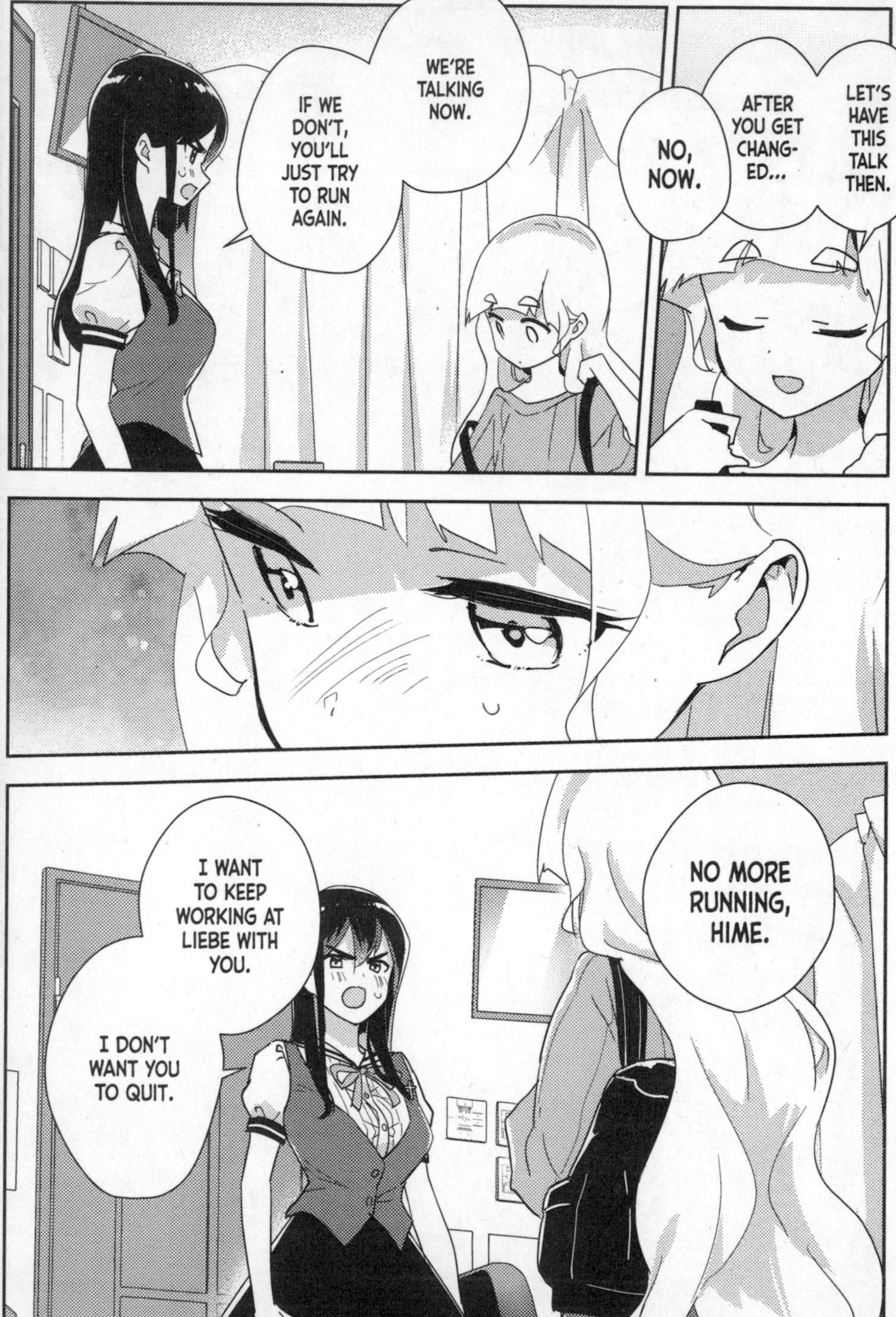
LET'S HAVE THIS TALK THEN.
AFTER YOU GET CHANG-ED...
NO, NOW.
WE'RE TALKING NOW.
IF WE DON'T, YOU'LL JUST TRY TO RUN AGAIN.
NO MORE RUNNING, HIME.
I WANT TO KEEP WORKING AT LIEBE WITH YOU.
I DON'T WANT YOU TO QUIT.

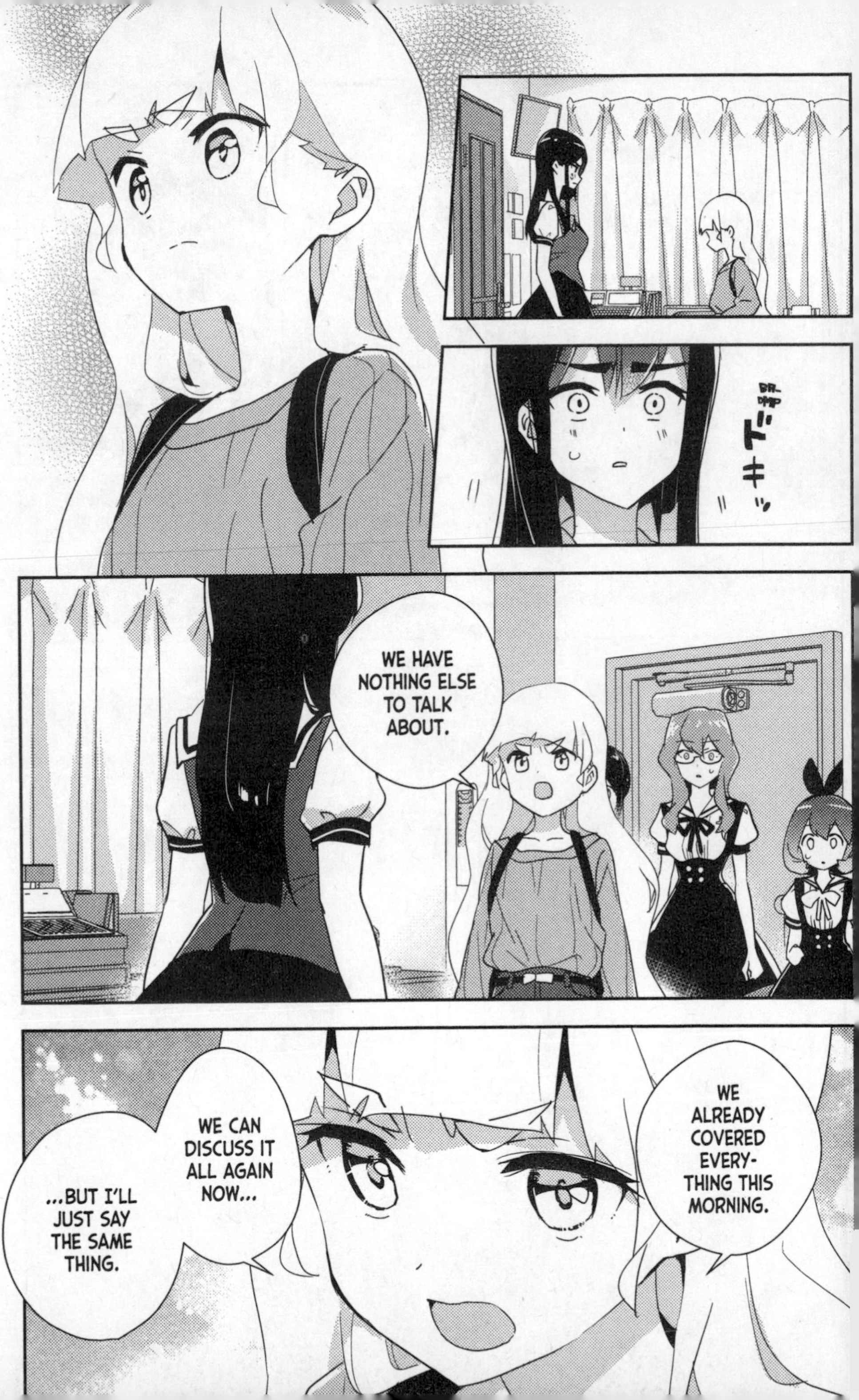
BA-DMP
ドキッ
WE HAVE NOTHING ELSE TO TALK ABOUT.
WE ALREADY COVERED EVERY-THING THIS MORNING.
WE CAN DISCUSS IT ALL AGAIN NOW...
...BUT I'LL JUST SAY THE SAME THING.

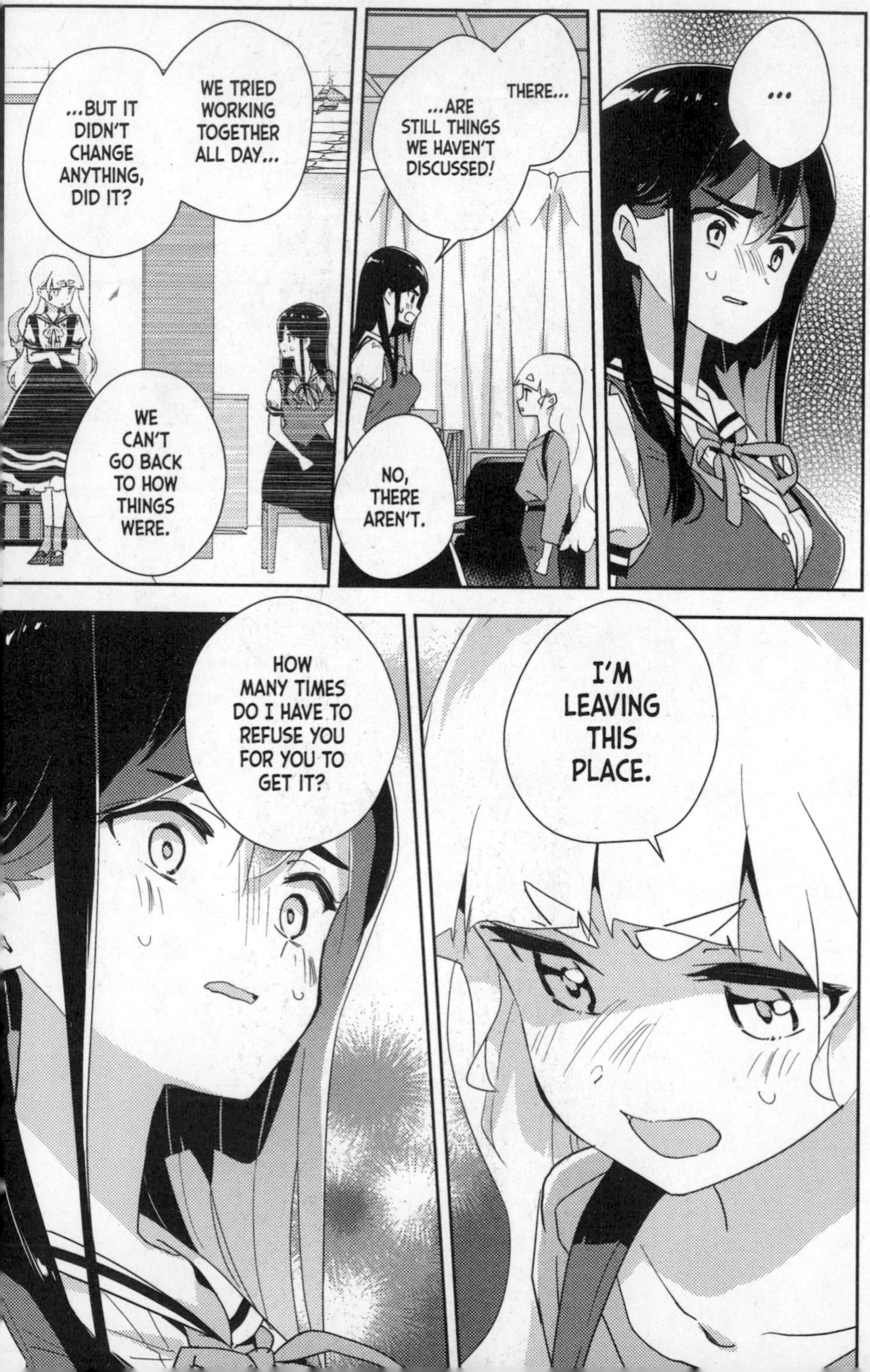
...
THERE...
...ARE STILL THINGS WE HAVEN'T DISCUSSED!
NO, THERE AREN'T.
WE TRIED WORKING TOGETHER ALL DAY...
...BUT IT DIDN'T CHANGE ANYTHING, DID IT?
WE CAN'T GO BACK TO HOW THINGS WERE.
I'M LEAVING THIS PLACE.
HOW MANY TIMES DO I HAVE TO REFUSE YOU FOR YOU TO GET IT?

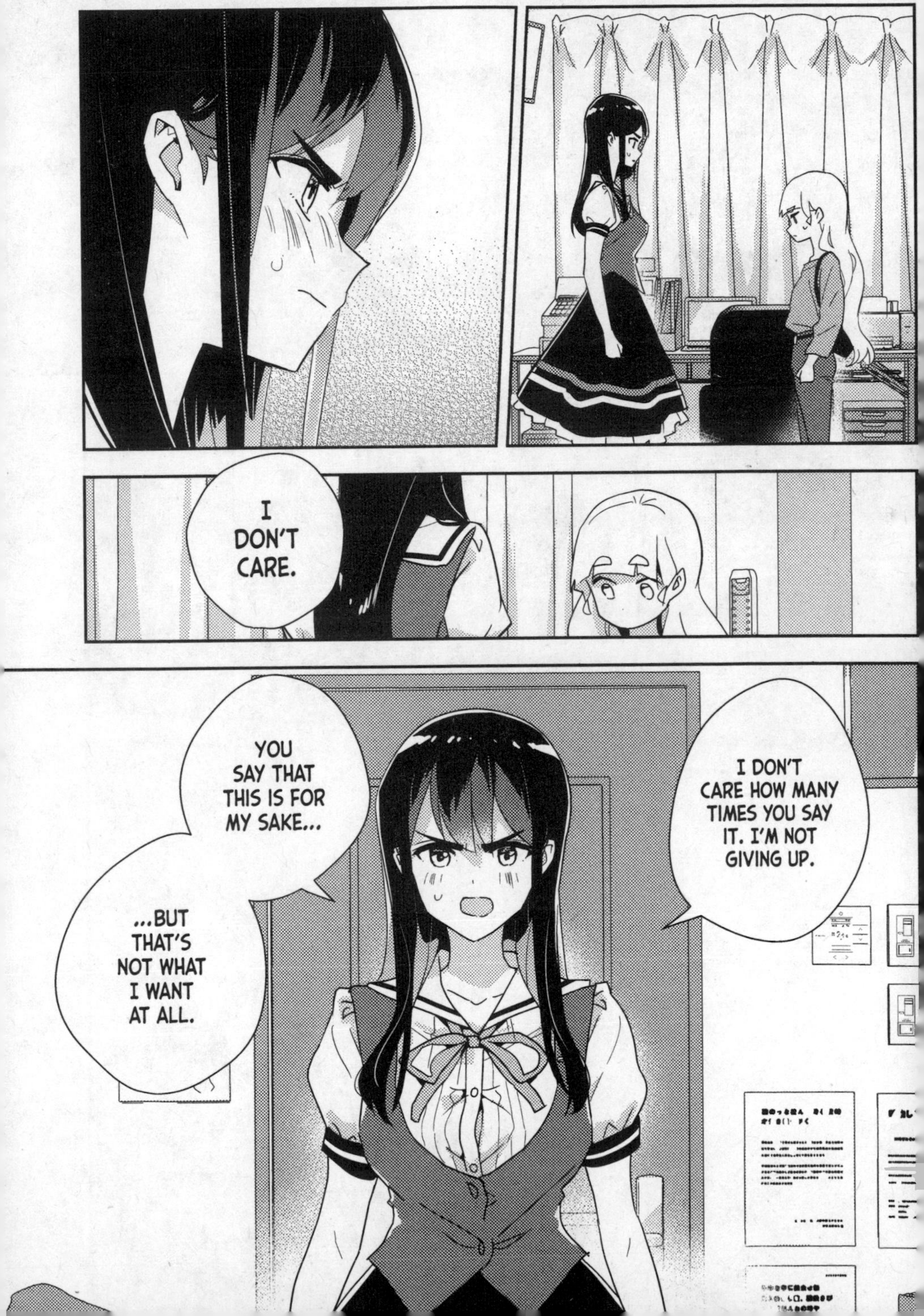
I DON'T CARE.
I DON'T CARE HOW MANY TIMES YOU SAY IT. I'M NOT GIVING UP.
YOU SAY THAT THIS IS FOR MY SAKE...
...BUT THAT'S NOT WHAT I WANT AT ALL.

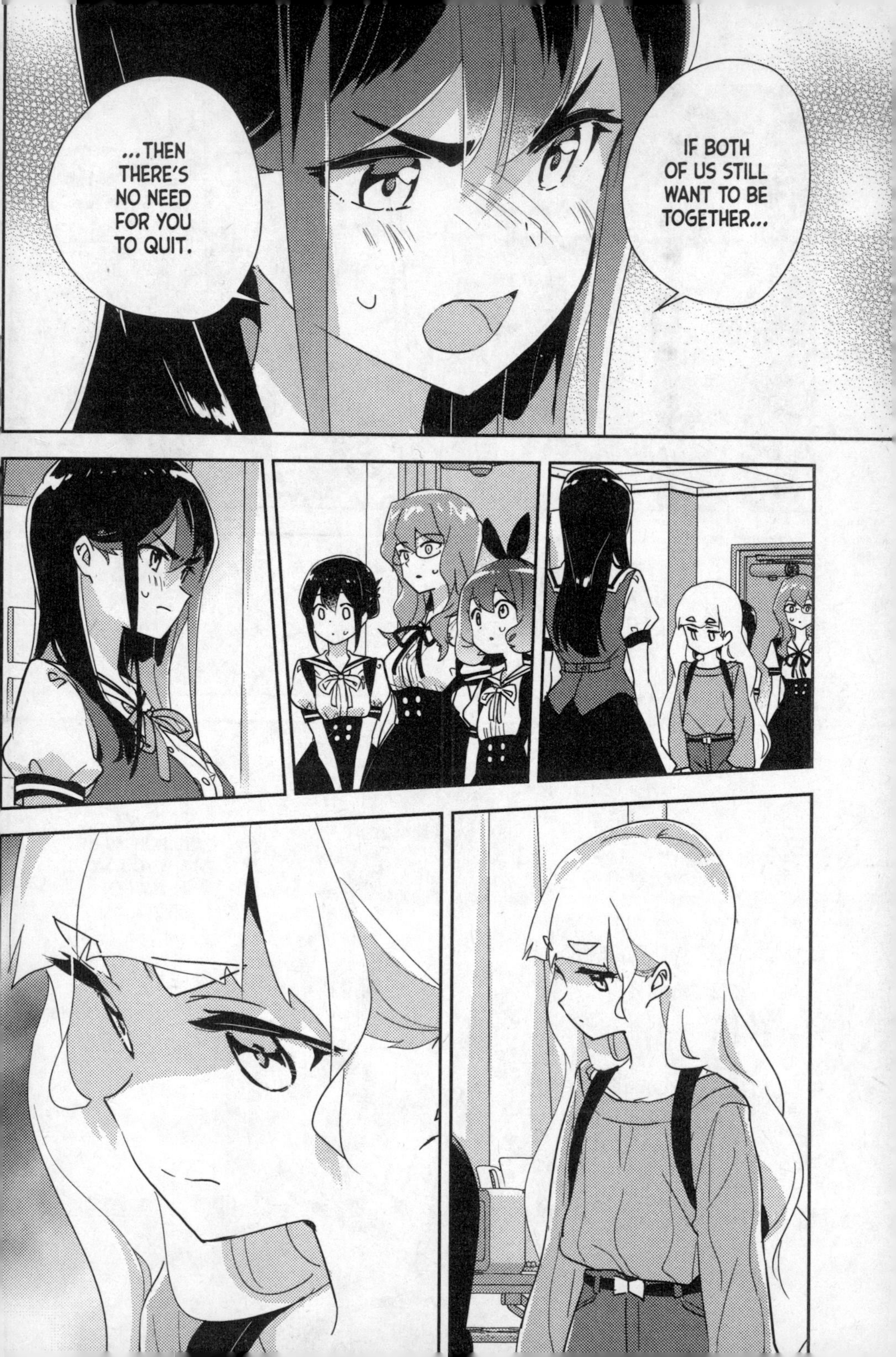
IF BOTH OF US STILL WANT TO BE TOGETHER...
...THEN THERE'S NO NEED FOR YOU TO QUIT.

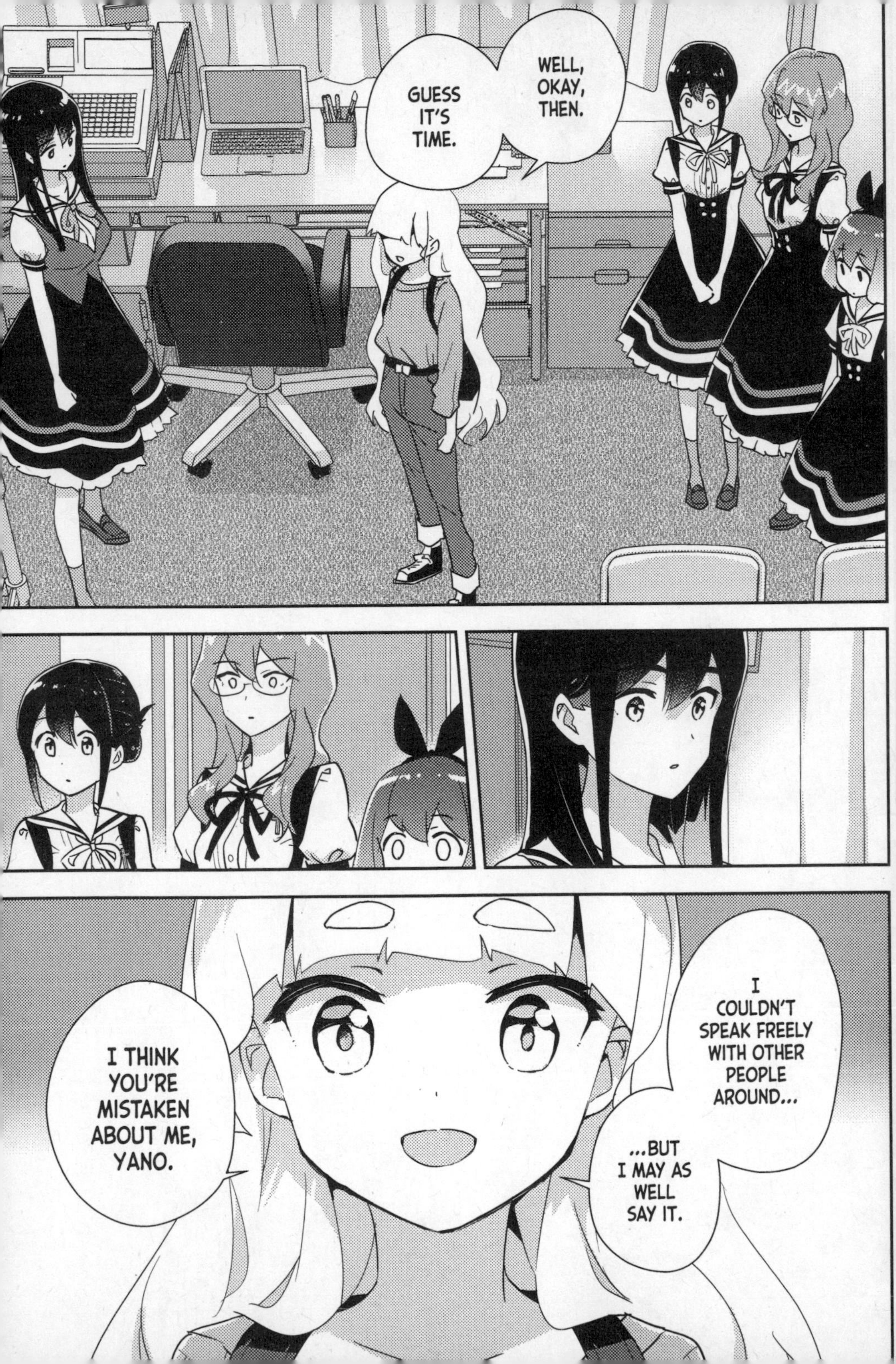
WELL, OKAY, THEN.
GUESS IT'S TIME.
I COULDN'T SPEAK FREELY WITH OTHER PEOPLE AROUND...
...BUT I MAY AS WELL SAY IT.
I THINK YOU'RE MISTAKEN ABOUT ME, YANO.

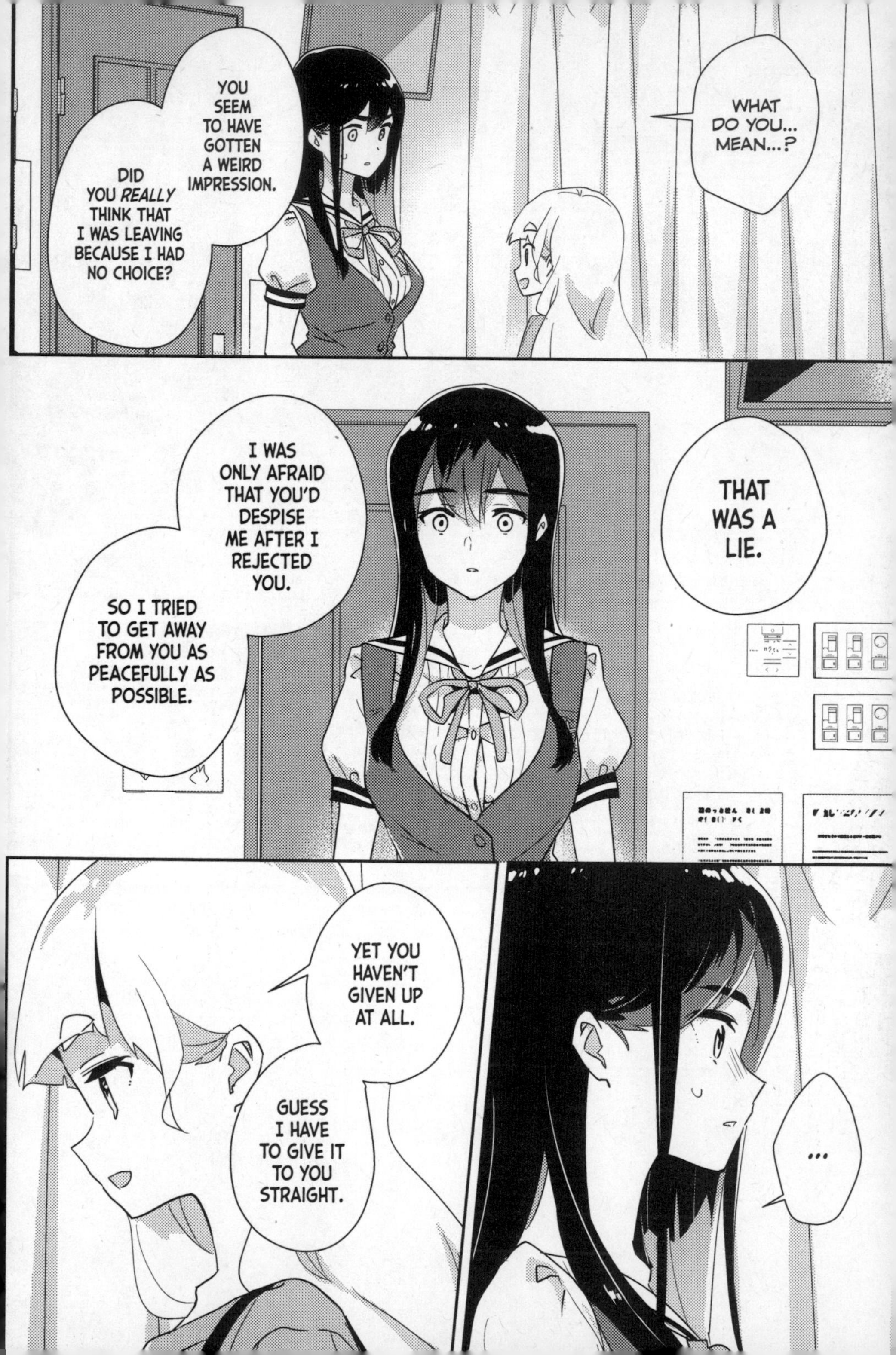
WHAT DO YOU... MEAN...?
YOU SEEM TO HAVE GOTTEN A WEIRD IMPRESSION.
DID YOU *REALLY* THINK THAT I WAS LEAVING BECAUSE I HAD NO CHOICE?
THAT WAS A LIE.
I WAS ONLY AFRAID THAT YOU'D DESPISE ME AFTER I REJECTED YOU.
SO I TRIED TO GET AWAY FROM YOU AS PEACEFULLY AS POSSIBLE.
...
YET YOU HAVEN'T GIVEN UP AT ALL.
GUESS I HAVE TO GIVE IT TO YOU STRAIGHT.

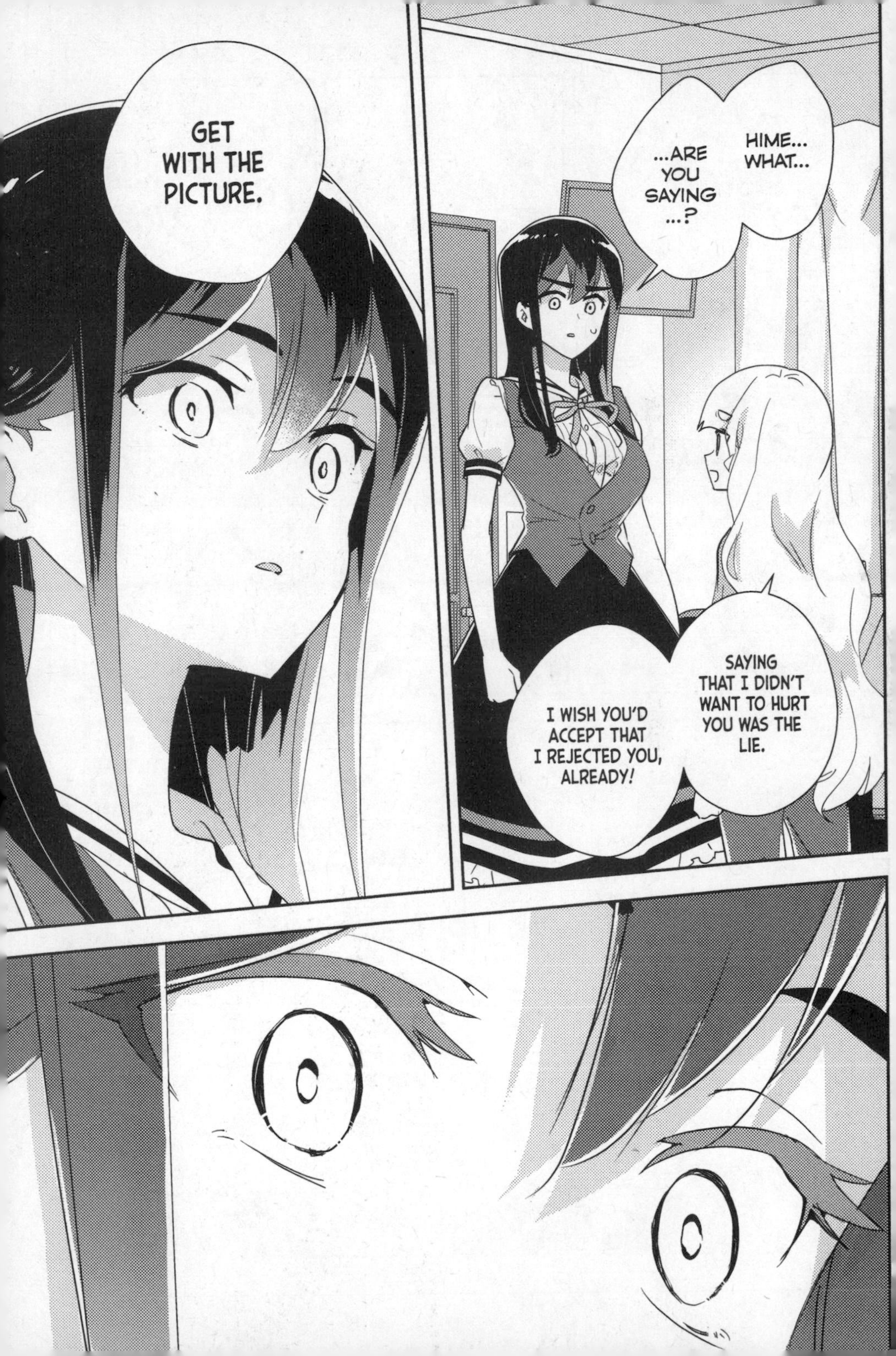
HIME... WHAT...
...ARE YOU SAYING ...?
SAYING THAT I DIDN'T WANT TO HURT YOU WAS THE LIE.
I WISH YOU'D ACCEPT THAT I REJECTED YOU, ALREADY!
GET WITH THE PICTURE.

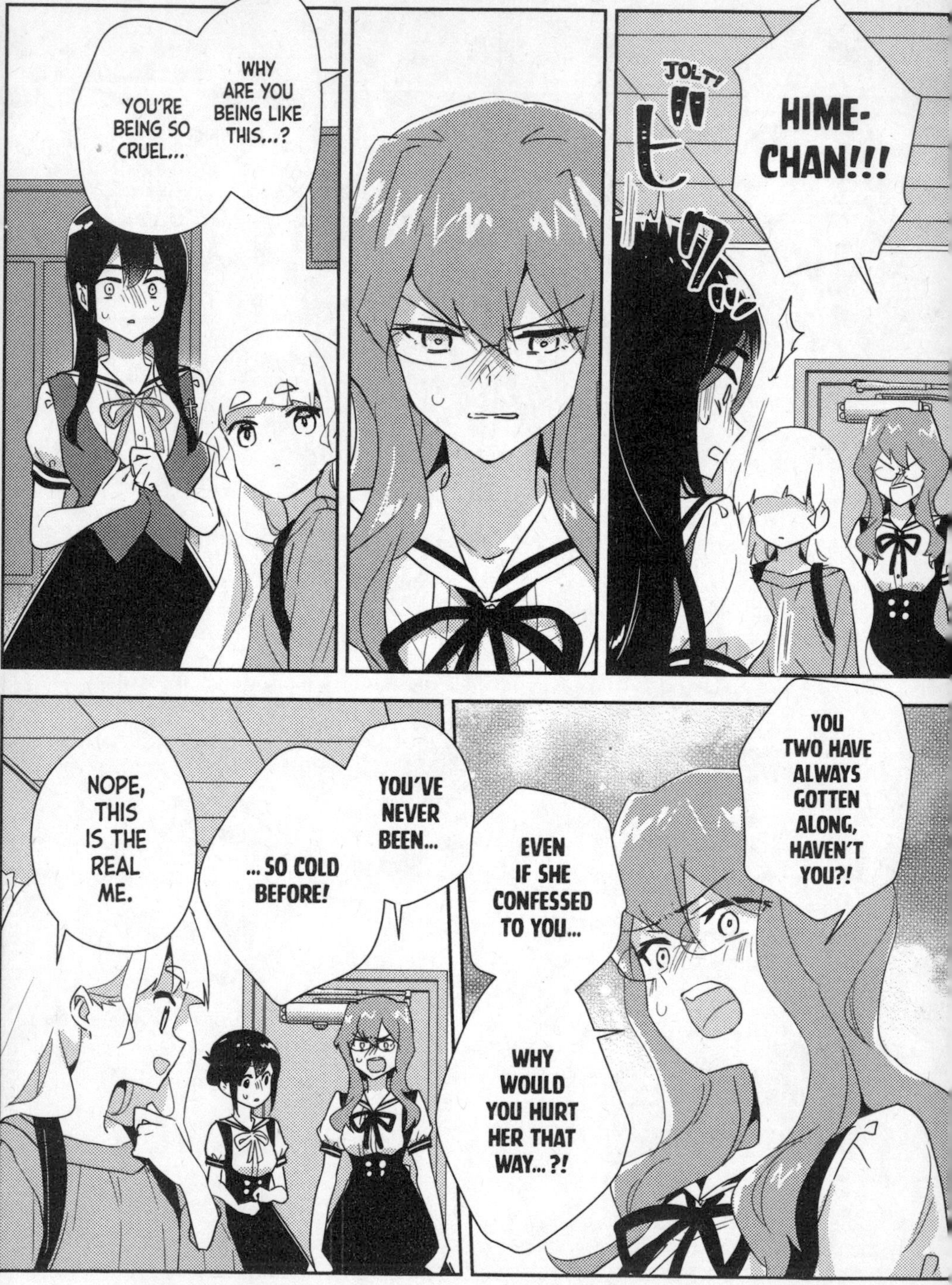
JOLT!
HIME-CHAN!!!
WHY ARE YOU BEING LIKE THIS...? YOU'RE BEING SO CRUEL...
YOU TWO HAVE ALWAYS GOTTEN ALONG, HAVEN'T YOU?!
EVEN IF SHE CONFESSED TO YOU...
WHY WOULD YOU HURT HER THAT WAY...?!
YOU'VE NEVER BEEN...
...SO COLD BEFORE!
NOPE, THIS IS THE REAL ME.

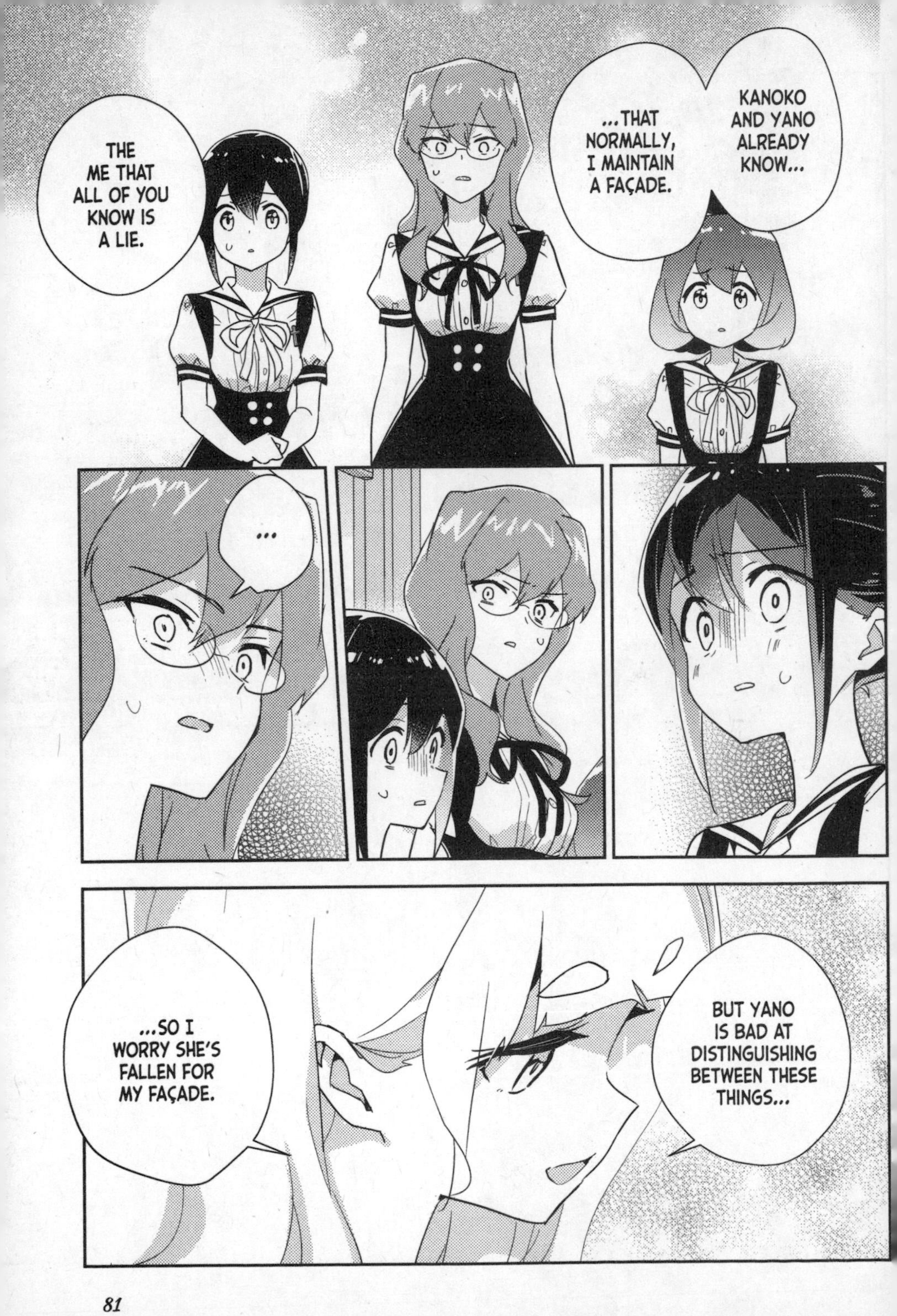
KANOKO AND YANO ALREADY KNOW...
...THAT NORMALLY, I MAINTAIN A FAÇADE.
THE ME THAT ALL OF YOU KNOW IS A LIE.
...
BUT YANO IS BAD AT DISTINGUISHING BETWEEN THESE THINGS...
...SO I WORRY SHE'S FALLEN FOR MY FAÇADE.

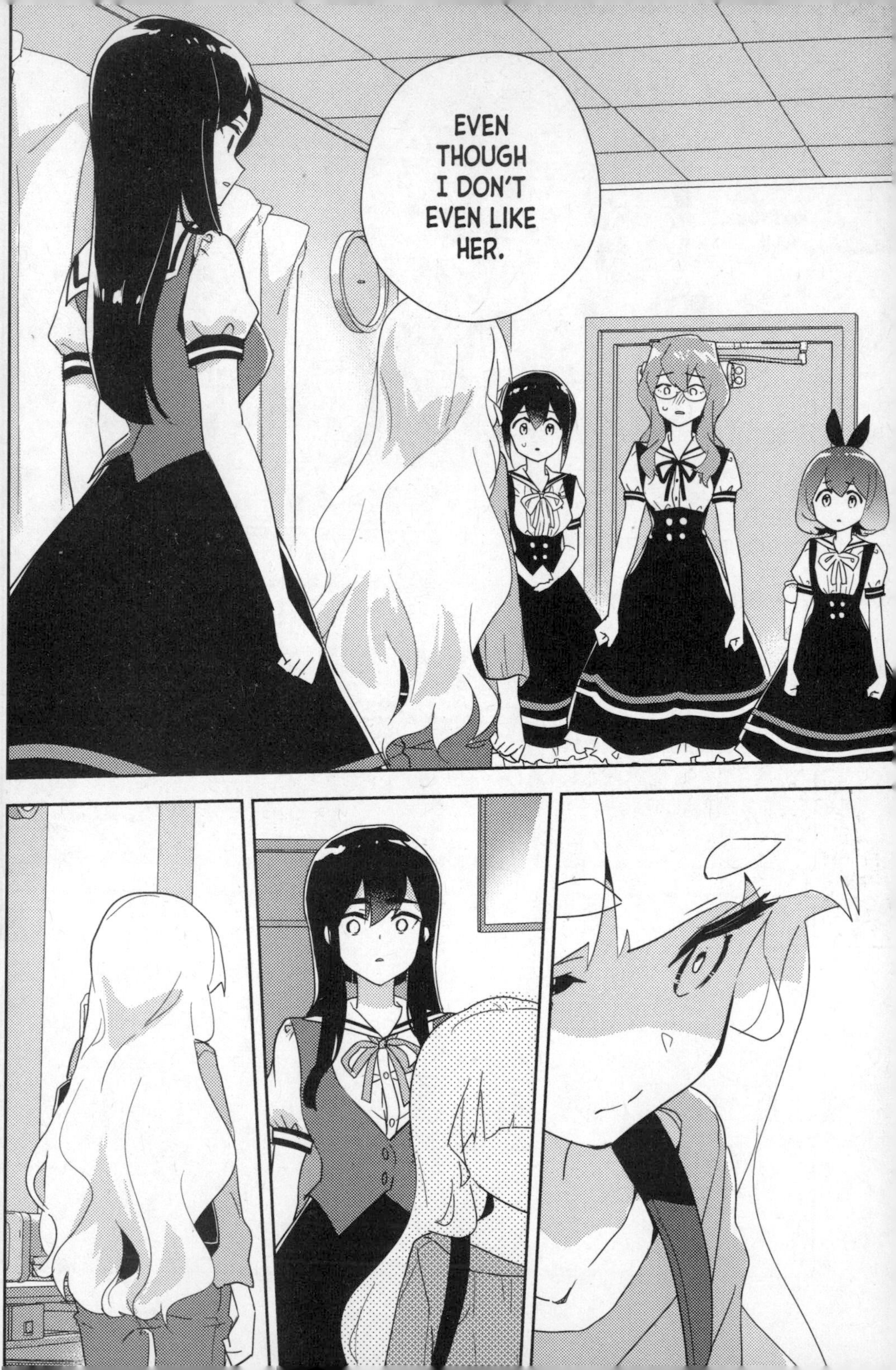
EVEN THOUGH I DON'T EVEN LIKE HER.

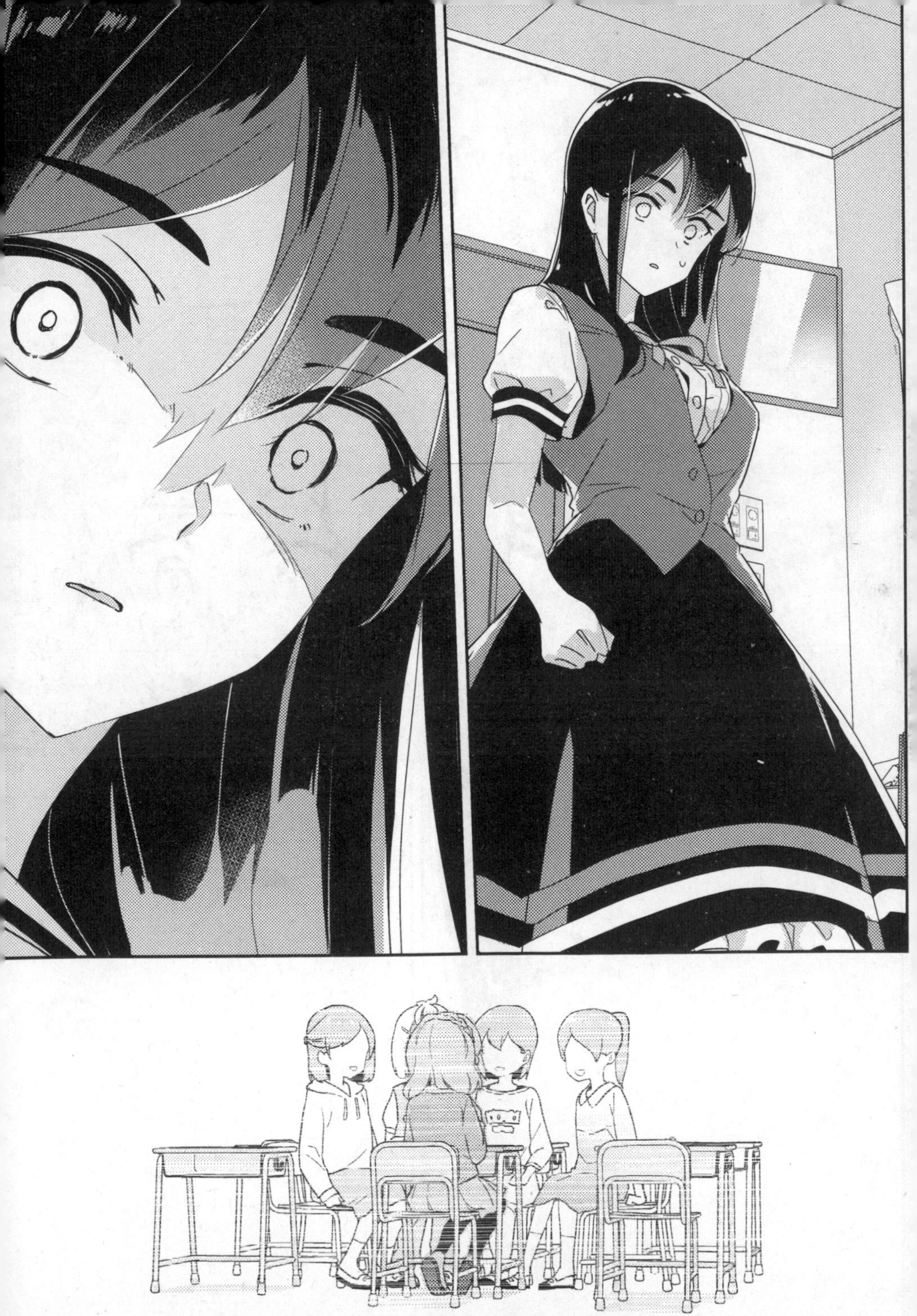

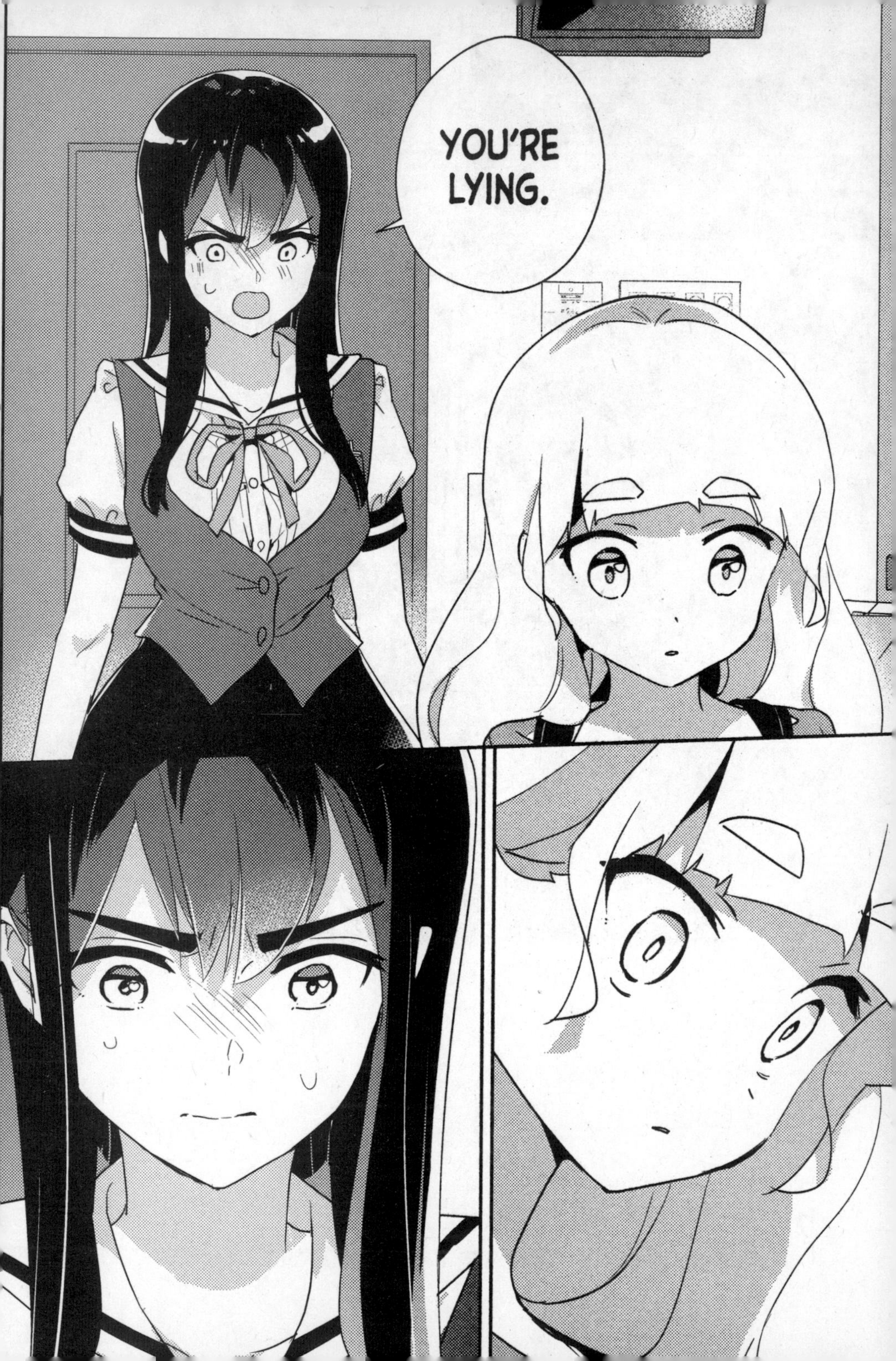
YOU'RE LYING.

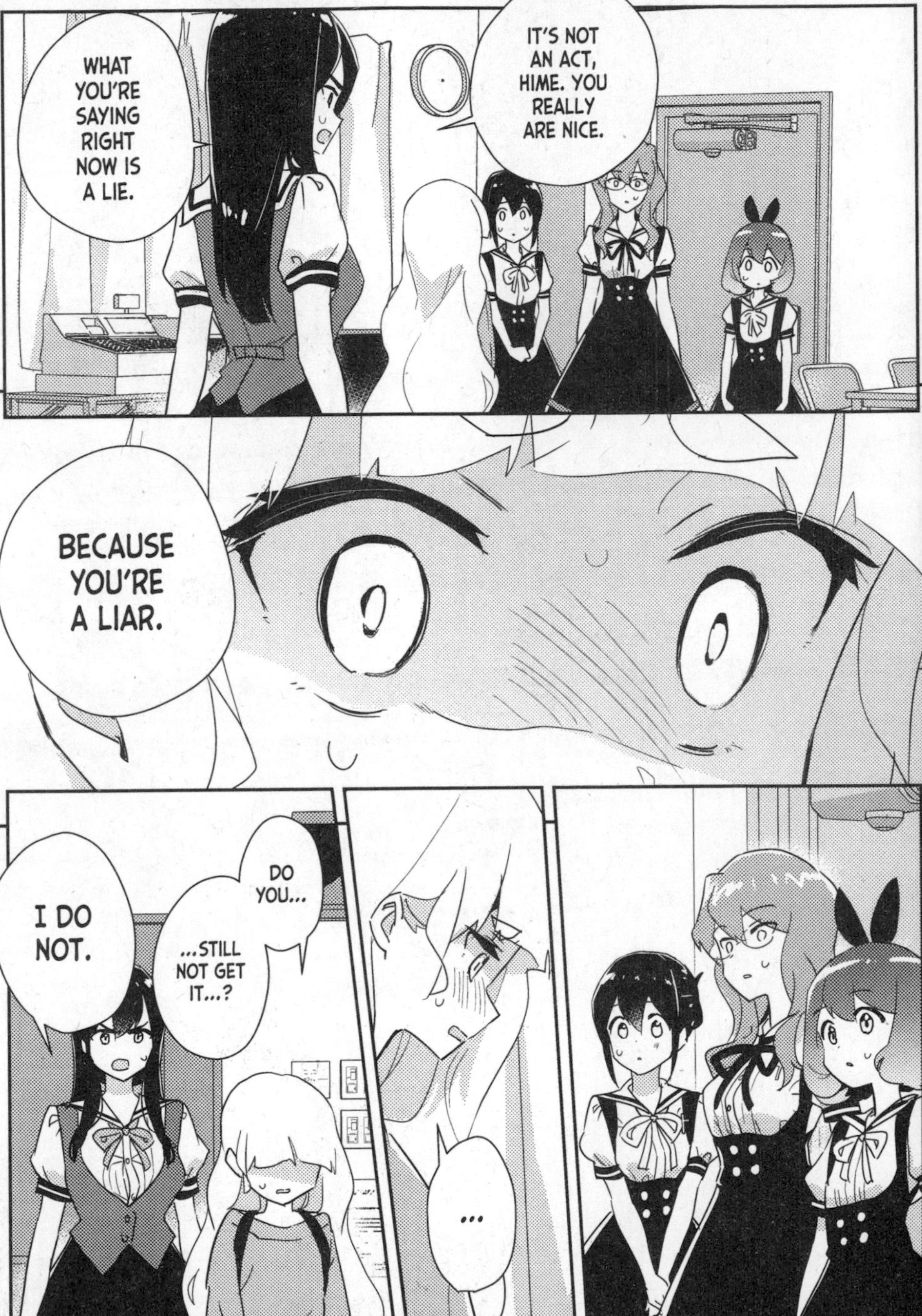
IT'S NOT AN ACT, HIME. YOU REALLY ARE NICE.
WHAT YOU'RE SAYING RIGHT NOW IS A LIE.
BECAUSE YOU'RE A LIAR.
...
DO YOU...
...STILL NOT GET IT...?
I DO NOT.

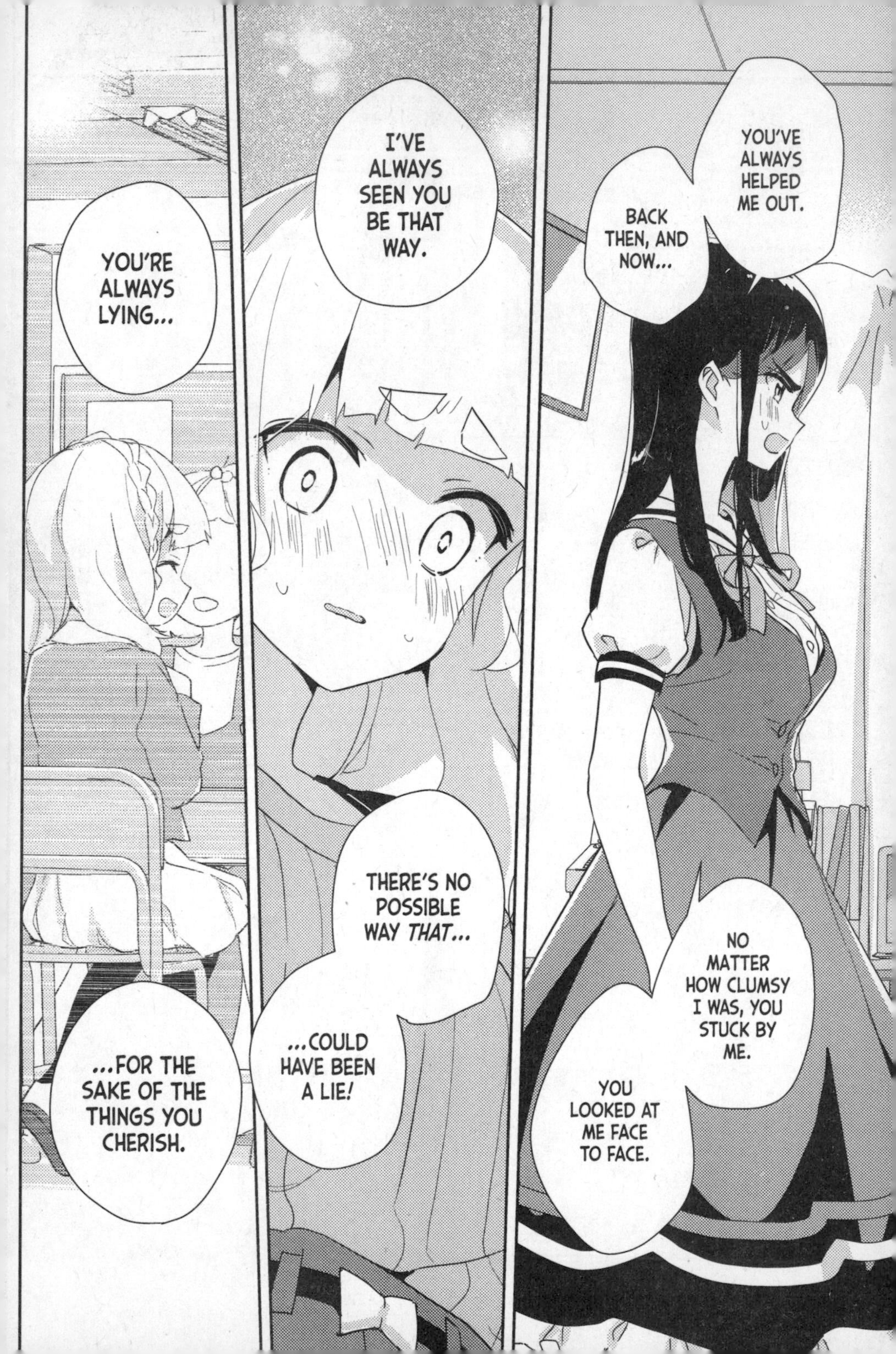
YOU'VE ALWAYS HELPED ME OUT.
BACK THEN, AND NOW...
NO MATTER HOW CLUMSY I WAS, YOU STUCK BY ME.
YOU LOOKED AT ME FACE TO FACE.
I'VE ALWAYS SEEN YOU BE THAT WAY.
THERE'S NO POSSIBLE WAY *THAT*...
...COULD HAVE BEEN A LIE!
YOU'RE ALWAYS LYING...
...FOR THE SAKE OF THE THINGS YOU CHERISH.

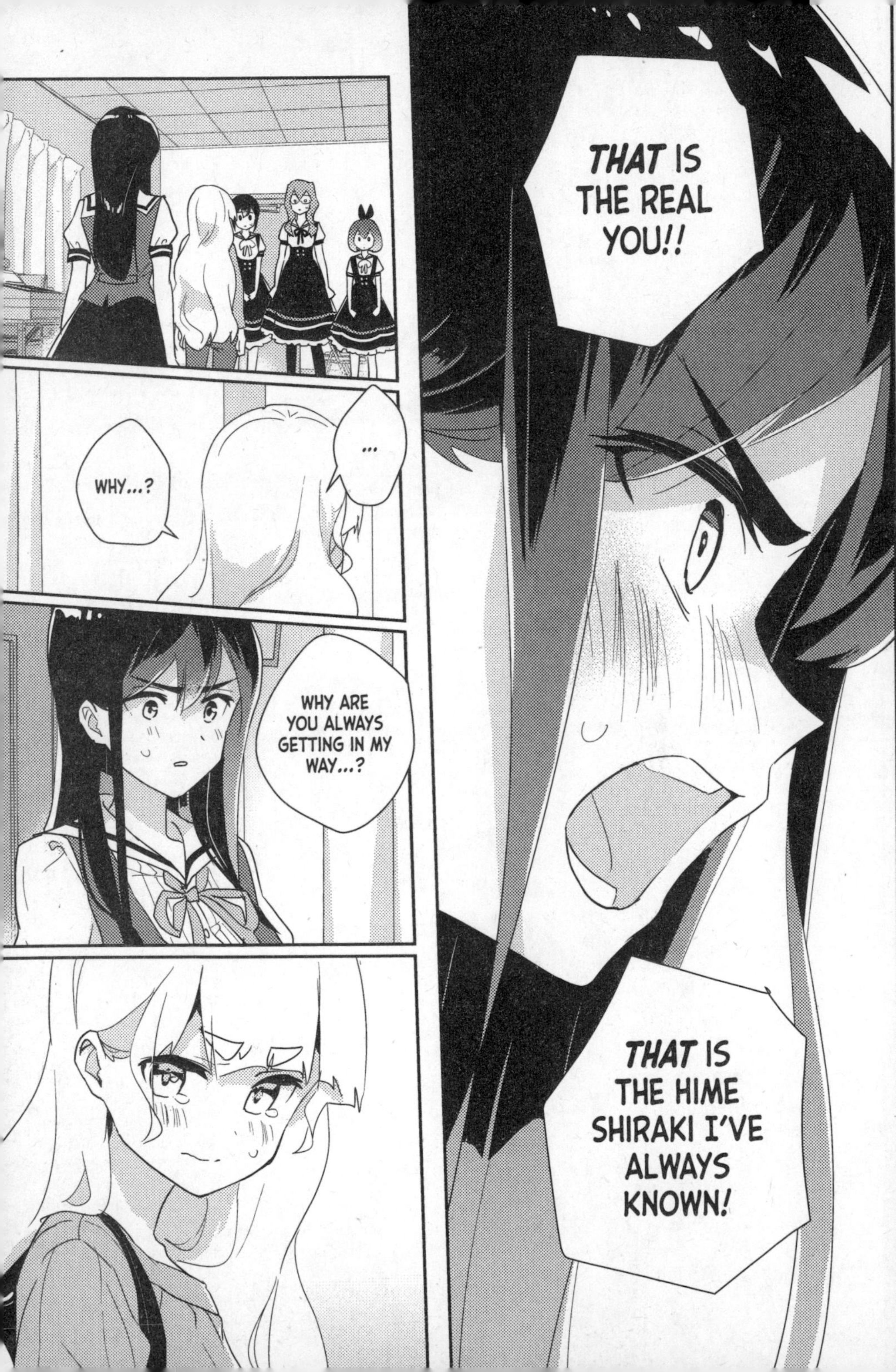
THAT IS THE REAL YOU!!
THAT IS THE HIME SHIRAKI I'VE ALWAYS KNOWN!
...
WHY...?
WHY ARE YOU ALWAYS GETTING IN MY WAY...?

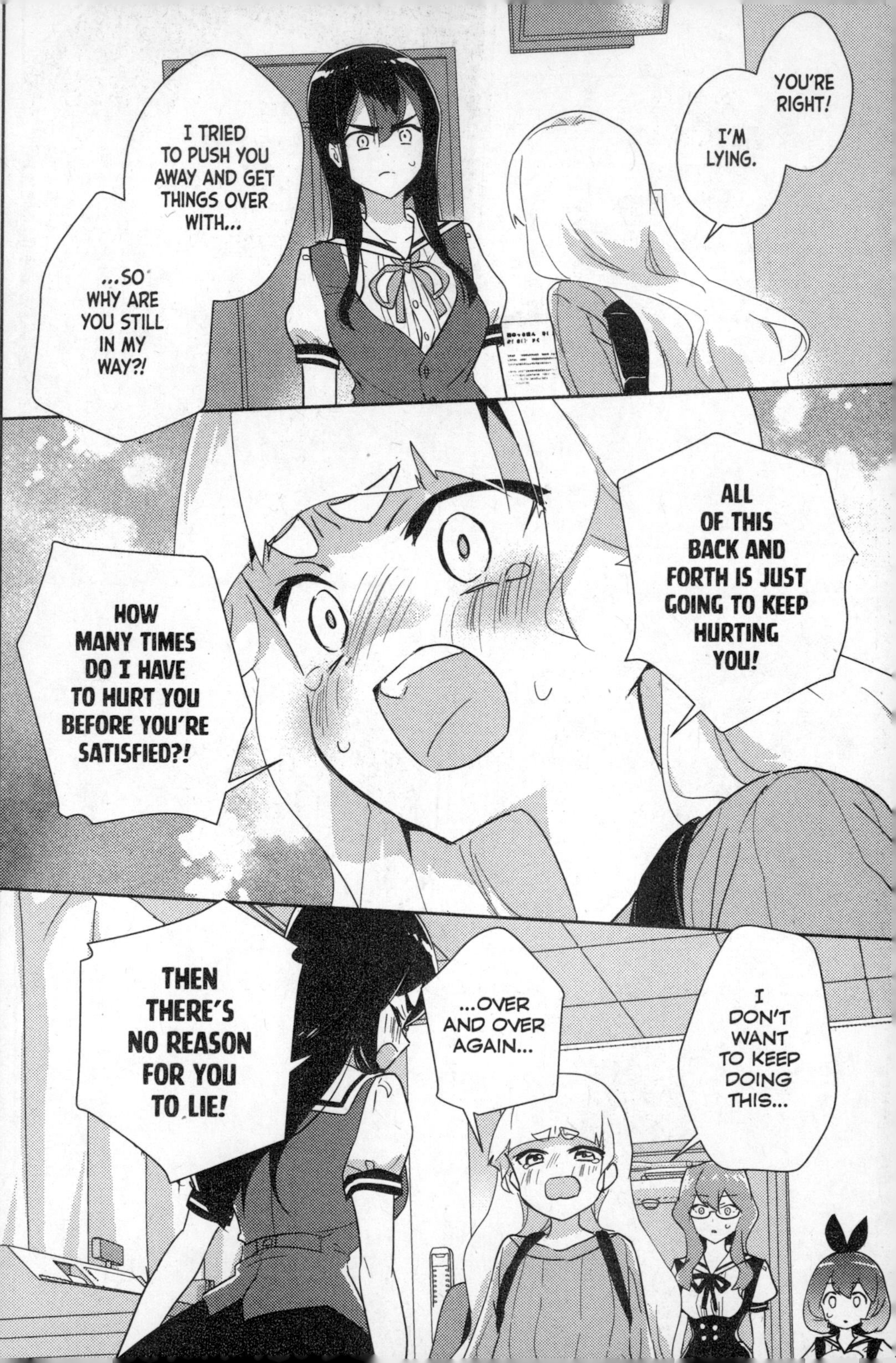
YOU'RE RIGHT! I'M LYING.
I TRIED TO PUSH YOU AWAY AND GET THINGS OVER WITH...
...SO WHY ARE YOU STILL IN MY WAY?!
ALL OF THIS BACK AND FORTH IS JUST GOING TO KEEP HURTING YOU!
HOW MANY TIMES DO I HAVE TO HURT YOU BEFORE YOU'RE SATISFIED?!
I DON'T WANT TO KEEP DOING THIS...
...OVER AND OVER AGAIN...
THEN THERE'S NO REASON FOR YOU TO LIE!

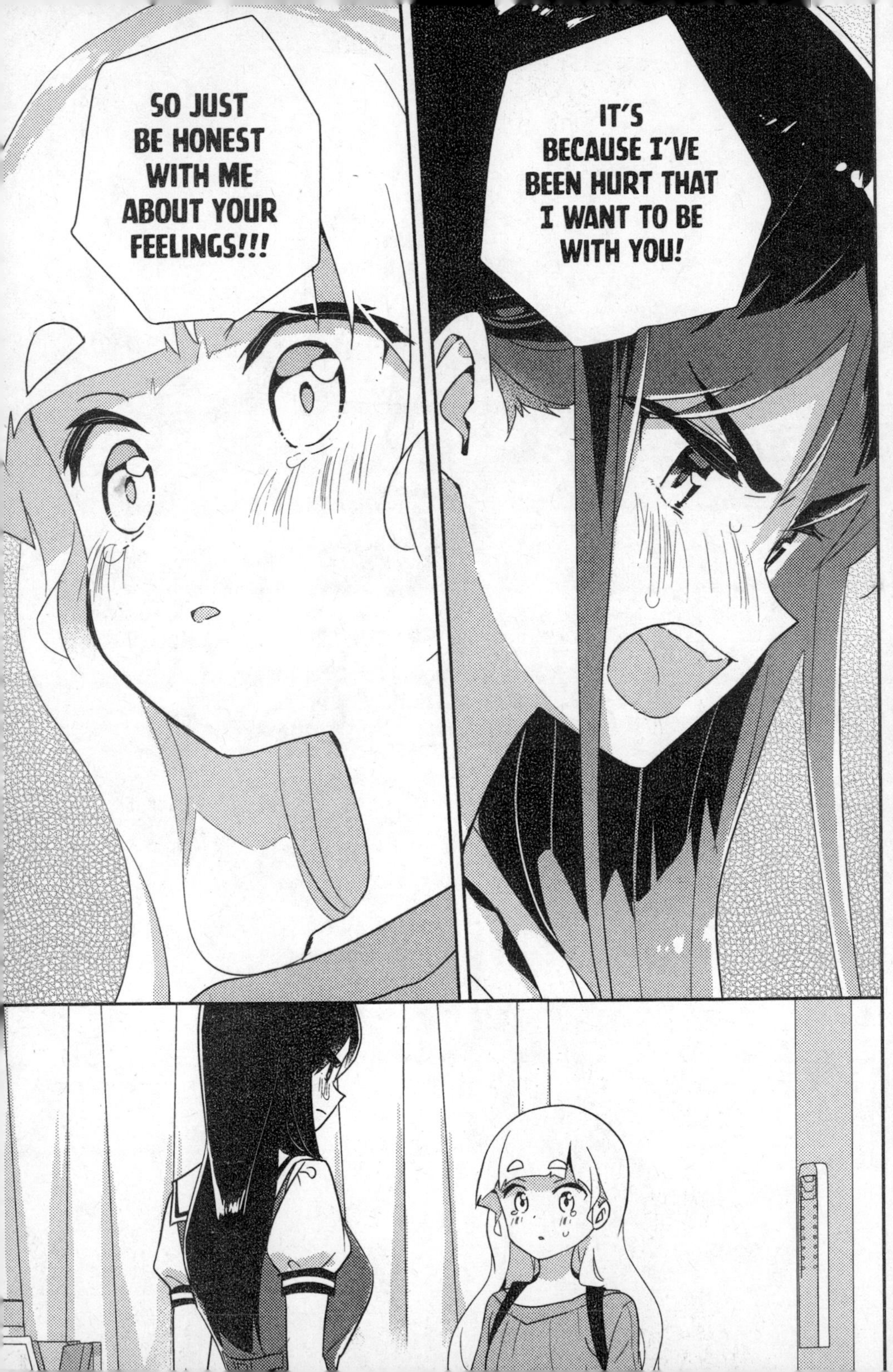
IT'S BECAUSE I'VE BEEN HURT THAT I WANT TO BE WITH YOU!
SO JUST BE HONEST WITH ME ABOUT YOUR FEELINGS!!!

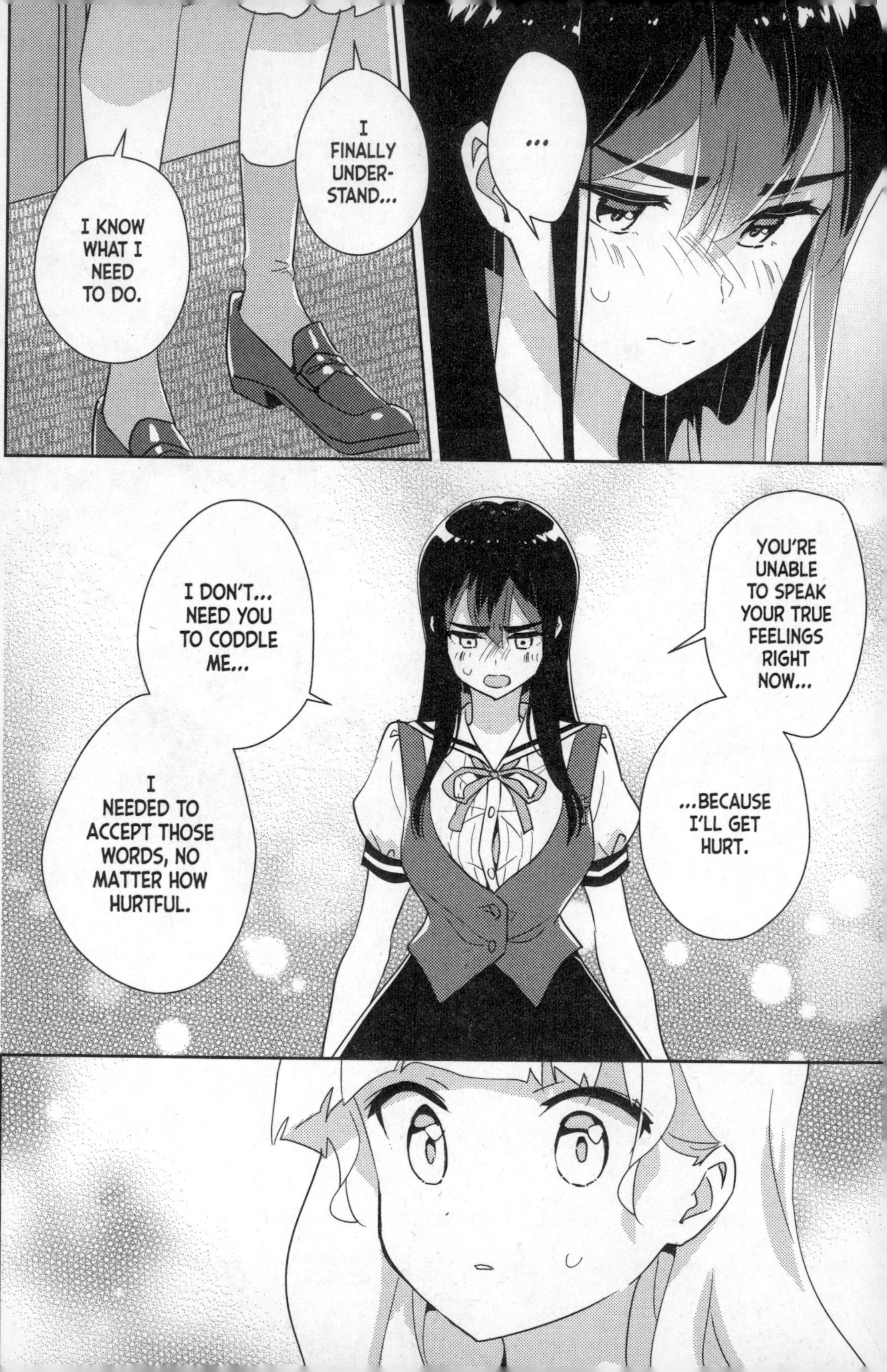
...
I FINALLY UNDER-STAND...
I KNOW WHAT I NEED TO DO.
YOU'RE UNABLE TO SPEAK YOUR TRUE FEELINGS RIGHT NOW...
...BECAUSE I'LL GET HURT.
I DON'T... NEED YOU TO CODDLE ME...
I NEEDED TO ACCEPT THOSE WORDS, NO MATTER HOW HURTFUL.

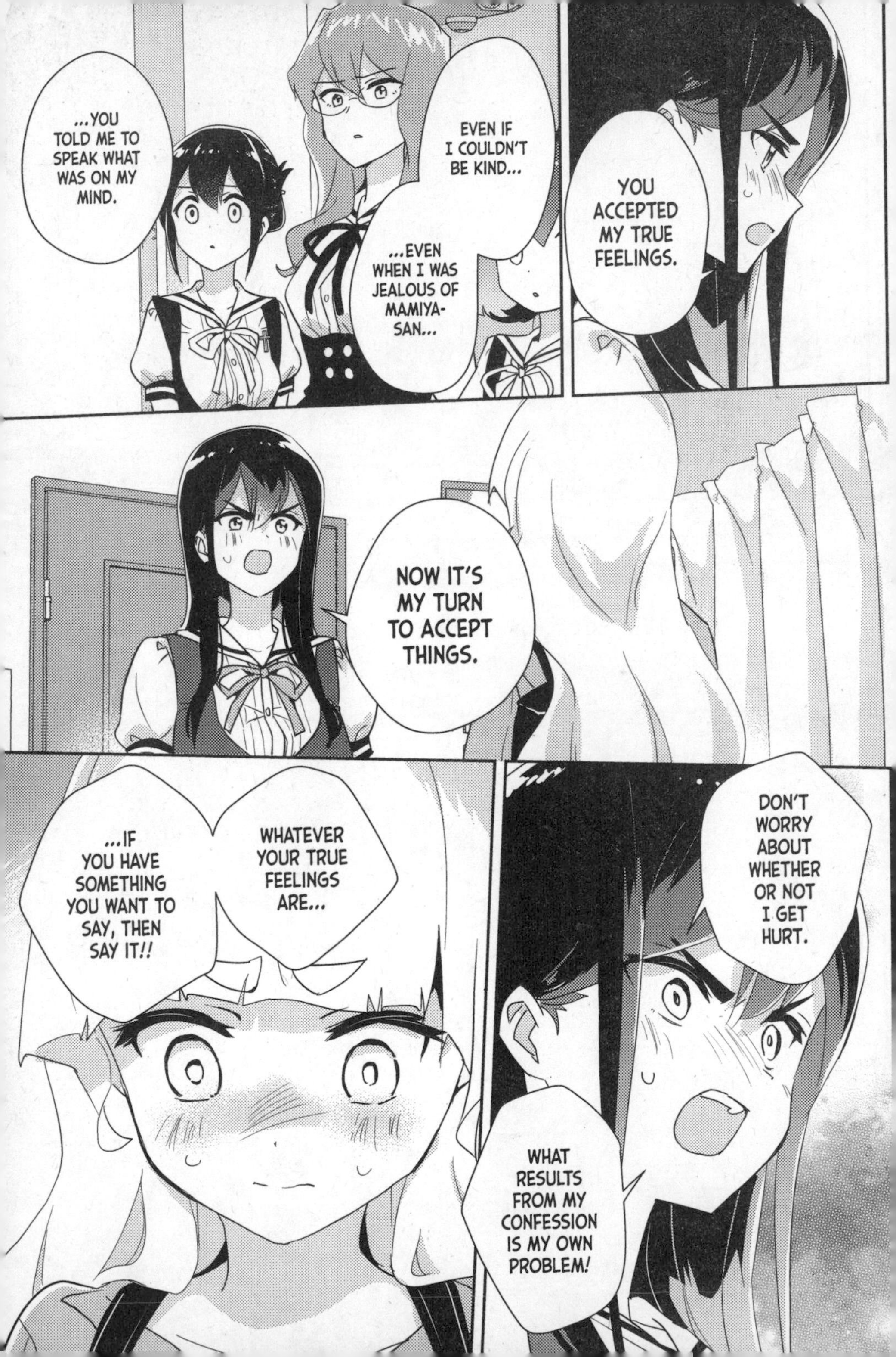
YOU ACCEPTED MY TRUE FEELINGS.
EVEN IF I COULDN'T BE KIND...
...EVEN WHEN I WAS JEALOUS OF MAMIYA-SAN...
...YOU TOLD ME TO SPEAK WHAT WAS ON MY MIND.
NOW IT'S MY TURN TO ACCEPT THINGS.
DON'T WORRY ABOUT WHETHER OR NOT I GET HURT.
WHAT RESULTS FROM MY CONFESSION IS MY OWN PROBLEM!
WHATEVER YOUR TRUE FEELINGS ARE...
...IF YOU HAVE SOMETHING YOU WANT TO SAY, THEN SAY IT!!

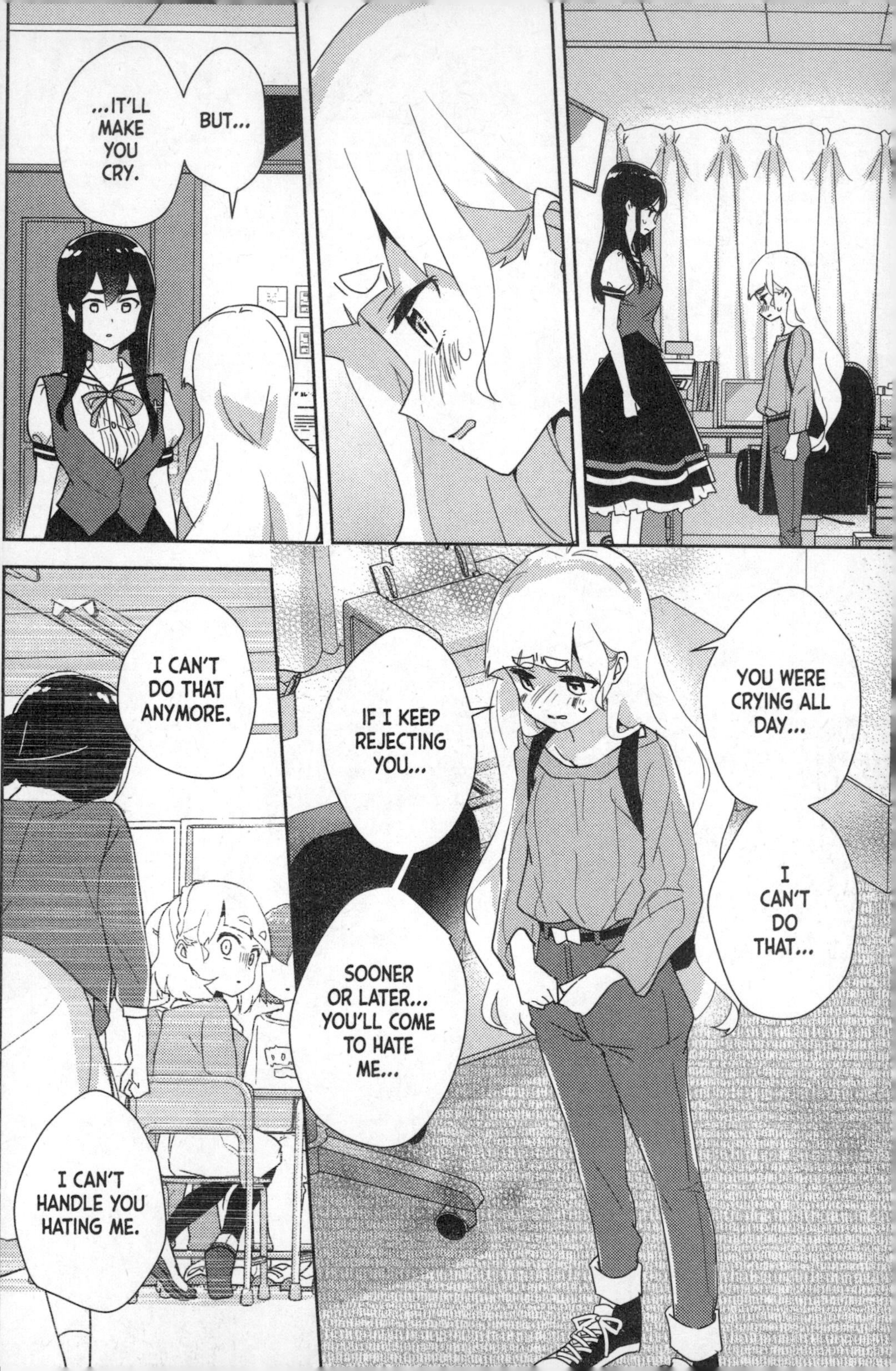
BUT...
...IT'LL MAKE YOU CRY.
YOU WERE CRYING ALL DAY...
I CAN'T DO THAT...
IF I KEEP REJECTING YOU...
SOONER OR LATER... YOU'LL COME TO HATE ME...
I CAN'T DO THAT ANYMORE.
I CAN'T HANDLE YOU HATING ME.

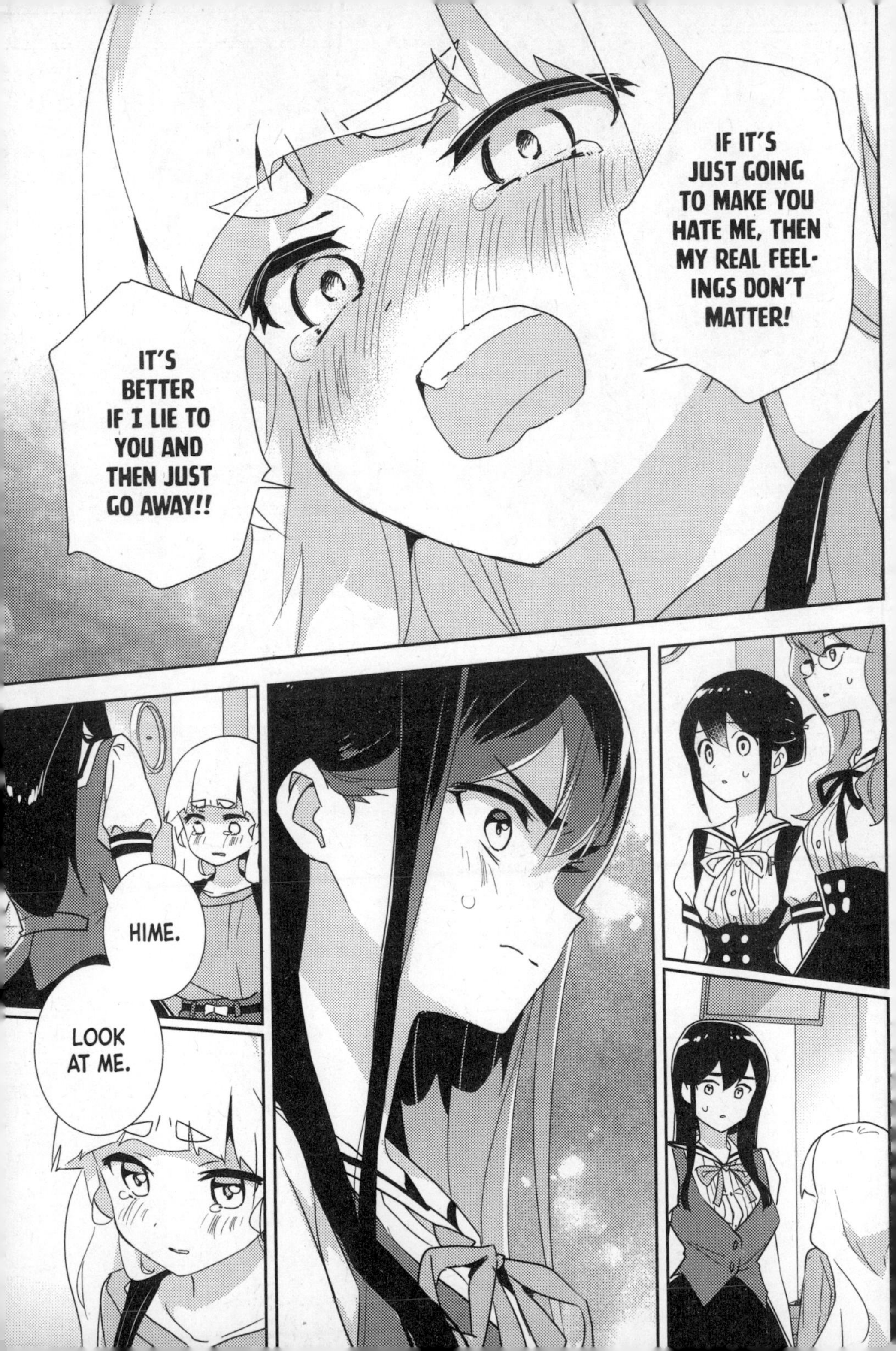
IF IT'S JUST GOING TO MAKE YOU HATE ME, THEN MY REAL FEEL-INGS DON'T MATTER!
IT'S BETTER IF I LIE TO YOU AND THEN JUST GO AWAY!!
HIME.
LOOK AT ME.

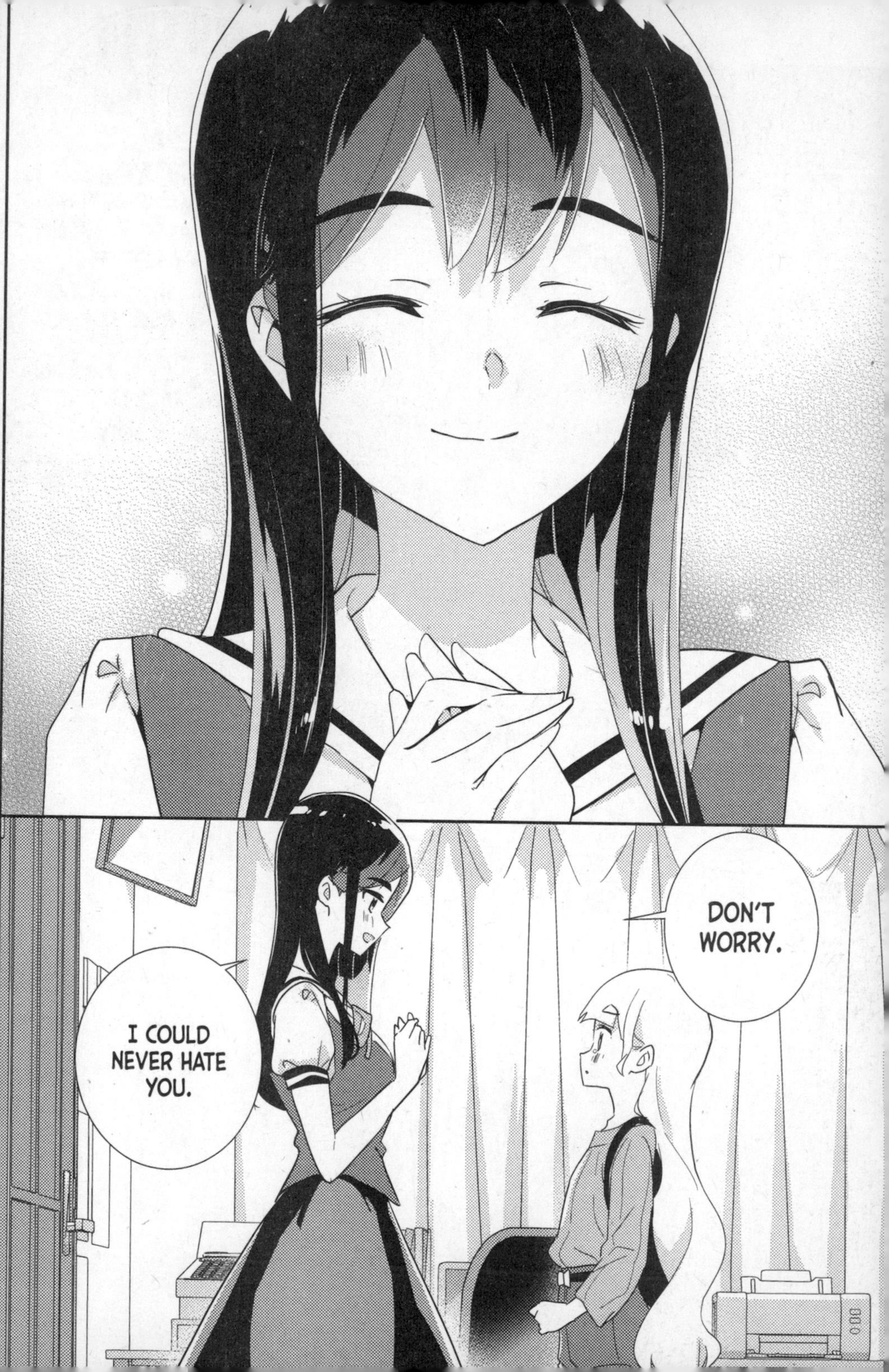
DON'T WORRY.
I COULD NEVER HATE YOU.

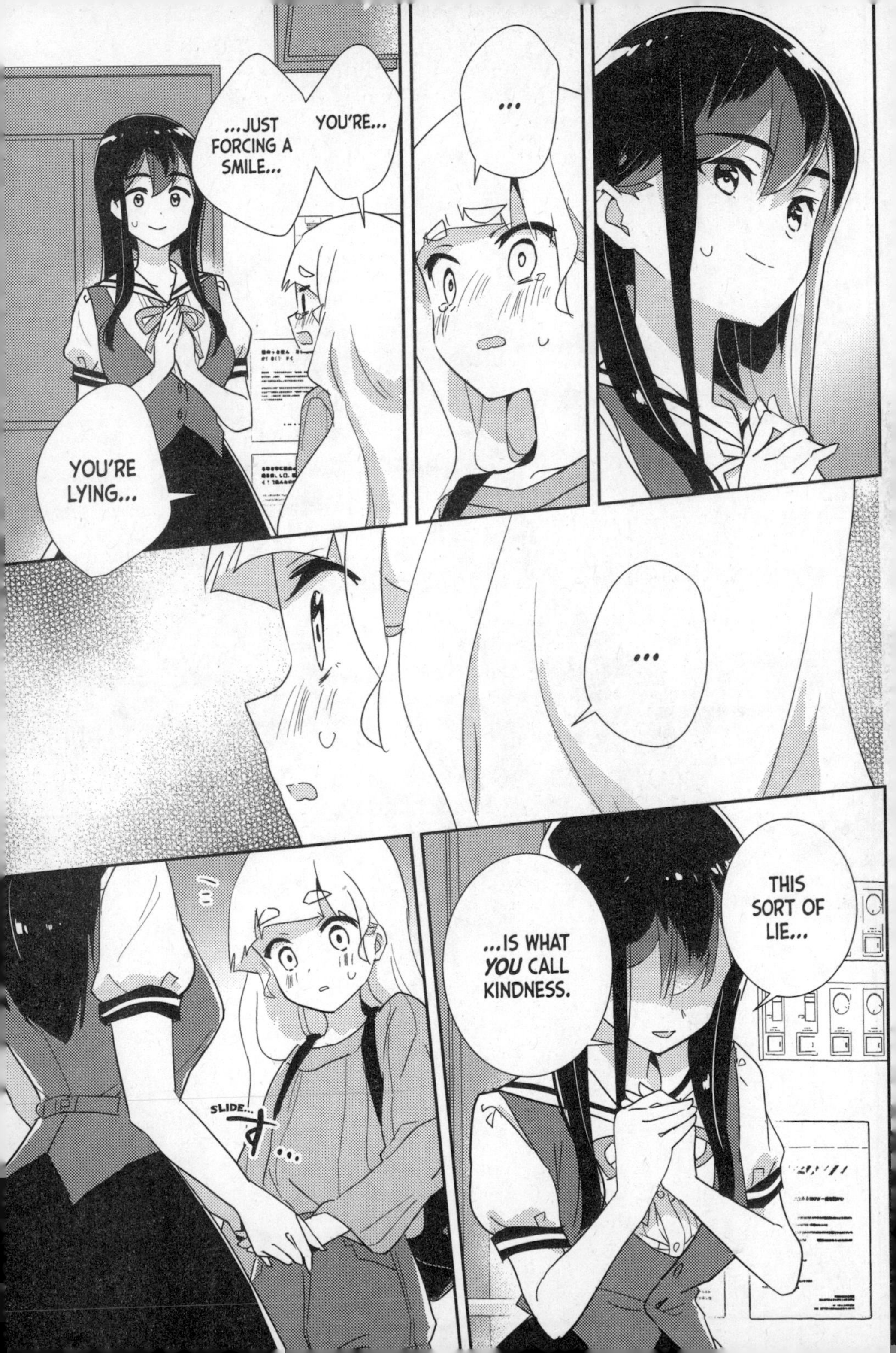
...
YOU'RE...
...JUST FORCING A SMILE...
YOU'RE LYING...
...
THIS SORT OF LIE...
...IS WHAT *YOU* CALL KINDNESS.
SLIDE...
...

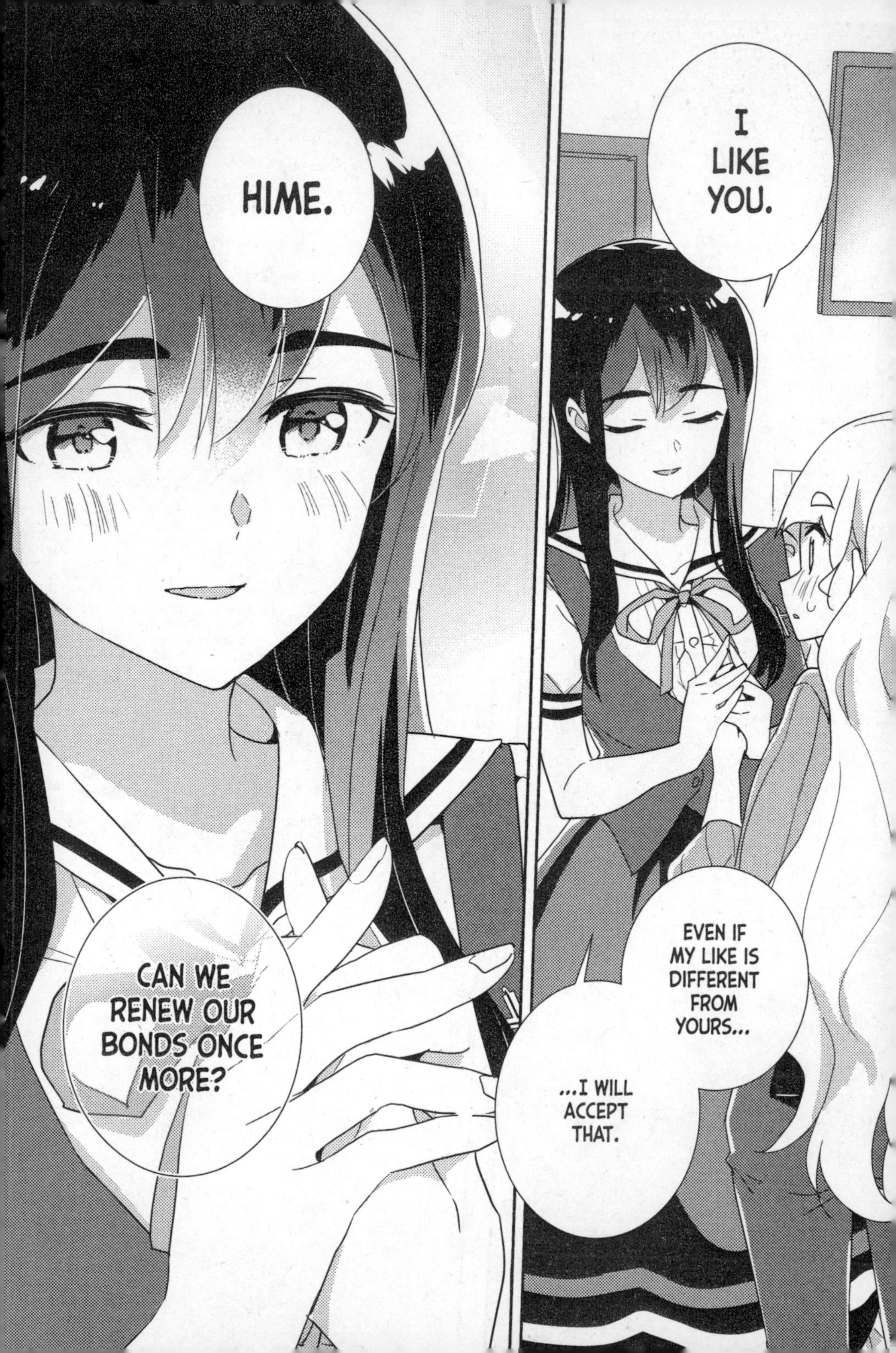
I LIKE YOU.
EVEN IF MY LIKE IS DIFFERENT FROM YOURS...
...I WILL ACCEPT THAT.
HIME.
CAN WE RENEW OUR BONDS ONCE MORE?

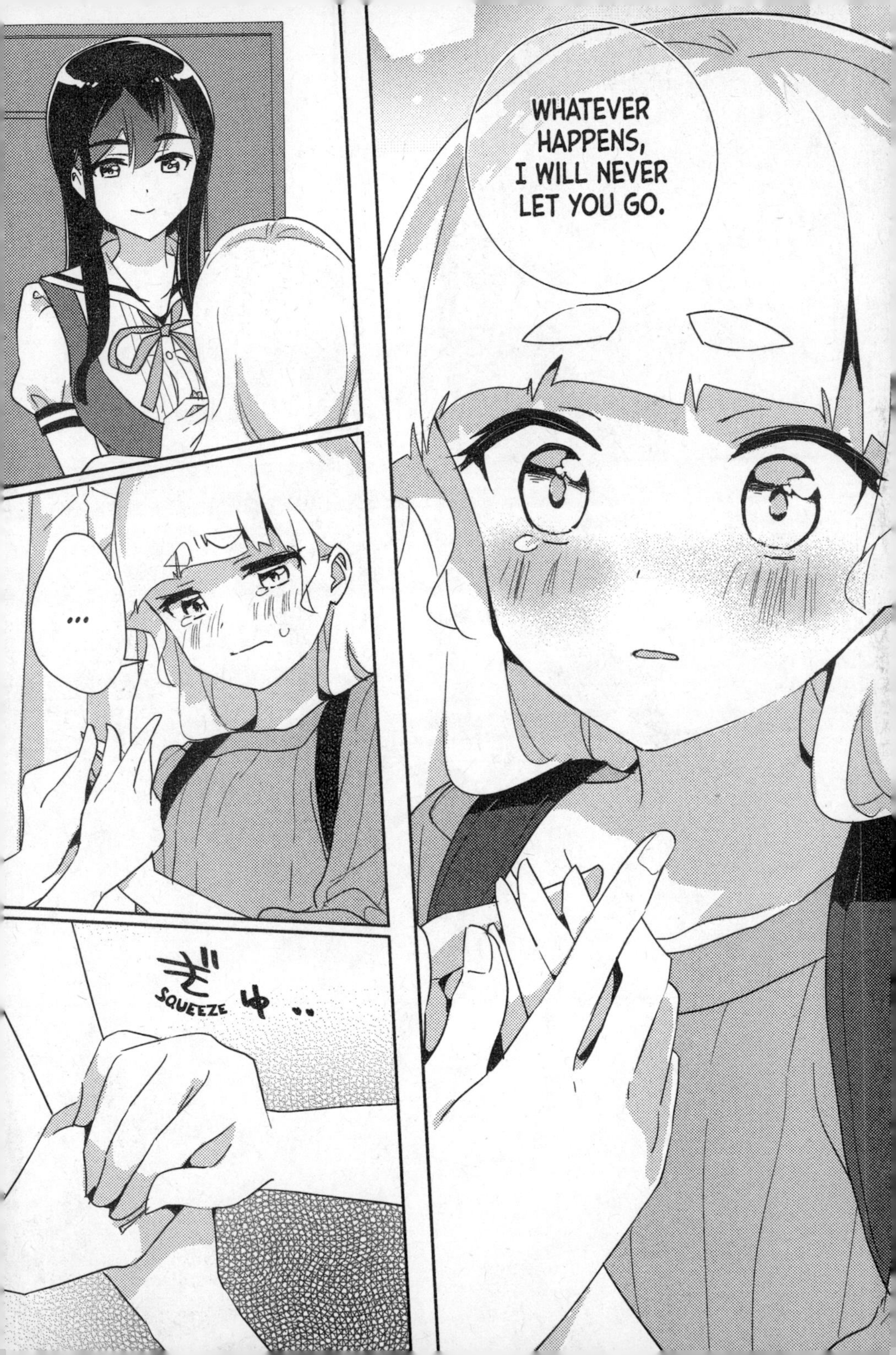
WHATEVER HAPPENS, I WILL NEVER LET YOU GO.
...
ぎゅ..
SQUEEZE

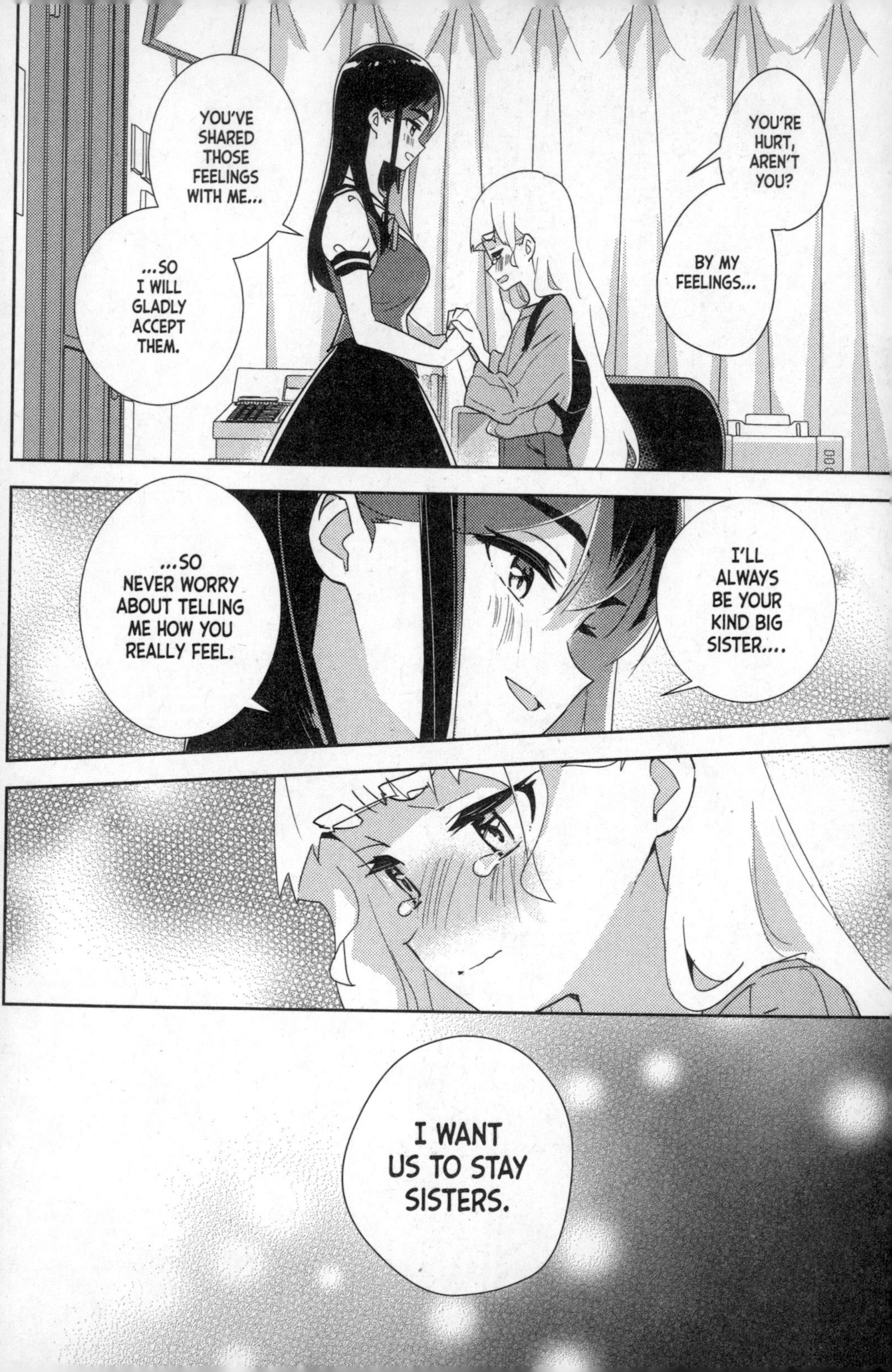
YOU'RE HURT, AREN'T YOU?
BY MY FEELINGS...
YOU'VE SHARED THOSE FEELINGS WITH ME...
...SO I WILL GLADLY ACCEPT THEM.
I'LL ALWAYS BE YOUR KIND BIG SISTER....
...SO NEVER WORRY ABOUT TELLING ME HOW YOU REALLY FEEL.
I WANT US TO STAY SISTERS.

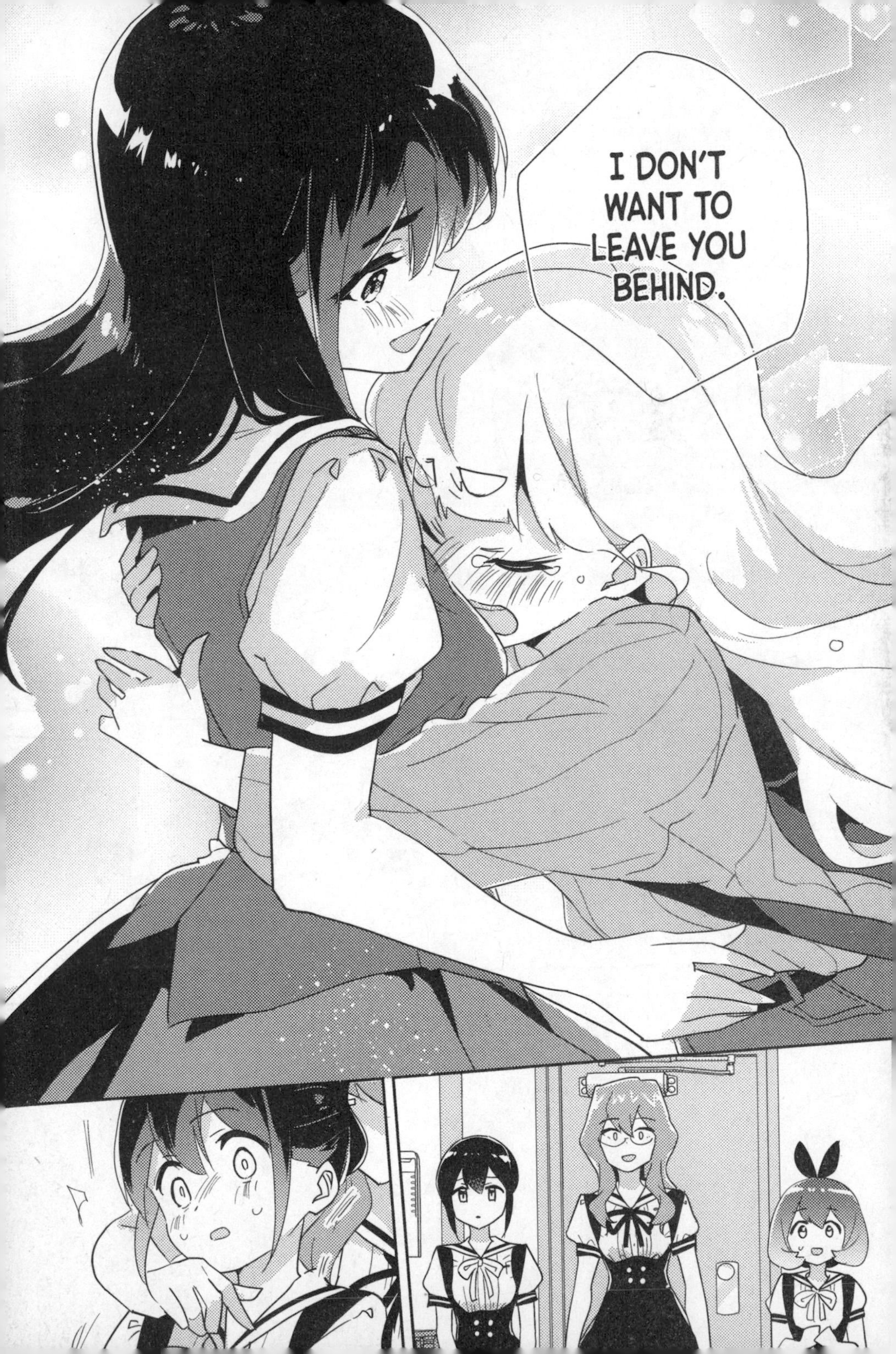
I DON'T WANT TO LEAVE YOU BEHIND.

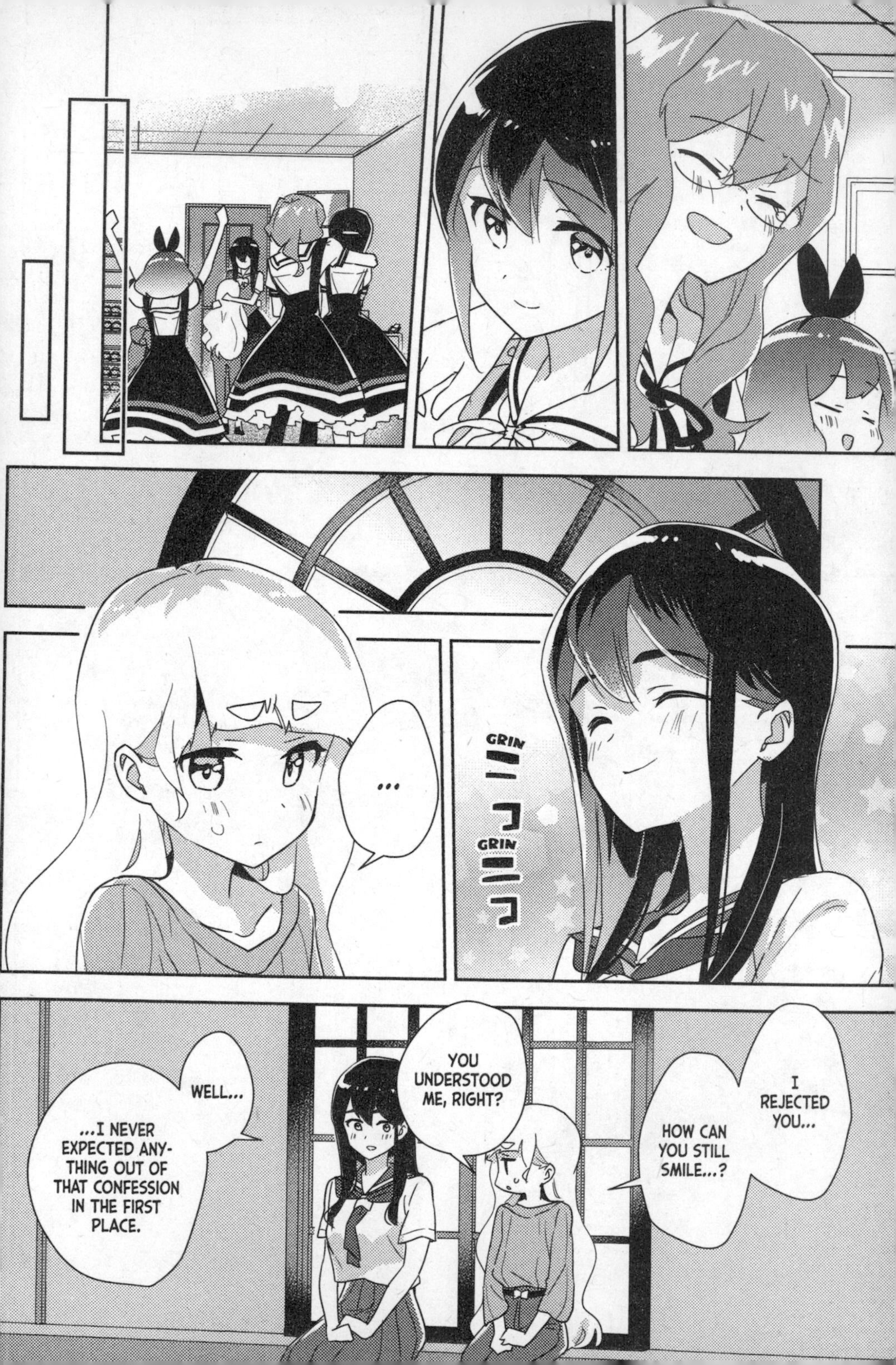
GRIN
GRIN
...
I REJECTED YOU...
HOW CAN YOU STILL SMILE...?
YOU UNDERSTOOD ME, RIGHT?
WELL...
...I NEVER EXPECTED ANY-THING OUT OF THAT CONFESSION IN THE FIRST PLACE.

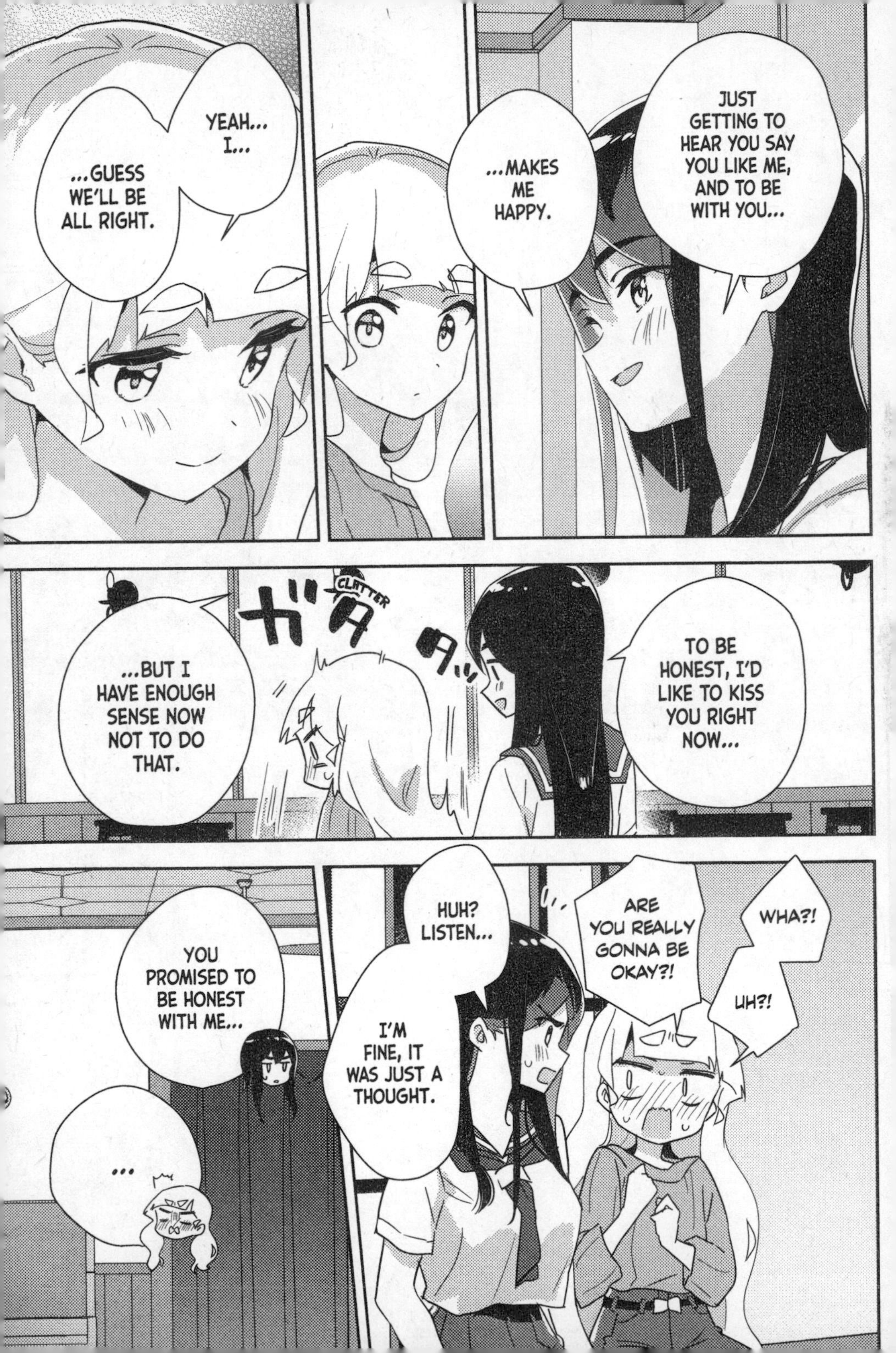
JUST GETTING TO HEAR YOU SAY YOU LIKE ME, AND TO BE WITH YOU...
...MAKES ME HAPPY.
YEAH... I...
...GUESS WE'LL BE ALL RIGHT.
TO BE HONEST, I'D LIKE TO KISS YOU RIGHT NOW...
タッ
ガタ
CLATTER
...BUT I HAVE ENOUGH SENSE NOW NOT TO DO THAT.
WHA?!
ARE YOU REALLY GONNA BE OKAY?!
UH?!
HUH? LISTEN...
I'M FINE, IT WAS JUST A THOUGHT.
YOU PROMISED TO BE HONEST WITH ME...
...

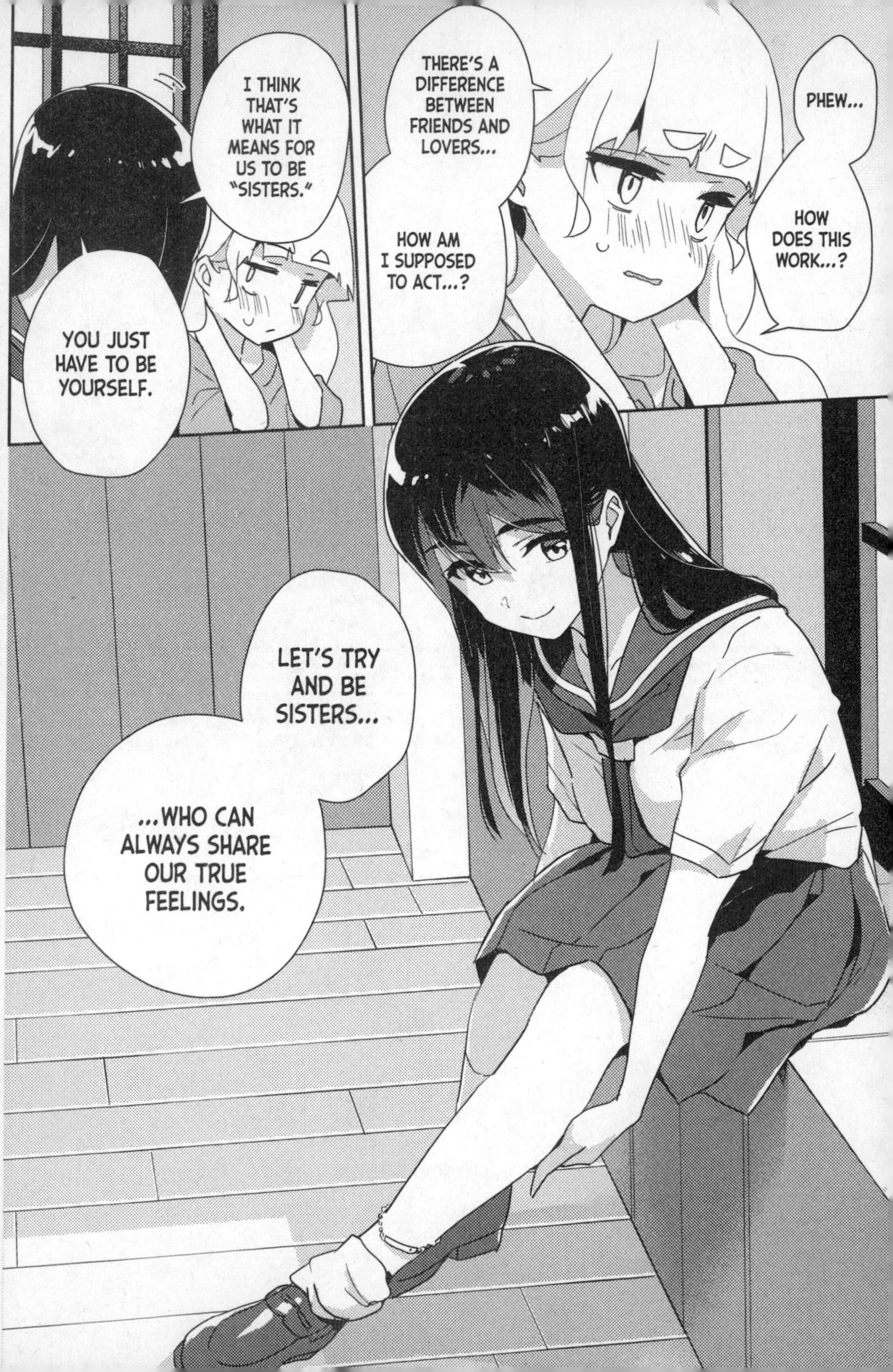
PHEW...
HOW DOES THIS WORK...?
THERE'S A DIFFERENCE BETWEEN FRIENDS AND LOVERS...
HOW AM I SUPPOSED TO ACT...?
I THINK THAT'S WHAT IT MEANS FOR US TO BE "SISTERS."
YOU JUST HAVE TO BE YOURSELF.
LET'S TRY AND BE SISTERS...
...WHO CAN ALWAYS SHARE OUR TRUE FEELINGS.

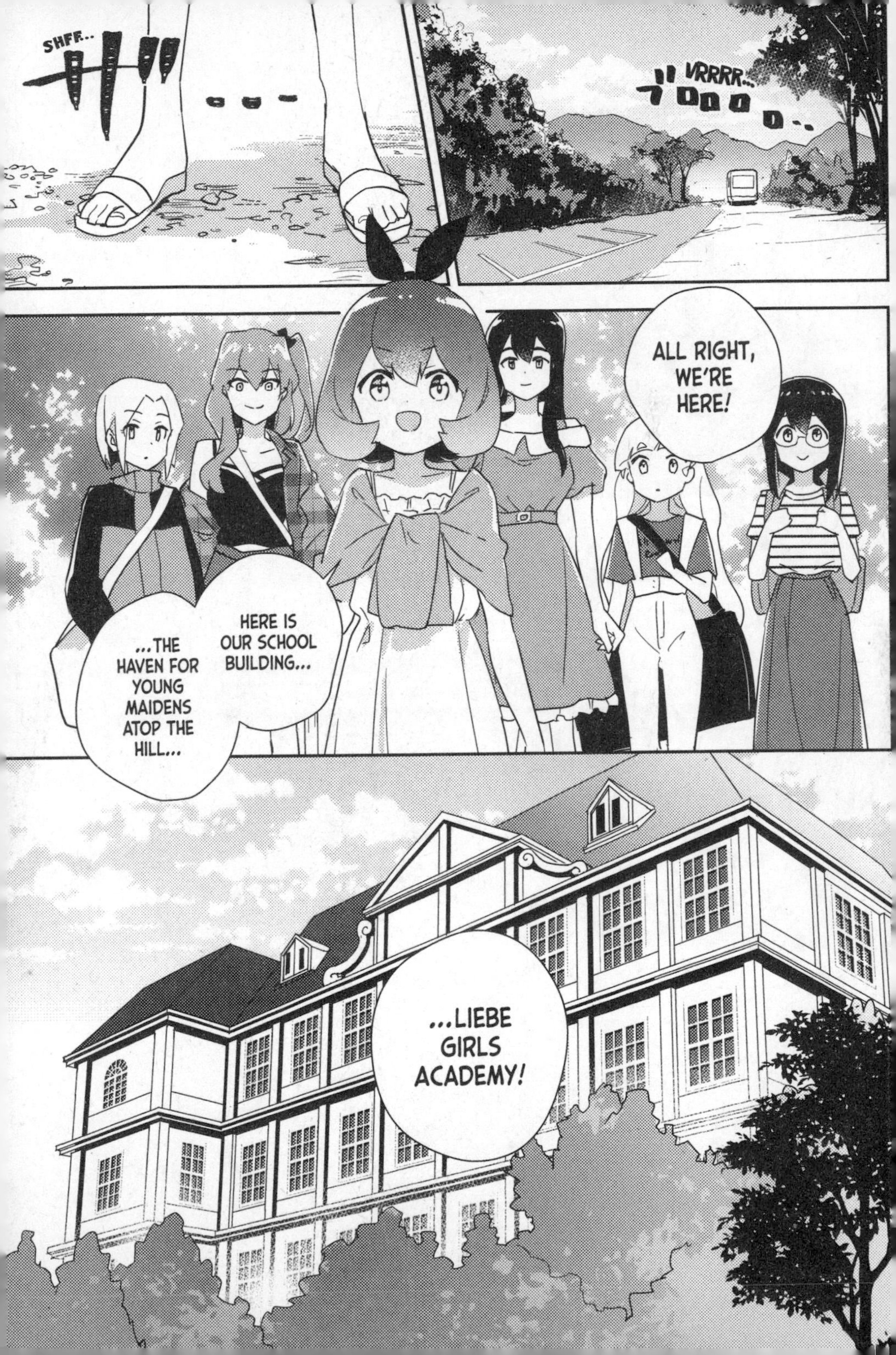
VRRRR...
SHFF...
...
ALL RIGHT, WE'RE HERE!
HERE IS OUR SCHOOL BUILDING...
...THE HAVEN FOR YOUNG MAIDENS ATOP THE HILL...
...LIEBE GIRLS ACADEMY!

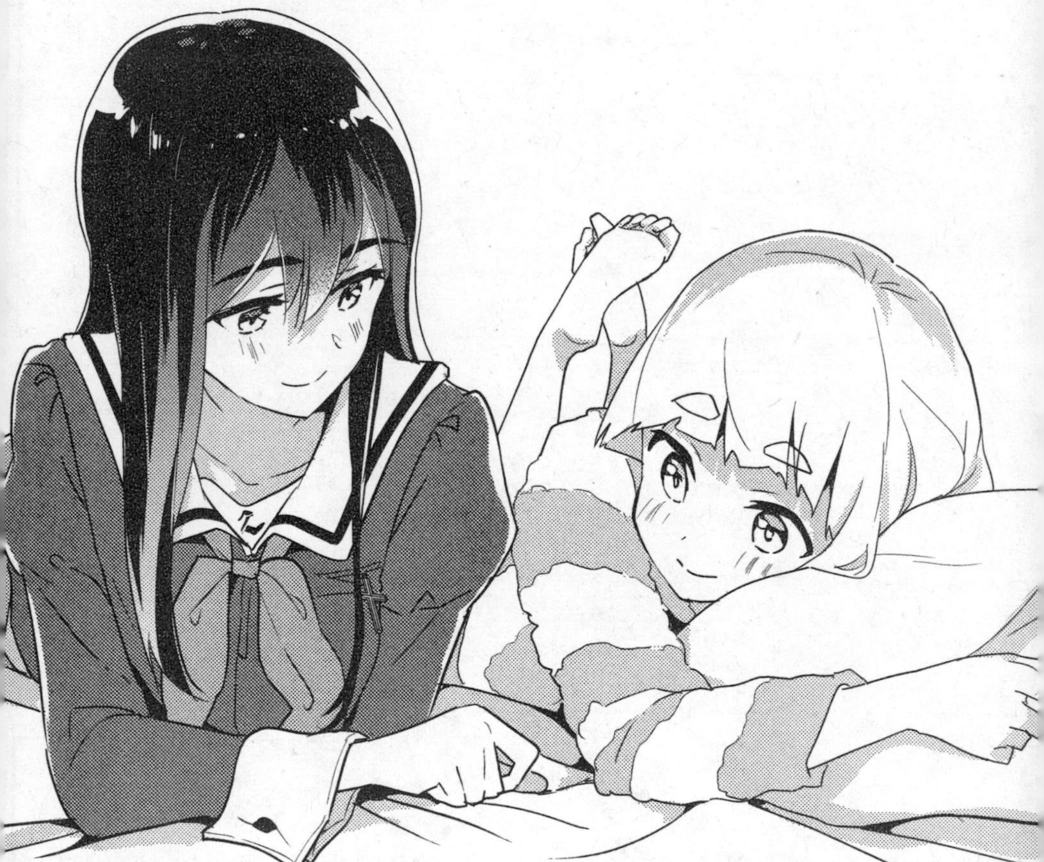

# Shift 40 Schoolhouse Sleepover!

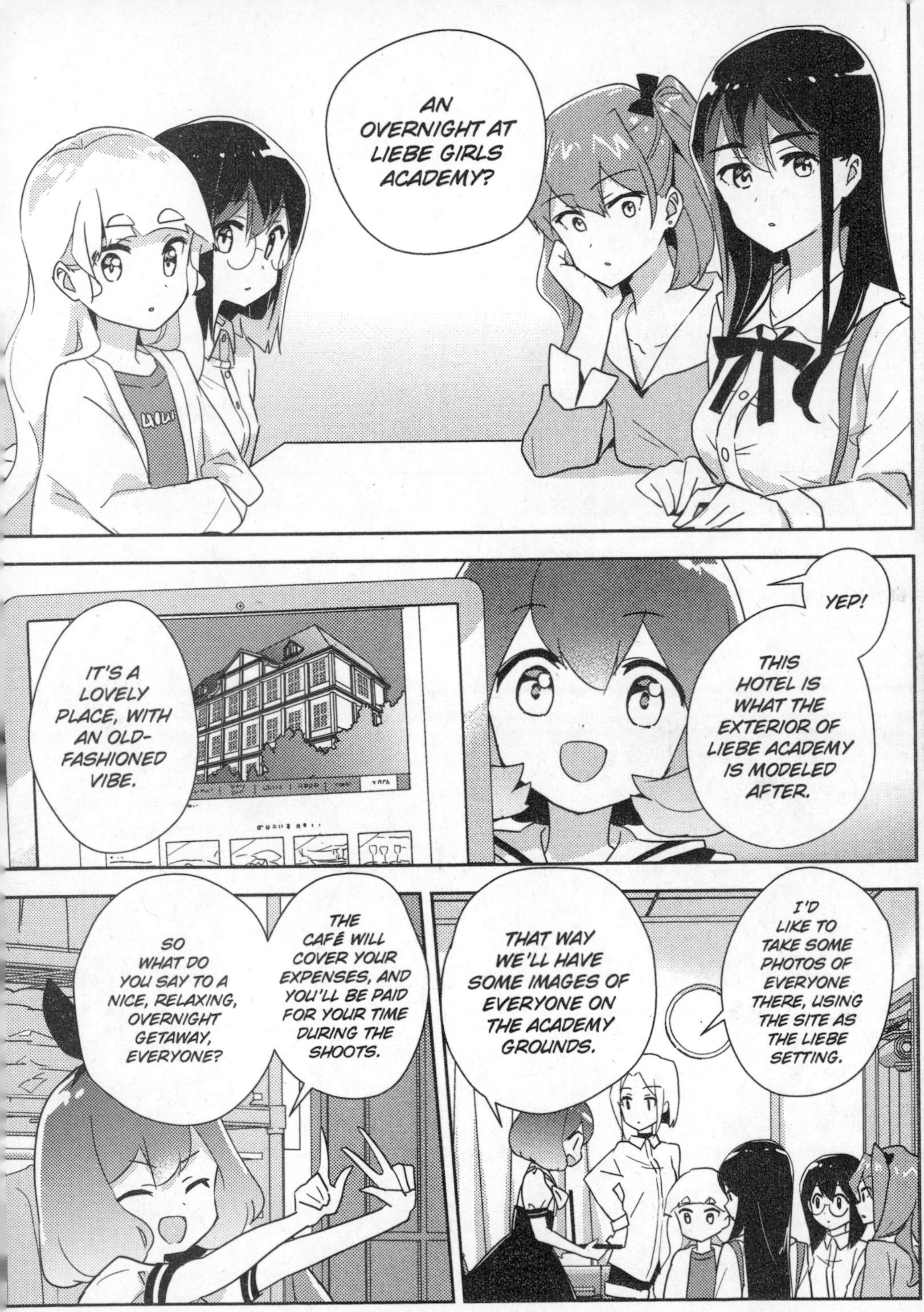
AN OVERNIGHT AT LIEBE GIRLS ACADEMY?
YEP!
THIS HOTEL IS WHAT THE EXTERIOR OF LIEBE ACADEMY IS MODELED AFTER.
IT'S A LOVELY PLACE, WITH AN OLD-FASHIONED VIBE.
I'D LIKE TO TAKE SOME PHOTOS OF EVERYONE THERE, USING THE SITE AS THE LIEBE SETTING.
THAT WAY WE'LL HAVE SOME IMAGES OF EVERYONE ON THE ACADEMY GROUNDS.
THE CAFÉ WILL COVER YOUR EXPENSES, AND YOU'LL BE PAID FOR YOUR TIME DURING THE SHOOTS.
SO WHAT DO YOU SAY TO A NICE, RELAXING, OVERNIGHT GETAWAY, EVERYONE?

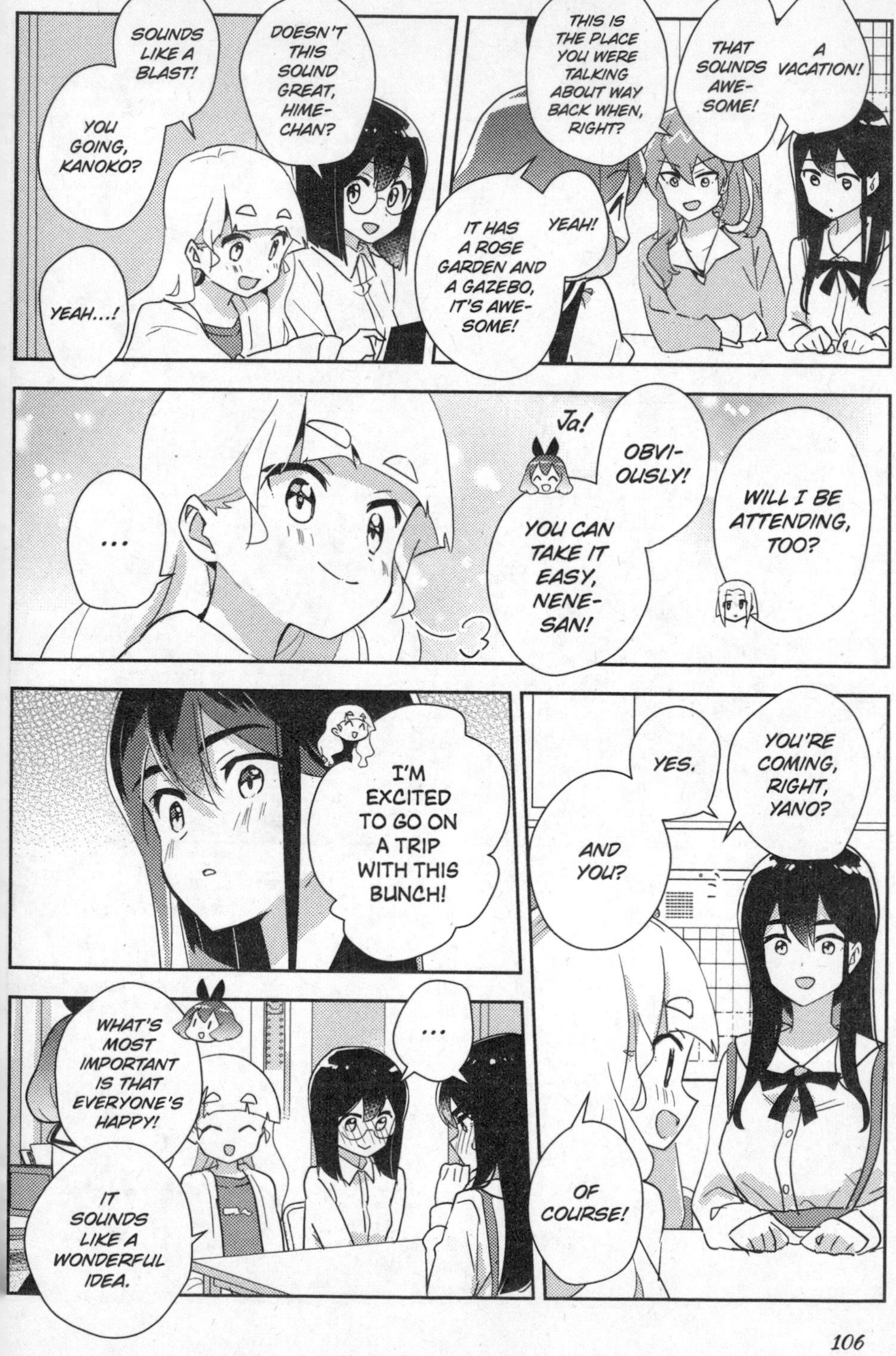
A VACATION!
THAT SOUNDS AWE-SOME!
THIS IS THE PLACE YOU WERE TALKING ABOUT WAY BACK WHEN, RIGHT?
YEAH!
IT HAS A ROSE GARDEN AND A GAZEBO, IT'S AWE-SOME!
DOESN'T THIS SOUND GREAT, HIME-CHAN?
SOUNDS LIKE A BLAST!
YOU GOING, KANOKO?
YEAH...!
WILL I BE ATTENDING, TOO?
Ja!
OBVI-OUSLY!
YOU CAN TAKE IT EASY, NENE-SAN!
...
YOU'RE COMING, RIGHT, YANO?
YES.
AND YOU?
OF COURSE!
I'M EXCITED TO GO ON A TRIP WITH THIS BUNCH!
...
WHAT'S MOST IMPORTANT IS THAT EVERYONE'S HAPPY!
IT SOUNDS LIKE A WONDERFUL IDEA.

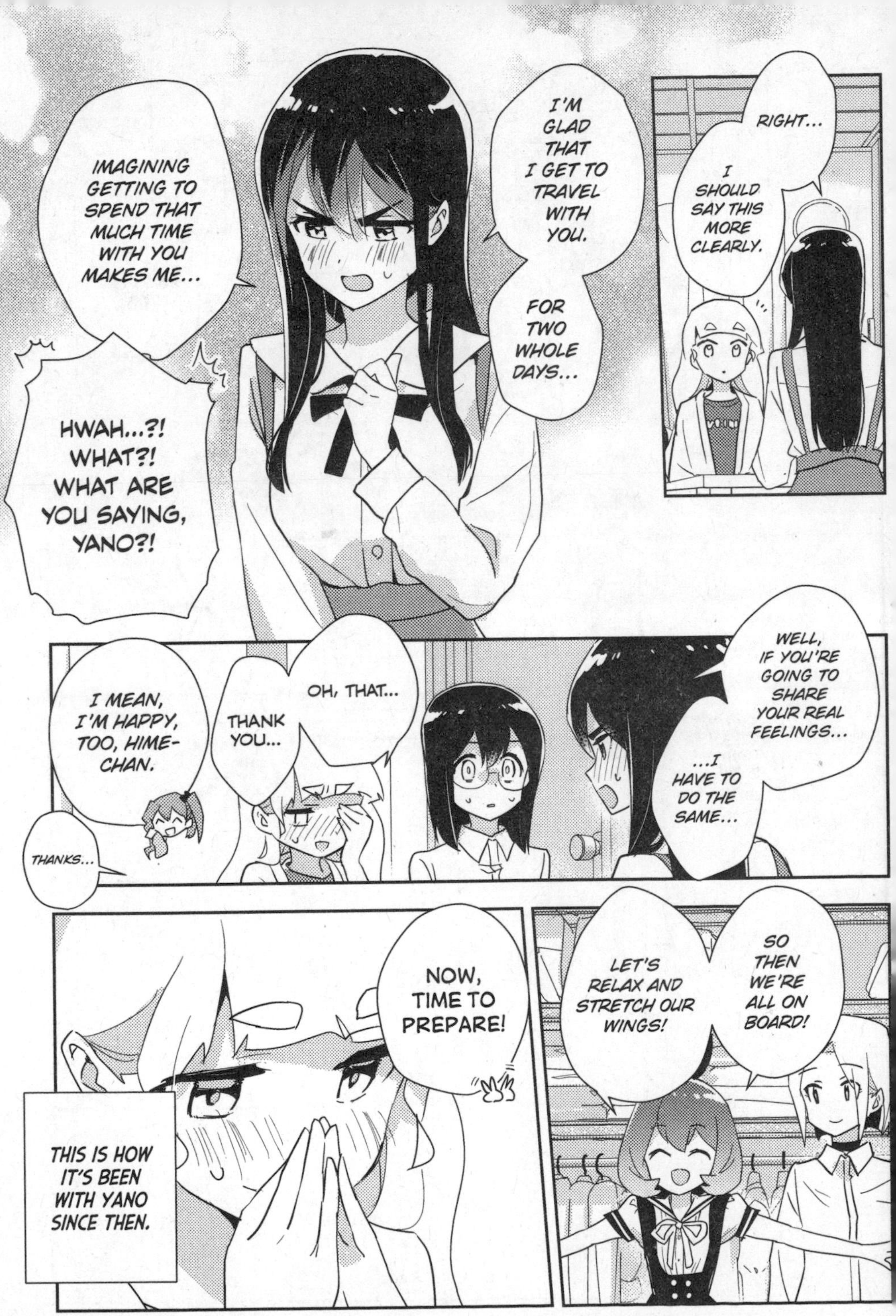
RIGHT...
I SHOULD SAY THIS MORE CLEARLY.
I'M GLAD THAT I GET TO TRAVEL WITH YOU.
FOR TWO WHOLE DAYS...
IMAGINING GETTING TO SPEND THAT MUCH TIME WITH YOU MAKES ME...
HWAH...?! WHAT?! WHAT ARE YOU SAYING, YANO?!
WELL, IF YOU'RE GOING TO SHARE YOUR REAL FEELINGS...
...I HAVE TO DO THE SAME...
OH, THAT...
THANK YOU...
I MEAN, I'M HAPPY, TOO, HIME-CHAN.
THANKS...
SO THEN WE'RE ALL ON BOARD!
LET'S RELAX AND STRETCH OUR WINGS!
NOW, TIME TO PREPARE!
THIS IS HOW IT'S BEEN WITH YANO SINCE THEN.

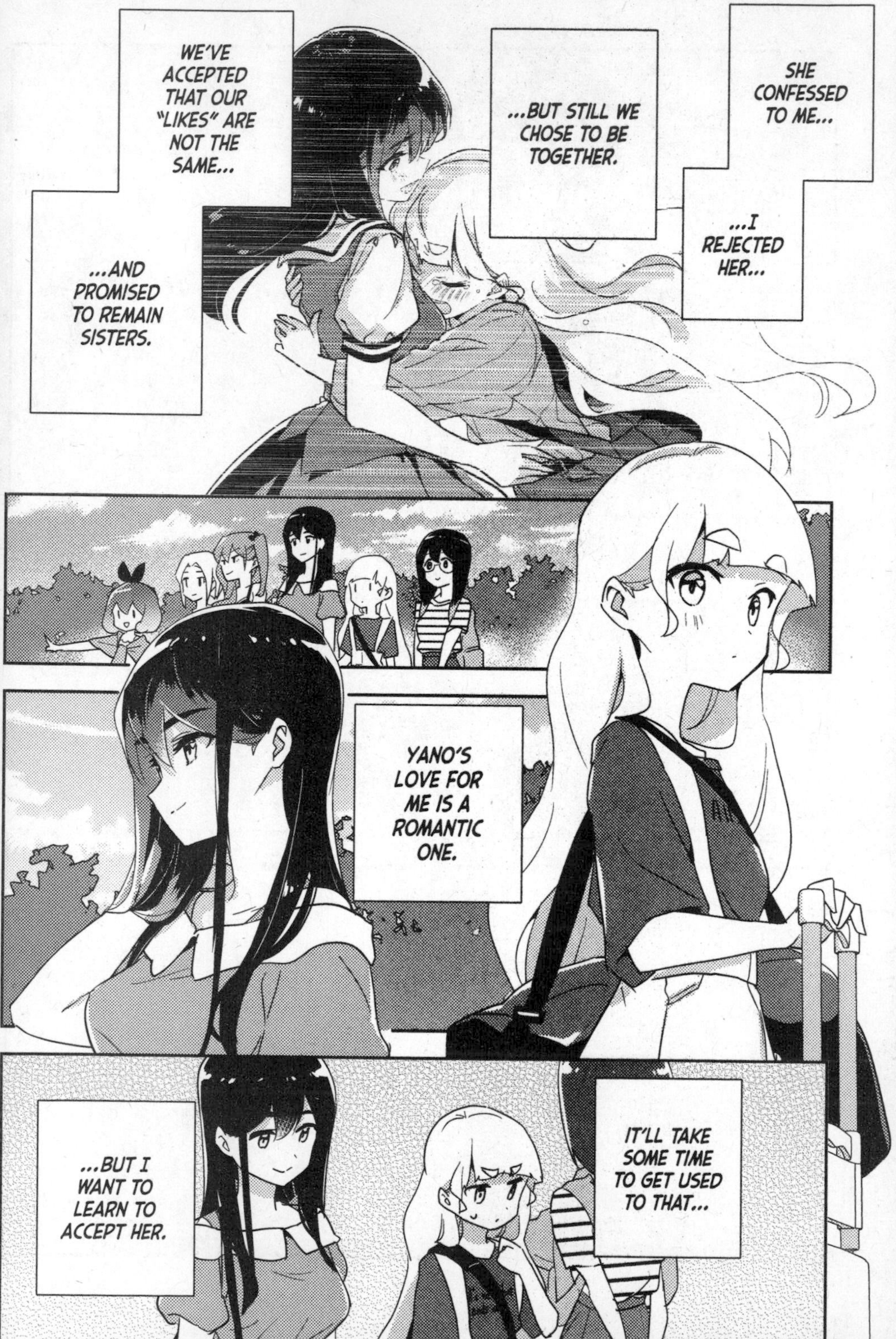
SHE CONFESSED TO ME...
...I REJECTED HER...
...BUT STILL WE CHOSE TO BE TOGETHER.
WE'VE ACCEPTED THAT OUR "LIKES" ARE NOT THE SAME...
...AND PROMISED TO REMAIN SISTERS.
YANO'S LOVE FOR ME IS A ROMANTIC ONE.
IT'LL TAKE SOME TIME TO GET USED TO THAT...
...BUT I WANT TO LEARN TO ACCEPT HER.

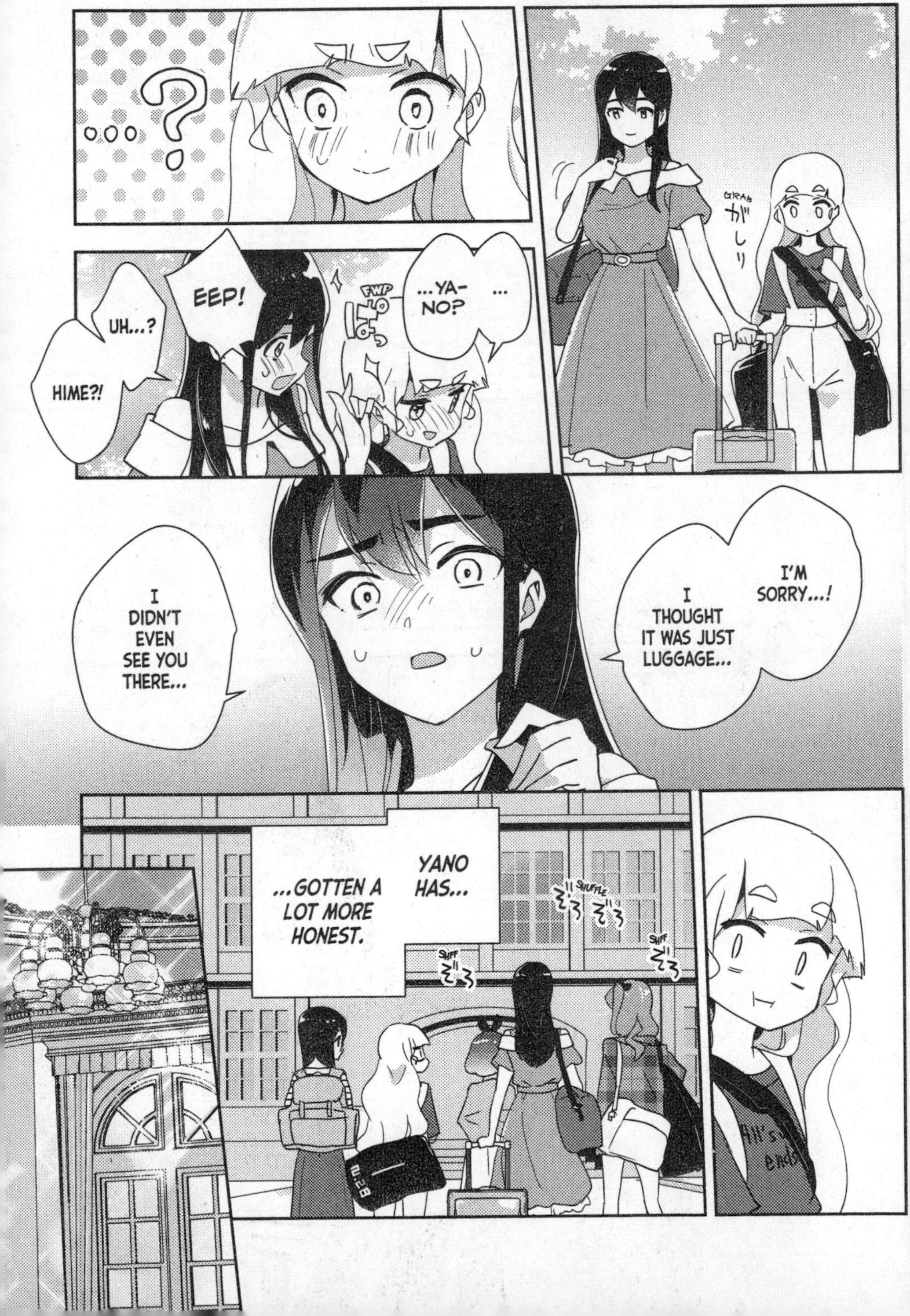
GRAB
がしり
?
FWP
...YA- NO?
...
EEP!
UH...?
HIME?!
I'M SORRY...!
I THOUGHT IT WAS JUST LUGGAGE...
I DIDN'T EVEN SEE YOU THERE...
YANO HAS...
...GOTTEN A LOT MORE HONEST.
SHUFFLE
ぞろぞろ
SHFF
ぞろ
SHFF
ぞろ

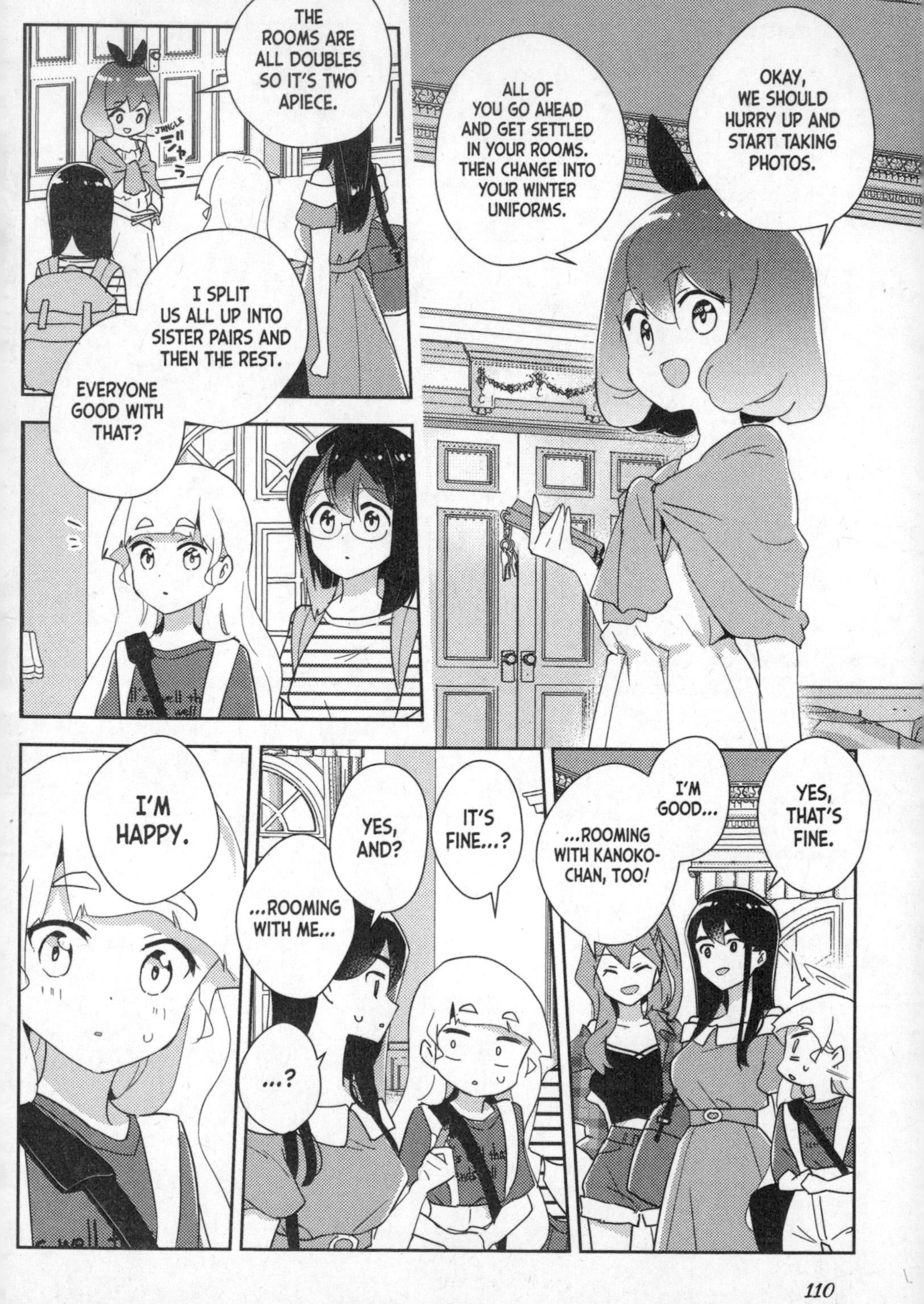
OKAY, WE SHOULD HURRY UP AND START TAKING PHOTOS.
ALL OF YOU GO AHEAD AND GET SETTLED IN YOUR ROOMS. THEN CHANGE INTO YOUR WINTER UNIFORMS.
THE ROOMS ARE ALL DOUBLES SO IT'S TWO APIECE.
JANGLE
I SPLIT US ALL UP INTO SISTER PAIRS AND THEN THE REST.
EVERYONE GOOD WITH THAT?
YES, THAT'S FINE.
I'M GOOD...
...ROOMING WITH KANOKO-CHAN, TOO!
IT'S FINE...?
YES, AND?
...ROOMING WITH ME...
...?
I'M HAPPY.

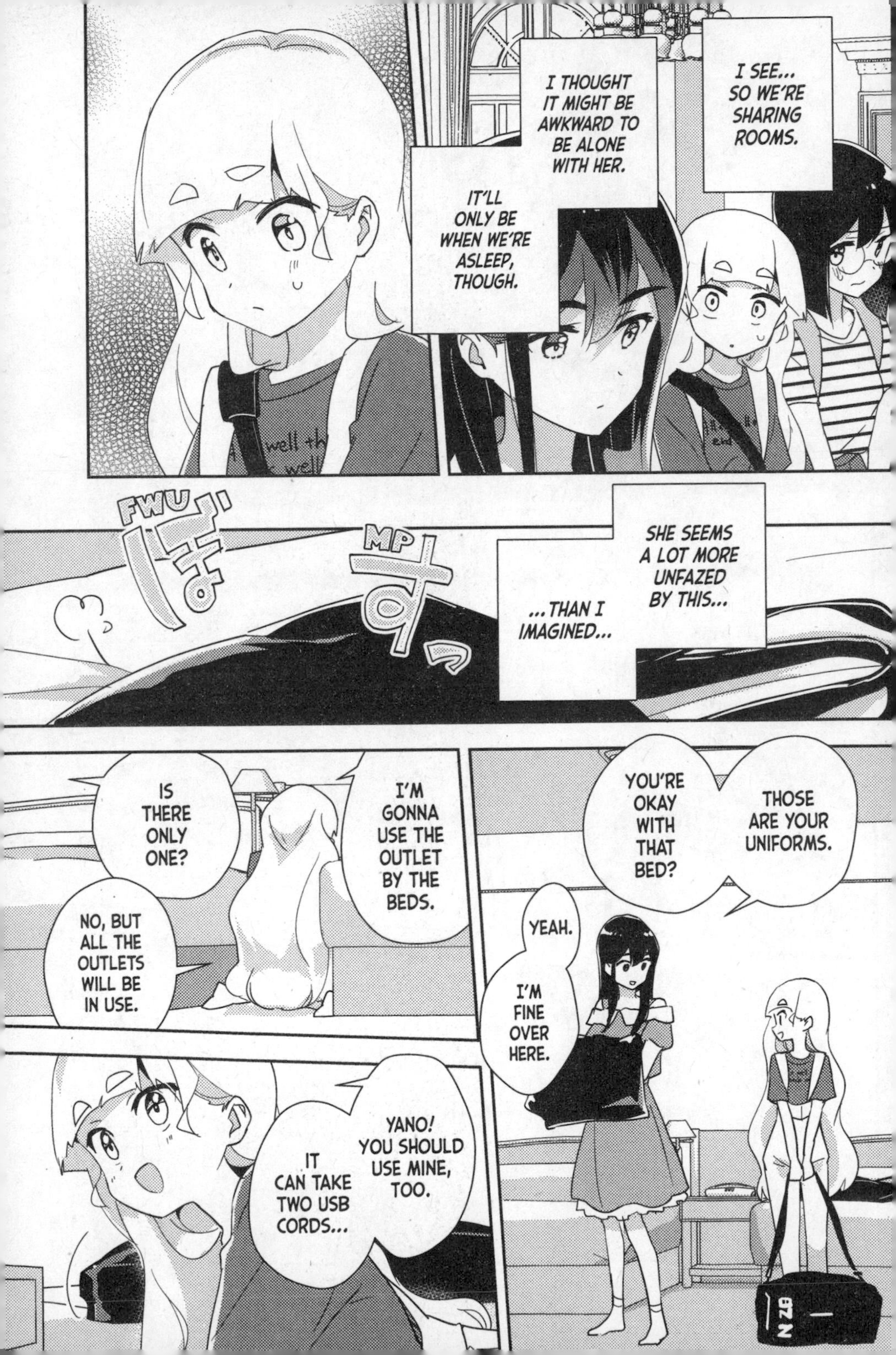
I SEE... SO WE'RE SHARING ROOMS.
I THOUGHT IT MIGHT BE AWKWARD TO BE ALONE WITH HER.
IT'LL ONLY BE WHEN WE'RE ASLEEP, THOUGH.
SHE SEEMS A LOT MORE UNFAZED BY THIS...
...THAN I IMAGINED...
MP
FWU
THOSE ARE YOUR UNIFORMS.
YOU'RE OKAY WITH THAT BED?
YEAH.
I'M FINE OVER HERE.
I'M GONNA USE THE OUTLET BY THE BEDS.
IS THERE ONLY ONE?
NO, BUT ALL THE OUTLETS WILL BE IN USE.
YANO! YOU SHOULD USE MINE, TOO.
IT CAN TAKE TWO USB CORDS...

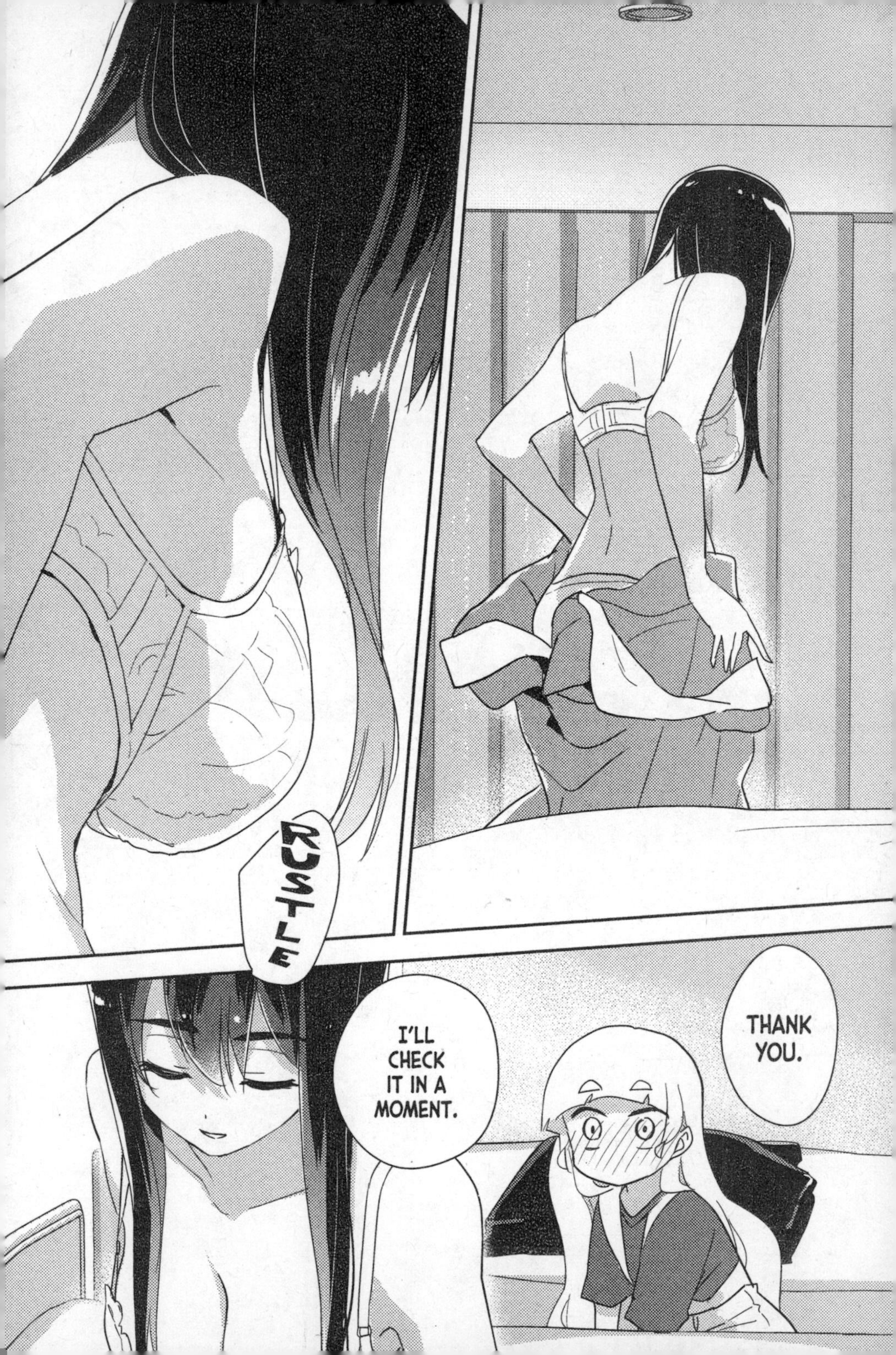
RUSTLE
THANK YOU.
I'LL CHECK IT IN A MOMENT.

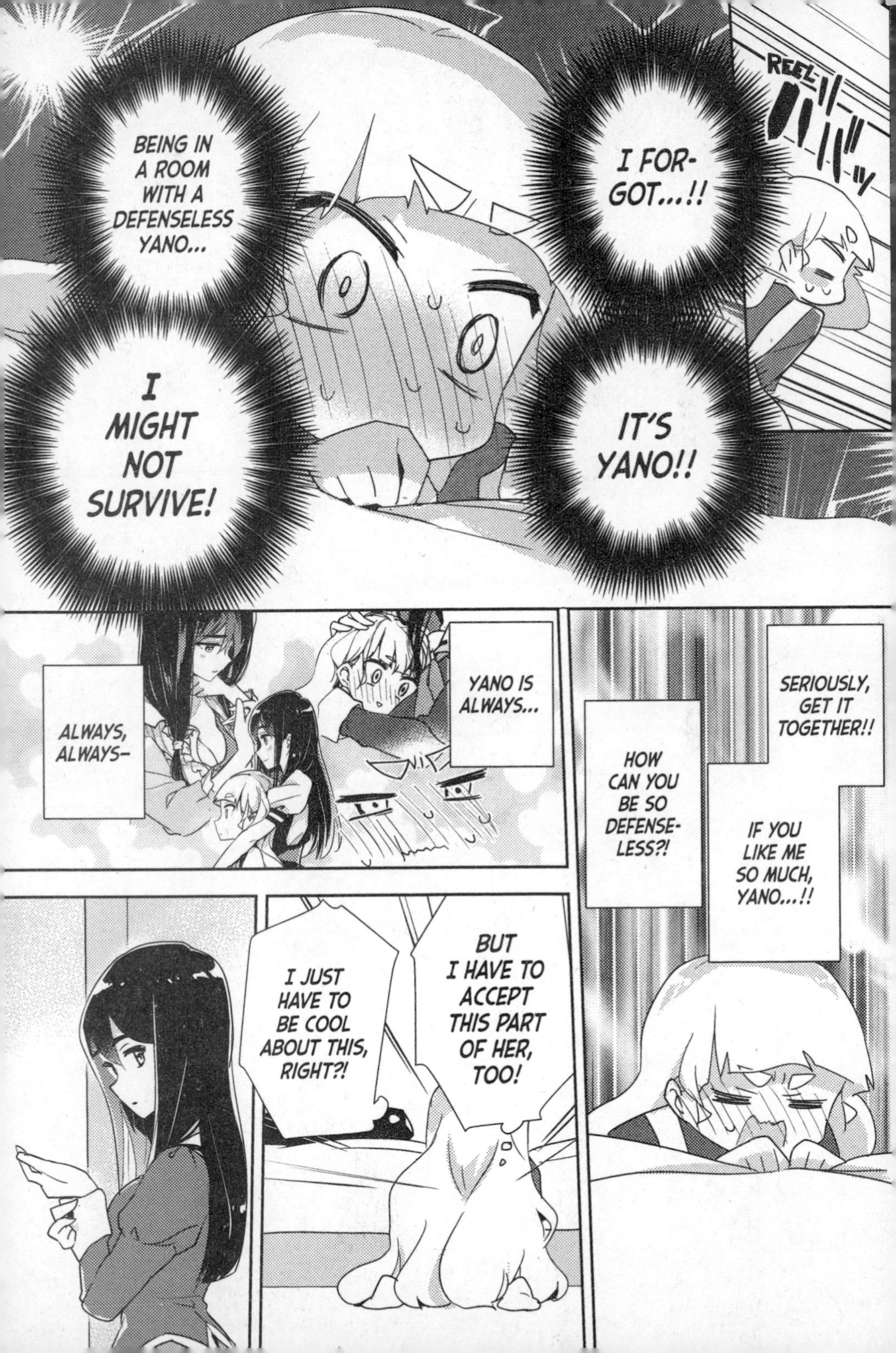
REEL
I FOR-GOT...!!
IT'S YANO!!
BEING IN A ROOM WITH A DEFENSELESS YANO...
I MIGHT NOT SURVIVE!
SERIOUSLY, GET IT TOGETHER!!
HOW CAN YOU BE SO DEFENSE-LESS?!
IF YOU LIKE ME SO MUCH, YANO...!!
YANO IS ALWAYS...
ALWAYS, ALWAYS–
BUT I HAVE TO ACCEPT THIS PART OF HER, TOO!
I JUST HAVE TO BE COOL ABOUT THIS, RIGHT?!

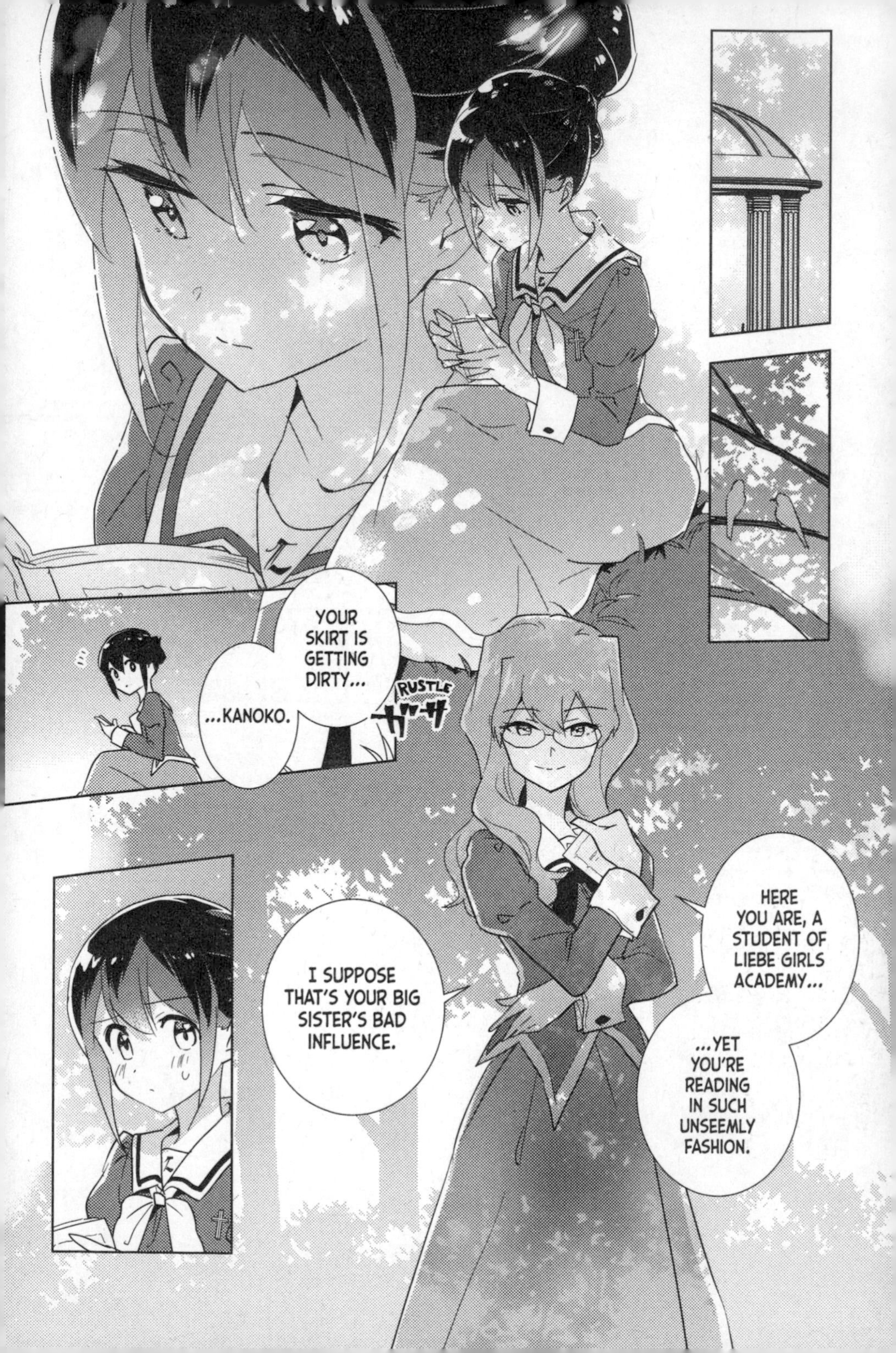
YOUR SKIRT IS GETTING DIRTY...
...KANOKO.
RUSTLE
HERE YOU ARE, A STUDENT OF LIEBE GIRLS ACADEMY...
...YET YOU'RE READING IN SUCH UNSEEMLY FASHION.
I SUPPOSE THAT'S YOUR BIG SISTER'S BAD INFLUENCE.

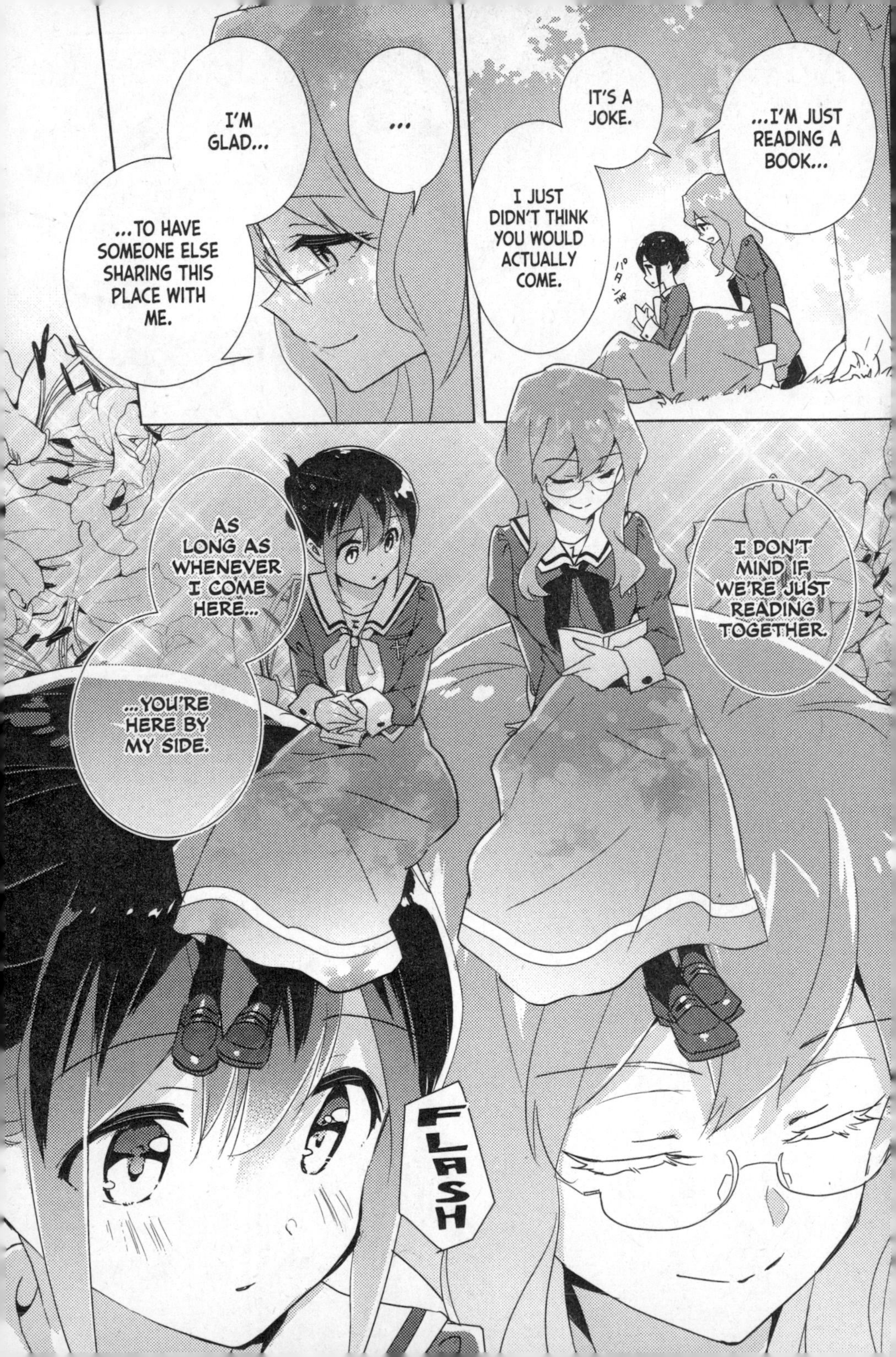
...I'M JUST READING A BOOK...
IT'S A JOKE.
I JUST DIDN'T THINK YOU WOULD ACTUALLY COME.
...
I'M GLAD...
...TO HAVE SOMEONE ELSE SHARING THIS PLACE WITH ME.
I DON'T MIND IF WE'RE JUST READING TOGETHER.
AS LONG AS WHENEVER I COME HERE...
...YOU'RE HERE BY MY SIDE.
FLASH

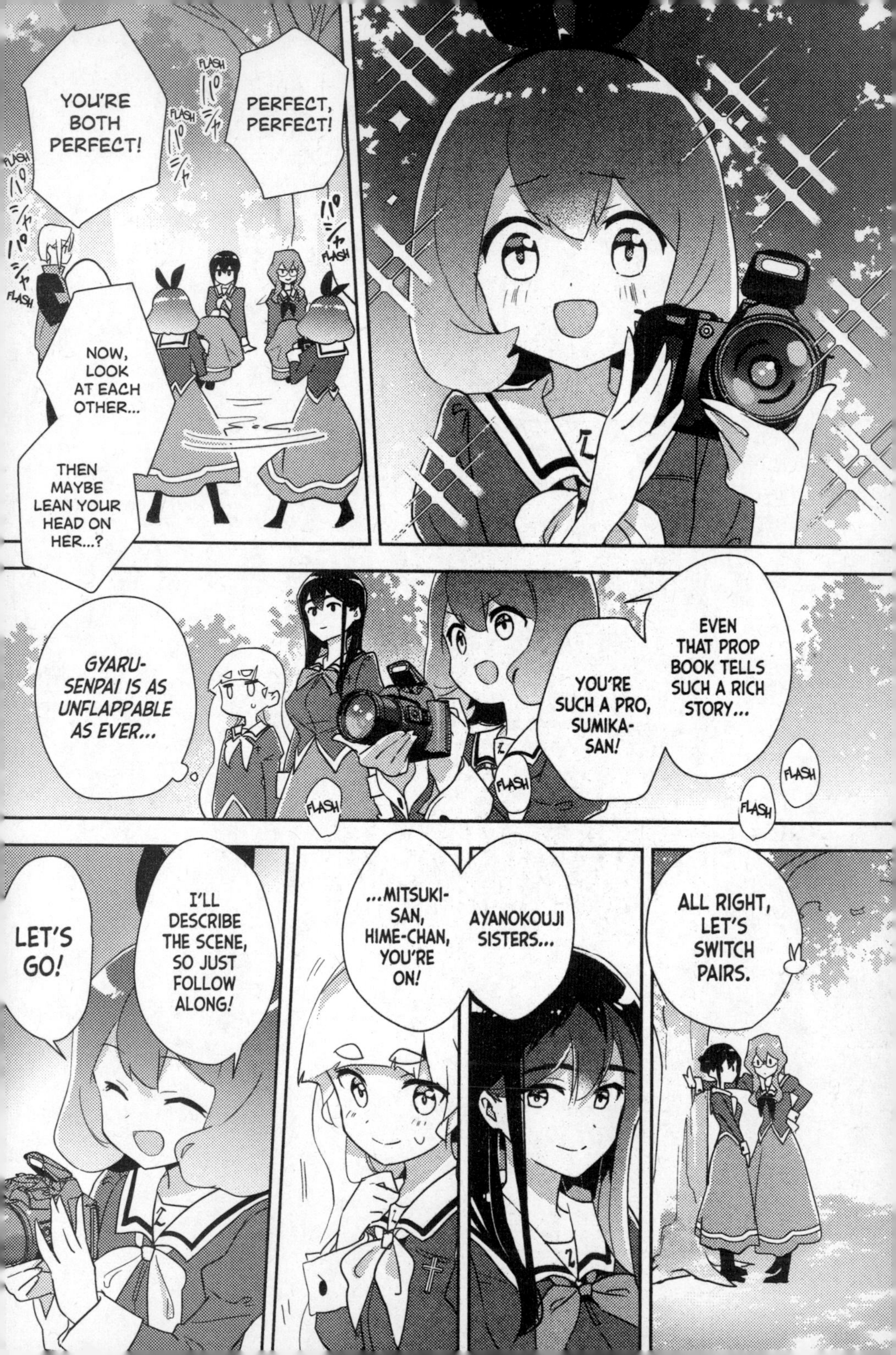
PERFECT, PERFECT!
FLASH
FLASH
YOU'RE BOTH PERFECT!
FLASH
FLASH
NOW, LOOK AT EACH OTHER...
THEN MAYBE LEAN YOUR HEAD ON HER...?
EVEN THAT PROP BOOK TELLS SUCH A RICH STORY...
YOU'RE SUCH A PRO, SUMIKA-SAN!
FLASH
FLASH
FLASH
FLASH
GYARU-SENPAI IS AS UNFLAPPABLE AS EVER...
ALL RIGHT, LET'S SWITCH PAIRS.
AYANOKOUJI SISTERS...
...MITSUKI-SAN, HIME-CHAN, YOU'RE ON!
I'LL DESCRIBE THE SCENE, SO JUST FOLLOW ALONG!
LET'S GO!

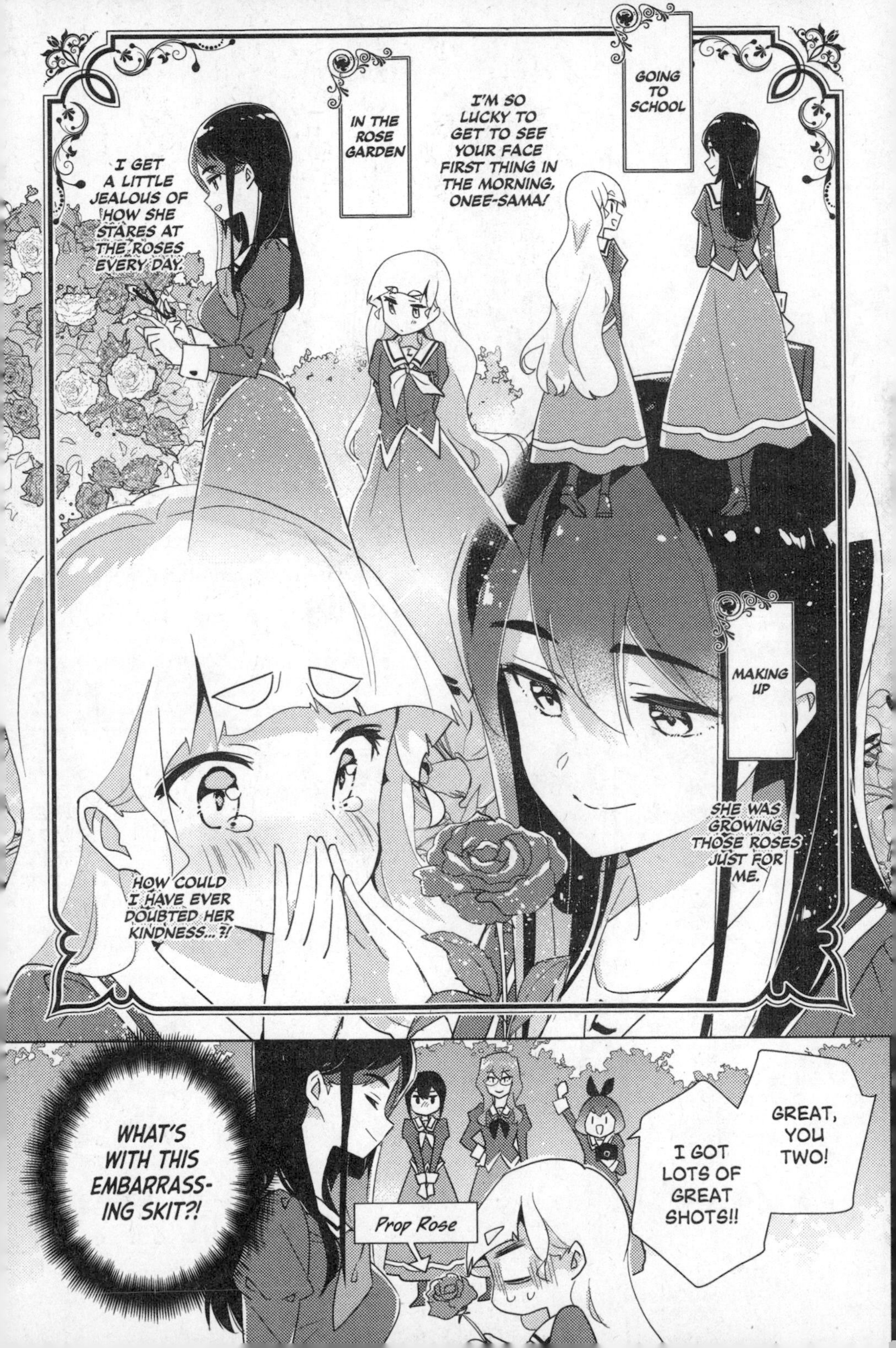
GOING TO SCHOOL
I'M SO LUCKY TO GET TO SEE YOUR FACE FIRST THING IN THE MORNING, ONEE-SAMA!
IN THE ROSE GARDEN
I GET A LITTLE JEALOUS OF HOW SHE STARES AT THE ROSES EVERY DAY.
MAKING UP
SHE WAS GROWING THOSE ROSES JUST FOR ME.
HOW COULD I HAVE EVER DOUBTED HER KINDNESS...?!
GREAT, YOU TWO!
I GOT LOTS OF GREAT SHOTS!!
Prop Rose
WHAT'S WITH THIS EMBARRASS-ING SKIT?!

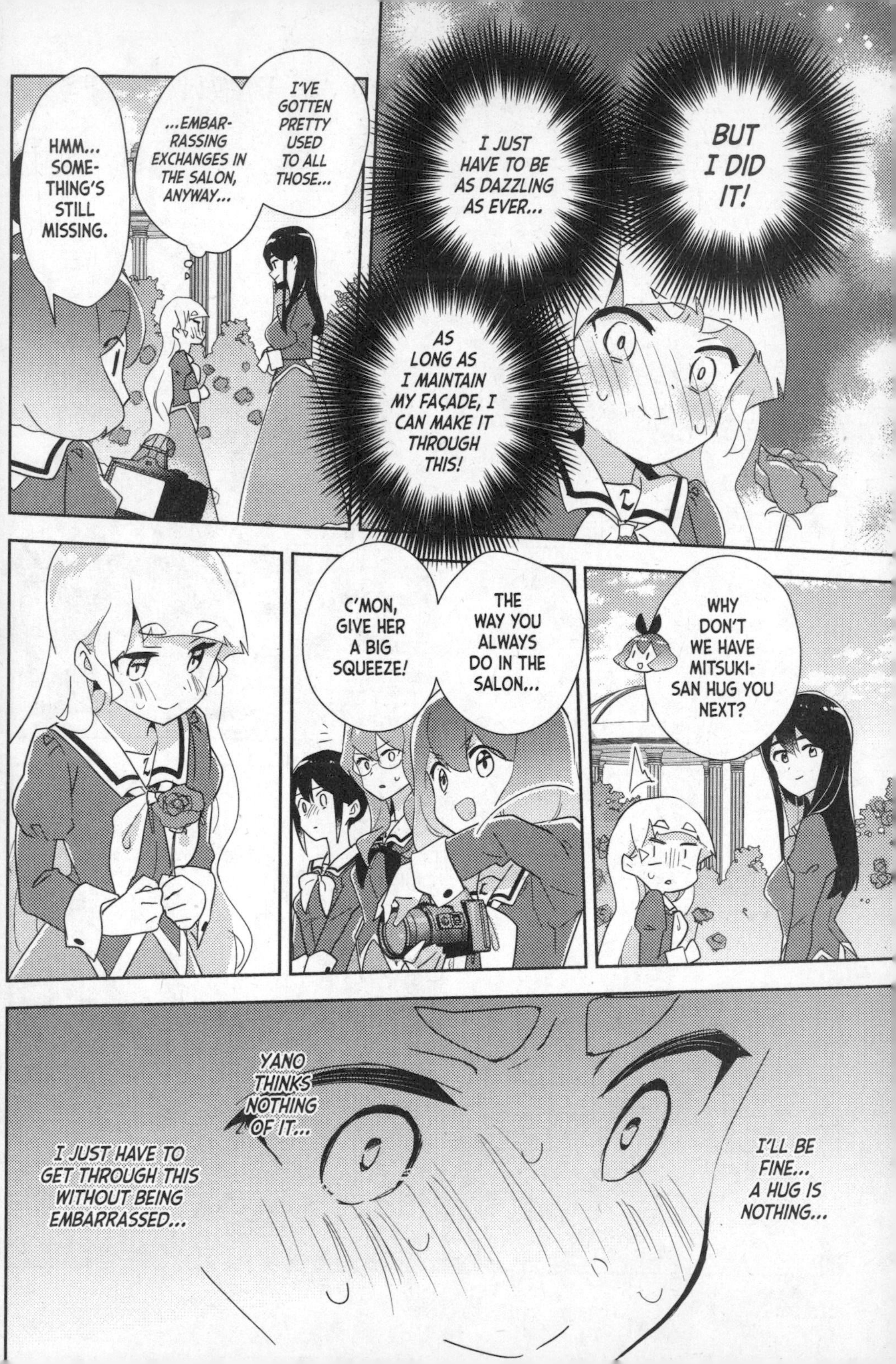
BUT I DID IT!
I JUST HAVE TO BE AS DAZZLING AS EVER...
AS LONG AS I MAINTAIN MY FAÇADE, I CAN MAKE IT THROUGH THIS!
I'VE GOTTEN PRETTY USED TO ALL THOSE...
...EMBARRASSING EXCHANGES IN THE SALON, ANYWAY...
HMM... SOMETHING'S STILL MISSING.
WHY DON'T WE HAVE MITSUKI-SAN HUG YOU NEXT?
THE WAY YOU ALWAYS DO IN THE SALON...
C'MON, GIVE HER A BIG SQUEEZE!
I'LL BE FINE... A HUG IS NOTHING...
YANO THINKS NOTHING OF IT...
I JUST HAVE TO GET THROUGH THIS WITHOUT BEING EMBARRASSED...

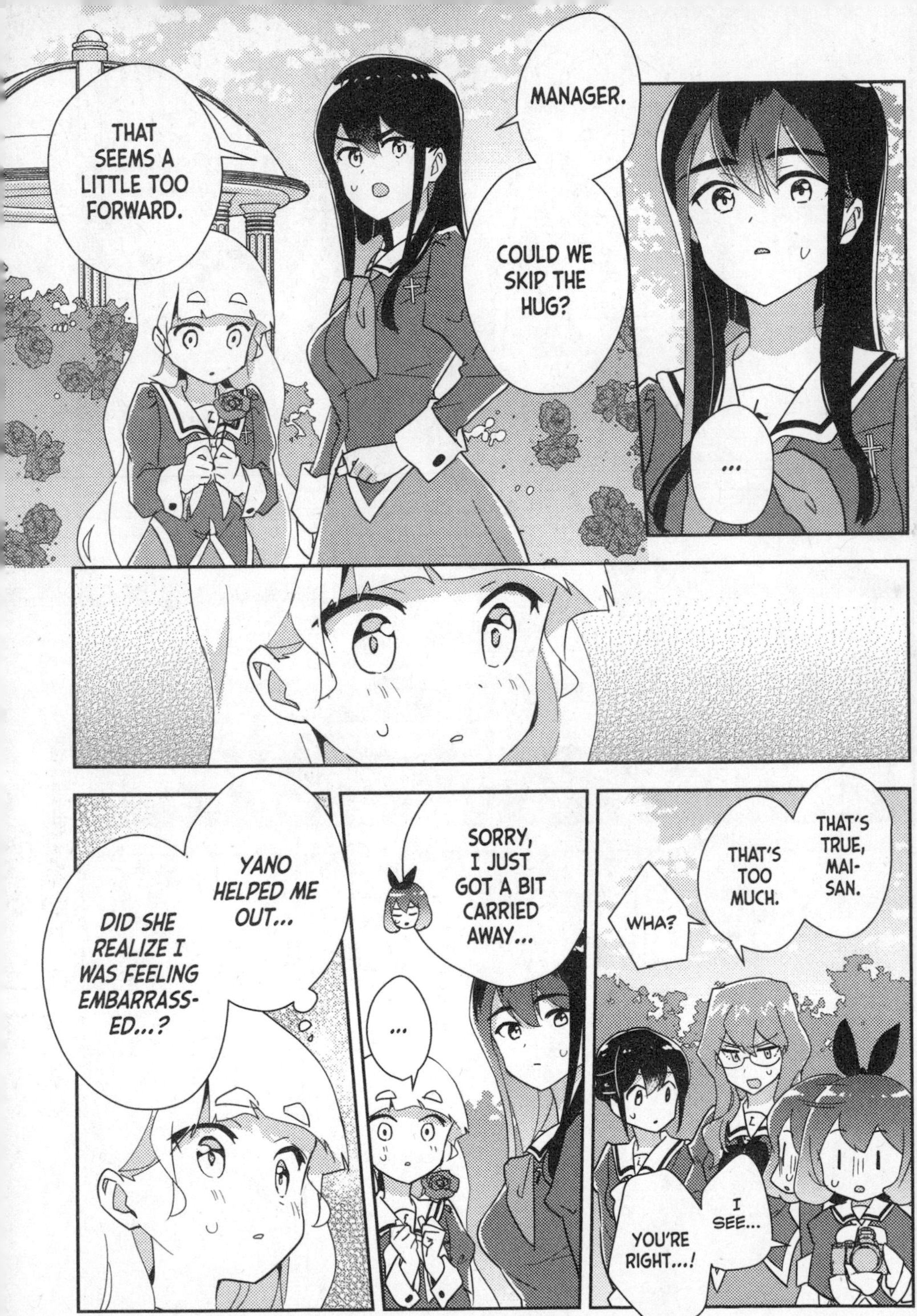
...
MANAGER.
COULD WE SKIP THE HUG?
THAT SEEMS A LITTLE TOO FORWARD.
THAT'S TRUE, MAI-SAN.
THAT'S TOO MUCH.
WHA?
I SEE...
YOU'RE RIGHT...!
SORRY, I JUST GOT A BIT CARRIED AWAY...
...
YANO HELPED ME OUT...
DID SHE REALIZE I WAS FEELING EMBARRASS-ED...?

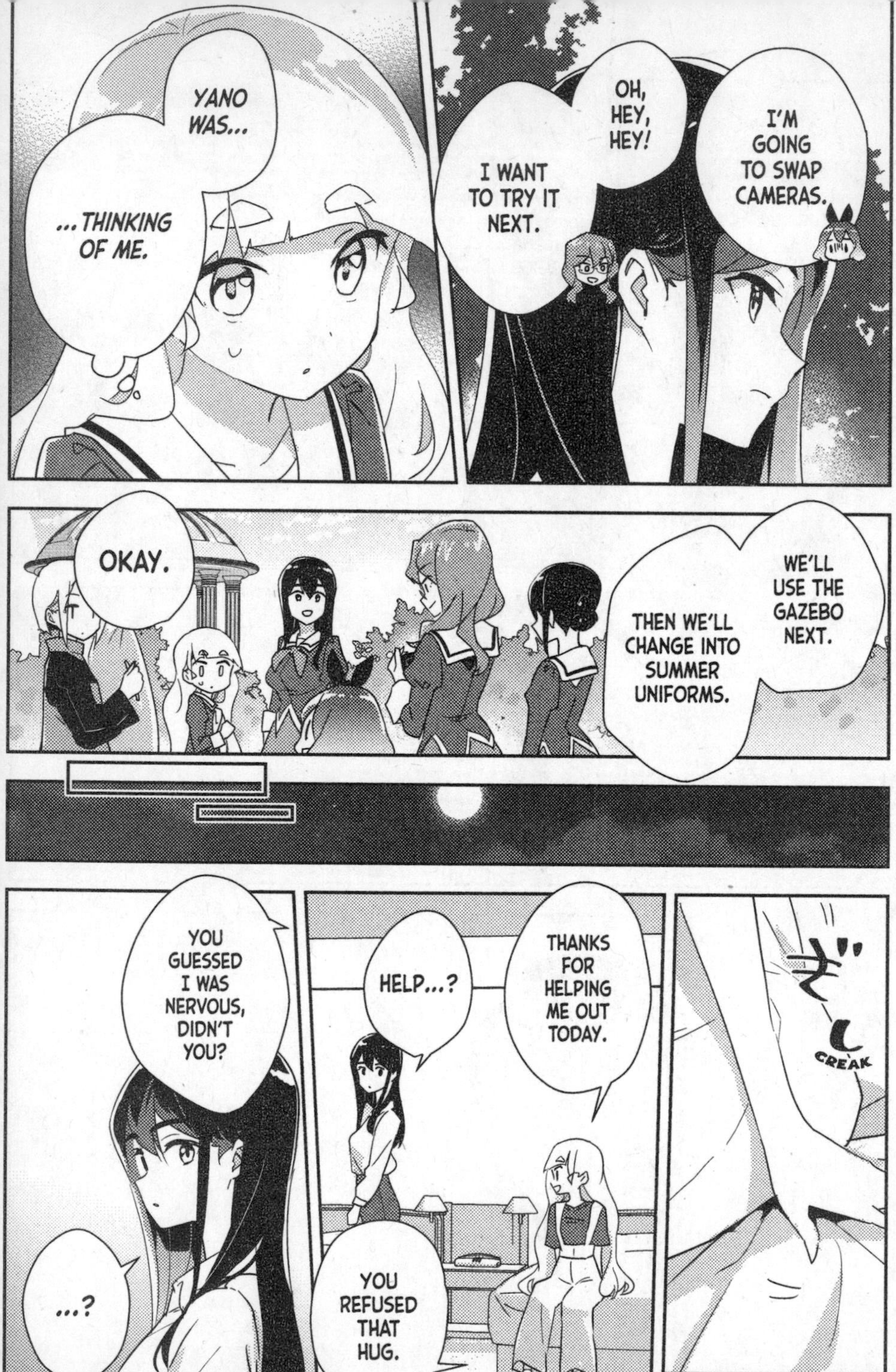

I'M GOING TO SWAP CAMERAS.
OH, HEY, HEY!
I WANT TO TRY IT NEXT.
YANO WAS...
...THINKING OF ME.
WE'LL USE THE GAZEBO NEXT.
THEN WE'LL CHANGE INTO SUMMER UNIFORMS.
OKAY.
CREAK
THANKS FOR HELPING ME OUT TODAY.
HELP...?
YOU REFUSED THAT HUG.
YOU GUESSED I WAS NERVOUS, DIDN'T YOU?
...?

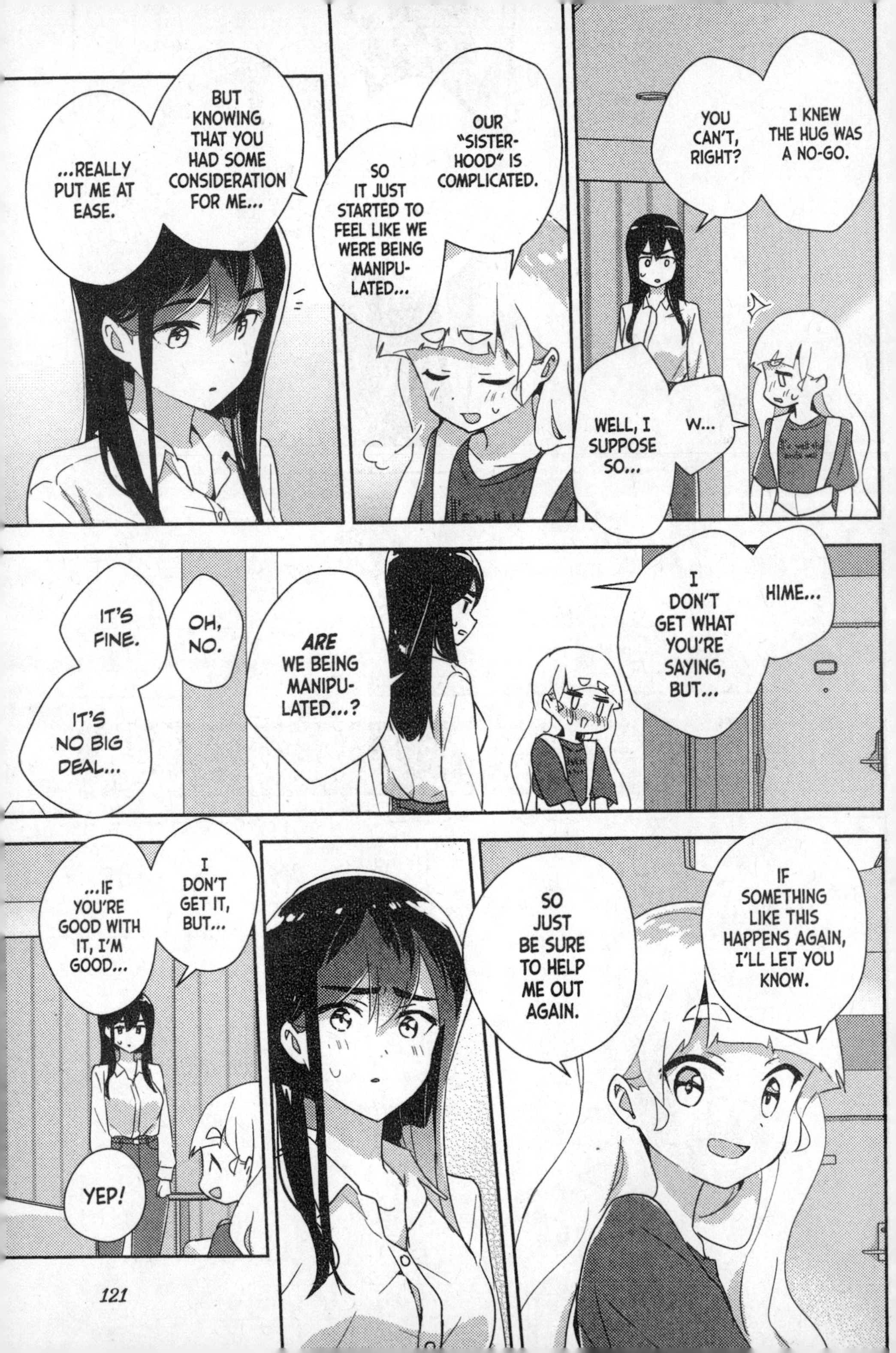
I KNEW THE HUG WAS A NO-GO.
YOU CAN'T, RIGHT?
W...
WELL, I SUPPOSE SO...
OUR "SISTER-HOOD" IS COMPLICATED.
SO IT JUST STARTED TO FEEL LIKE WE WERE BEING MANIPU-LATED...
BUT KNOWING THAT YOU HAD SOME CONSIDERATION FOR ME...
...REALLY PUT ME AT EASE.
HIME...
I DON'T GET WHAT YOU'RE SAYING, BUT...
*ARE* WE BEING MANIPU-LATED...?
OH, NO.
IT'S FINE.
IT'S NO BIG DEAL...
IF SOMETHING LIKE THIS HAPPENS AGAIN, I'LL LET YOU KNOW.
SO JUST BE SURE TO HELP ME OUT AGAIN.
I DON'T GET IT, BUT...
...IF YOU'RE GOOD WITH IT, I'M GOOD...
YEP!

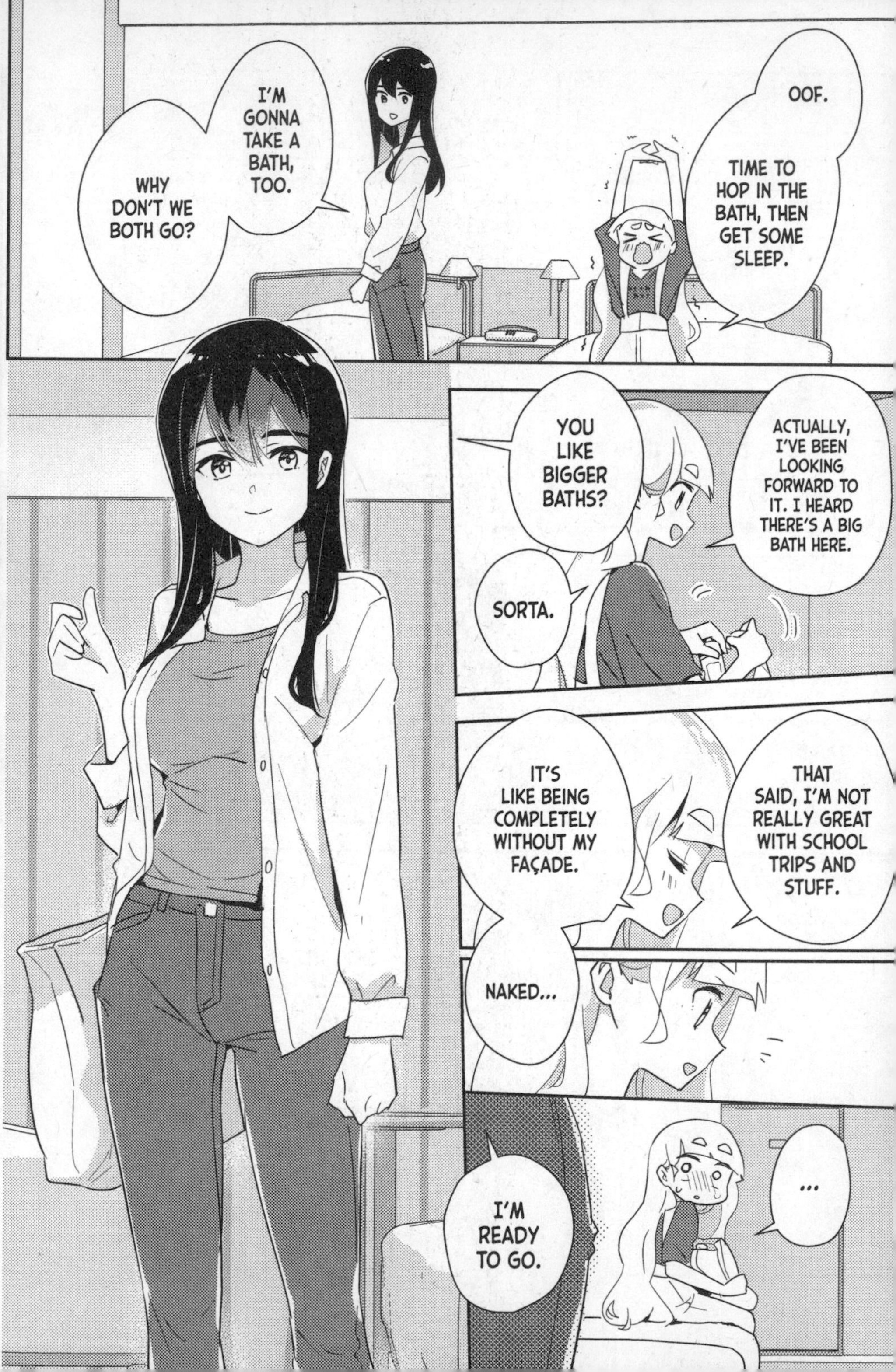
OOF.
TIME TO HOP IN THE BATH, THEN GET SOME SLEEP.
I'M GONNA TAKE A BATH, TOO.
WHY DON'T WE BOTH GO?
ACTUALLY, I'VE BEEN LOOKING FORWARD TO IT. I HEARD THERE'S A BIG BATH HERE.
YOU LIKE BIGGER BATHS?
SORTA.
THAT SAID, I'M NOT REALLY GREAT WITH SCHOOL TRIPS AND STUFF.
IT'S LIKE BEING COMPLETELY WITHOUT MY FAÇADE.
NAKED...
...
I'M READY TO GO.

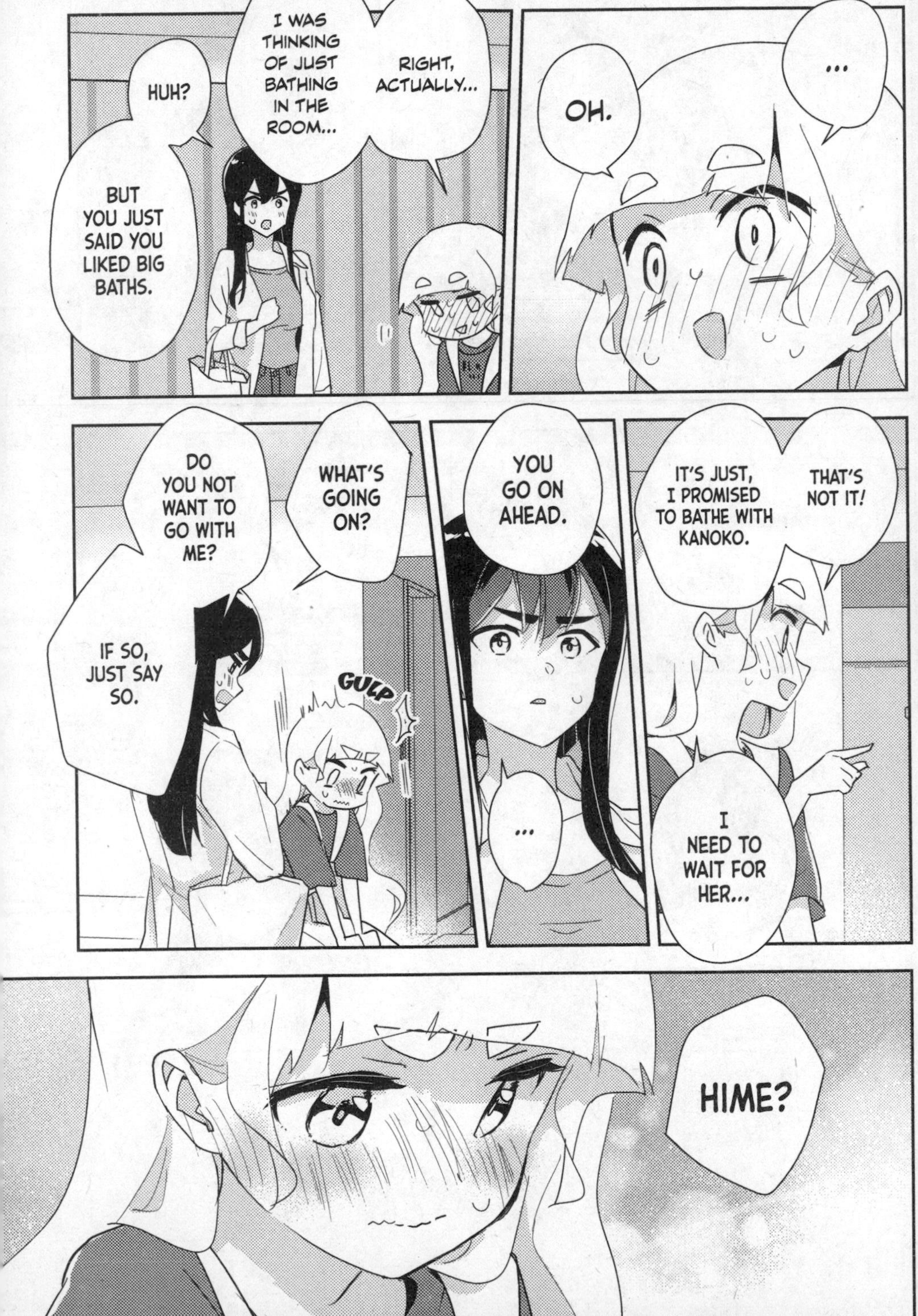
...
OH.
RIGHT, ACTUALLY...
I WAS THINKING OF JUST BATHING IN THE ROOM...
HUH?
BUT YOU JUST SAID YOU LIKED BIG BATHS.
THAT'S NOT IT!
IT'S JUST, I PROMISED TO BATHE WITH KANOKO.
I NEED TO WAIT FOR HER...
YOU GO ON AHEAD.
...
WHAT'S GOING ON?
DO YOU NOT WANT TO GO WITH ME?
GULP
IF SO, JUST SAY SO.
HIME?

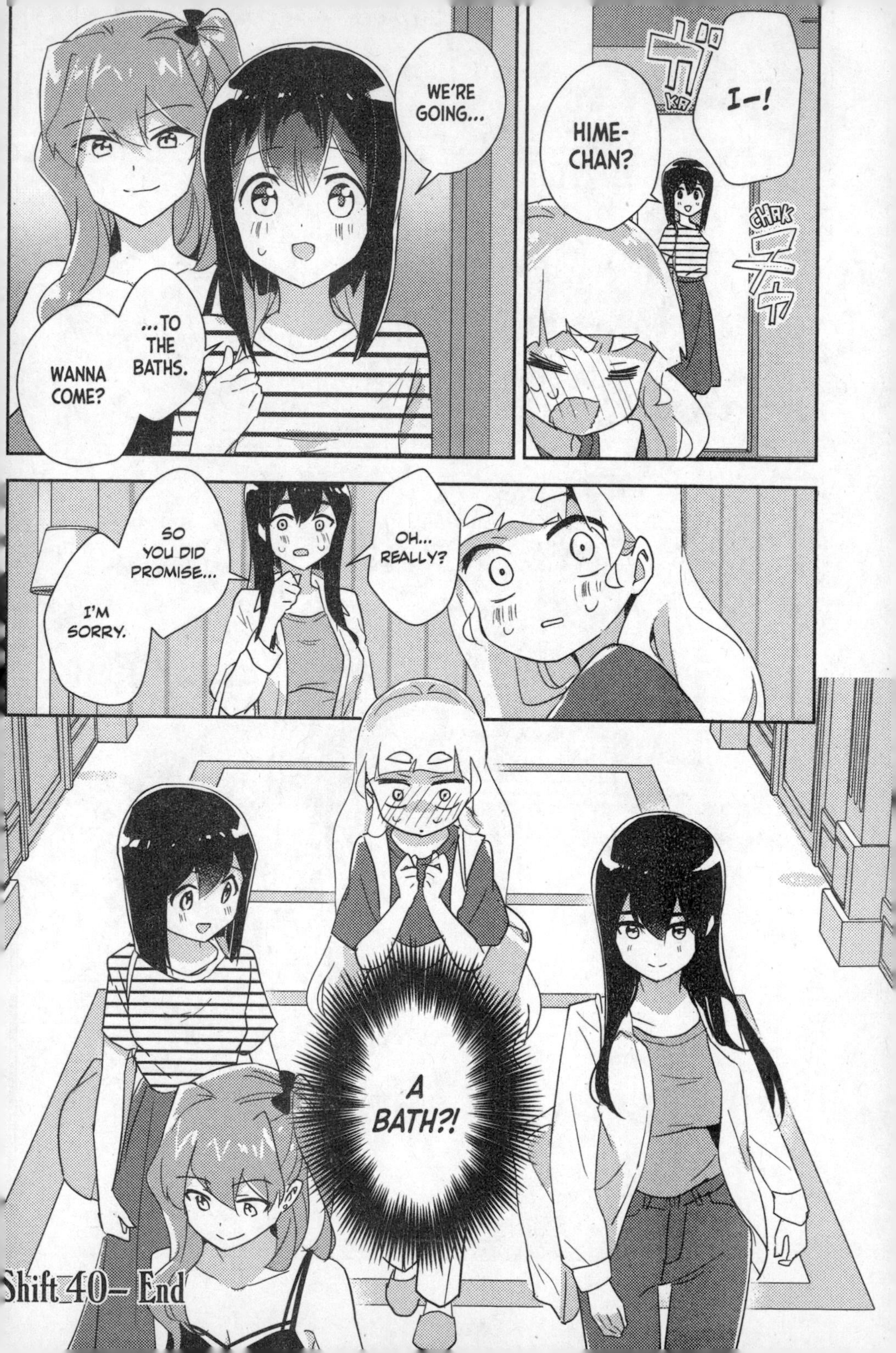
ガ
KA
I–!
HIME-CHAN?
CHAK
ガチャ
WE'RE GOING...
...TO THE BATHS.
WANNA COME?
OH... REALLY?
SO YOU DID PROMISE...
I'M SORRY.
A BATH?!

Shift 40– End

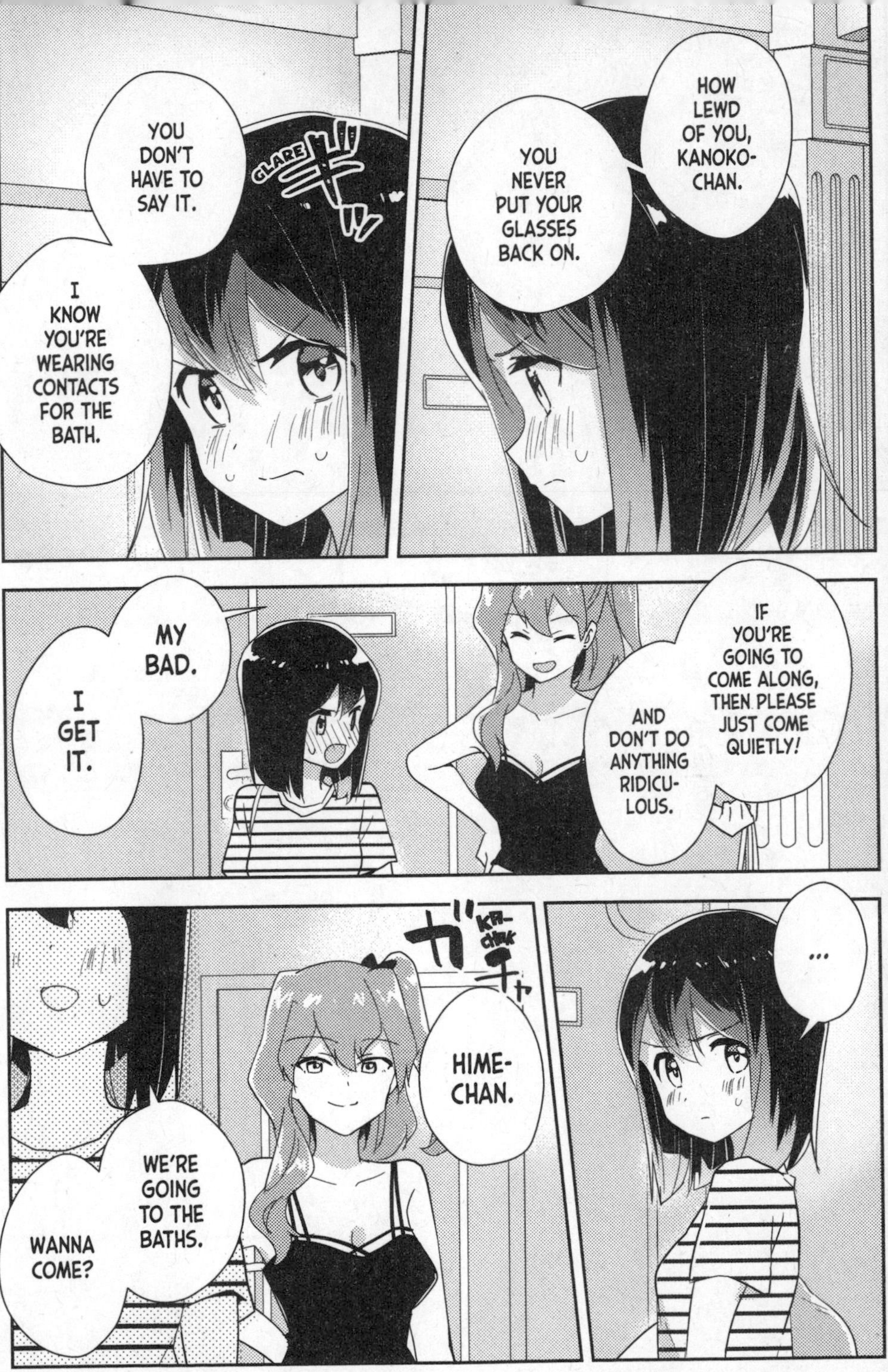
HOW LEWD OF YOU, KANOKO-CHAN.
YOU NEVER PUT YOUR GLASSES BACK ON.
GLARE
YOU DON'T HAVE TO SAY IT.
I KNOW YOU'RE WEARING CONTACTS FOR THE BATH.
IF YOU'RE GOING TO COME ALONG, THEN PLEASE JUST COME QUIETLY!
AND DON'T DO ANYTHING RIDICU-LOUS.
MY BAD.
I GET IT.
...
KA-CHAK
HIME-CHAN.
WE'RE GOING TO THE BATHS.
WANNA COME?

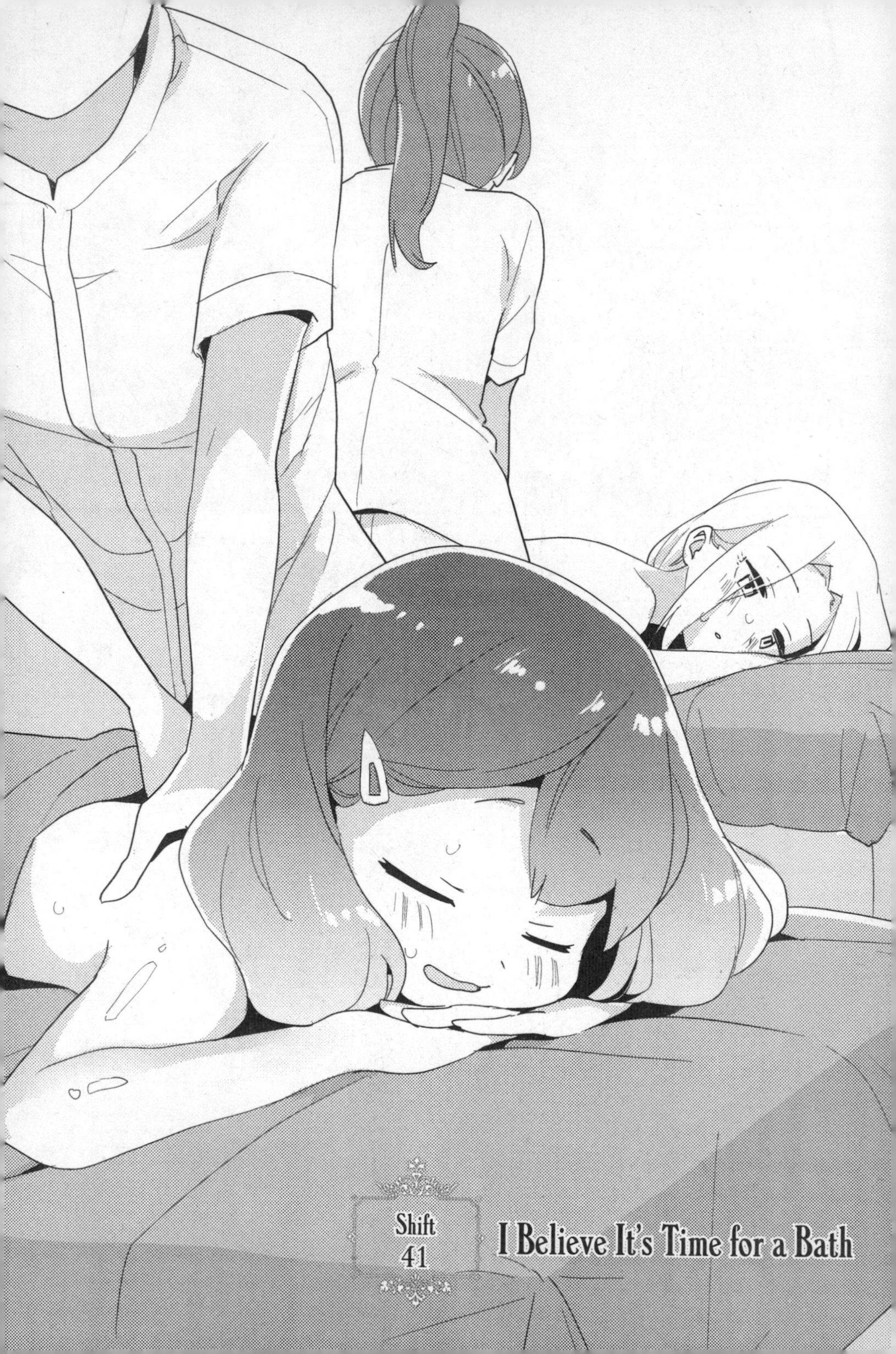
Shift 41
I Believe It's Time for a Bath

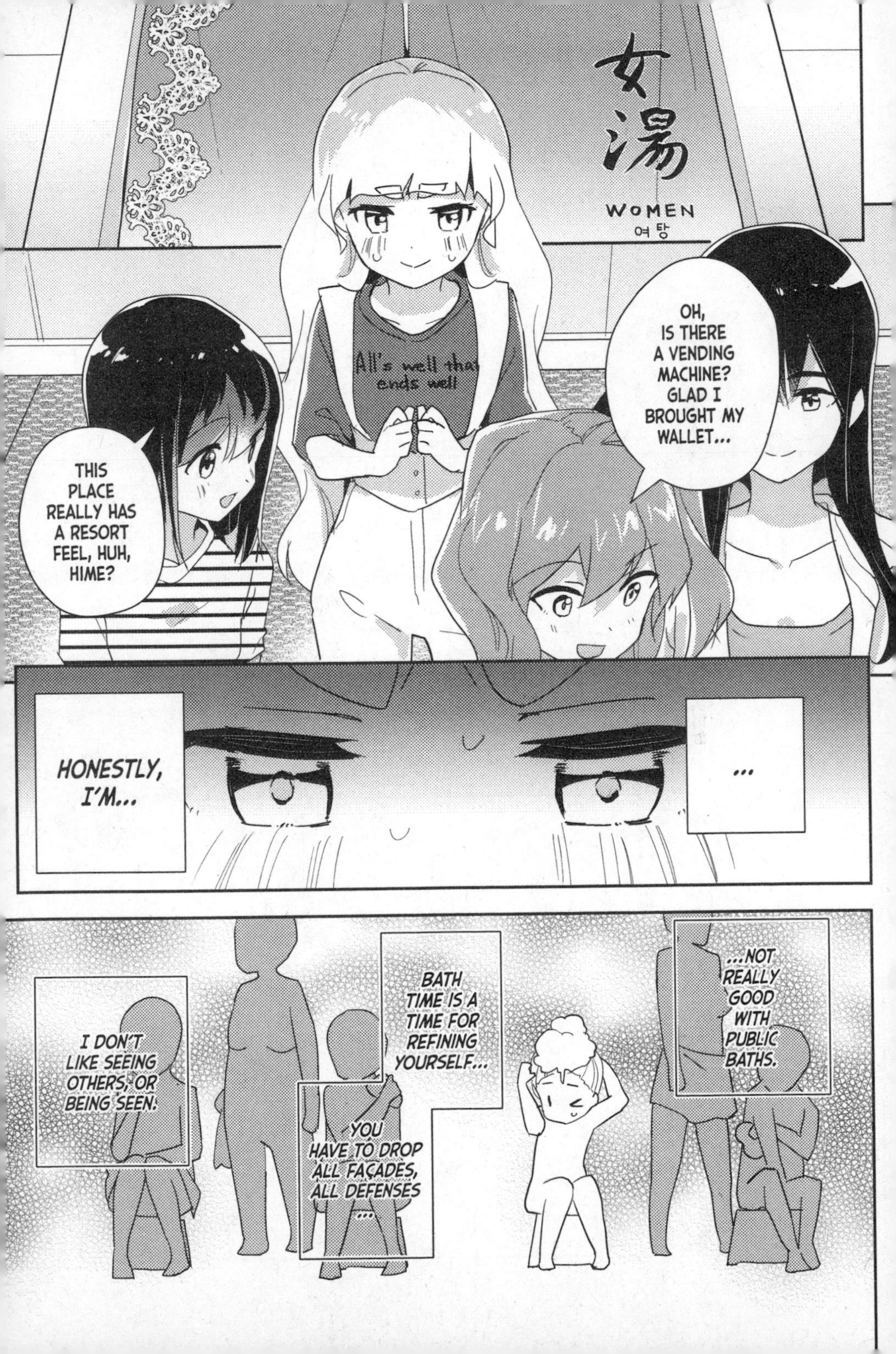
女湯
WOMEN
여탕
OH, IS THERE A VENDING MACHINE? GLAD I BROUGHT MY WALLET...
All's well tha
ends well
THIS PLACE REALLY HAS A RESORT FEEL, HUH, HIME?
...
HONESTLY, I'M...
...NOT REALLY GOOD WITH PUBLIC BATHS.
BATH TIME IS A TIME FOR REFINING YOURSELF...
YOU HAVE TO DROP ALL FAÇADES, ALL DEFENSES...
I DON'T LIKE SEEING OTHERS, OR BEING SEEN.

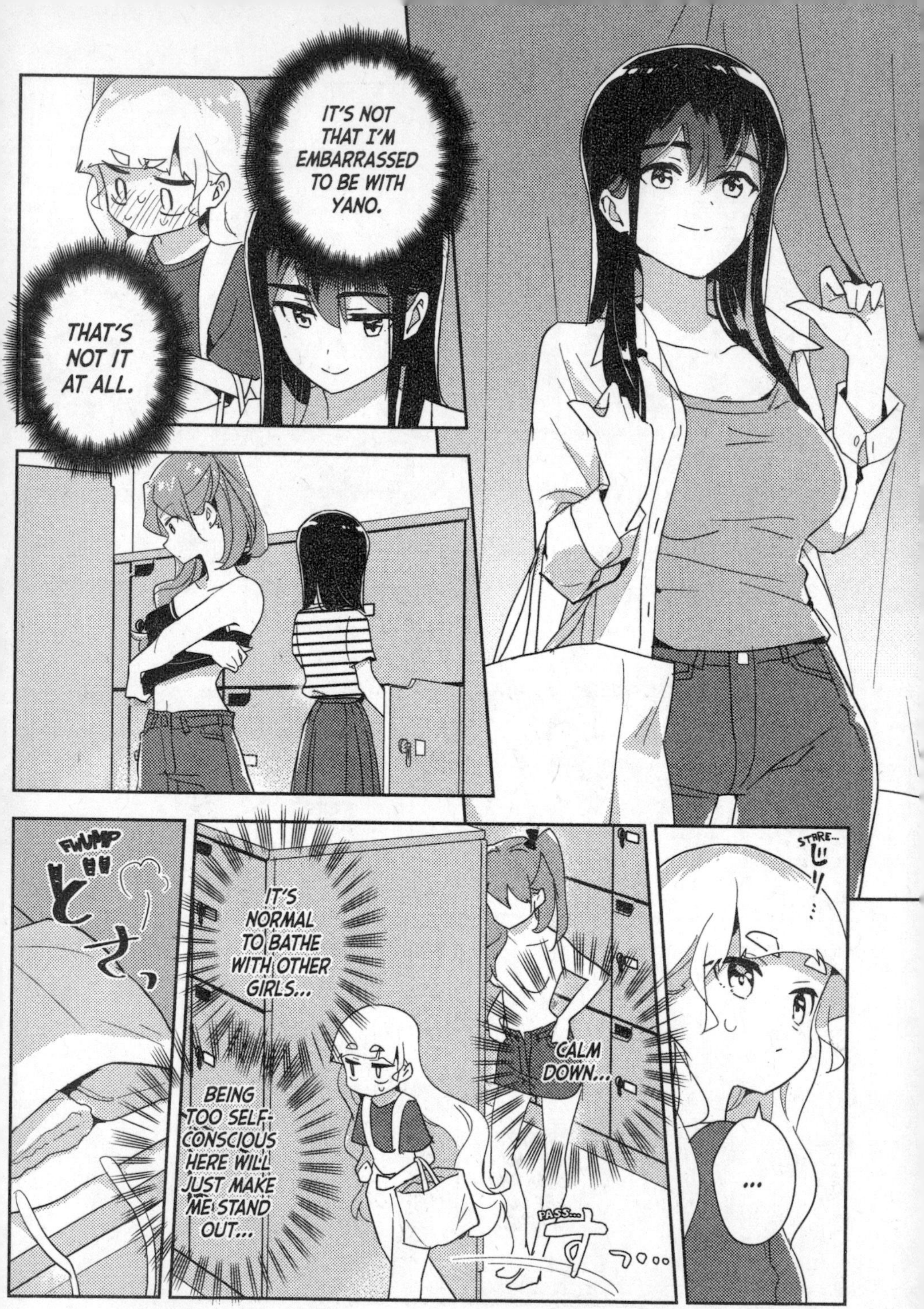
IT'S NOT THAT I'M EMBARRASSED TO BE WITH YANO.
THAT'S NOT IT AT ALL.
STARE...
...
IT'S NORMAL TO BATHE WITH OTHER GIRLS...
CALM DOWN...
BEING TOO SELF-CONSCIOUS HERE WILL JUST MAKE ME STAND OUT...
PASS...
すっ…
FWUMP
どさっ

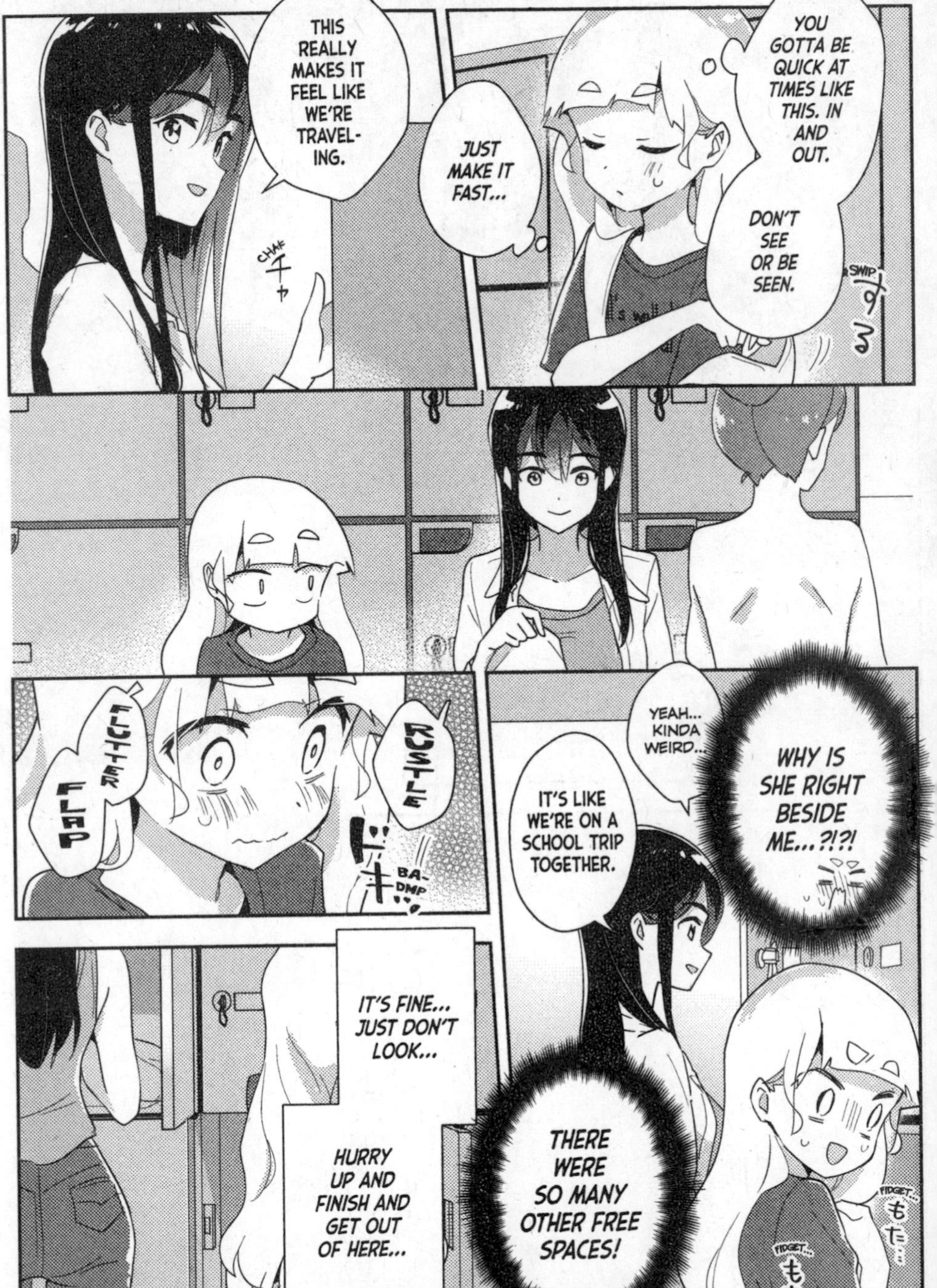
YOU GOTTA BE QUICK AT TIMES LIKE THIS. IN AND OUT.
DON'T SEE OR BE SEEN.
JUST MAKE IT FAST...
SWIP
THIS REALLY MAKES IT FEEL LIKE WE'RE TRAVEL-ING.
CHAK
WHY IS SHE RIGHT BESIDE ME...?!?!
YEAH... KINDA WEIRD...
IT'S LIKE WE'RE ON A SCHOOL TRIP TOGETHER.
FIDGET...
FIDGET...
THERE WERE SO MANY OTHER FREE SPACES!
RUSTLE
FLUTTER FLAP
BA-DMP
IT'S FINE... JUST DON'T LOOK...
HURRY UP AND FINISH AND GET OUT OF HERE...

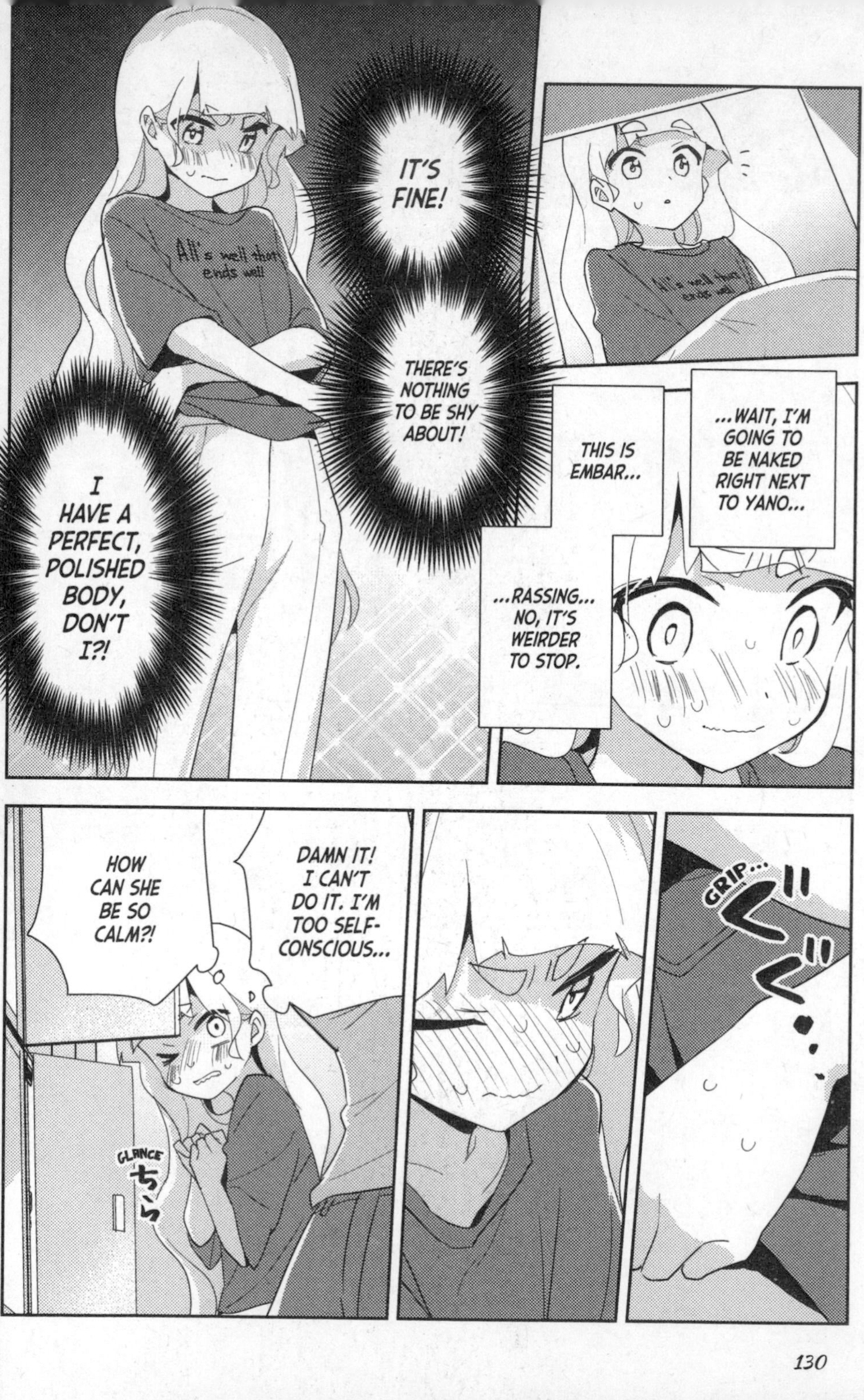
...WAIT, I'M GOING TO BE NAKED RIGHT NEXT TO YANO...
THIS IS EMBAR...
...RASSING... NO, IT'S WEIRDER TO STOP.
IT'S FINE!
All's well that ends well
THERE'S NOTHING TO BE SHY ABOUT!
I HAVE A PERFECT, POLISHED BODY, DON'T I?!
GRIP...
DAMN IT! I CAN'T DO IT. I'M TOO SELF-CONSCIOUS...
HOW CAN SHE BE SO CALM?!
GLANCE
ちら

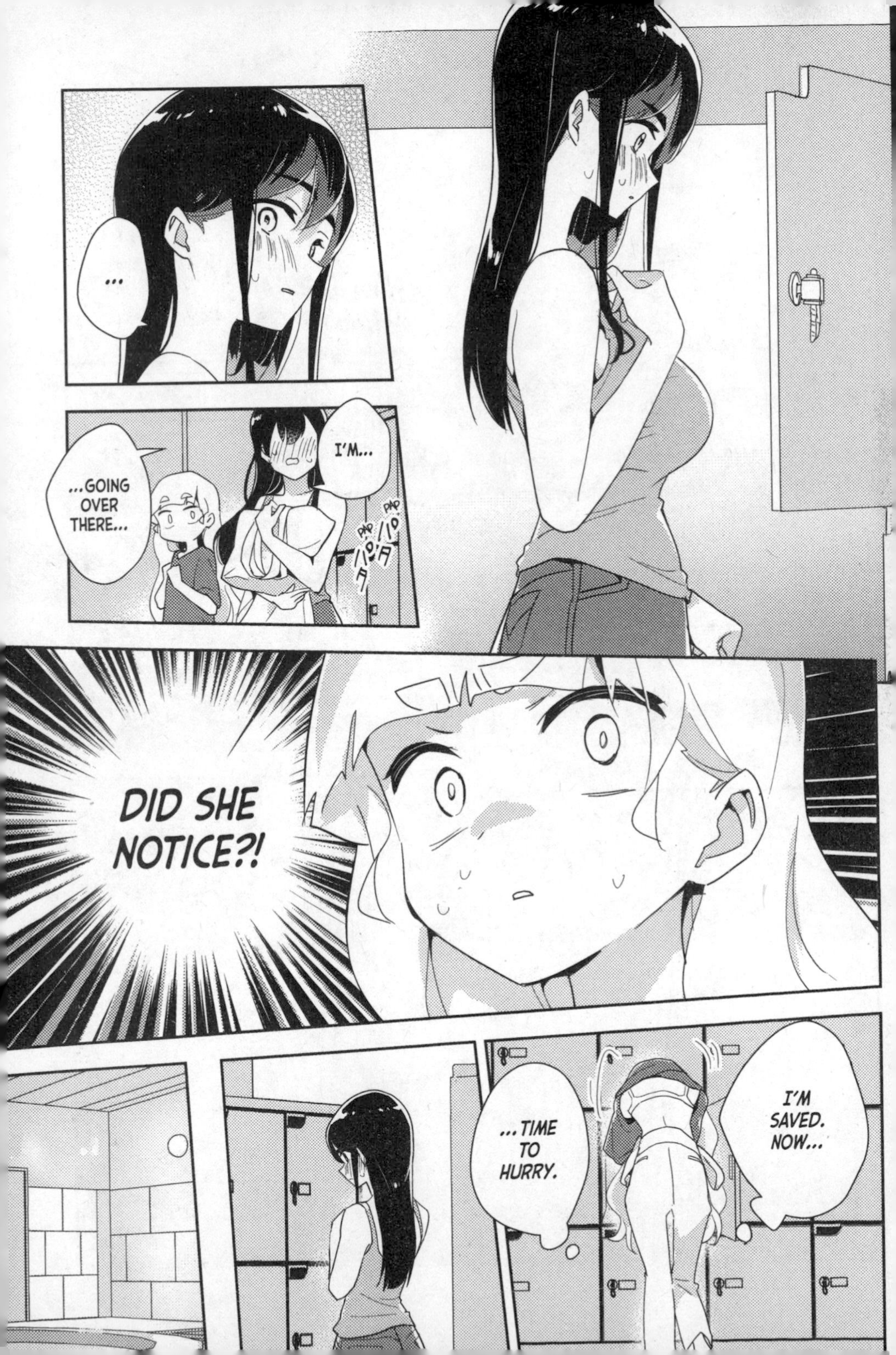
...
I'M...
PAD PAD
...GOING OVER THERE...
DID SHE NOTICE?!
I'M SAVED. NOW...
...TIME TO HURRY.

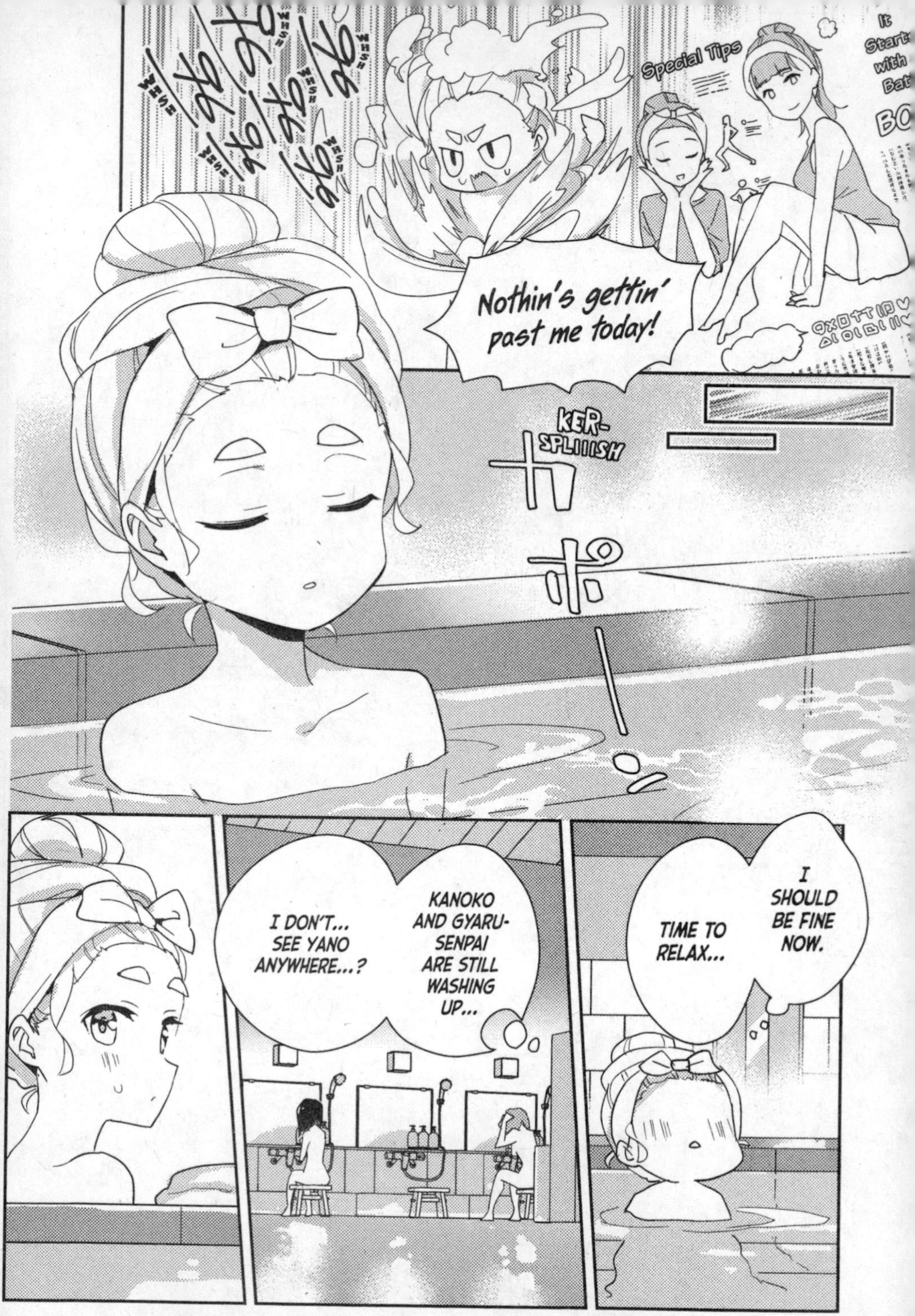
WHSH WHSH WHSH WHSH WHSH
Special Tips
Nothin's gettin' past me today!
KER-SPLIIISH
TIME TO RELAX... I SHOULD BE FINE NOW.
I DON'T... SEE YANO ANYWHERE...? KANOKO AND GYARU-SENPAI ARE STILL WASHING UP...

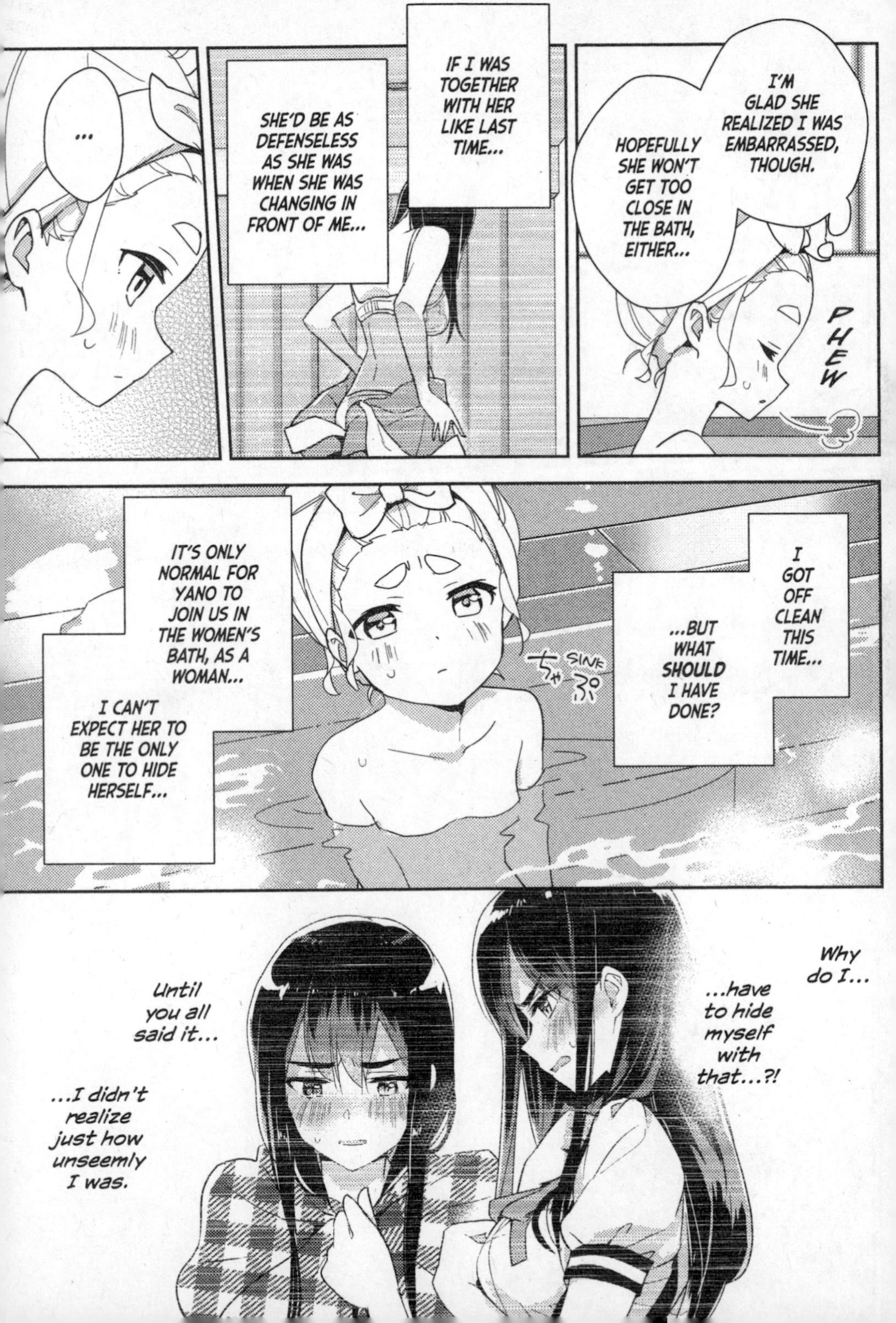
I'M GLAD SHE REALIZED I WAS EMBARRASSED, THOUGH.
HOPEFULLY SHE WON'T GET TOO CLOSE IN THE BATH, EITHER...
PHEW
IF I WAS TOGETHER WITH HER LIKE LAST TIME...
SHE'D BE AS DEFENSELESS AS SHE WAS WHEN SHE WAS CHANGING IN FRONT OF ME...
...
I GOT OFF CLEAN THIS TIME...
...BUT WHAT **SHOULD** I HAVE DONE?
ちゃぷ SINK
IT'S ONLY NORMAL FOR YANO TO JOIN US IN THE WOMEN'S BATH, AS A WOMAN...
I CAN'T EXPECT HER TO BE THE ONLY ONE TO HIDE HERSELF...
Why do I...
...have to hide myself with that...?!
Until you all said it...
...I didn't realize just how unseemly I was.

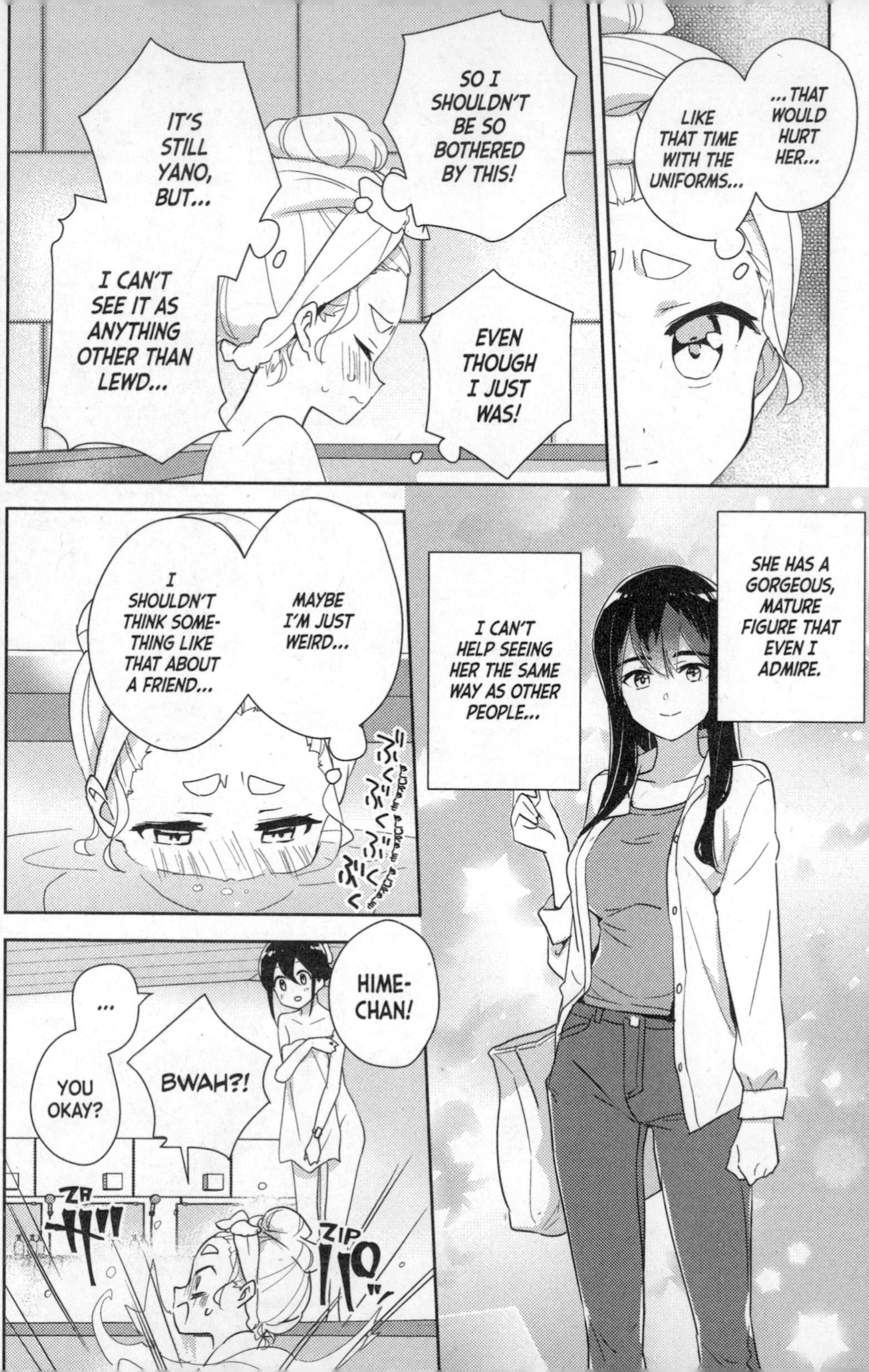
...THAT WOULD HURT HER...
LIKE THAT TIME WITH THE UNIFORMS...
SO I SHOULDN'T BE SO BOTHERED BY THIS!
IT'S STILL YANO, BUT...
I CAN'T SEE IT AS ANYTHING OTHER THAN LEWD...
EVEN THOUGH I JUST WAS!
SHE HAS A GORGEOUS, MATURE FIGURE THAT EVEN I ADMIRE.
I CAN'T HELP SEEING HER THE SAME WAY AS OTHER PEOPLE...
MAYBE I'M JUST WEIRD...
I SHOULDN'T THINK SOME-THING LIKE THAT ABOUT A FRIEND...
HIME-CHAN!
BWAH?!
...
YOU OKAY?
ZIP
ZA

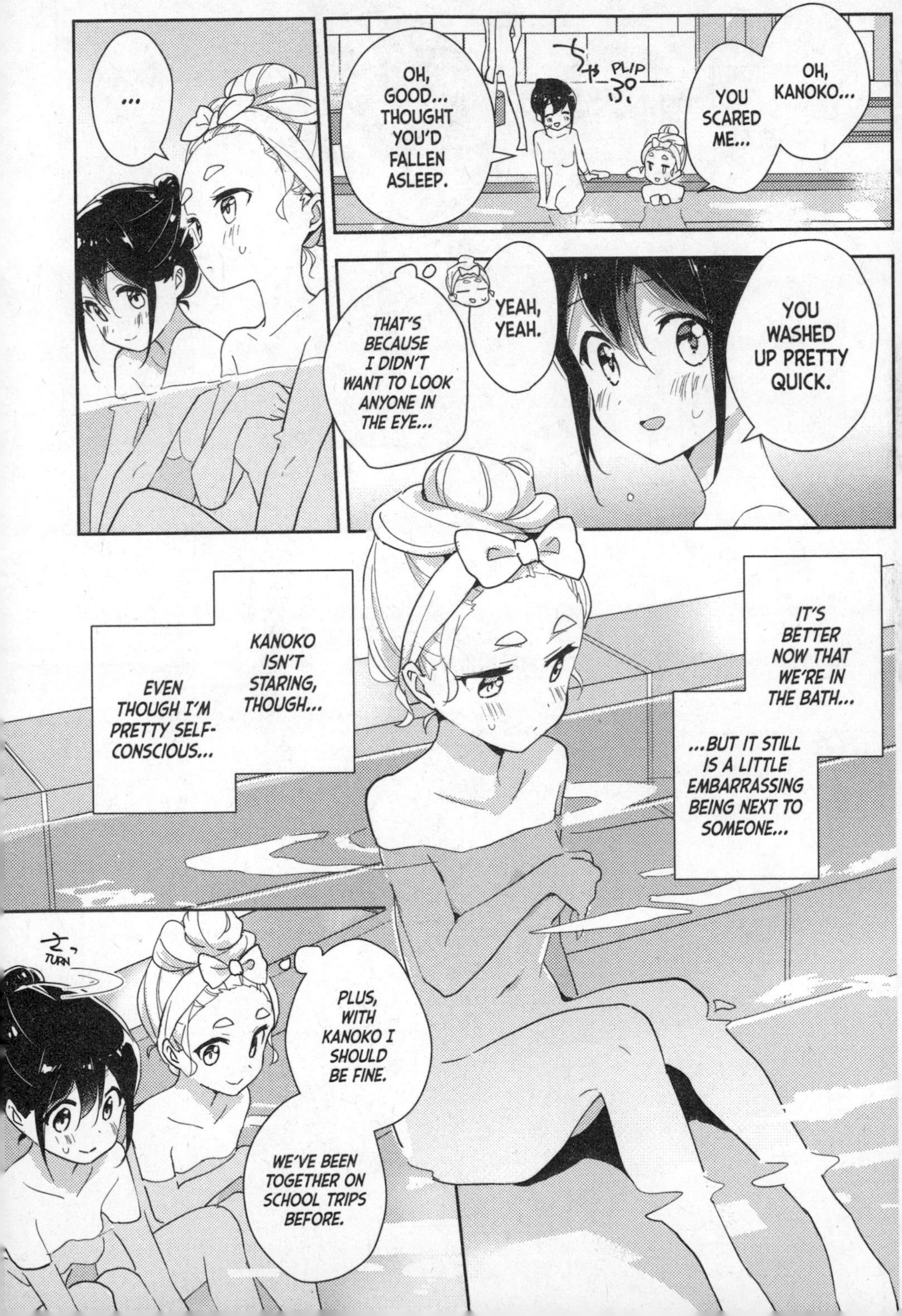
OH, KANOKO... YOU SCARED ME...
PLIP
OH, GOOD... THOUGHT YOU'D FALLEN ASLEEP.
...
YOU WASHED UP PRETTY QUICK.
YEAH, YEAH.
THAT'S BECAUSE I DIDN'T WANT TO LOOK ANYONE IN THE EYE...
IT'S BETTER NOW THAT WE'RE IN THE BATH...
...BUT IT STILL IS A LITTLE EMBARRASSING BEING NEXT TO SOMEONE...
KANOKO ISN'T STARING, THOUGH...
EVEN THOUGH I'M PRETTY SELF-CONSCIOUS...
TURN
PLUS, WITH KANOKO I SHOULD BE FINE.
WE'VE BEEN TOGETHER ON SCHOOL TRIPS BEFORE.

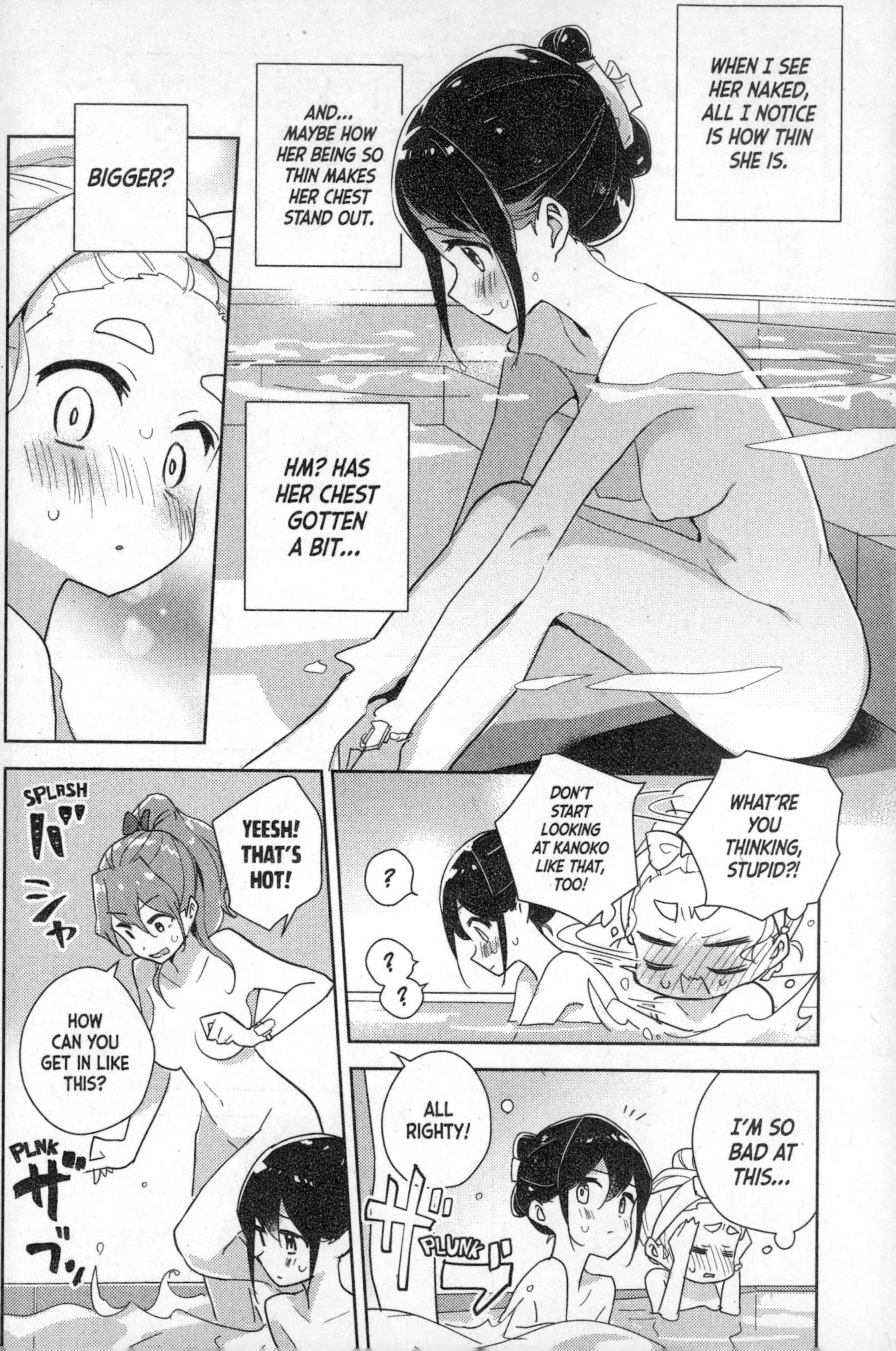
WHEN I SEE HER NAKED, ALL I NOTICE IS HOW THIN SHE IS.
AND... MAYBE HOW HER BEING SO THIN MAKES HER CHEST STAND OUT.
HM? HAS HER CHEST GOTTEN A BIT...
BIGGER?
WHAT'RE YOU THINKING, STUPID?!
DON'T START LOOKING AT KANOKO LIKE THAT, TOO!
?
??
I'M SO BAD AT THIS...
ALL RIGHTY!
PLUNK
SPLASH
YEESH! THAT'S HOT!
HOW CAN YOU GET IN LIKE THIS?
PLNK

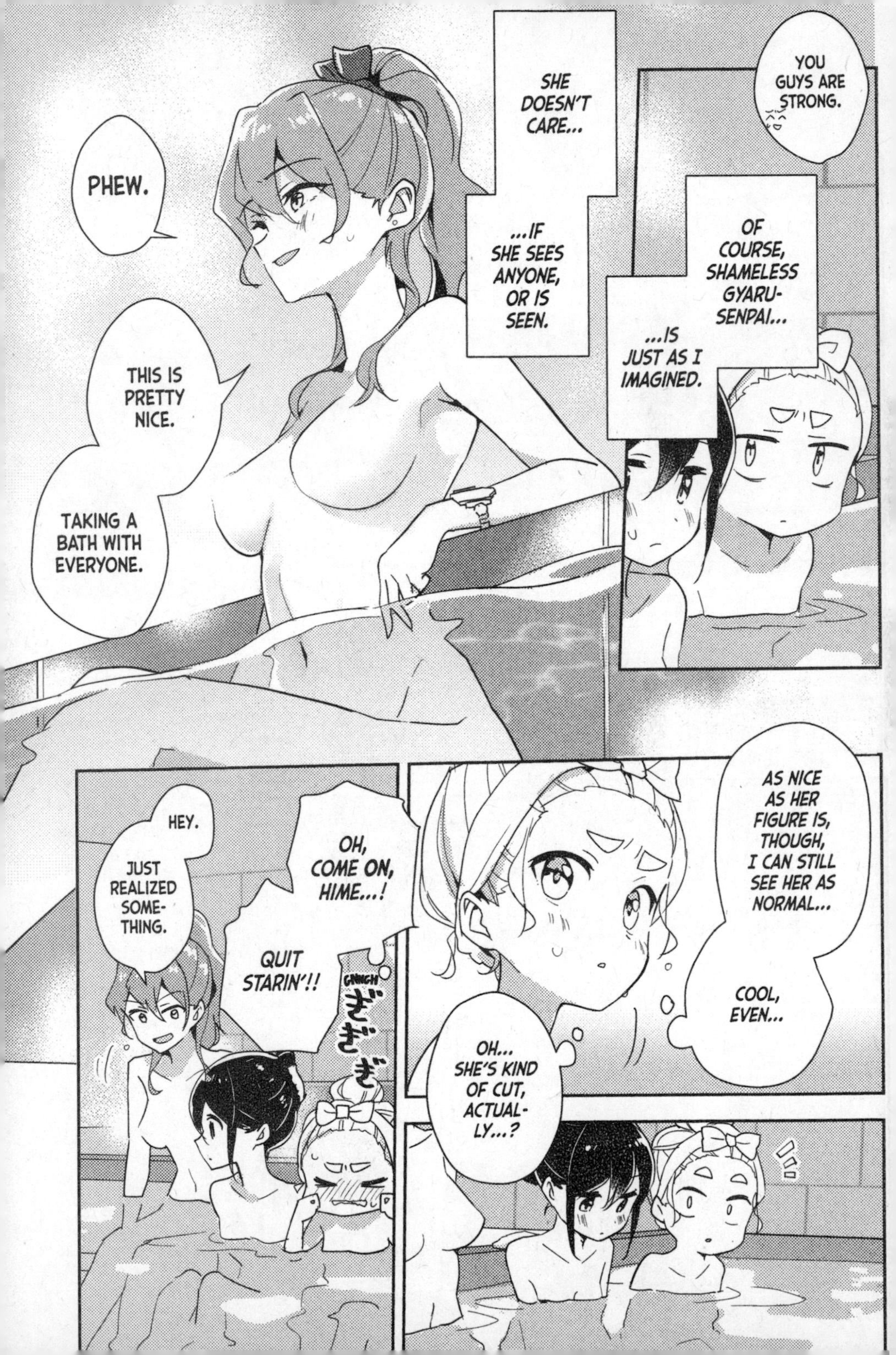
YOU GUYS ARE STRONG.
OF COURSE, SHAMELESS GYARU-SENPAI...
...IS JUST AS I IMAGINED.
SHE DOESN'T CARE...
...IF SHE SEES ANYONE, OR IS SEEN.
PHEW.
THIS IS PRETTY NICE.
TAKING A BATH WITH EVERYONE.
AS NICE AS HER FIGURE IS, THOUGH, I CAN STILL SEE HER AS NORMAL...
COOL, EVEN...
OH... SHE'S KIND OF CUT, ACTUAL-LY...?
!!
OH, COME ON, HIME...!
QUIT STARIN'!!
GNGH
HEY.
JUST REALIZED SOME-THING.

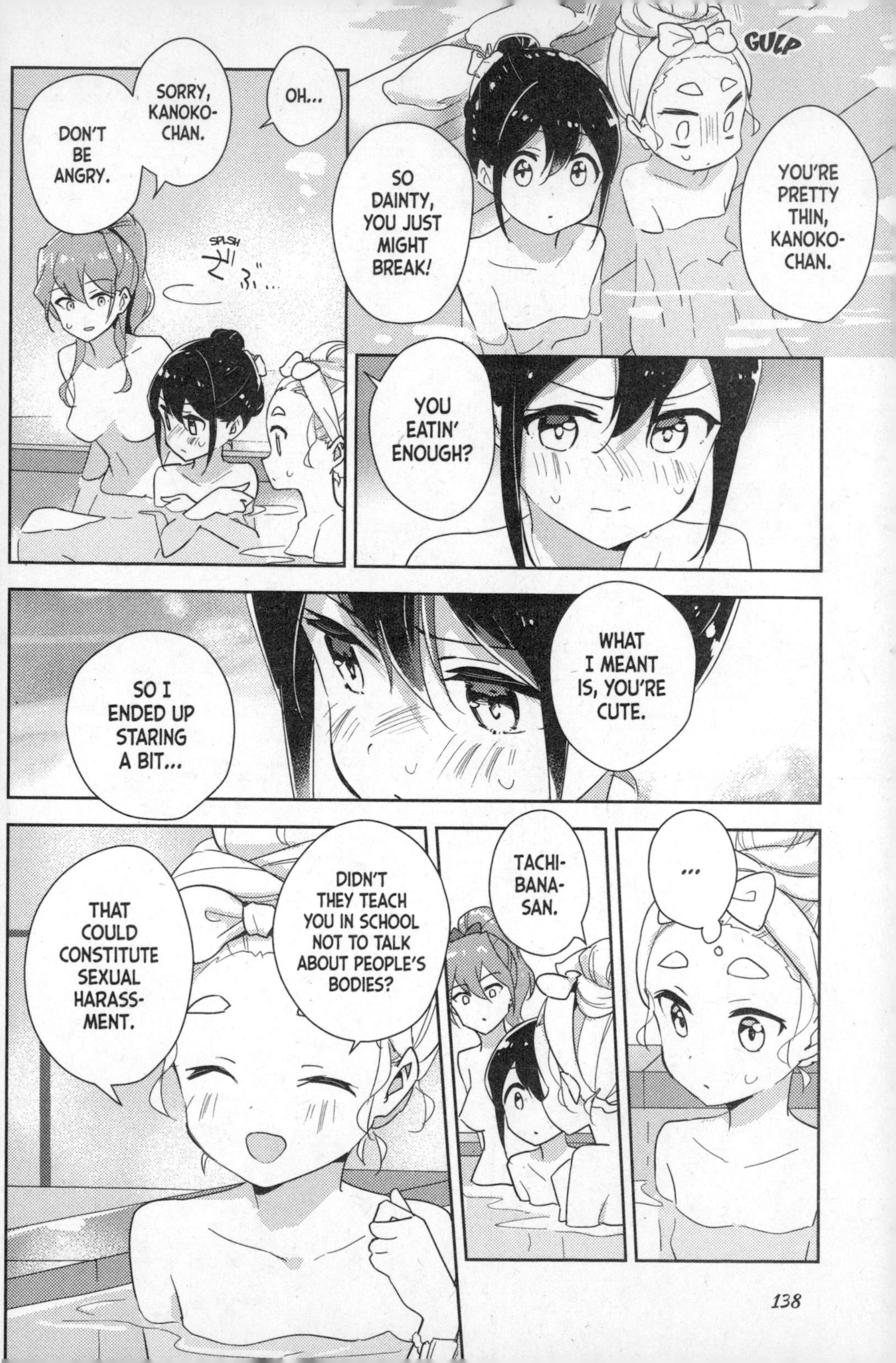
GULP
YOU'RE PRETTY THIN, KANOKO-CHAN.
SO DAINTY, YOU JUST MIGHT BREAK!
YOU EATIN' ENOUGH?
OH...
SORRY, KANOKO-CHAN.
DON'T BE ANGRY.
SPLSH
WHAT I MEANT IS, YOU'RE CUTE.
SO I ENDED UP STARING A BIT...
...
TACHIBANA-SAN.
DIDN'T THEY TEACH YOU IN SCHOOL NOT TO TALK ABOUT PEOPLE'S BODIES?
THAT COULD CONSTITUTE SEXUAL HARASS-MENT.

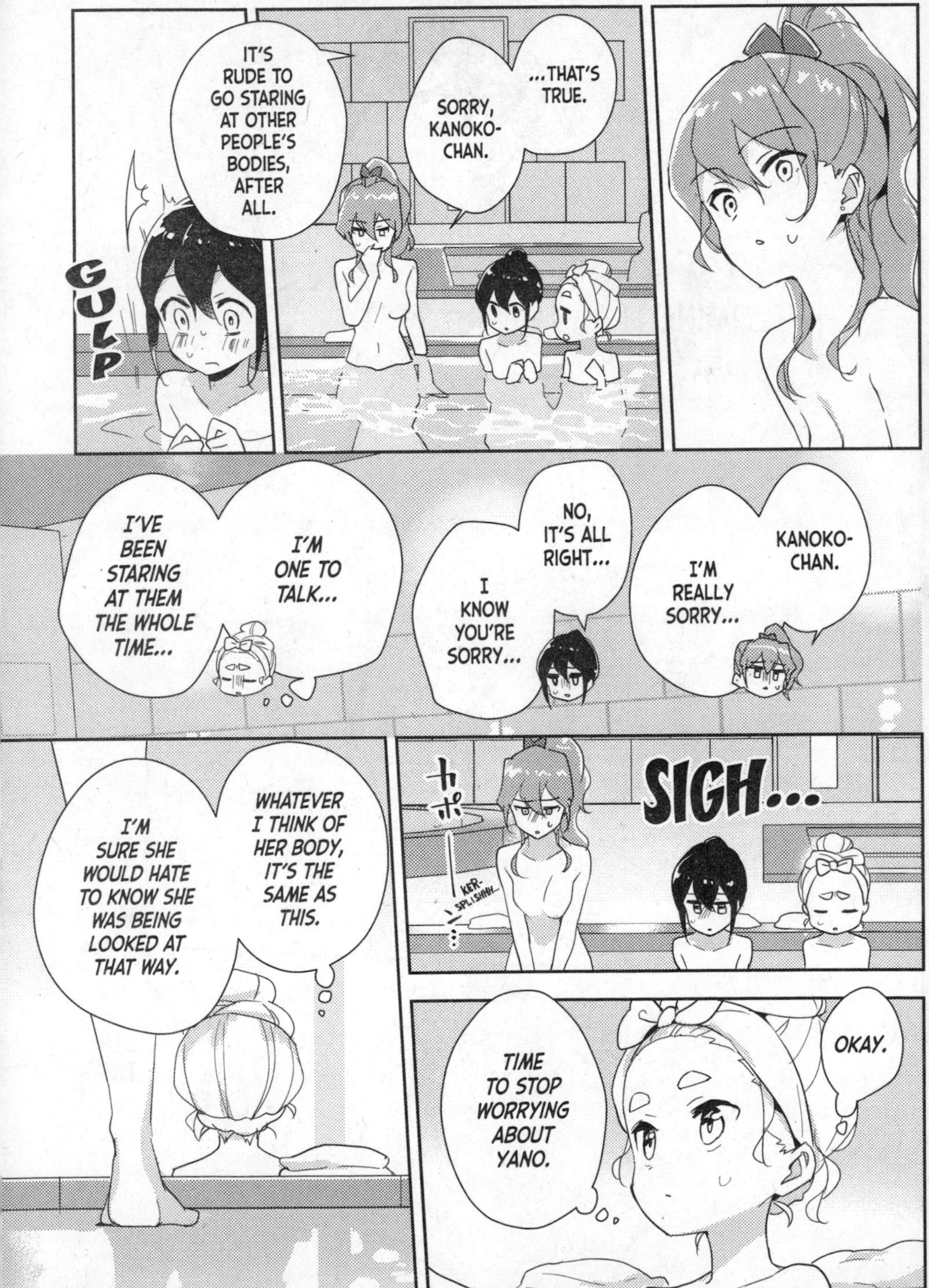
...THAT'S TRUE.
SORRY, KANOKO-CHAN.
IT'S RUDE TO GO STARING AT OTHER PEOPLE'S BODIES, AFTER ALL.
GULP
KANOKO-CHAN.
I'M REALLY SORRY...
NO, IT'S ALL RIGHT...
I KNOW YOU'RE SORRY...
I'M ONE TO TALK...
I'VE BEEN STARING AT THEM THE WHOLE TIME...
SIGH...
カポ
KER-SPLISHHH...
OKAY.
TIME TO STOP WORRYING ABOUT YANO.
WHATEVER I THINK OF HER BODY, IT'S THE SAME AS THIS.
I'M SURE SHE WOULD HATE TO KNOW SHE WAS BEING LOOKED AT THAT WAY.

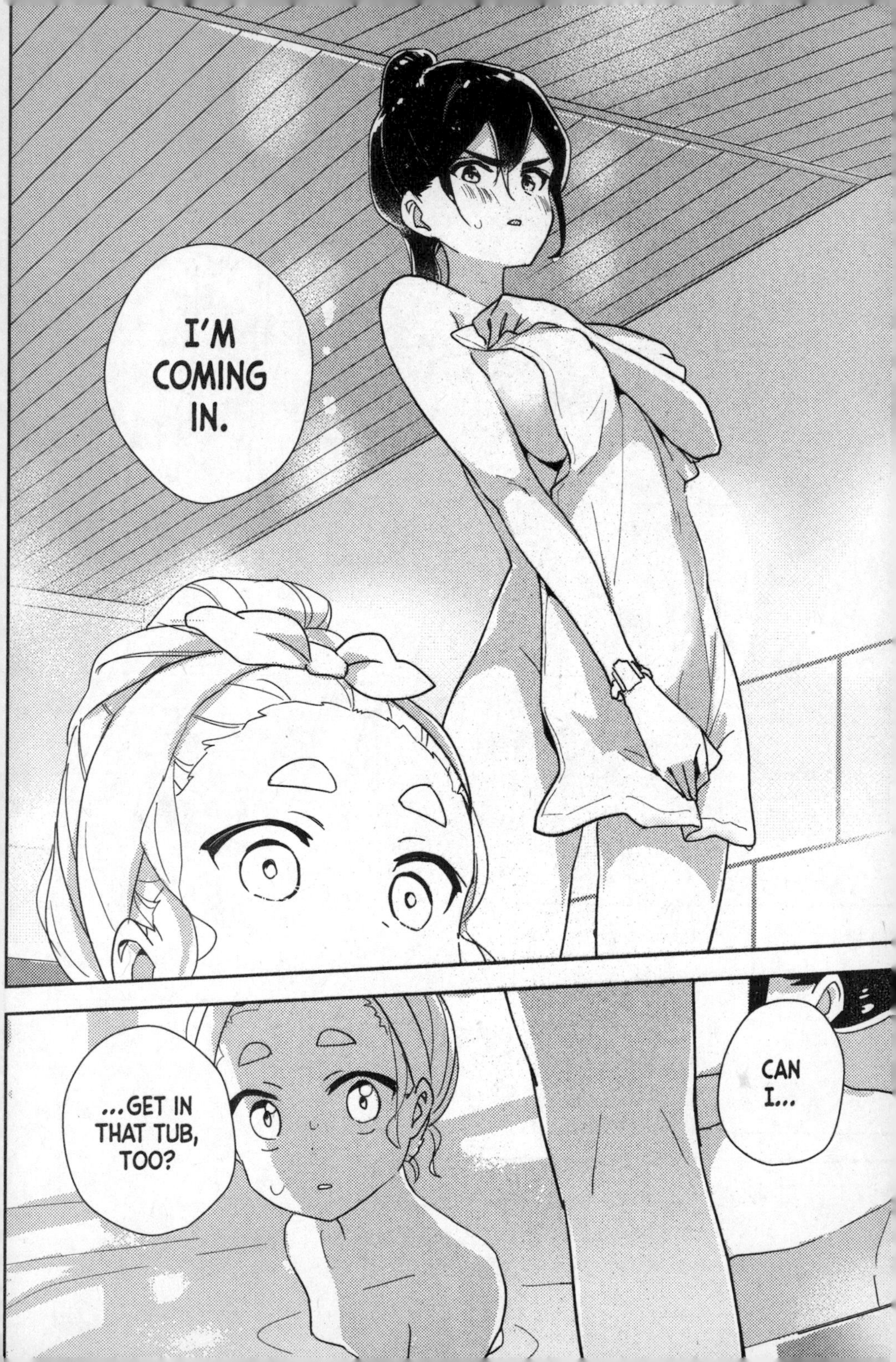
I'M COMING IN.
CAN I...
...GET IN THAT TUB, TOO?

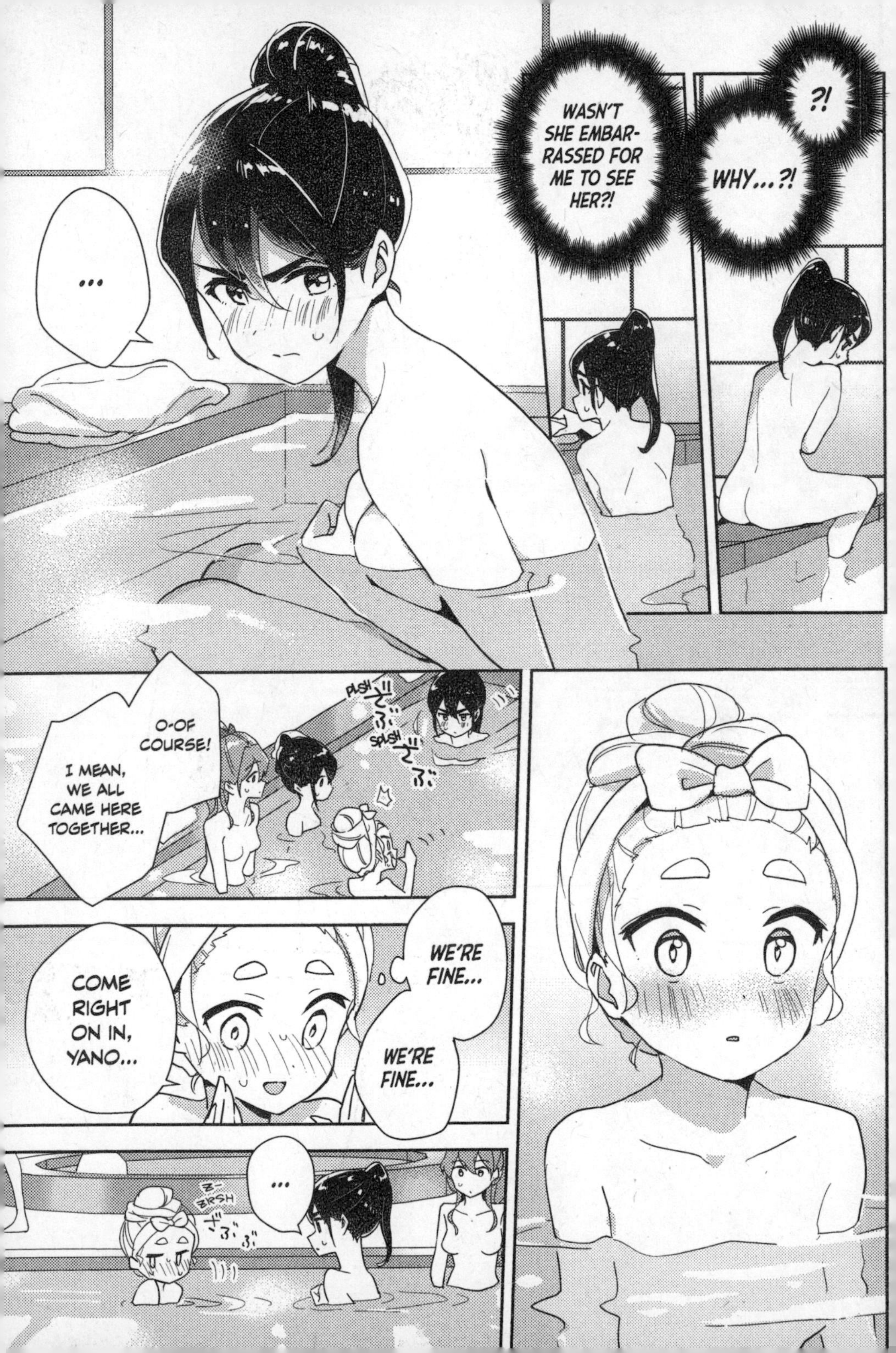

?!
WHY...?!
WASN'T SHE EMBARRASSED FOR ME TO SEE HER?!
...
O-OF COURSE!
I MEAN, WE ALL CAME HERE TOGETHER...
PLSH
SPLSH
WE'RE FINE...
WE'RE FINE...
COME RIGHT ON IN, YANO...
...
B-BRSH

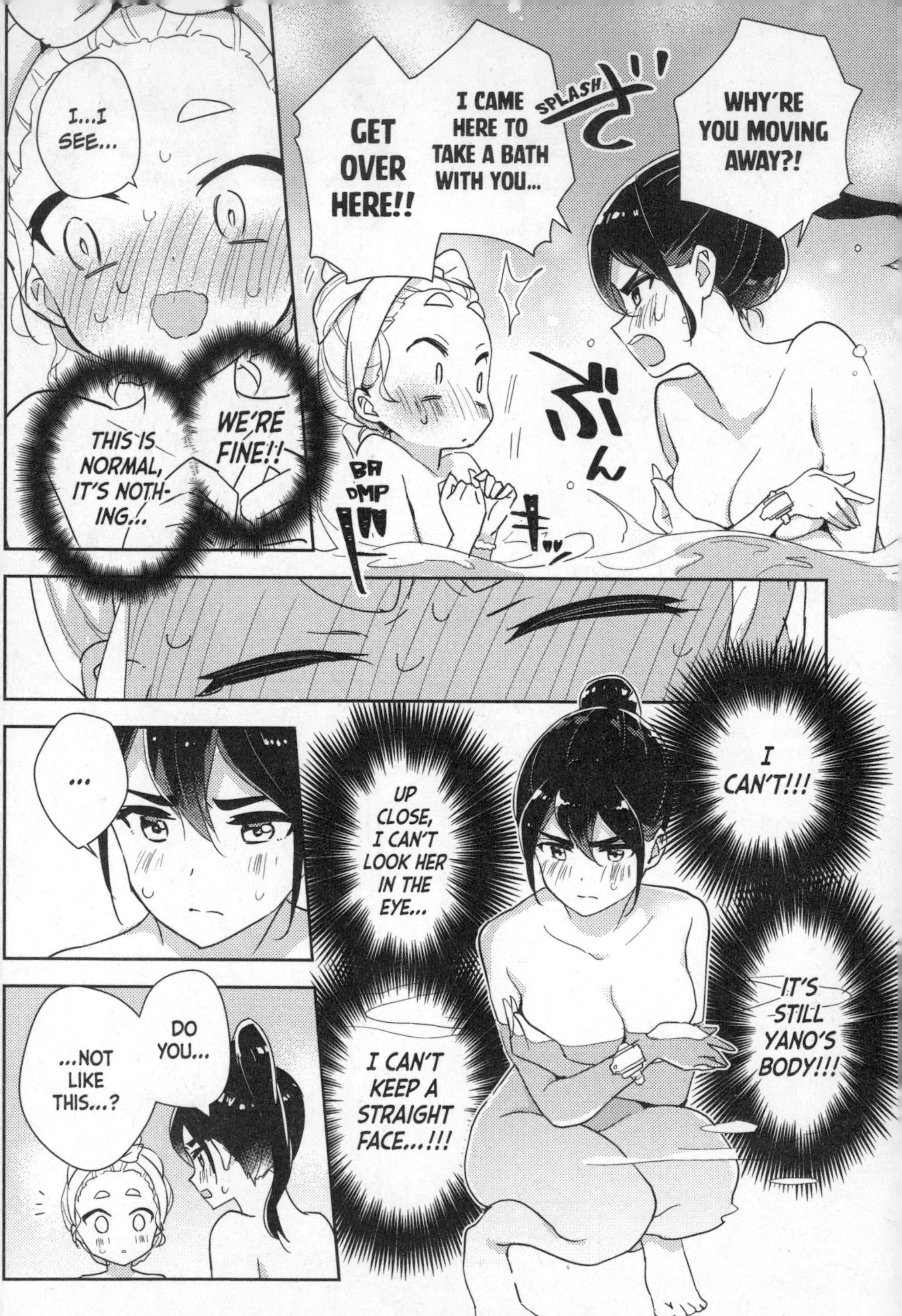
WHY'RE YOU MOVING AWAY?!
SPLASH
ざ
I CAME HERE TO TAKE A BATH WITH YOU...
GET OVER HERE!!
ぶん
BA DMP
I...I SEE...
WE'RE FINE!!
THIS IS NORMAL, IT'S NOTHING...
I CAN'T!!!
UP CLOSE, I CAN'T LOOK HER IN THE EYE...
IT'S STILL YANO'S BODY!!!
I CAN'T KEEP A STRAIGHT FACE...!!!
...
DO YOU...
...NOT LIKE THIS...?

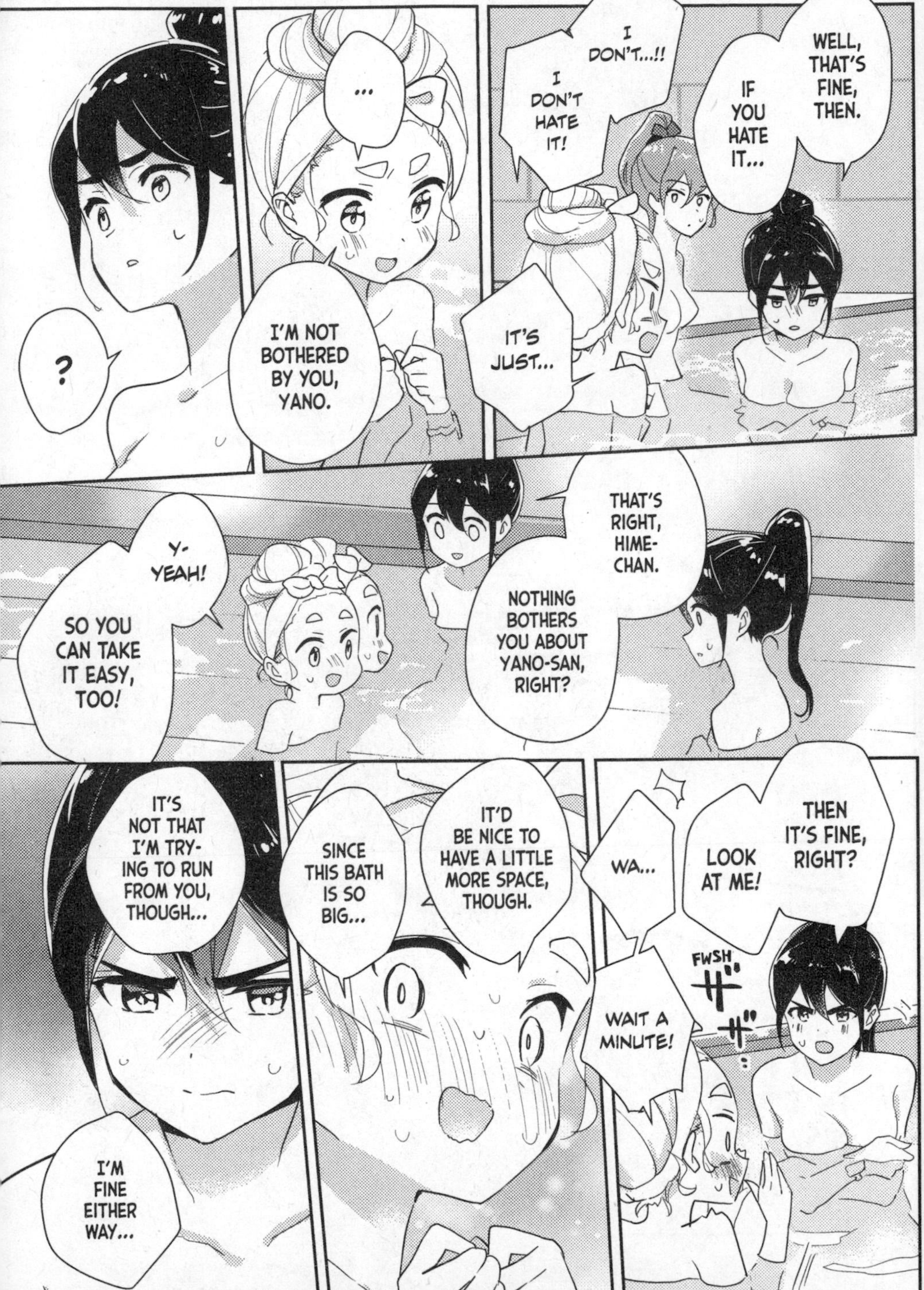
WELL, THAT'S FINE, THEN.
IF YOU HATE IT...
I DON'T...!!
I DON'T HATE IT!
IT'S JUST...
...
I'M NOT BOTHERED BY YOU, YANO.
?
THAT'S RIGHT, HIME-CHAN.
NOTHING BOTHERS YOU ABOUT YANO-SAN, RIGHT?
Y-YEAH!
SO YOU CAN TAKE IT EASY, TOO!
THEN IT'S FINE, RIGHT?
LOOK AT ME!
WA...
FWSH
WAIT A MINUTE!
IT'D BE NICE TO HAVE A LITTLE MORE SPACE, THOUGH.
SINCE THIS BATH IS SO BIG...
IT'S NOT THAT I'M TRYING TO RUN FROM YOU, THOUGH...
I'M FINE EITHER WAY...

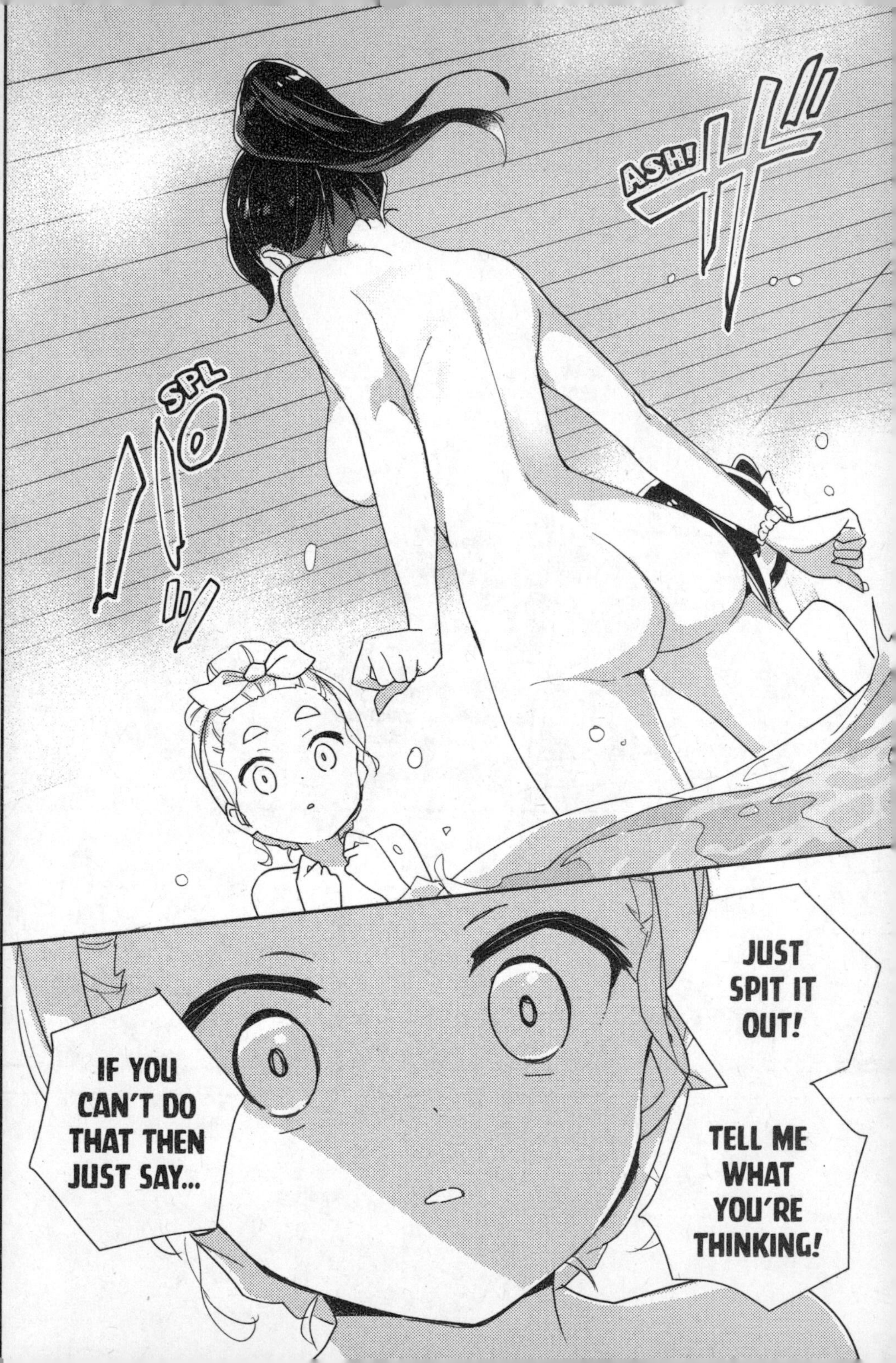
ASH!
SPL
JUST SPIT IT OUT!
TELL ME WHAT YOU'RE THINKING!
IF YOU CAN'T DO THAT THEN JUST SAY...

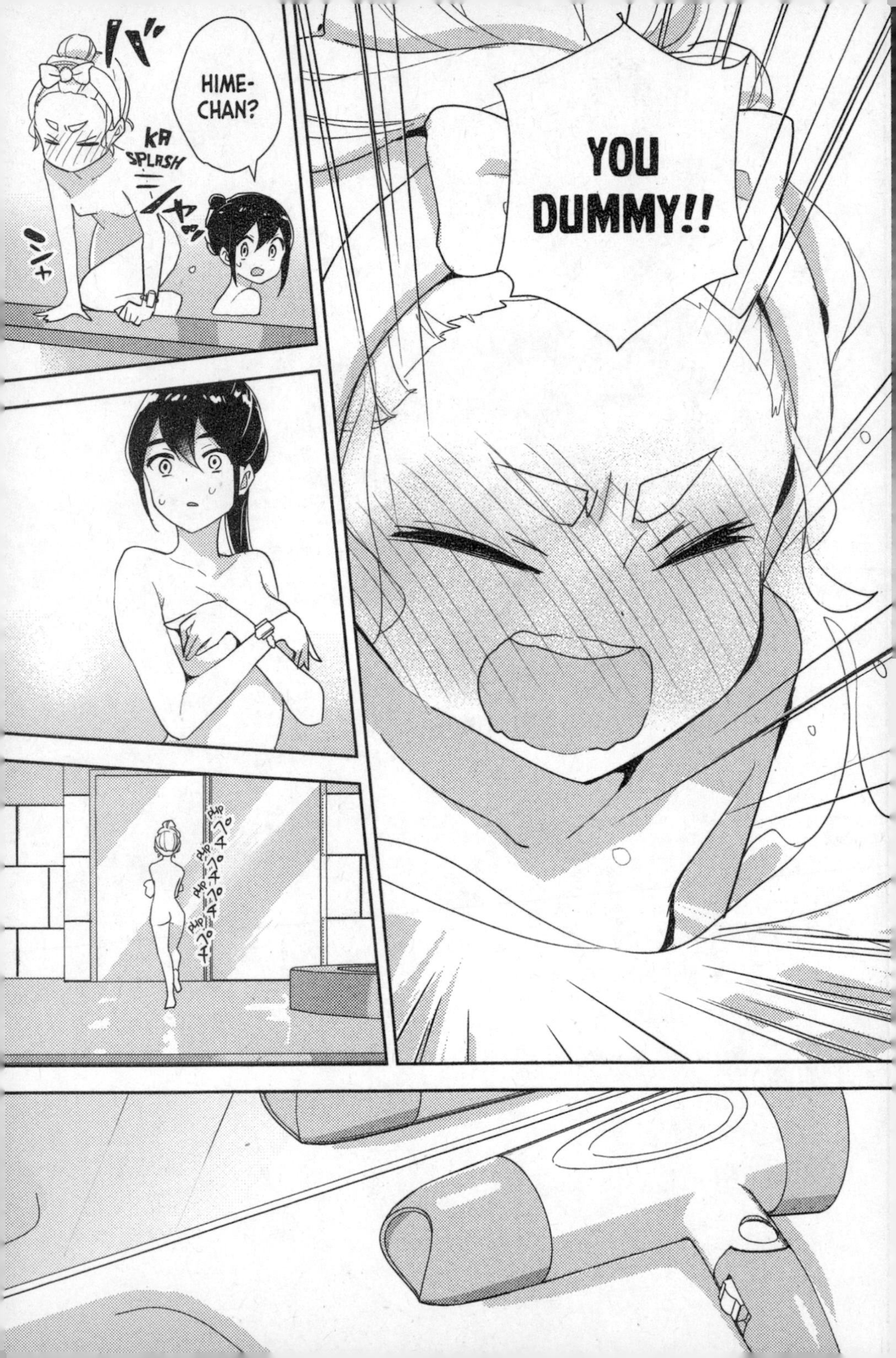
YOU DUMMY!!
HIME-CHAN?
KA SPLASH
pup
pup
pup
pup

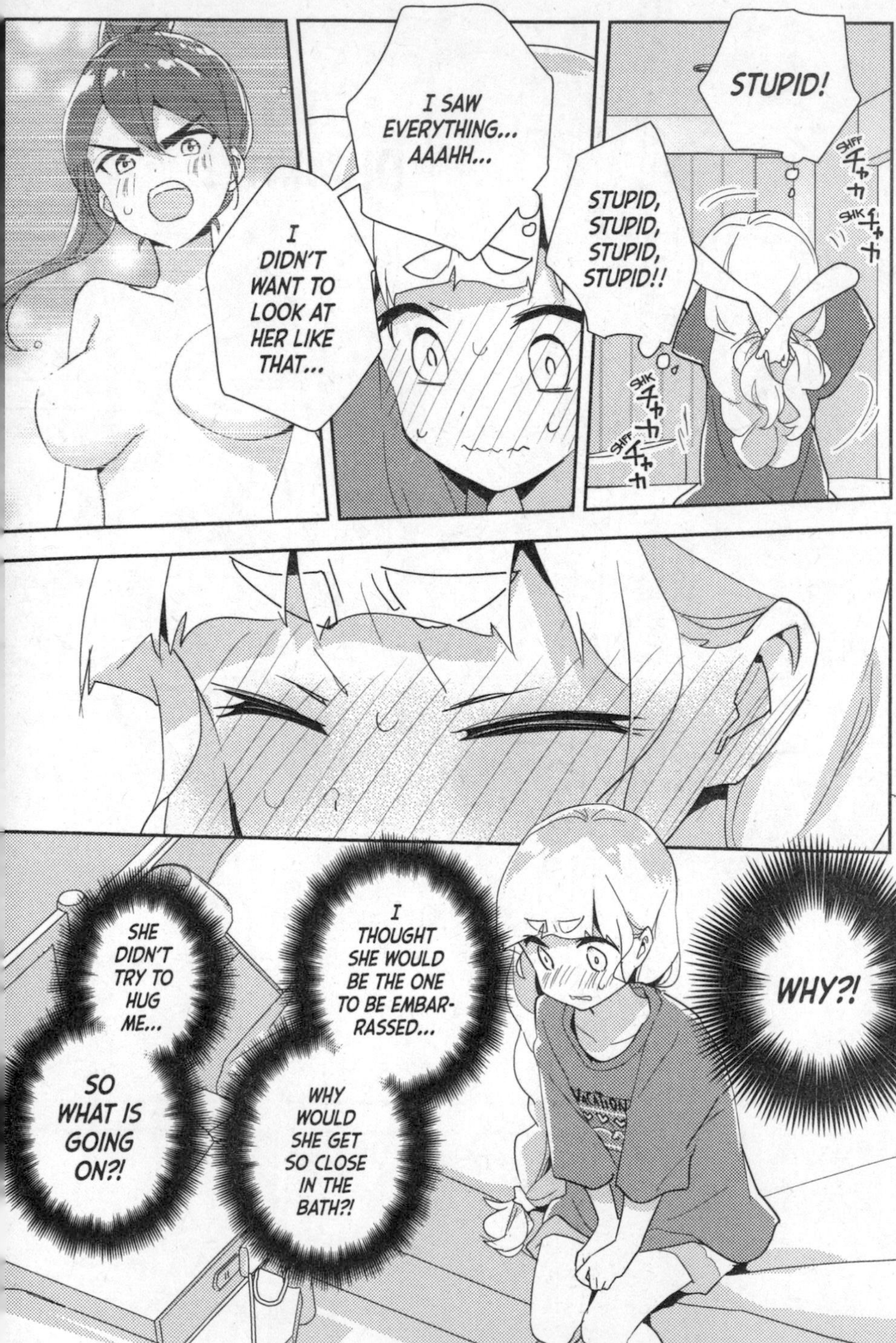
STUPID!
STUPID, STUPID, STUPID, STUPID!!
SHFF
SHK
SHK
SHFF
I SAW EVERYTHING... AAAHH...
I DIDN'T WANT TO LOOK AT HER LIKE THAT...
WHY?!
I THOUGHT SHE WOULD BE THE ONE TO BE EMBARRASSED...
WHY WOULD SHE GET SO CLOSE IN THE BATH?!
SHE DIDN'T TRY TO HUG ME...
SO WHAT IS GOING ON?!

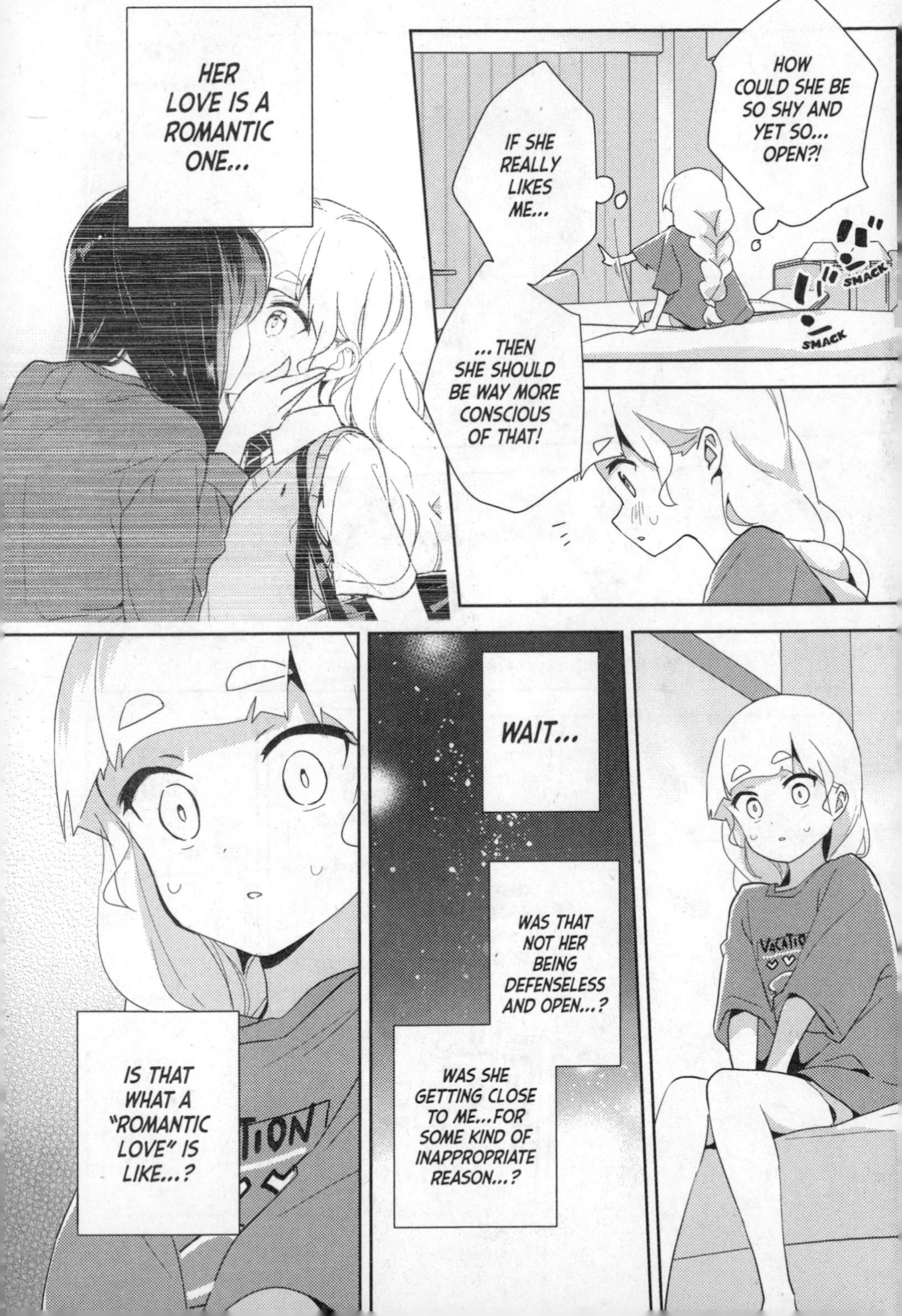
HOW COULD SHE BE SO SHY AND YET SO... OPEN?!
IF SHE REALLY LIKES ME...
SMACK
SMACK
...THEN SHE SHOULD BE WAY MORE CONSCIOUS OF THAT!
HER LOVE IS A ROMANTIC ONE...
WAIT...
WAS THAT NOT HER BEING DEFENSELESS AND OPEN...?
WAS SHE GETTING CLOSE TO ME...FOR SOME KIND OF INAPPROPRIATE REASON...?
IS THAT WHAT A "ROMANTIC LOVE" IS LIKE...?

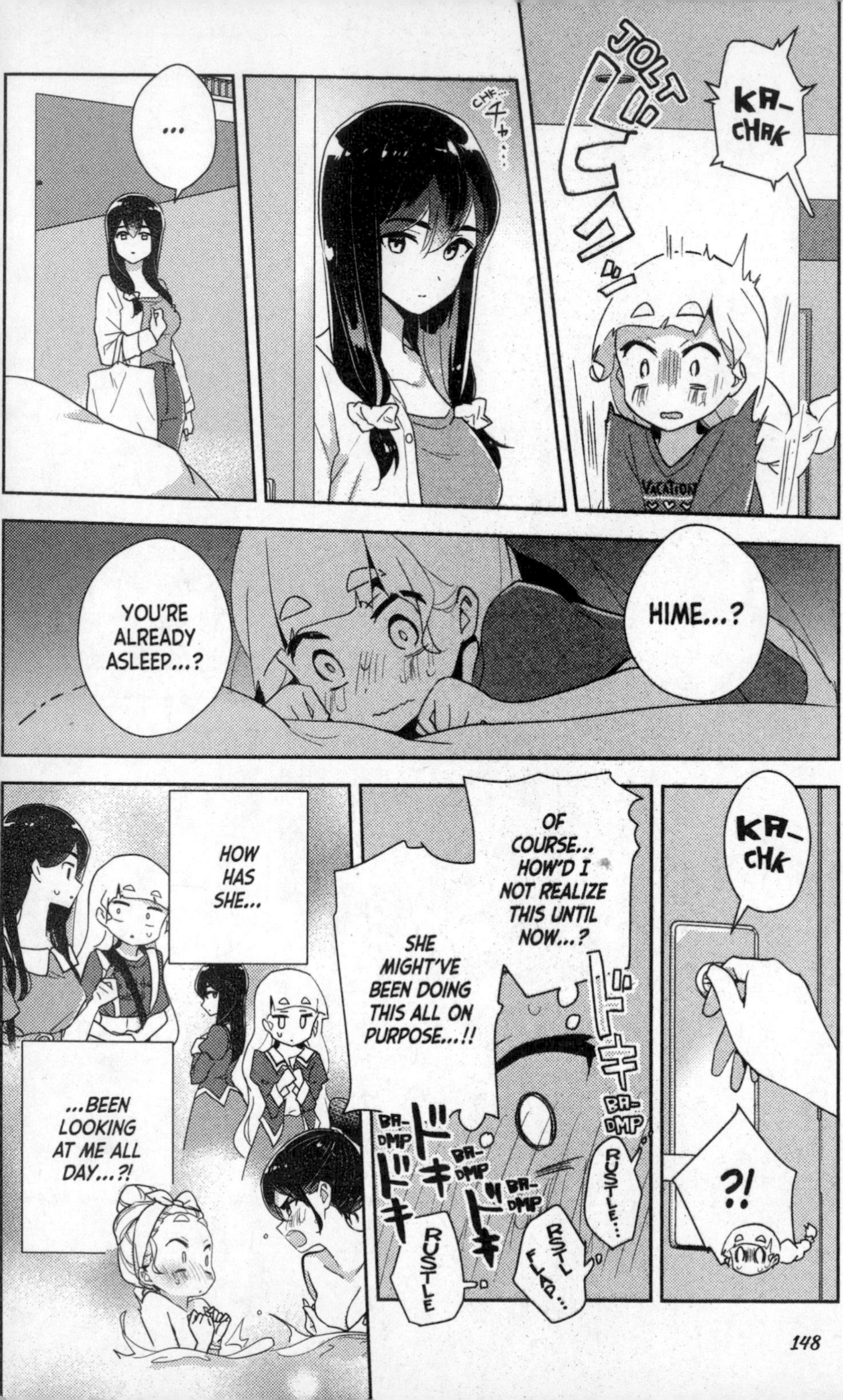
JOLT
KA-CHAK
CHK...
...
HIME...?
YOU'RE ALREADY ASLEEP...?
KA-CHK
?!
OF COURSE... HOW'D I NOT REALIZE THIS UNTIL NOW...?
SHE MIGHT'VE BEEN DOING THIS ALL ON PURPOSE...!!
BA-DMP
RUSTLE...
RSTL FLAP...
BA-DMP
BA-DMP
BA-DMP
RUSTLE
HOW HAS SHE...
...BEEN LOOKING AT ME ALL DAY...?!

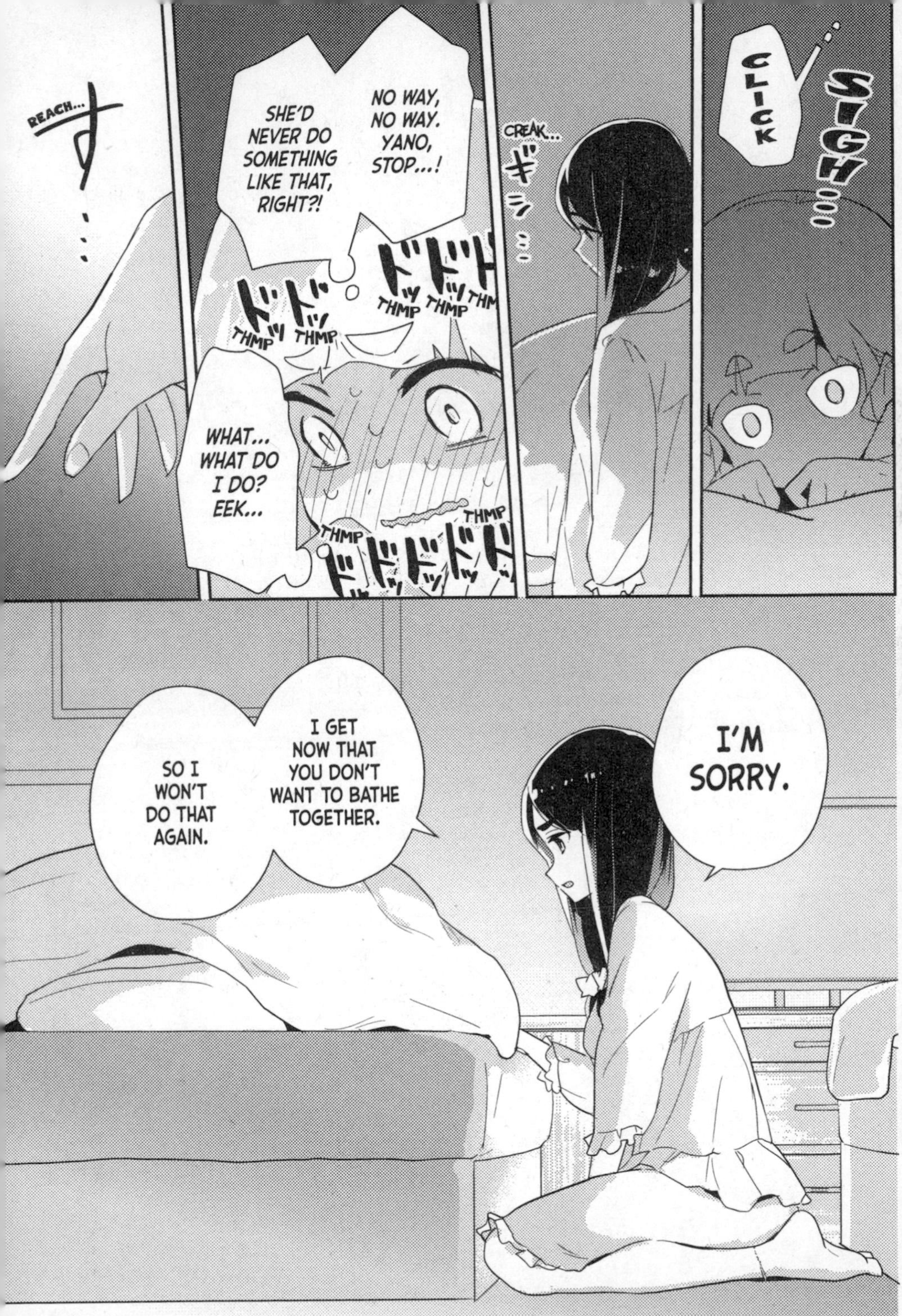
CLICK
SIGH...
CREAK...
NO WAY, NO WAY. YANO, STOP...!
SHE'D NEVER DO SOMETHING LIKE THAT, RIGHT?!
THMP THMP THMP
THMP THMP
WHAT... WHAT DO I DO? EEK...
THMP THMP
REACH...
I'M SORRY.
I GET NOW THAT YOU DON'T WANT TO BATHE TOGETHER.
SO I WON'T DO THAT AGAIN.

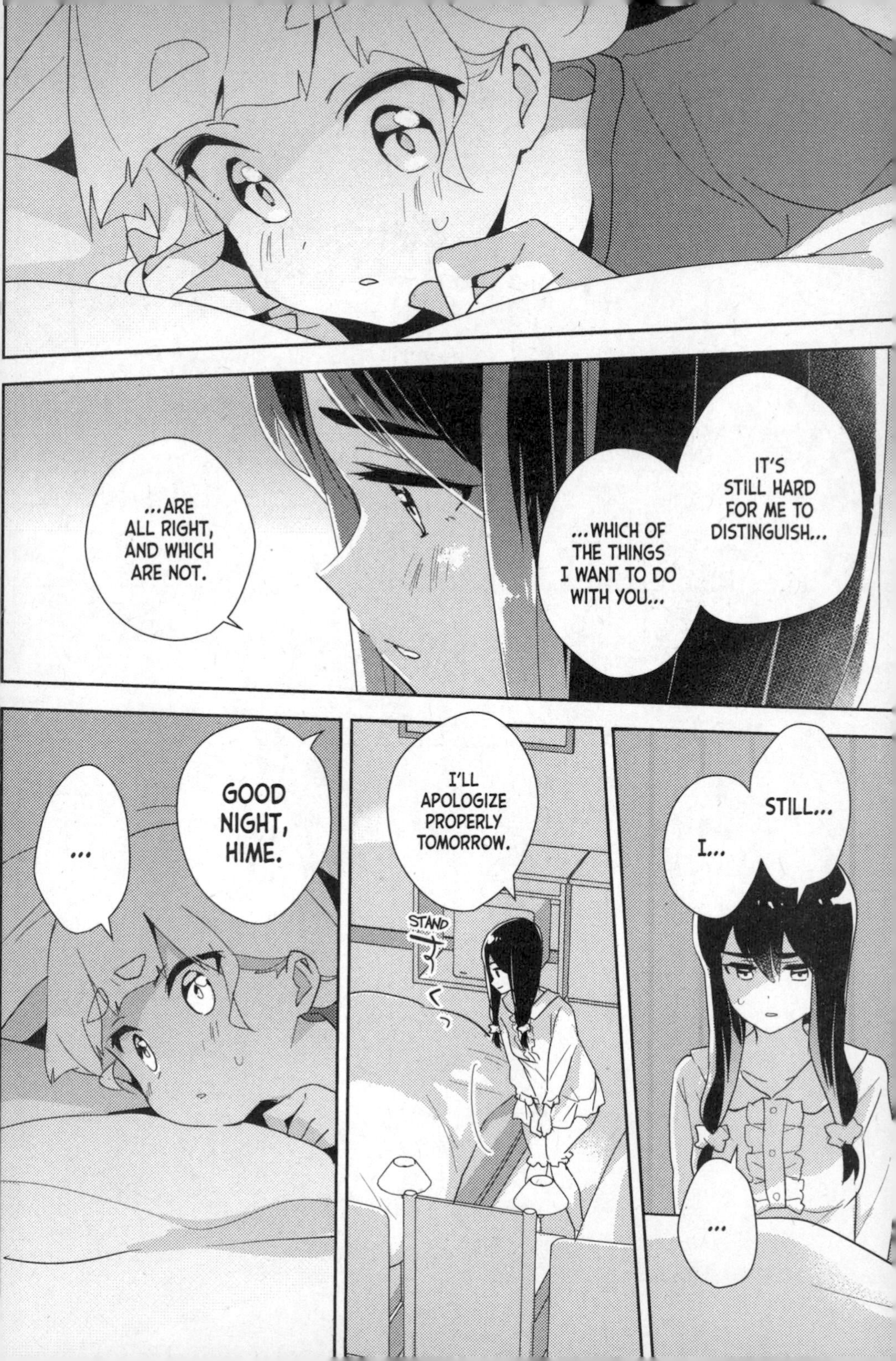
IT'S STILL HARD FOR ME TO DISTINGUISH...
...WHICH OF THE THINGS I WANT TO DO WITH YOU...
...ARE ALL RIGHT, AND WHICH ARE NOT.
STILL...
I...
...
I'LL APOLOGIZE PROPERLY TOMORROW.
STAND
GOOD NIGHT, HIME.
...

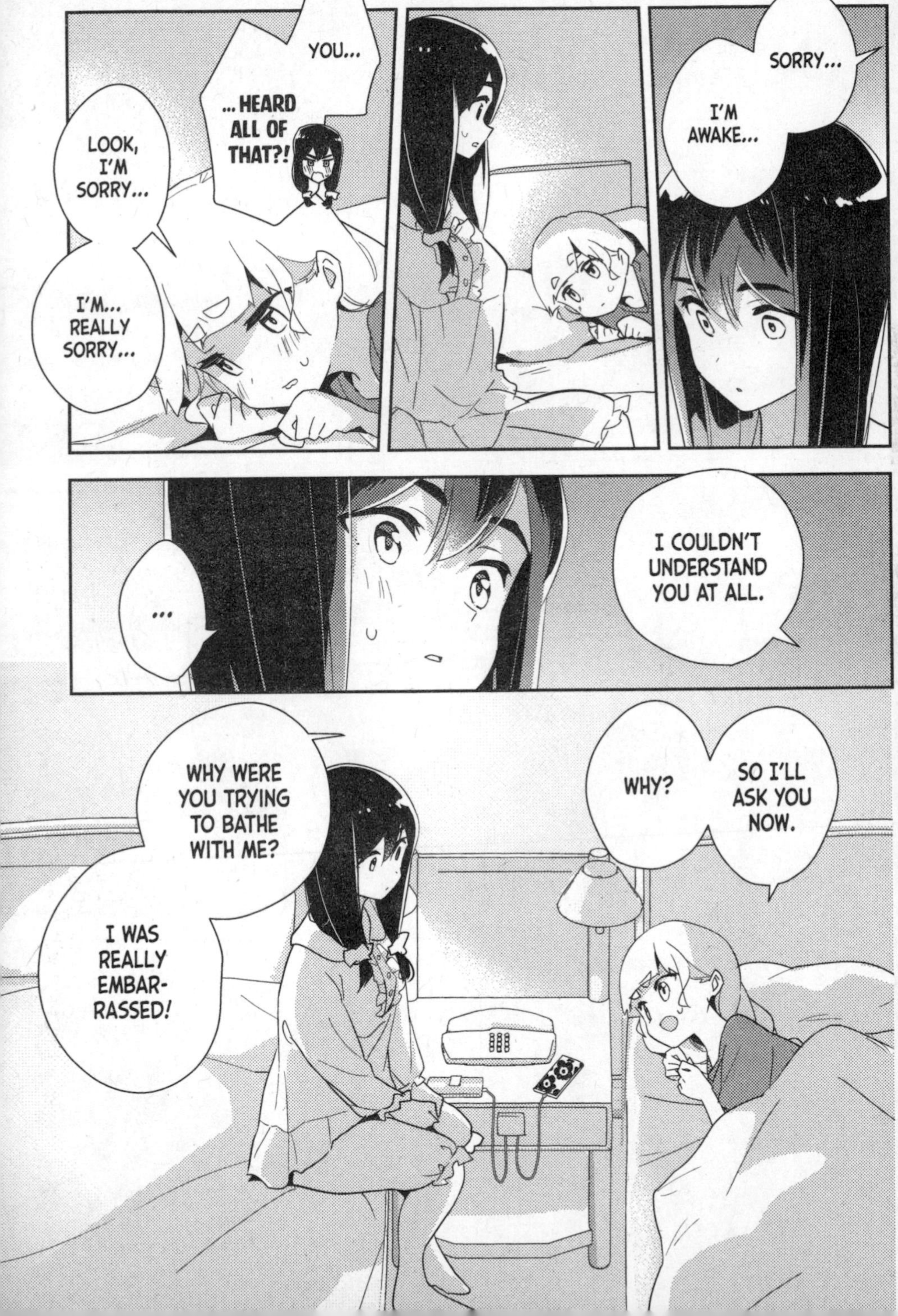
SORRY...
I'M AWAKE...
YOU...
...HEARD ALL OF THAT?!
LOOK, I'M SORRY...
I'M... REALLY SORRY...
I COULDN'T UNDERSTAND YOU AT ALL.
...
SO I'LL ASK YOU NOW.
WHY?
WHY WERE YOU TRYING TO BATHE WITH ME?
I WAS REALLY EMBARRASSED!

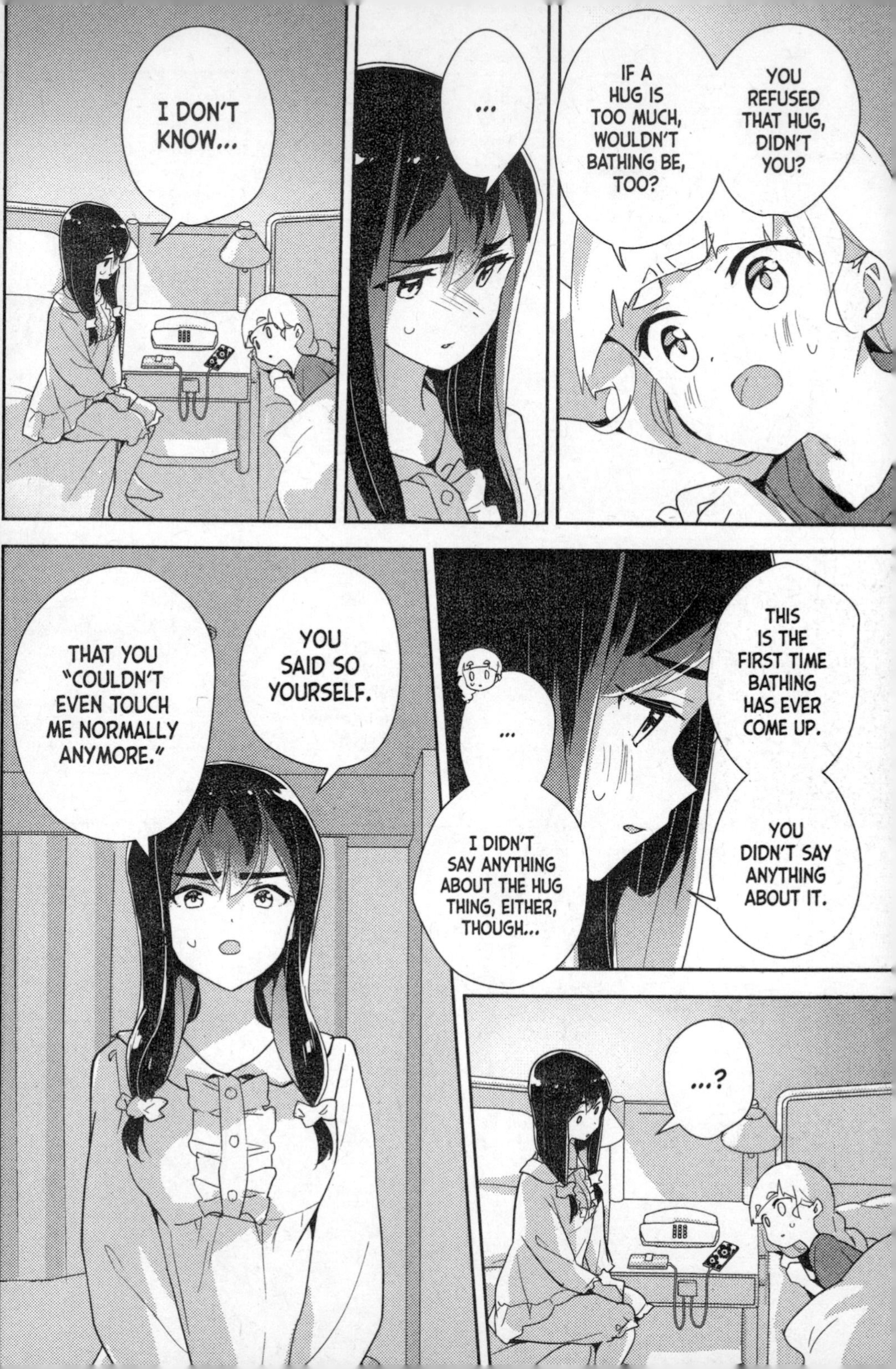
YOU REFUSED THAT HUG, DIDN'T YOU?
IF A HUG IS TOO MUCH, WOULDN'T BATHING BE, TOO?
...
I DON'T KNOW...
THIS IS THE FIRST TIME BATHING HAS EVER COME UP.
YOU DIDN'T SAY ANYTHING ABOUT IT.
...
I DIDN'T SAY ANYTHING ABOUT THE HUG THING, EITHER, THOUGH...
...?
YOU SAID SO YOURSELF.
THAT YOU "COULDN'T EVEN TOUCH ME NORMALLY ANYMORE."

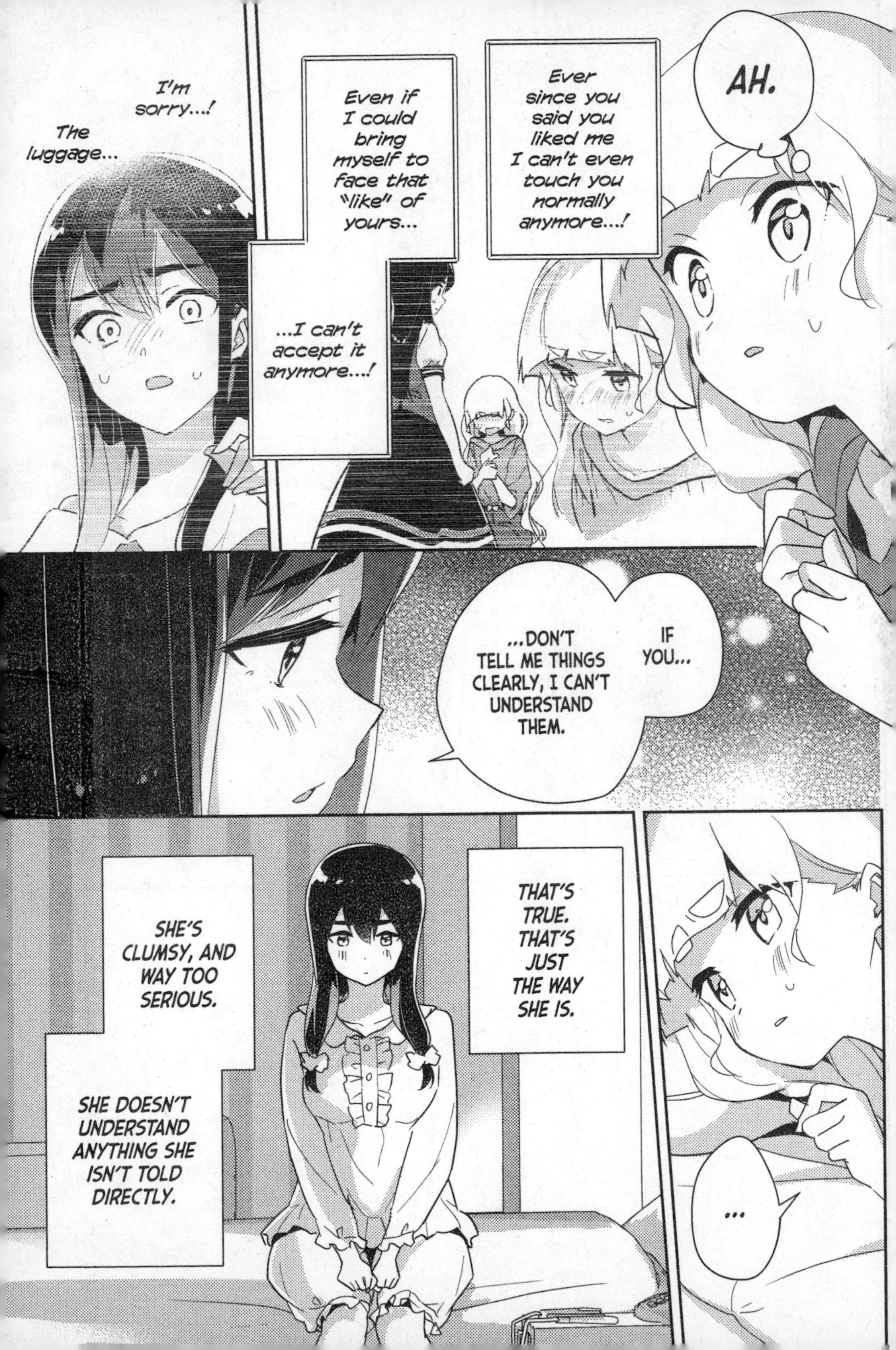
AH.
Ever since you said you liked me I can't even touch you normally anymore...!
Even if I could bring myself to face that "like" of yours...
...I can't accept it anymore...!
I'm sorry...!
The luggage...
IF YOU...
...DON'T TELL ME THINGS CLEARLY, I CAN'T UNDERSTAND THEM.
...
THAT'S TRUE. THAT'S JUST THE WAY SHE IS.
SHE'S CLUMSY, AND WAY TOO SERIOUS.
SHE DOESN'T UNDERSTAND ANYTHING SHE ISN'T TOLD DIRECTLY.

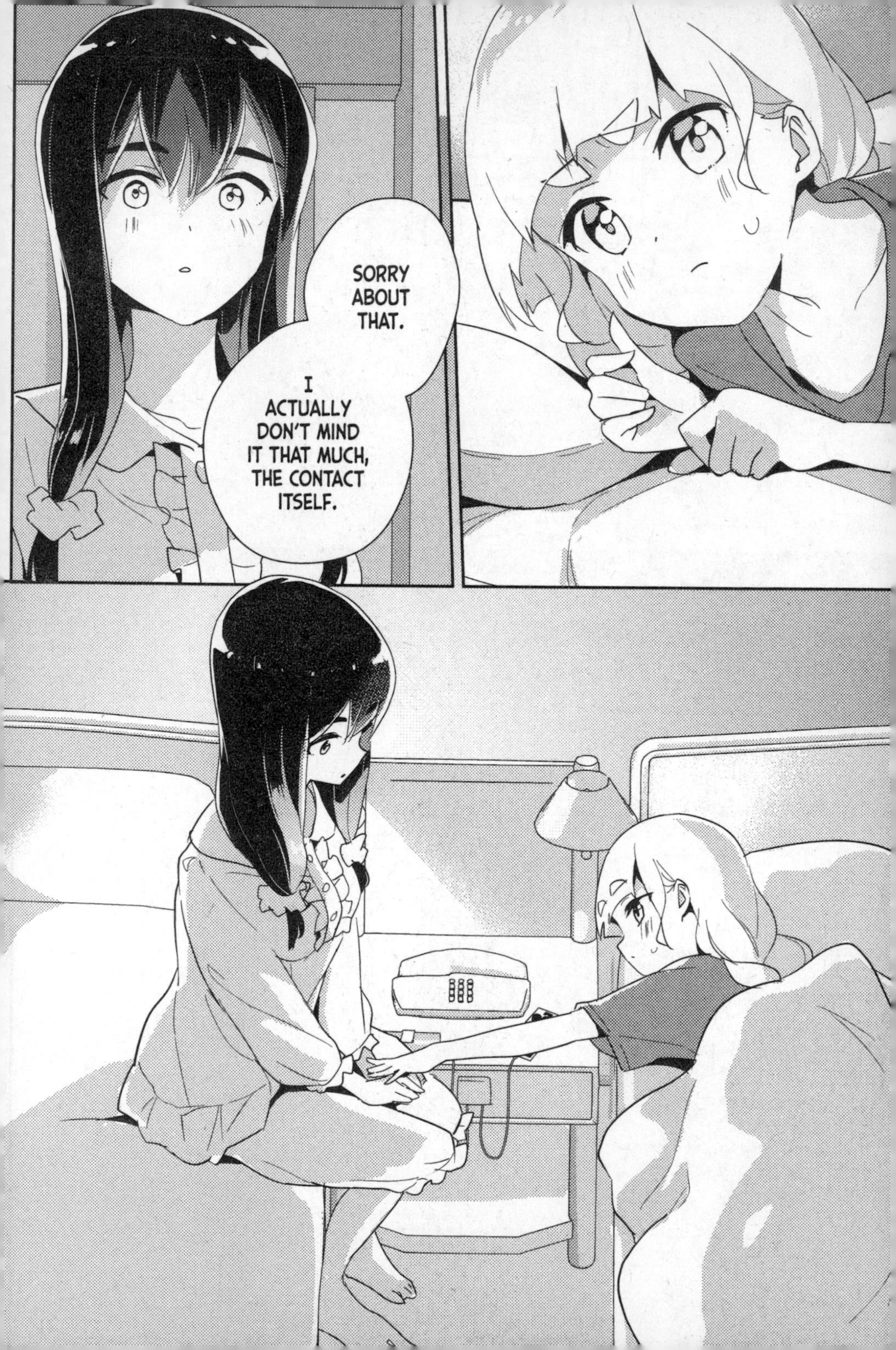

SORRY ABOUT THAT.
I ACTUALLY DON'T MIND IT THAT MUCH, THE CONTACT ITSELF.

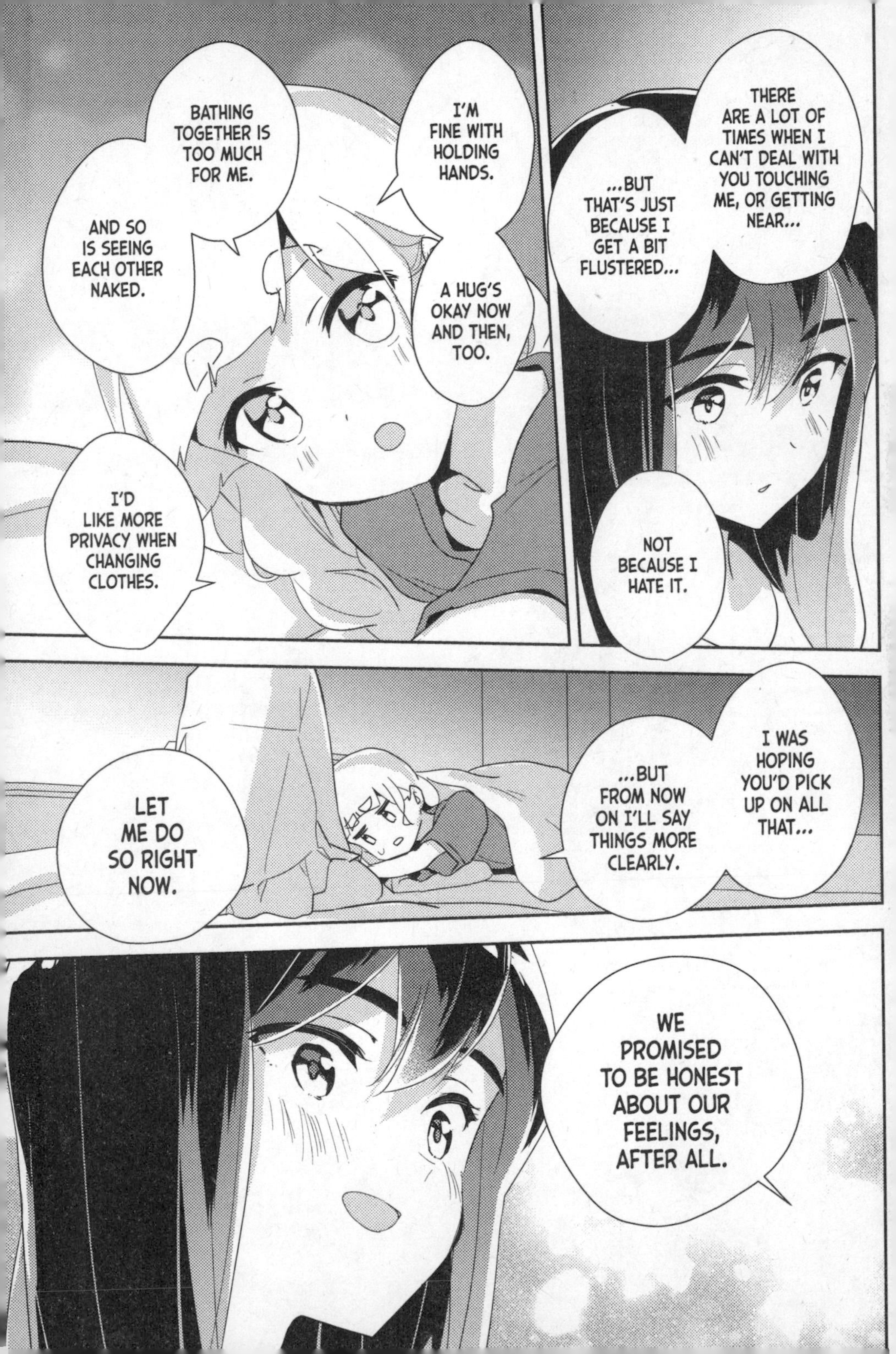
THERE ARE A LOT OF TIMES WHEN I CAN'T DEAL WITH YOU TOUCHING ME, OR GETTING NEAR...
...BUT THAT'S JUST BECAUSE I GET A BIT FLUSTERED...
NOT BECAUSE I HATE IT.
I'M FINE WITH HOLDING HANDS.
A HUG'S OKAY NOW AND THEN, TOO.
BATHING TOGETHER IS TOO MUCH FOR ME.
AND SO IS SEEING EACH OTHER NAKED.
I'D LIKE MORE PRIVACY WHEN CHANGING CLOTHES.
I WAS HOPING YOU'D PICK UP ON ALL THAT...
...BUT FROM NOW ON I'LL SAY THINGS MORE CLEARLY.
LET ME DO SO RIGHT NOW.
WE PROMISED TO BE HONEST ABOUT OUR FEELINGS, AFTER ALL.

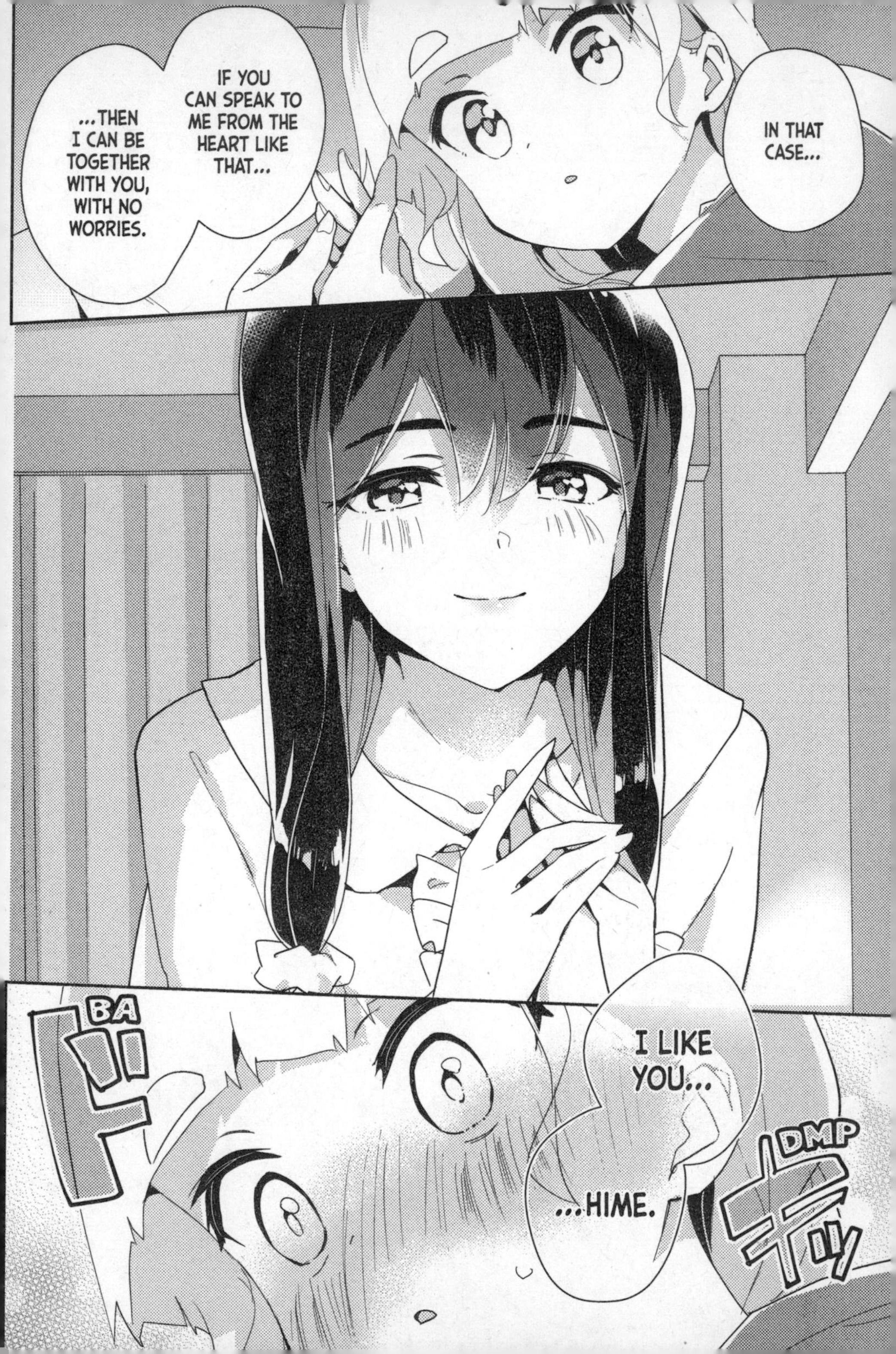
IN THAT CASE...
IF YOU CAN SPEAK TO ME FROM THE HEART LIKE THAT...
...THEN I CAN BE TOGETHER WITH YOU, WITH NO WORRIES.
I LIKE YOU... ...HIME.
DMP
BA

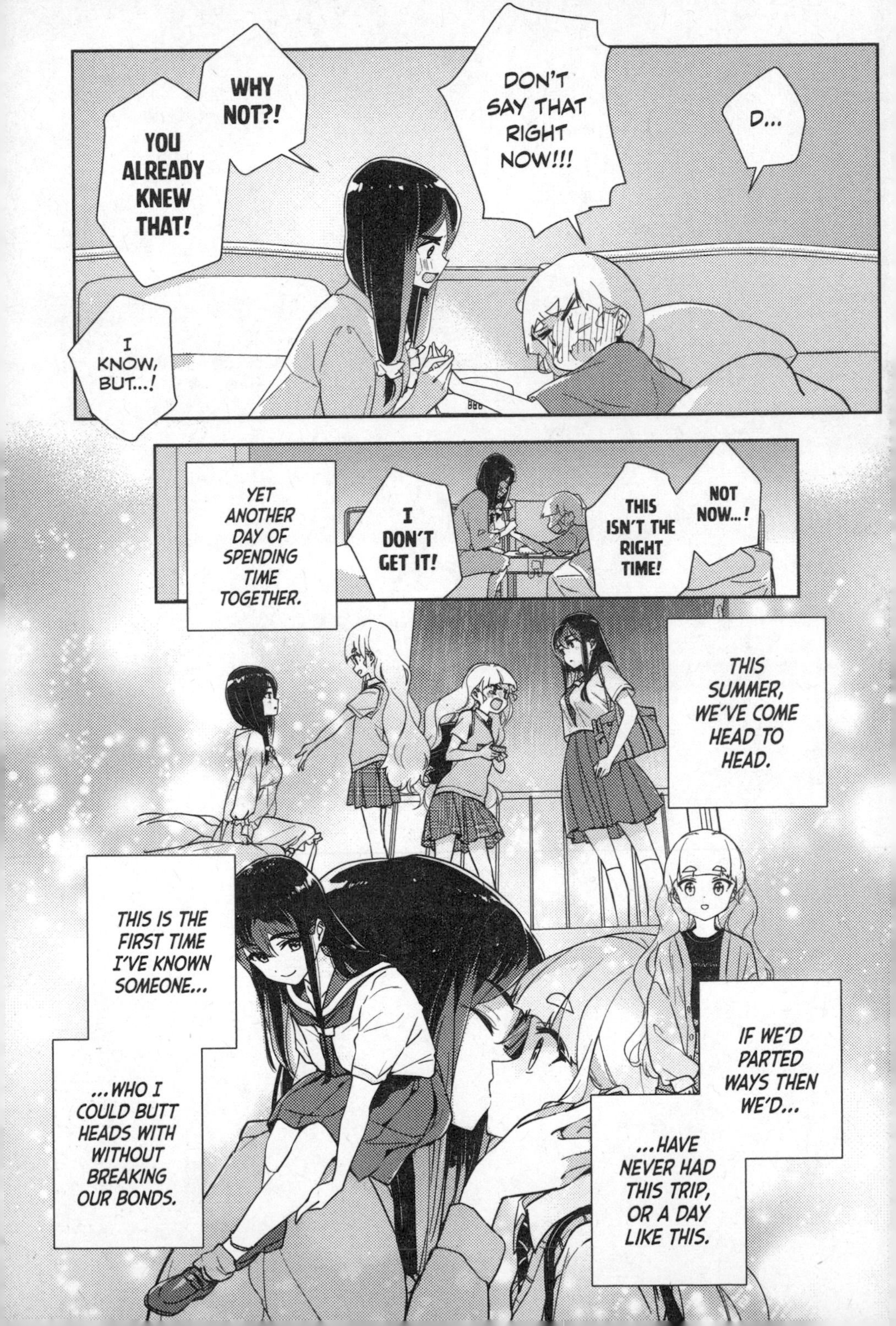
D...
DON'T SAY THAT RIGHT NOW!!!
WHY NOT?!
YOU ALREADY KNEW THAT!
I KNOW, BUT...!
NOT NOW...!
THIS ISN'T THE RIGHT TIME!
I DON'T GET IT!
YET ANOTHER DAY OF SPENDING TIME TOGETHER.
THIS SUMMER, WE'VE COME HEAD TO HEAD.
IF WE'D PARTED WAYS THEN WE'D...
...HAVE NEVER HAD THIS TRIP, OR A DAY LIKE THIS.
THIS IS THE FIRST TIME I'VE KNOWN SOMEONE...
...WHO I COULD BUTT HEADS WITH WITHOUT BREAKING OUR BONDS.

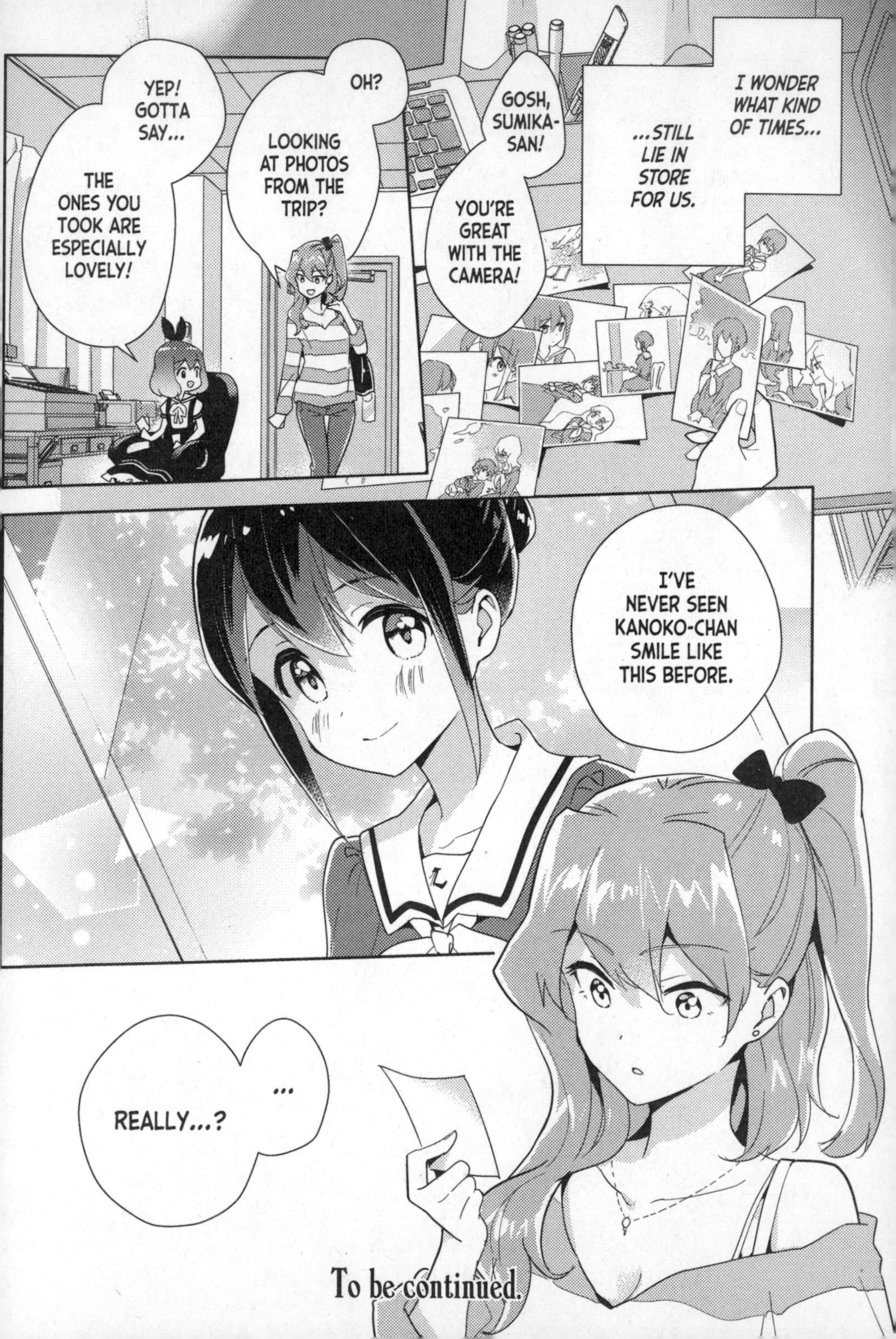
I WONDER WHAT KIND OF TIMES...
...STILL LIE IN STORE FOR US.
GOSH, SUMIKA-SAN!
YOU'RE GREAT WITH THE CAMERA!
OH?
LOOKING AT PHOTOS FROM THE TRIP?
YEP! GOTTA SAY...
THE ONES YOU TOOK ARE ESPECIALLY LOVELY!
I'VE NEVER SEEN KANOKO-CHAN SMILE LIKE THIS BEFORE.
...
REALLY...?
To be continued.

Yuri Is My Job!

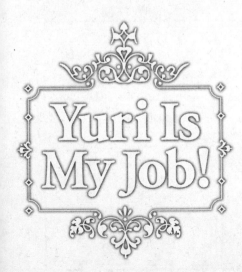

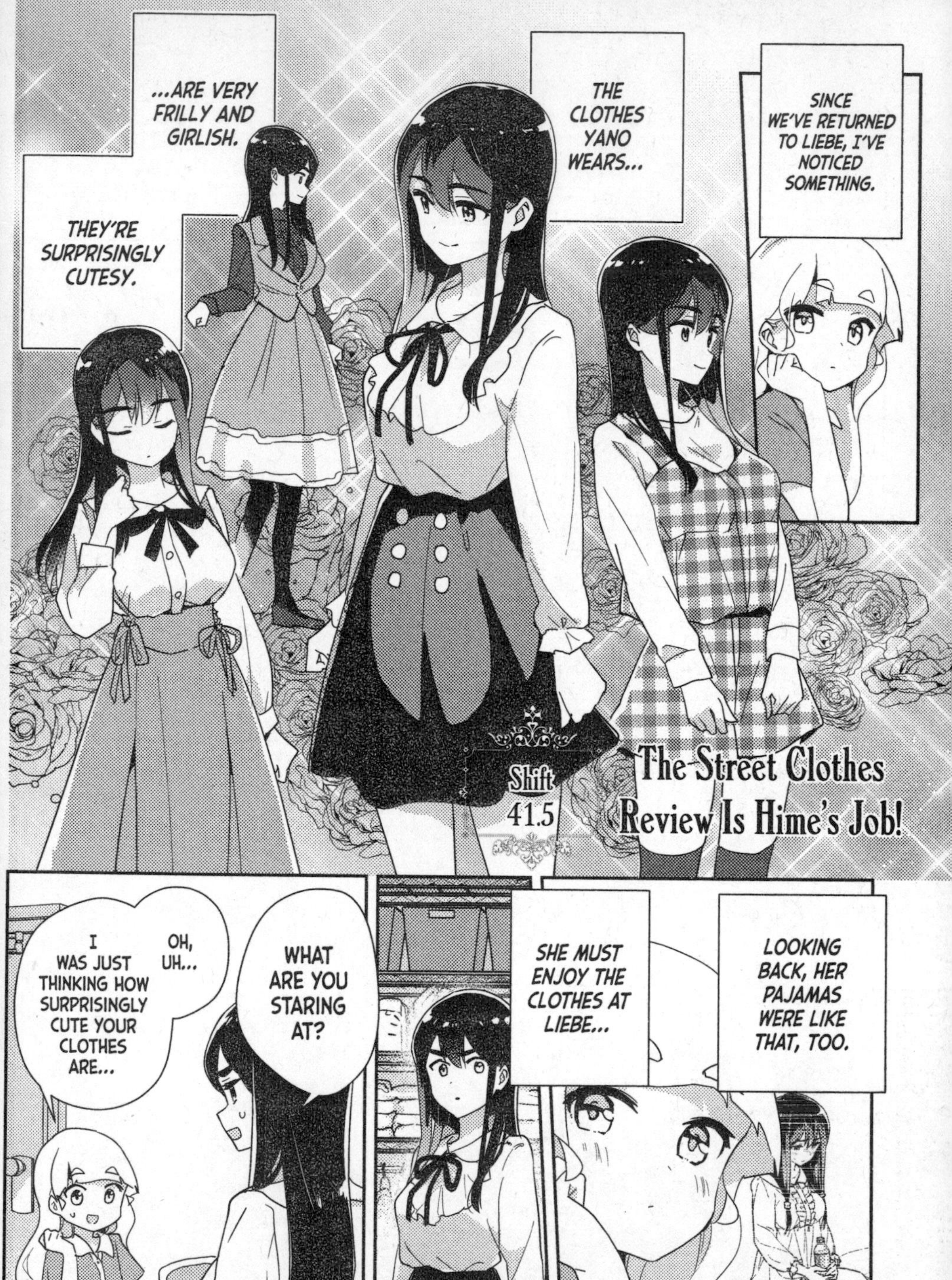
SINCE WE'VE RETURNED TO LIEBE, I'VE NOTICED SOMETHING.
THE CLOTHES YANO WEARS...
...ARE VERY FRILLY AND GIRLISH.
THEY'RE SURPRISINGLY CUTESY.
Shift 41.5
The Street Clothes Review Is Hime's Job!
LOOKING BACK, HER PAJAMAS WERE LIKE THAT, TOO.
SHE MUST ENJOY THE CLOTHES AT LIEBE...
WHAT ARE YOU STARING AT?
OH, UH...
I WAS JUST THINKING HOW SURPRISINGLY CUTE YOUR CLOTHES ARE...

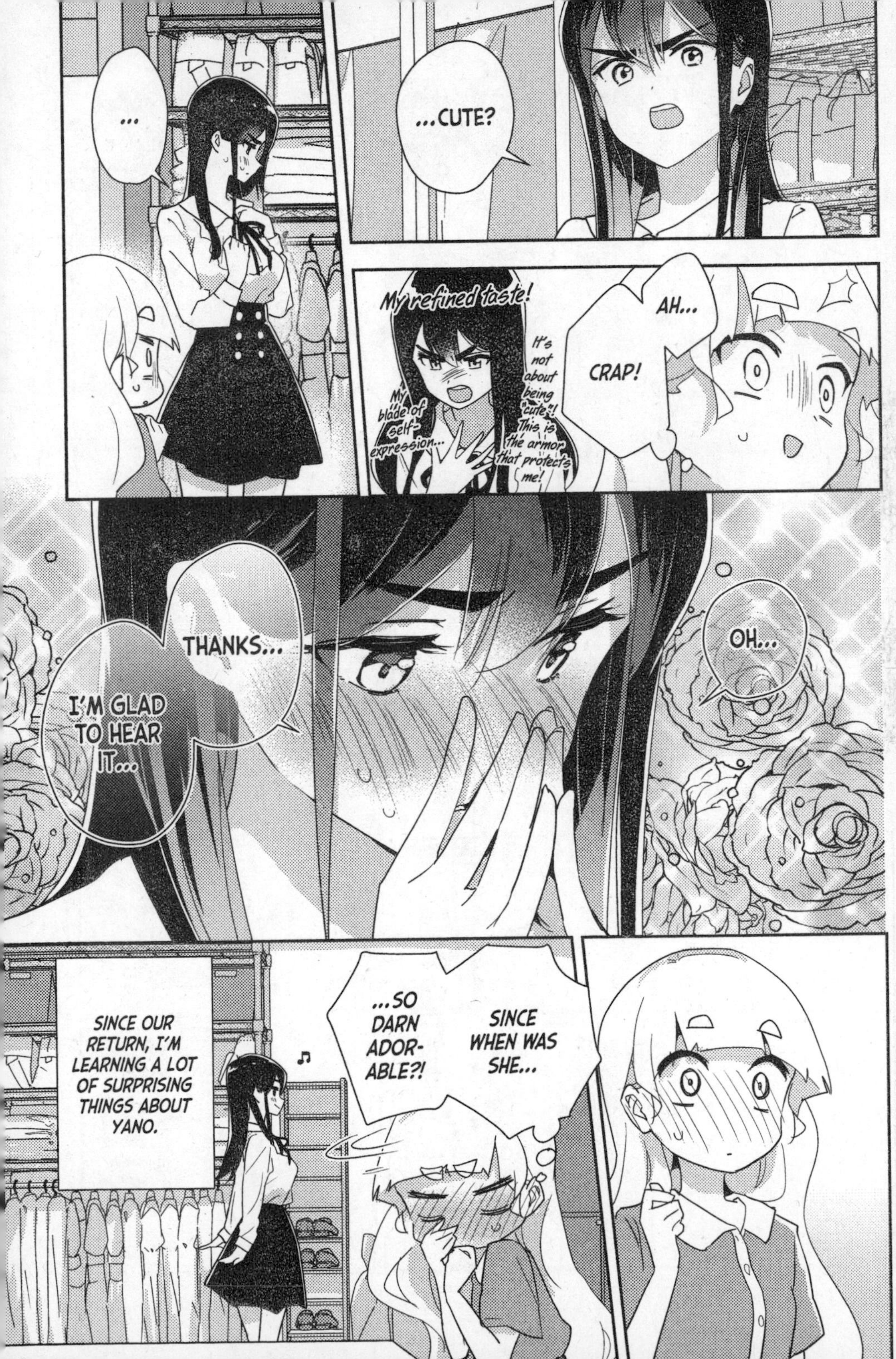
...CUTE?
...
AH...
CRAP!
My refined taste!
It's not about being "cute"! This is the armor that protects me!
My blade of self-expression...
OH...
THANKS...
I'M GLAD TO HEAR IT...
SINCE WHEN WAS SHE...
...SO DARN ADORABLE?!
SINCE OUR RETURN, I'M LEARNING A LOT OF SURPRISING THINGS ABOUT YANO.

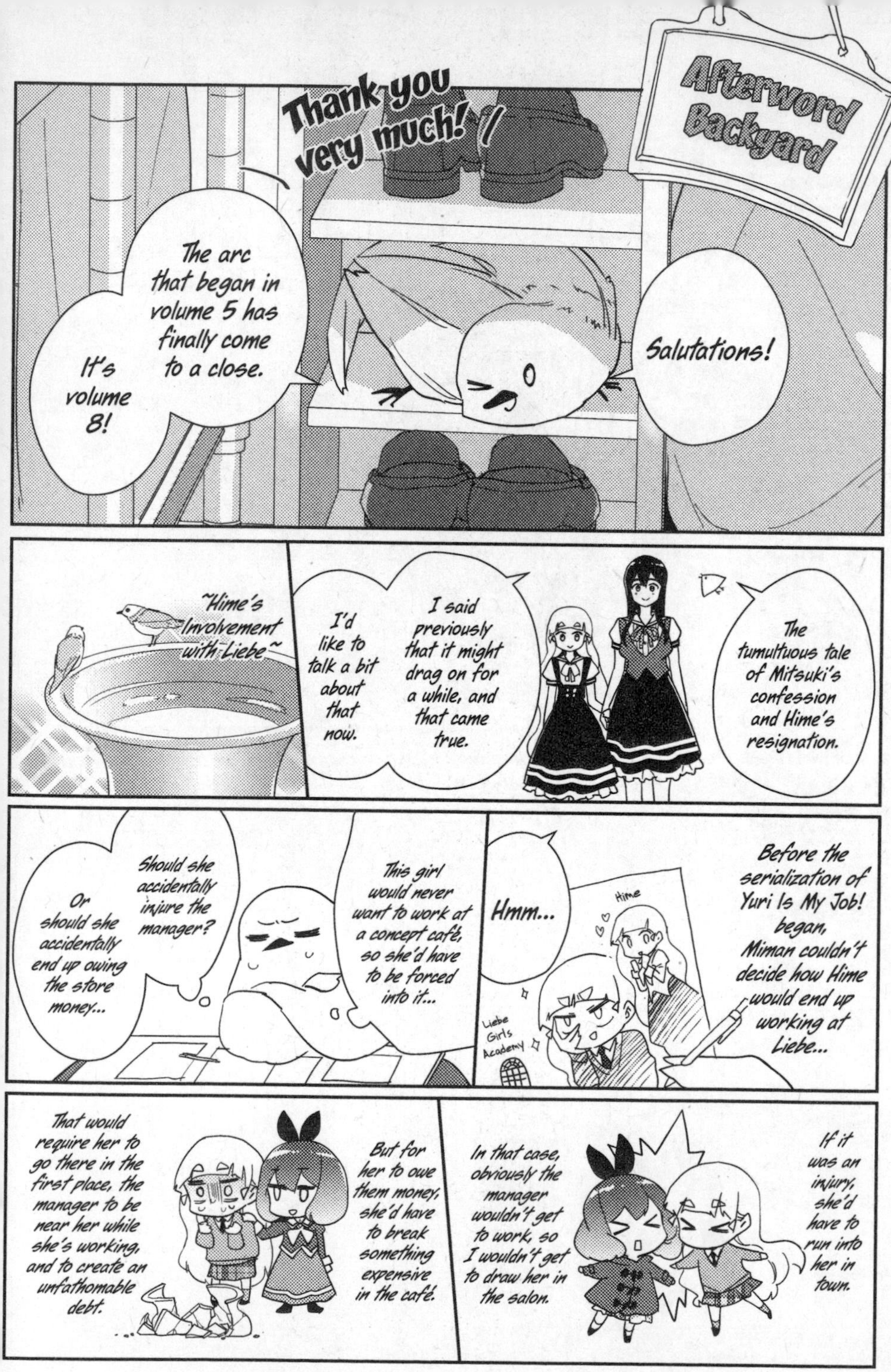
Afterword Backyard
Thank you very much!
Salutations!
It's volume 8!
The arc that began in volume 5 has finally come to a close.
The tumultuous tale of Mitsuki's confession and Hime's resignation.
I said previously that it might drag on for a while, and that came true.
I'd like to talk a bit about that now.
~Hime's Involvement with Liebe~
Before the serialization of Yuri Is My Job! began, Miman couldn't decide how Hime would end up working at Liebe...
Hime
Liebe Girls Academy
Hmm...
This girl would never want to work at a concept café, so she'd have to be forced into it...
Should she accidentally injure the manager?
Or should she accidentally end up owing the store money...
If it was an injury, she'd have to run into her in town.
In that case, obviously the manager wouldn't get to work, so I wouldn't get to draw her in the salon.
But for her to owe them money, she'd have to break something expensive in the café.
That would require her to go there in the first place, the manager to be near her while she's working, and to create an unfathomable debt.

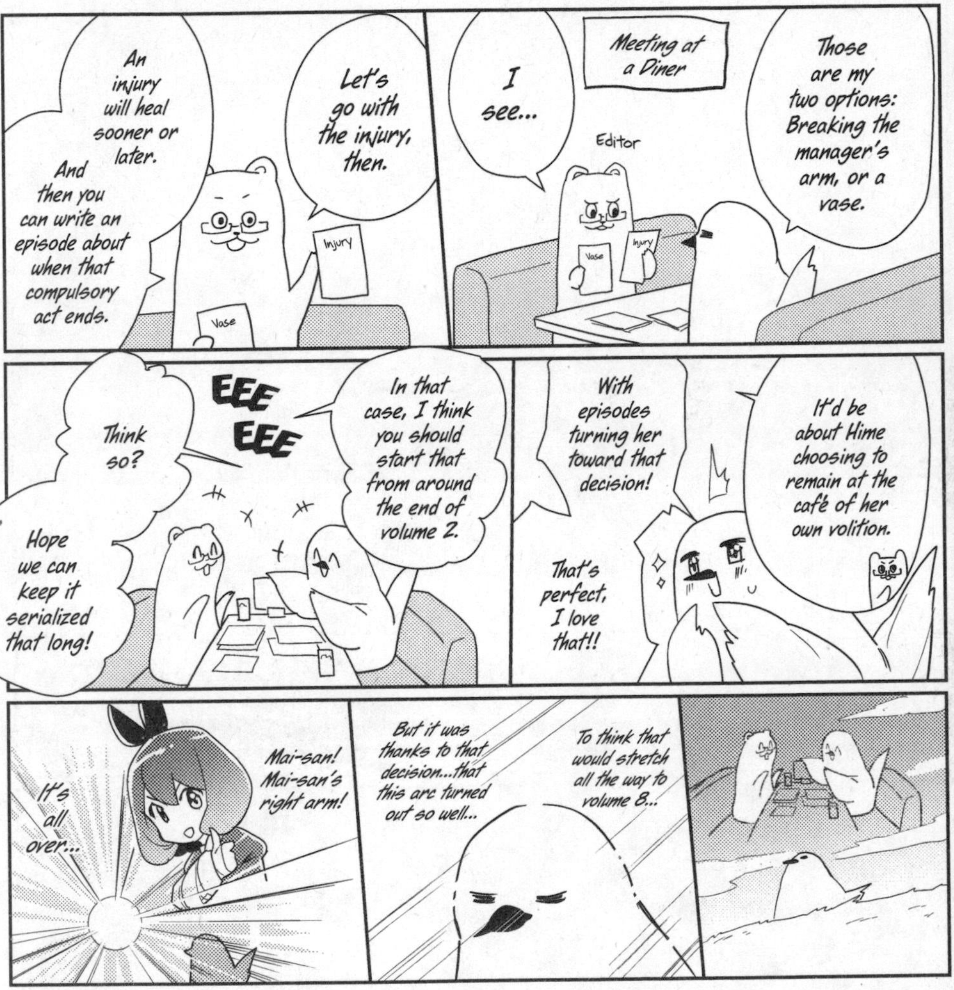
Those are my two options: Breaking the manager's arm, or a vase.
Meeting at a Diner
I see...
Editor
Injury
Vase
Let's go with the injury, then.
An injury will heal sooner or later.
And then you can write an episode about when that compulsory act ends.
Injury
Vase
It'd be about Hime choosing to remain at the café of her own volition.
With episodes turning her toward that decision!
That's perfect, I love that!!
In that case, I think you should start that from around the end of volume 2.
EEE
EEE
Think so?
Hope we can keep it serialized that long!
To think that would stretch all the way to volume 8...
But it was thanks to that decision...that this arc turned out so well...
Mai-san! Mai-san's right arm!
It's all over...

Anyway, that's been volume 8! I'm glad to have been able to provide the travel chapter as a nice break after all that seriousness.

By the way, Mai-san and Nene-san also went to the baths and had massages and beauty treatments.

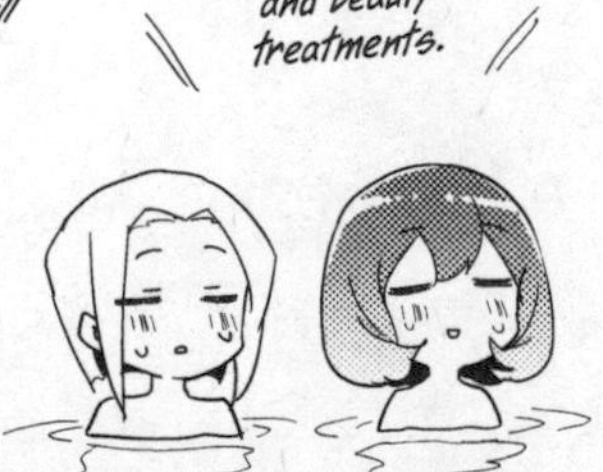

There's so much more I want to draw. The stories will continue yet...

...so please look forward to the next volume as well!!

Until the day that we might meet again!

2021

special thanx

Yuuri

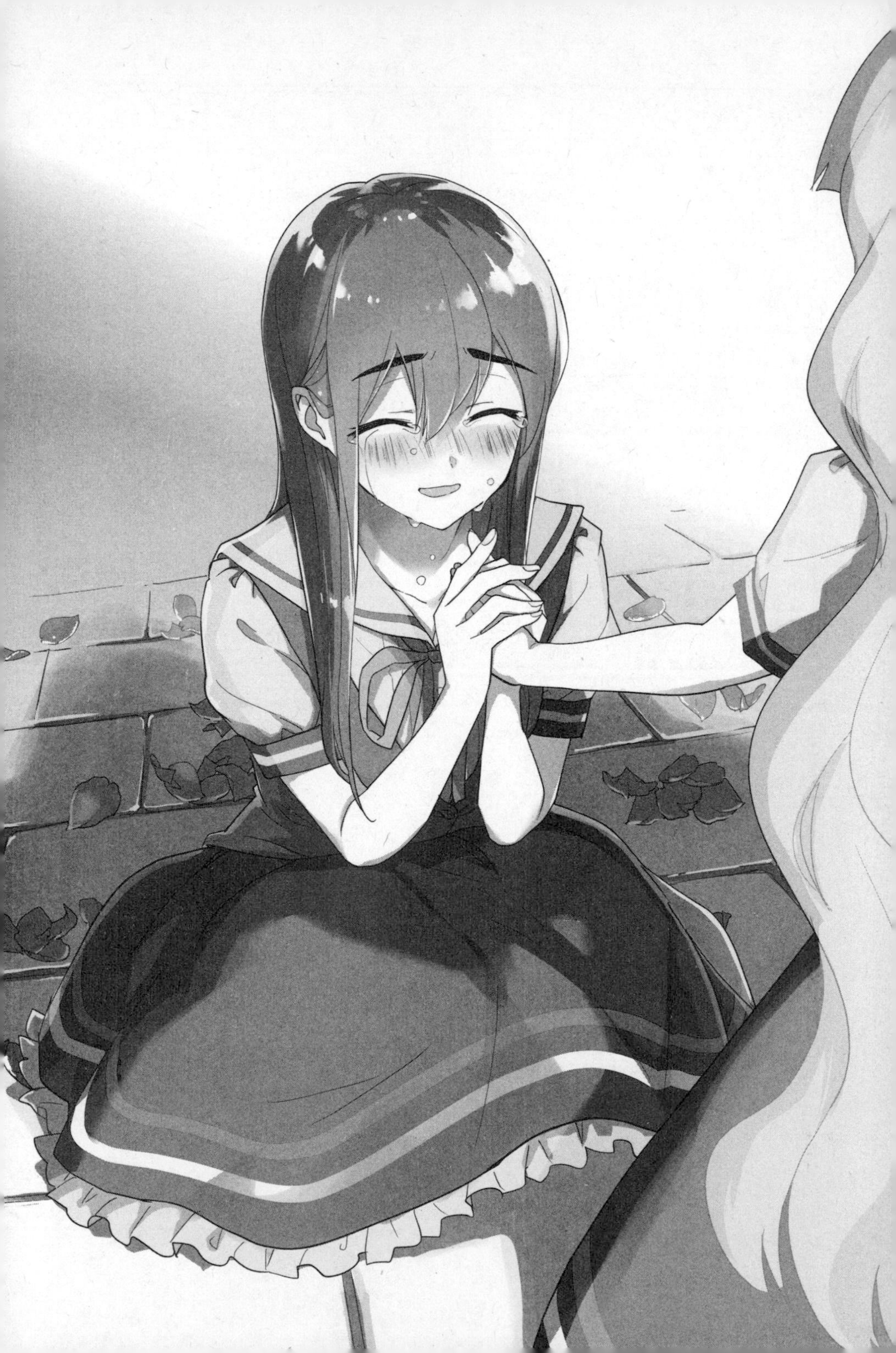

Hime-chan's

# Review! Café Liebe Operation Manual

## Liebe Girls Academy Uniforms

The Liebe Girls Academy uniforms are provided as different layers of varying sizes. The summer shirts are washed every time, the other uniform pieces as necessary. They are collected in a large bag in the back room and collected by a cleaning service.

The loafers are ordered in bulk, so there's one pair for each person. This is a food service job, so they're water-resistant and anti-slip. The inner layers we provide ourselves, and we're each responsible for washing our own socks and stockings as they are store-issued. Thank you for keeping up with this.

On this past trip, we brought the uniforms outside, but they looked pretty good out in natural light, too. The winter uniforms are from the first round of creations, so they've gotten fairly mussed up over time. Perhaps it's about time we put together some new ones.

## miman

Salutations.

Here comes the stormy cloud

cast upon Liebe by Hime...

Will daybreak ever come?

This arc concludes here!

Yuri Is My Job!

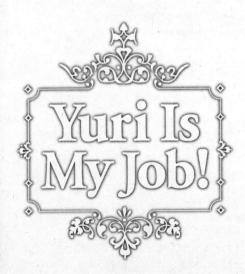

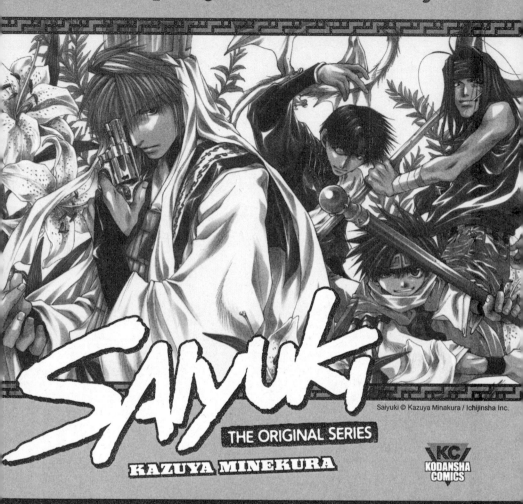

# SAINT ☆ YOUNG MEN

## A LONG AWAITED ARRIVAL IN PREMIUM 2-IN-1 HARDCOVER

After centuries of hard work, Jesus and Buddha take a break from their heavenly duties to relax among the people of Japan, and their adventures in this lighthearted buddy comedy are sure to bring mirth and merriment to all!

"Brilliant...the physical comedy and facial expressions will make you literally LOL."
—Sam Humphries (host of *DC Daily*; writer, *Green Lanterns*, *Legendary Star-Lord*)

KC KODANSHA COMICS

# The art-deco cyberpunk classic from the creators of *xxxHOLiC* and *Cardcaptor Sakura!*

"Starred Review. This experimental sci-fi work from CLAMP reads like a romantic version of *AKIRA*."
—Publishers Weekly

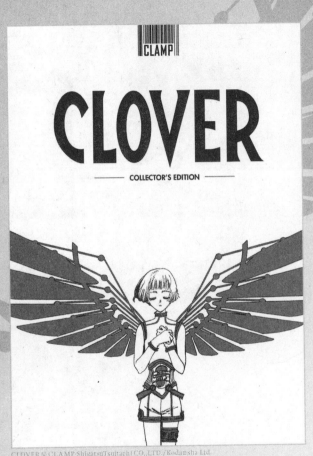

Su was born into a bleak future, where the government keeps tight control over children with magical powers—codenamed "Clovers." With Su being the only "four-leaf" Clover in the world, she has been kept isolated nearly her whole life. Can ex-military agent Kazuhiko deliver her to the happiness she seeks? Experience the complete series in this hardcover edition, which also includes over twenty pages of ravishing color art!

# THE SWEET SCENT OF LOVE IS IN THE AIR! FOR FANS OF OFFBEAT ROMANCES LIKE *WOTAKOI*

Sweat and Soap © Kintetsu Yamada / Kodansha Ltd.

In an office romance, there's a fine line between sexy and awkward... and that line is where Asako — a woman who sweats copiously — meets Koutarou — a perfume developer who can't get enough of Asako's, er, scent. Don't miss a romcom manga like no other!

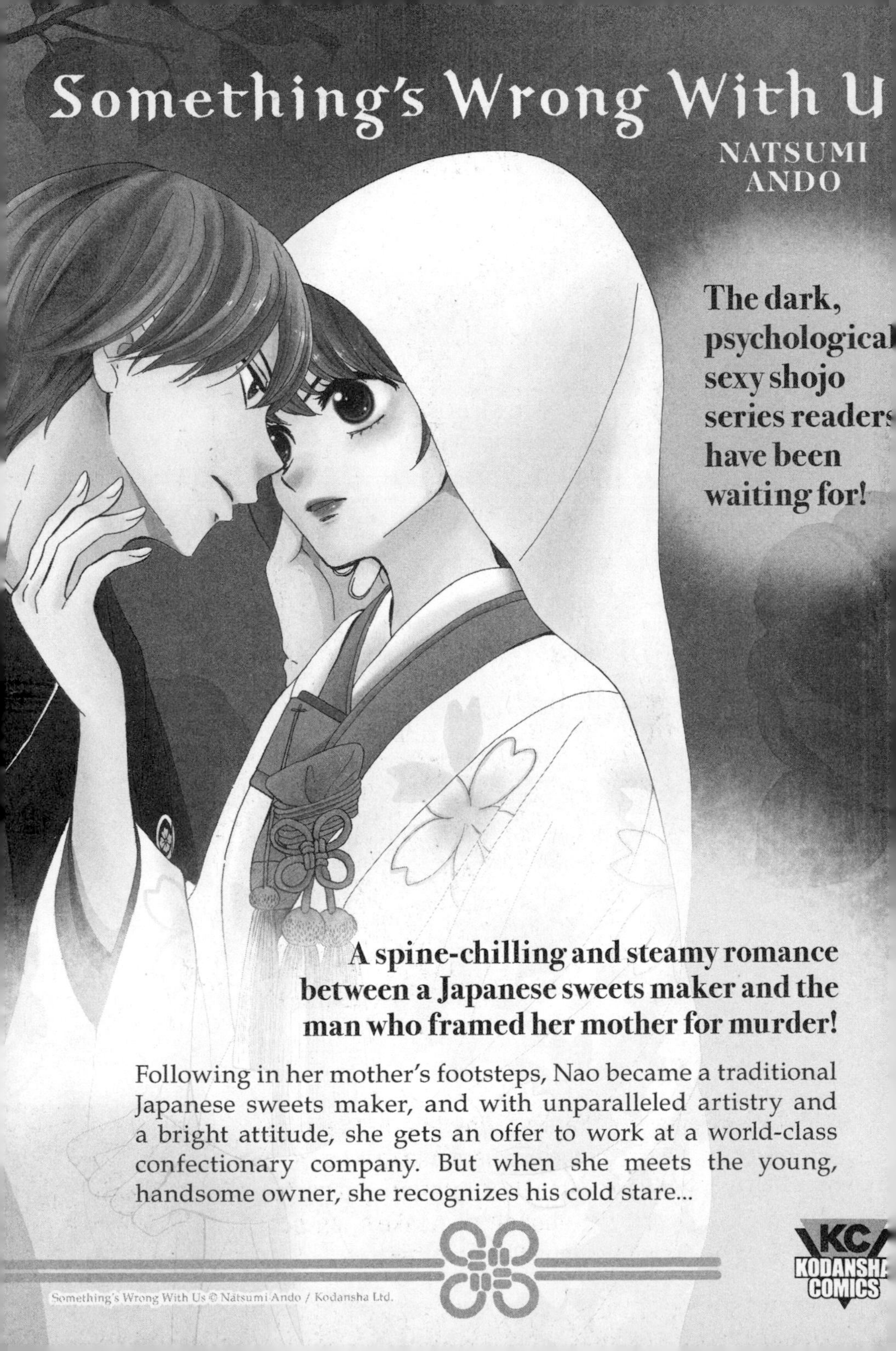
Something's Wrong With U
NATSUMI ANDO
The dark, psychologica sexy shojo series reader have been waiting for!
A spine-chilling and steamy romance between a Japanese sweets maker and the man who framed her mother for murder!
Following in her mother's footsteps, Nao became a traditional Japanese sweets maker, and with unparalleled artistry and a bright attitude, she gets an offer to work at a world-class confectionary company. But when she meets the young, handsome owner, she recognizes his cold stare...
Something's Wrong With Us © Natsumi Ando / Kodansha Ltd.
KC KODANSHA COMICS

# PERFECT WORLD

## Rie Aruga

A TOUCHING NEW SERIES ABOUT LOVE AND COPING WITH DISABILITY

An office party reunites Tsugumi with her high school crush Itsuki. He's realized his dream of becoming an architect, but along the way, he experienced a spinal injury that put him in a wheelchair. Now Tsugumi's rekindled feelings will butt up against prejudices she never considered — and Itsuki will have to decide if he's ready to let someone into his heart...

"Depicts with great delicacy and courage the difficulties some with disabilities experience getting involved in romantic relationships... Rie Aruga refuses to romanticize, pushing her heroine to face the reality of disability. She invites her readers to the same tasks of empathy, knowledge and recognition."
—Slate.fr

"An important entry [in manga romance]... The emotional core of both plot and characters indicates thoughtfulness... [Aruga's] research is readily apparent in the text and artwork, making this feel like a real story."
—Anime News Network

KC
KODANSHA
COMICS

# A SMART, NEW ROMANTIC COMEDY FOR FANS OF *SHORTCAKE CAKE* AND *TERRACE HOUSE*!

A romance manga starring high school girl Meeko, who learns to live on her own in a boarding house whose living room is home to the odd (but handsome) Matsunaga-san. She begins to adjust to her new life away from her parents, but Meeko soon learns that no matter how far away from home she is, she's still a young girl at heart — especially when she finds herself falling for Matsunaga-san.

# Young characters and steampunk setting, like *Howl's Moving Castle* and *Battle Angel Alita*

Beyond the Clouds © 2018 Nicke / Ki-oon

A boy with a talent for machines and a mysterious girl whose wings he's fixed will take you beyond the clouds! In the tradition of the high-flying, resonant adventure stories of Studio Ghibli comes a gorgeous tale about the longing of young hearts for adventure and friendship!

A Kodansha Comics Trade Paperback Original
*Yuri Is My Job!* 8 copyright © 2021 miman
English translation copyright © 2022 miman

Published in the United States by Kodansha Comics, an imprint of Kodansha USA Publishing, LLC, New York.

Publication rights for this English edition arranged through Kodansha Ltd., Tokyo.

First published in Japan in 2021 by Ichijinsha Inc., Tokyo as *Watashi no Yuri wa Oshigotodesu!*, volume 8.

ISBN 978-1-64651-238-6

Printed in the United States of America.

www.kodansha.us

1st Printing
Translation: Diana Taylor
Lettering: Jennifer Skarupa
Editing: Haruko Hashimoto
Kodansha Comics edition cover design by Phil Balsman

Publisher: Kiichiro Sugawara

Director of publishing services: Ben Applegate
Associate director, publishing operations: Stephen Pakula
Publishing services managing editor: Madison Salters, Alanna Ruse
Production managers: Emi Lotto, Angela Zurlo